HOW ORGANIZATIONAL BEHAVIOR INFLUENCES ECONOMIC GROWTH

JOHN LOK

Contents

Preface

Introduction

How social change influences human behavioral change ? Why human behavior may be influenced by social change? Our individual behavior whether can be influenced to bring negative or positive attitude by social change? I shall attempt to indicate cases to explain whether our individual behavior can be influenced to changed by social environment change. Readers can have more understand how and why social change may influence our behavior in possible. Behavioral economy is one useful and fun social subject. Behavioral economists ususally research how and why human behaviors may influence economy growth or recession, or how and why economy environment changing factor may influence human behavior changes.

I write this book aims to let students can have more clear concerns whether how behavioral economy theory can help our society to evaluate why whether the consumer will make the decision, how our societies will be influenced to change, how any why our organizations employees decide to make the performance.

In my this book, I shall attempt to explain why and how organizational behavior may influence economic growth or recession as well as how and why ecommerce may be one kind network human job to influence economic growth. Also, I shall indicate reasons to explain why human network behavior may bring direct or indirect influences to economy growth or recession in our global societies in macro and micro economy view.

How farmer individual agriculture behavior may influence economic development. Farming industry is important food industry, farming industry may include farming products and non-farming products, it may include: farming of wheat, fruit, meat,corn , cotton etc.food and non-food products. So, any countries governments and farmers ought need to concern how to learn farming technology to improve and help them to achieve farming economic development. In my this book, I shall attempt to explain what farming technology means and how learning farming technology can help any countries to bring economy growth , how raising farming and non-farming productivities to bring farmer individual profit methods.

On employee productive efficient raising method aspect, I shall explain how to apply behavioral economy methods to influence employee individual psychology to achieve to raise productivity of long term incentive invention. I shall apply behavioral economy method to explain why increasing salary is short term incentive productivity method,how to improve the design of incentive structures to encourage productivities organizations, how to build employees and managers kindly co-operational relationship method, explain whether bonus method can encourage service performance to be raised as well as how to apply behavioral economy method to explain how to predict human motivation natural behaviors.

In the final, I shall apply behavioral economic method to explain that why under-level productive efficiency is not represent low production number to the manufacturer as well as low-consumption desire is not represent less consumer demands or customers lose confidence to the product. The most importance, you can learn how to apply marketing strategies to analyze to solve your further problems to threaten your business. Besides, you can learn how to use strategy to analyze any business case study to prepare your studying. I shall give reasons to explain why I shall apply this kind of marketing strategy to solve every problem to every company case study. Hence, students can understand what reasons to be judged to make these strategic decision more clearly. I shall explain future how artificial intellignt technology may be applied to implement in order to assist organizations to implement more accurate prediction to consumer behaviors how change and evaluat the most reasonable sale price to increase sale number.I hope that my readers can feel why and how organizational behavior can influence economic growth or recession in possible.

Prologue

ethnographic method measures
stable income consumer purchase desire

Quantitative and qualitative method measures stable income consumer purchase desire

China future digital product market development

New economic social development causes China is as the world factory p.66-75

New economic society influences human right marginal social cost and benefit social analysis need

- Environment Economy-Pollution and illness influences c consumer behavior
- How artificial intelligence impacts energy consumers using behaviours
- Is the low income and rising price of modern fuels both factors best to influence Nigeria householders choose to use energy efficiently?
- Urbanization level and income per capita both tangible factors as well as temperature (weather variation factor) will have close relationship to influence China householder energy consumption or useful needs at home every day
- Does season factor influence New Zealand householders' energy consumption behaviors at homes

- Employment rates or gross domestic product macro economic variation factor, residential space size factor, and the government's implementation of energy labeling schemes provide significant impacts on Taiwan residential electricity consumption .

p.76-90

Explaining how organizational strategy solving problem
Engagement (Building good organizational culture) Strategy solves Hill Wood Medical Centre organization international different culture difficult cooperation problem

How and why can engagement strategy solve medical organizational departments difficult culture cooperate problem ?

- suggestion engagement strategy influences to medical centre departments' staffs build kindly culture efficient cooperative method

.What barriers did this medical centre face in implementing the strategies or achieving success?

.Did it overcome those obstacles and if so, how?

England NHS public hospital patient price structure of marketing strategy

1. What do you understand by the concept of a pricing model? Critically discuss their relevance to a public sector service ,such as the NHS.
2. What factors should influence the level of charges at an NHS car park?

What are the important factors that the leaders of Willard and Eastern must consider in order to be effective?
What could each have done to be more effective?

- Outsourcing service Strategy solves Unversity cost raising challenges
  - Outsoucing service strategy can help this university to solve staff management challenge.

Building effective organizational international communication strategy solves broadcasting television department and file producing entrepreneur cooperation challenge

- upward communication strategy solves broadcasting television department communication challenge
- film producing entrepreneur downward communincation strategy solves team cooperation challenge

Fair compensation strategy solves factory workers and baseball players cooperation challenge

- Factors cause electronic assemblies factory workers team performance
- What factors seem to be influencing team performance?
- If I was Dave, shop supervisor, what team concepts should I apply? why?
- Fair compensation solve baseball organization players cooperation challenge
- Describe the types of conflict that seem to exist within the Bluebirds organization.
- Fair compensation strategy solves compensation director poor working performance challenge

Crisis management and time management strategy solves nuclear factory team cooperation challenge

- Nuclear factory team making the most right decision challenge
- What alternatives do you use for reducing the possibility of a similar problem in the future?
- Time management hotel staff workplace stress emotion challenge

Marketing mix strategy solves supermarket store organizational cooperation challenge

- Critically discuss the factors influencing Tesco's sourcing of fresh fruit and vegetables.
- Assess the level of power that Tesco exercises in the supply chain for fruit and vegetables.

A national chain of restaurant mobile advertising promotion strategy

● Discuss methods that could be used to assess the effectiveness of mobile advertising.

● Discuss the relationship between mobile advertising and other elements of the promotion in campaign planning. p.91-125

Chapter 4 Learning AI assists organizational development

Management accounting science how applies to Amazon ecommerce organization

● How management accounting cocept can help Amazon publish to manage its cost effectively in order to increase its profit or e-books or paper books sale ability.

How management accounting concept applies to investment

● How to apply mental accouting method to predict investor behavior?

● How mental (managerial) accounting concept helps Amazon publish to make investment decision?

Management science accounting concept how predicts market changing

Accounting science how predicts e-commerce consumer behavior

Can robots perform management accounting analysis tasks

● How robotic process automation impact on accouting industry changes?

● Can robots perform the same management accounting analytical decision making skills to human management accountants tasks?

Applying HR management accounting learns consumer behavior

● Computer sale applies management accounting to predict consumer behavior

● How can the laptop computer seller applies management accounting data to analyze whether which is the main factor to influence laptop buyer behavior changes?

● Management accounting data can also help this laptop seller to predict future market development or whether which market will have high sale effort

Organization management accounting strategy

● The relationship between organizational management accounting strategy and avoiding resource waste

● What are the source of resource mobilization to any organizations?

● Can resource mobilization change improve organizational performance?

● Why does organizational resource budget need?

● What does organization office , shop , warehouse space resource management strategy?

● The relationship netween organization behavior and resource using management accounting

How applying artificial intelligent management accounting solution accounting challenges

● Future AI management accountant may help human to the honest accounting record

● Can AI be applied to help organizations to implement management account strategies ? p.126-140

Chapter 5 Organizational behavior how influence economic growth

Human Behavioral network job brings social economic benefits

What does human network job mean

Why human network job behavior may influence economy

Robots take our jobs behavioral and economy influences

Robot job behavior brings economy influences

Intellectual human economic behaviors

What does intellectual human economic behaviors
mean ?

The relationship between social change and human
behavior

How human productive behavior may influence economic development

- New Zealand farmer individual wine productive behavior
- America high technological productive behavior
- China share market investing behavior

Why has any individual country have many people invest share behavior which can influence the country's macro consumption desire?

Can technology influence human shopping behavioral change?

Why and how human behavior may influence the country's economic growth or recession?

Technology how impacts human behavior changing?

How and why employees behaviors may influence economy development? p.141-160

CHAPTER ONE

LEARNING ORGANIZATION BEHAVIOR AND SOCIAL ECONOMY RELATIONSHIP

What behavioral economic means

(BE) Behavioral economics is primarily concerned with the bounds of rationality of economic agents. Behavioral models typically bring insights from psychology and microeconomic theory. The study of behavioral economics includes how market decisions are made and the mechanisms that drive public choice. Moreover, behavioral economic plays a important role in our lives and in the economy because it can help businesses to explain why we consume the kind of goods and services , the way we do, why we make certain choices of action, the key contibution to behavioral economics, it uses psychological and experimentation to develop theories about human decision making, and has identified a range of biases as a result of the way people think and feel . (BE) is trying to change the way economics think about people's perception of value and expresses preferences.

● Have they relationship between consumer behaviors and economy ?

The success or failure of a nation's economy can greatly affect consumer behavior based on a variety of economic factors. If the economy is strong, consumers have more purchase power and money is spent , f the economy is poor, the reverse is true. Consumer behavior in economics means to explain of how individual cstomers, groups or organizations select, buy, use and dispose ideas, goods and services. A such, consumers play a vitual role in the economic system of a capitalist economy. Without consumer demand, producers would lack one of the key motivations to produce to sell to consumers.

The motivates consumers behavioral economic perspective, it is the new field of behavioral economics has shown them, in practice, people's decisions can be greatly influenced by seemingly irrelevant aspects of their personalities and by the environment in which their decisions are made. So, it seems that consumer buying behavior changes during economic crisis.

In organization how resources choices to use in behavioral economy view, though the number and variety of the different resources businesses require is limitless. Economists divide factors of production into three basic categories: Land, labour and capital. Land refers to all of the natural resources that businessed need to make and distribut goods and services, labours to make and distribute goods and services, labours refers how the organization chooses to employ the employee skill to make the kind of job, capital refers to how much the organization plans to spend in order to operate its business. Hence, behavioral economy can explains the economic model of employee, human behavior, working performance. It is a representation of people action. The concept is based on traditional economics, where human behavior is believed to spring from absolute rationality.

On behavioral economics in consumer lives and in the economy aspect, it explains it is a game theory, behavioral game theory. It is a game theory , behavioral game theory extened standard analytical game theory by taking into account how players (consumers) feel about the payoffs other players receive, limits in strategic thinking, as well as the effects of learning , the consumer individual past purchase experience, games (choices of purchases) are usually about cooperation or fairness.

For advertising how plays beneficial roles in a healthy economy example, advertising plays a strong role in the economy. It provides useful informatin to consumers that tells them about products and services choices as well as comparing features, benefits and prices, with more complete information, consumers and businesses often choose to purchase additional products and services . Hence, behavioral eonomics draws instead on psychology and economics to explore why people sometimes make irrational decisions, and why and how their behavior does not follow the predictionsof economic models. Because humans are emotional and easily distracted being, they make decisions that are not in their self-interest.

So, behavioral economics is the study of the effects that psychological factors have on the economic decisions making process of individuals. The importance of understanding behavioral economics for marketers is immeasurable as it shows for a better factors that can lead to irrational economic decision, e.g. overspend because of lack of availabiliey, such as buying expense gad because you are in the desert. Another irrational economic decision may be impluse buying or pressure.

- How to apply behavioral economic to explain why the employee does peformance behavior?

A study on human behavior has revealed that 90% of the working population can be classified into four basic personality types: Optimistic, pessimistic, trusting. However, the latter of the four types. Envious is the most common, with 30% compared to 20% of each of the organization whole employee individual economic behavior, economic behavior occurs in a climate of formal and informal organizational rukes. These rules often act as incentives, e.g. appreciation, job promotion, increasing salary. These rules often act as incentives and influence the choices employees make , in general employees chooce to work desk jobs that do not keep to fit, and how they have to make more time to stay healthy.

So, behavioral economic theory explain any organization will need have behavioral skills to dominate employee individual performance to raise. Behavioral skills are interpersonal, self-regulatory, and task-related behaviors that connect to successful performance in education and workplace settings. The behavioral skills are designed to help individuals succeed thorough effecttive interactions, stress management and persistent effort in any organizations. for task-oriented behavioral skills examples, they may include: active always buy with something, ambitious, strongly wants to succeed, cautious, being very careful, conscientious, taking time to do things right and creative, someone who can make up things easily or think of new things. The six important employee behaviors in organizations are employee productivity, absenteeism, turnover, organizational citizenship behavior, job satisfaction and workplace misbehavior. So, managers need have good behavioral management skills. They are all about learnings appreciation and growth. Take the time to learn, try and grow oen strategies and leadership style.

- How to apply behavioral eocnomic skill to help society to solve challenges ?

The three principles of social economics theory describes how the economy as a whole woks are (1) a country's standard of living depends on its ability to produce goods and services . (2) prices rise when the government prints too much money and (3) society faces a short-run tradeoff between inflation and unemployment. How to use behavioral economics for social impact. According to the American psychological association, social psychology is the study of how individuals affects and are affected by physical environment. Behavioral economics applies these concepts to the economic decisions that people make in addition to the ration thinking. It helps us understand how consumer participate in contest buy products and brand familiar choice in order to make the most rational purchase decison. Also, behavioral economists ask questions mostly about the way people make economic choices, judgements or the way particular financial purchase choice.

Hence, behavioral economic is the study of psychology as it relates to the economic decision making processes of individuals and organizations. In general, our societies ask two important questions: Are economists‘ assumptions of utility of profit maximization good approximations of real people's behavior? So individuals maximize subjective expected utility?

IN our societies, we need to satisfy and earn the greatest benefit, in economics, rational choice theory, states that when humans are presented with various options under the conditions of scarcity, they would choose the option that maximizes their individual satisfaction. Behavioral economics draws on psychology and economics to explain

why people sometimes make irrational decisions and why and how their behavior does not follow the predictions of economic models, e.g. decisions such as how much to pay for a cup of coffee, whether to go to graduate school, whether to pursue a healthy lifestyle , how much to contribute toward retirement.
Because humans are emotional and easily distracted beings, they make decisions that are not in their self interest. For companies are increasingly incorpoarting behavioral economics to incrase sales of their products case example, in 2007, the price of the 8 GB iphone was introduced for $600 and quickly reduced to $400, what if the intrinsic value of the phone was $400? If Apple introduced the iphone for $400, the initial reaction the price in the smartphone market might have been negative as the iphone might be thought to have too pricely. Buy by introdicing the phone at a hgh-pricing and bringing it down to $400, consumers believed they were getting a pretty iphone deal for Apple. So, Apple iphone began to understand tht its phone consumers are irrational, an effective way to behavioral economics in the Apple iphone's decision making policies that concern its internal and external stakeholders may prove to be worthwhile of done properly .

Consumer leisure behavioral economy

- Consumer leisure need whether is more and less whether it has what relationship between economy?

Consumer leisure need whether is more and less whether it has what relationship between economy? Also whether the country's economy recession or growth, can it influence consumer leisure need to increase or decrease ? I shall attempt to apply behavioral economy theory to explain whether they have cause and effect relationship as below:
In our societies, there are so many different kinds of leisure activities, also any kinds of leisure consumers can follow the kind of leisure activity's price factor, enjoyable feeling factor, satisfactory feeling factor, lesiure time need factor to influence the leisure consumer individual final choice to which kind of leisure activity among the different kinds of leisure needs. For example, travel leisure activity ought be the most experience, spending of leisure expense to compare general sport lesiure, e.g. swimming , playing basketballs , table tennis, tennis, football, purchae tickets seeing movies, purchase tickets listening music, purchase electronic playing games to stay at homes to play.
In simiarity, it uses only considers leisure price aspect, we shall do the comparable and reasonable decision is that travelling activity ought be the kind of leisure activity, any leisure consumers ought spend the least leisure times to enjoy this kind of leisure activity, e.g. one year has only one time or two-to-five times for overseas for overseas travel. But, in fact, in global there are many travellers, they can make many times of travelling frequent decision, e.g. they can spend one week at least time to go to overseas to travel per month. Hence, it means that global some travellers like to buy air ticket to go to overseas to travel, they spend average one month and one time overseas travel.
In fact, tourism agents hope to attract travellers to choose travelling leisure activity, they will attempt to decrease air ticket price in order to increase travellers number. However, some cheap travelling package price can persuade global some travellers accept to pay cheap price to bu air ticket to spend several days to go to the country to travel enjoy their holidays.
So, it seems that cheap air tcket price strategy, it can attract some countries travellers to accept to spend some time for their overseas holiday their overseas travelling leisure activity can explain why leisure price must be main element factor to influence leisure consumers to reduce spending amount to pay for the kind of leisure activity , such as travelling lesiure activity is one kind of good lesiure activity example.
Otherwise, some kinds of leisure activities, ever their lesiure prices are cheap, it must not influence them to like to spend much time to enjoy them, e.g. swimming, riding bicycles leisure activities, although those kinds of sport leisure activities prices must be very cheap to compare travelling activities , it can must influence many young people like to buy bicycles to ridem even they are proficient bicycle riders or they like to buy tickets to go public swimming pools to swin. The factors may include these both kinds of sports are tired sport leisures, any one must need more body energy to do these sports. Moreover, for student leisure consumers, although these both kinds sports prices, such as bicycles and swimming pool purchase tickets, they are cheap to students, but in fact, students must need to spend time to learn, if they often spend time to enjoy these both of sport activities, they will feel fear that they can not concentrate on spending learning time, if they spend on sport leisure time.

Hence, in behavioral economy view, it explains that lesiure price whether it is high or low, it is not main factor to influence any leisure consumers to do leisure kind of choice, such as sport case to student leisure consumers, they will not choose to spend much time on sport lesiure aspect, because the hard students must feel fear to influence their learning effort when they often spend time on sport leisure aspect. Otherwise, for a sport professonal, e.g. proficient riding bicycle sportman, he may accept to spend expensive price to buy one expensive bicycle , e.g. when he feels the US$3,000 bicycle, it can help him to improve riding speed skills, he won't choose to buy the another US$1,000 bicycle, when he feels that it can not help him to improve riding speed skill, hence, it also explains that the leisure produt high price , it must not influence lesisure consumers number to reduce, it depends on whether the leisure product function to the leisure consumer, e.g. for riding bicycle sport men , they may accept to pay higher price to buy more expensive bicycles , because the hope that the bicyces can help them to comprove their riding speed to more rapid. Otherwise, for student bicycle consumers, they won't compare different kinds of bicycles prices in order to decide whether which kind of bicycles are the most suitable to them to buy to ride.

Hence, behavioral economic theory can explain that price must not be the main factor to influence lesiure consumers' lesiure activities choices, their lesiure need psychological and leisure product individual function factors was also influence their lesiure activities choices.

Behavioral economy view how DINA biological medical science impact our societies

● Can DNA reproductive technology bring only positive impact to influence our social behavior change?

Human's medical technology had been continue developed to improve to satisfy our medical need, such as cancer patient medical different new drug research, it aims to help future cancer patients to avoid death. However, future human's new medical research will research on DNA biological medical improvement . So, future DNA biological medical technology may bring good or bad social impact, e.g. reproductive animal, such as pig, cow animals . So, when many pigs and cows can be reproduced. Then, pigs and cows number can increase. Consequently, porks beefs meats food number can be also been increased by DNA biological medical reproductive cell technology improvement.

It is good aspect to bring enough meats supply to global , when future DNA biological medical technology can be developed to the reprodctive many cows and pigs number stage in order to raise porks and beefs food number. However, DNA biological cell reproductive technology can also bring bad impact to our society, if one day human can apply DNA biological cell reprodutive technology to reproduce another ourselves, it means that reproductive human why is it bad new? if ne DNA scientist decides to help one country ambitious leader to reproduce himself, then when the country ambitious leader dies, but his another reproductive himself person can aontiue to bring war crisis to global, such as Japan's past leader, he was one ambitious leader to dominate global countries. If DNA reproductive technology is applied to help him to reproduce this Japan ambitious another himself . Then, the another new world war may be occurred easily. So, I also worry about future DNA reproductive technology may be applied to help the ambitous bad people to reproduce themselves to bring our societies safety and economic recession negative impact. So, it brings this question: Can DNA reproductive technology bring only positive impact to influence our social behavior change? I shall attempt to explain as below:

How does DNA attract our behavior? In some situations, genes play a larger role in determining your behavior. How can genetic technologies impact society ? Although, genetic technology has a great potential to change the medical practice as we know it also has a potential to be misused , it also has a potential to be misused, and lead to further health disparities, discrimination and inequality in the human societies around the world.

However, I believe that those the ways that genetic engineering can help human society. Several works have been done on genetic engineering with major focus on its importance ranging from increasing plant and animal food productio, diagnosing disease condition, medical treatment improvement, as well as production of vaccines and other useful drugs.

● What is the focus of behavioral generics?

Behavioral genetics is the study of genetic and environmental influences on behaviors. By examining genetic influence, more information can be gleaned about how the environment operates to affect behavior. So, in behavioral economic view, gene DNA reproductive cell technology may seem to bring these benefits. Some benefits of genetic engineerinf in agricultures are increased crop yoelds, reduced need for food or drug production, reduced need for pesticides, enhanced nutrient composition and food quality , resistance to past and disease , greater food security, and medical benefits to the world's growing population . Also, the intangible , non economic measurement, possible benefit of genetic engineering may include more nutritious food, tastier food, disease -and-drought resistant plants that require fewer environment resources , such as water and fertilizers, less use of pesticides, increased supply of food with reduced cost and larger shelf life, faster growing plants and animals.

All of these benefits, they can not measured by economic calculation, but they can be felt by us. So, in our social behevioral economic view to genetic engineering, it may bring both positive and negative impact to our societies. On negative impact, these are many risks involves in genetic engineering, the release of genetically altered organisms in the environment can increase human suffering, disease animal welfare, and lead to ecological disasters are positive impact aspect, it can help to defeat diseases, getting rid of all illnesses in young and unborn children potential to live longer, produce new foods, organisms can be tailor-made , faster growth in animals and plants, pests and diseases resistance. But genetic engineering can also bring risks to our societies, e.g. new allergens in the food supply, antibiotic reistance, production of new toxins, concentration of toxic metals, enhancement of the environment for toxic fungi, unknown harms, gene transfer to wild ot weedy relations, change in herbicide use patterns.

By knocking out genes repsonsible for certain conditions, it is possible to create animal model organism of " human disease" as well as producing hotmenes, vaccies and other drugs. So, if DNA can bring human diseases, it means that it can also bring economic loss to our societies, because human disease may bring illness to any one to cause low productivity to any industry development, if the factory has many people human disease from reproductive animal cell accident risk. Then, the ill worker number increases, low productivities and inefficiencies will cause to the factory. If global has many factory workers got human disease from reproductive animal cell accidently. Then, global factries products producing number must have been influenced to fallen down.

Consequently, global manufacturers will encountered serious loss, due to their products producing speed is slow and their different kinds of products supply number must decrease, if global will workers number increases, they are caused by reproductive animal cell disease. Hence, DNA genetic reproductive technology may also bring global economic loss crisis in possible.

Explaining the relationship between increasing proficient workers number and avoiding excess resource waste

- In organizational behavioral economic view, whether they have cause and effect relationship between employees how to use resources behaviors and organizational resource excess use within organizations ?

In organizational behavioral economic view, whether they have cause and effect relationship between employees how to use resources behaviors and organizational resource excess use within organizations. For example, if the organization has many employees number, whether the organization will use its any internal tangible and intangible resources easily per day.

For construction organization example, one construction organization must need to buy different kinds of construction materials to prepare to let workers to help it to manufacture different kinds of properties or houses (products) in order to sell to property buyers. In its every building construction site, it will need more or less workers, they are needed to use different kinds of construction materials to build housess in different construction sites. I assume that construction site (A), it has 100 construction workers number, every day, construction site (A) 100 workers need to use different kinds of construction materials to help them to build 3 building floors wall at least floor number in the construction site (A).

I assume that these 100 construction workers , they include proficient workers and not proficient workers. For proficient construction workers group, they have 50 number, and not proficient construction workers group, they also have 50 number . Hence, the proficient construction workers only need to spend 3 hours maximum and use less number of constructoin materials, then they can finish to build 3 building floors wall per day.

I also assume that all constructoin material supply number is limited. It means that due to this construction firm needs to pre-booking to purchase this kind of the best quality of constructoin material from overseas before three worths. So, it must not have enough time to pre-booking to purchase this kind of best quality of constructoin materials when they are used rapaidly within one month, due to this one month is the final finishing time to this construction firm within one month. Hence, limited construction material supply number and limited finishing time to build this new 40 floors house within this final one month .

So , not proficient construction workers number , limit number of construction material and per day 8 hours which is its limited resources in behavioral eocnomy view. Moreover, total 50 proficient and not proficient 50 construction workers (human resource employees number) will cause this constructoin firm , it will possible need to build this new 40 floors house are more than one month, if these 50 proficient construction workers , they have more than 30 at least number, they are absent to cause their overall construction workers' efficiency to be fallen down, due to the other 50 not proficient constuction numbers must need their teaching how to cooperate ad how use less materials to build this new 40 floor hourse rapidly in order to raise overall constructon team efficiency and avoid to delay more than one month time to build this 40 floors new house successfully within this final one month time.

Hence, it explains that when one organization has more employees, it does not represent that this organization must need to use more resource to achieve its any mission, such as this construction firm case, although it has 50 not proficient construction workers, they need to use more construction materials to build this new 40 floors house in this construction site (A). But, in fact, it has other 50 proficient construction workers, they know how to reduce construction materials to build every building floor wall for this new 40 floors building house. So, they can teach the not proficient building workers to know hoe to avoid to use extra excess constructon material to finish to construct every building fllor wall. SO, although, it has 50 not proficient construction workers number, but they can be taught to learn how to reduce to use these limited the best quality of construction materials to build this 40 floors new house. It implies that if the construction workers number can increase, e.g. increases more 50 not proficient construction workers, this the best quality of construction material resource number must not need to increase demand, because this construction site (A) has 50 proficient construction workers , they can teach these 50 not proficient construction workers how to avoid to use extra excess this kind of high quality construction material to build this new 40 floor house efficiently and effectively within this one month.

Hence, if this construction firm won't have more than 30 proficient workers number is absent in this final one month, it will have enough proficient construction workers to teach these 50 not proficient construction workers to know how to use this high quality of construction materials to build this 40 floors new house building in order to avoid waste or construction material need shortage challenge occurs in this final one month time.

Consequently , it ought finish to build this 40 floors new house building within this month. Hence, it explains why its this kind of high quality of construction material resource need must not increase, because if its all proficient construction workers is absent and their absent number is less than 30, then they have enough proficient construction workers number , they can teach this 50 not proficient construction workers how to avoid to use extra excess construction materials resource number in order to have enough construction material resource supply to satisfy this new 40 floors building house to finish construction within one month finishing date need.

On conclusion, in organizational behavioral economic view, it explains that resource use need must not be influenced to increase when the organization's employees number increase. It depends on whether the organization has how many talent and proficient workers number in order to assist them and teach the not proficient employees how to use resource to manufacture any kinds of products in order to avoid to spend extra excess of resource need. Hence, organizational behavioral economic view, it can explain that any organization's increase to employees number, it does not mean that its resource number is also needed to increase. Moreover, in organizational behavioral economic view, it also explains that if the organization can have many proficient workers to help it to do any complex tasks, they will help it to bring avoiding waste or excess extra resource to use advantage, because they ought know whether how they work, they can help the organization to improve performance or raise efficiency e.g. car manufacture, computer manufacture, television manufcture etc. home electronic products or car leisure products. Due to that manufacturre processes are complex, if the organization can have more proficient high skillful workers to help it to manufacture their products. They ought help it to use lesser manufacturing time and less manufacturing resource to finish any above these products to compare not proficient or low skillful manufacture workers. So, in long time, the organization must may earn economic low cost benefits from proficient worker individual high manufacturing skillful knowledge behavior or performance. So, organizational behavioral economic theory explains why even the organization plans to increase employees number, it's resources number won't be influenced to increase rapidly because when the organization's proficient high skillful workers number is more 2 times at least than not proficient low skillful workers number. They ought have enough effort to train and teach and cooperate with the not proficient low skillful manufacture workers to improve their manufacture skills in order to raise manufacturing efficiency and reduce extra excess resources waste and avoid to bring long term resource waste economic loss. So, any manufacturing organizations must need to increase proficient workers number to assist the not proficient low skillful workers to learn how to improve their skills and know how to reduce to use excess resources to keep to manufacture the highest number of products aim frequently. Consequently, the organization will bring long term low resource use manufacturing economic benefit.

Can ethics behavior help organizations to bring economic benefit

- How ethic help organizations to bring economic benefit

Organizational ethic behavior concerns with explaining employee individual behavior in organization, e.g. ethical decision making, ethical conduct for example, when one marketing department manager does not attempt to carrying on any data research about new market research to sell the new model iphone to any country. He only depends on his personal judgement, he believes that this new invention of US iphone producs, they ought to be sell to Korean new iphone market, because he feels Korean must prefer to choose to buy US drand of new iphone products to compare other countries iphone product. However, this iphone marketing development manager lacks enough data research for different Korean iphone buyer age target, purchase experience, purchase desire to conclude Korean iphone buyers must like to buy any brand of US iphone products in preference.

His non ethical new iphone invention decision making to choice Korean ipohone buyers market will bring time waste rick to satisfy Korean iphone buyers' needs to replace other new model ipone users market, e.g. Hong KOng, China, ipone market. So, his ethical decision making to Korean iphone buyers ne iphone invention market may bring less economic benefit to this US iphone manufacture firm. So, this new model ipohone marketing development immoral judgement of this iphone marketing development manager individual decision making to Korean new model ipone invention to Korean ipone users, it can bring high economic loss to this US iphone firm.Otherwise, if this marketing department manager can spend time to carry on data gathering to make more accurate new model iphone invention decision making to choose which one country, then his ethical decision making may help his this US iphone firm to reduce new iphone invention loss risk. So, it explains that why ethic organizational behavior may influence the firm can earn more or less economic benefit. SO, ethic or moral behavior can influence the organization can earn how much economic benefit in long term significantly in organizational behavioral economic view.

- Can improve energy efficiency by organization building occupant's energy consumption relative behavior to bring economic benefit?

Reducing energy consumption in building , it must improve efficiency by building, but whether they have close cause and effect relationship between occupant's energy consumption behavior and improvement energy efficiency to the building? IN fact, high efficiency equipment is being developed, it can help any building to save energy and economic effectiveness, if building energy is subject to uncertainties, such as whether variations, human operations, human behavior changes and government policies. So, building technology equipment improvement may be one main factor to help buildings to save energy . But why occupant behavior may help building to save energy by their daily energy consumption behavior.

The occupant energy behavioral user inputs factor may include: Weather influences, internal heat gain, efficiencies, simplied/ normal occupant behaviors, e.g. a high efficiency chiller can save very limited energy in cold climates due to minimal cooling load, and a good designed natural ventilation building won't work if the occupants do not open windows when outdoor air favors cooling. So, it seems that if one living building hopes to reduce energy consumption, instead of building equipment technological change , e.g. air condition facilities, building occupants , artificial intelligent light, life, their daily energy consumption behaviors, they can influence the living building's energy consumption level in occupant energy consumption behavior and building energy saving economic benefit view.

In fact, when the occupant considers hot water, air condition, energy gas electricity expenditure, he won't use excess electricity, gas resources, because he needs to pay more energy expenditure , when gas and electricity energy consumption expenditure is applied to any business organization offices, warehouses , shops working facilities environment, such as offices, warehouses , shops can often use less electricity, gas energy far ther employees daily work . In long time, the organization must may reduce much electricity, gas energy expenditure for whole organizations business activities. In organizational behavior economic view, organizational energy consumption reduces it can help it to bring less expenditure spending economic benefit.

How to apply behavioral economic theory to explain
Amazon business e-commerce organizational behavior
can bring economic benefit to our societies

● Can Amazon e-commerce organization business activities bring
ecoonomic benefit to global societies?

Amazon e-commerce is one online product sale e-commerce organization. Any one country e-buyer can use his/her home computer to click to Amazon webstores, when he/she saw the product phone and price, then he/she feels the product's price is reasonable and he/she believes that he/she can make the best choice to buy the product. Then, he/she can pay visa to buy the product from Amazon webstore.

Amazon can bring the most convenient online sale channel to global any one e-buyer. The e-buyer can buy the oveseas product from its e-webstores . He does not need to catch air plane to fly to the e-sellers‘ shop. he can pay visa to pay the product from Amazon e-webstores any time immediately. All Amazon e-webstores . He can open 24 hours, so all webstores have no close time. So , it can bring busy working people, they do not need to spend long time to visit any shops to make purchase decision. For busy working people example, time has important value to them, they do not want to waste time to make any purchase choice. So, Amazon gives " economic purchase time benefit " to global any one full time working people. In their psychology, Amazon can help them to save much time to go to online shopping purchase chance at homes. They can stay at homes to shopping. Even, when they give their their address to Amazon to know, Amazon will deliver their products to their homes within several days rapidly. Also , they do not need to pay money to buy its products immediately. They can only pay visa to buy the product from Amazon webstores. So, they can save " consumption money" to use for another need in short time. So, one individual e-air ticket buyer, Amazon can bring economic benefit to him, he does not need to buy air ticket to fly to another country to buy the product. Amazon webstores are given more different kinds of similar brand products to let him to choose in order to pay the most reasonable price, working people do not need to spend much visiting shop time to choose any products in order to make the final purchase decision at home rapidly, any one has visa card , he/she can buy the product from Amazon webstores at homes.

Instead of individual e-buyer ecommerce time benefit, spending little time product choice, reducing catching air plane to visit another country seller shop to pay air ticket expense and travelling time spending activities to every e-buyer . Amazon also brings global economic benefits to any one country. When the e-buyer lives in one country to buy the product, it is saved in the overseas country's warehouse. Then, the product must need to deliver to his home by air plane. So, all of Amazon products can bring global goods air transport delivering service to any one overseas buyer, when the product is saved in the overseas seller's warehouse. Any one Amazon product overseas transpor delivery service activity, it can help air goods transport service need increases as well as their goods air transport service income will also increase. Amazon can bring global air goods transport service need increases. It can assist global GDP air goods transport industry grows, and economic benefit for the country's air plan goods delivery service industry development in long term. Hence, on behavioral economic view, Amazon online sale channel ,it can help global economic benefit to air plane goods delviery service industy as well as individual differeent country e-buyer individual time saving and short term money saving economic benefit by visa payment method.

Moreover, Amazon alsoo creates more high technology employment chance to any one country because Amazon owns many offices and warehouses in different countries, due to it is one high technological e-commerce online sale organization, It must need many high skillful website designers to help it to design different countries webstores in order to satisfy any one e-buyer online purchase need. So, it creates high technology job chance to any one country webstore designers . It can help them to raise competitive effort when any one graduate pursues website designer career. IN Amazon provides good employent chance for any one country computer ecommerce designers in order to let them to earn high salary. Also, Amazon public e-commerce organization provides good chance for any one country author to earn royalty income when he/she publishes any electronic or paper books to sell from Amazon publish. It gives good writing skillful authors have more writing chance to help them to sell electronic books and /or paper books from its different countries webbook stores to different countries' readers in short time. It can help them to increase book sale chance to let different countries book buyers can know whether new book topic to the author, he/she will publish soon. So, it brings author's new writing mind training chance when he/she needs to compare book sale rank from Amazon webstores.

Hence, Amazon can bring social employment benefit and author individual skillful training advantage and royalty income benefit to any on country author in nowadays online published industty. So, Amazon online business activities can increase global social employment chance, encourages global authors attempt to train writing skill, helps e-buyers to save visiting shops shopping time and air ticket expenditure for global overseas buyers.

- How and why Amazon e-commerce organization influence global consumee behavioral changes to bring ecommerce benefits to sellers?

In behavioral economic view, Amazon changes consumers behavior as well as product sellers sale method, such as global consumer sellers began to accept online purchase method to replace frequent visiting shop purchase method and global sellers began to accept to apply Amazon webstores to help them to sell products from its online sale channel to replace opening shops locate to the country sale channel.

The advantages to global sellers may include they do not need to pay rent or buy the shops, they can use Amazon webstores to show their different kinds of products photos and prices to let any one online buyer to know . The advantage to global buyers, they do not need to spend time to visit any countries shops to choose products in order to make purchase decision. They only need to spend some time to visit amazon any one country's webstore to see any brands of product photos and know their prices to different kinds of products to compare design and price and functions among of them in the online visiting short time when they stay at home to trun on themselves home computers . So, future home consumption behavior may replace visiting shop consumption behavior. Amazon 's online purchase method will encourage global many sellers have began to believe traditional visiting shop purchase model can not be accepted to global any one consumer more easily, when any one owns computer and internet service at home in common. Then, global shops number will reduce, due to different kinds of product websites purchase model needs number increases to global product sellers, they will close their shops and open themselves webstores or choose Amazon webstore to help them to sell their products conveniently. Consequently, global online purchase and sale transactions number will be influenced to increase by e-commerce organization development.

Why can global consumer behavioral change influence global economic change

- Have they close relationship between consumer behavioral change and economic change?
- How does consumer behavioral change impact economic change?
- How does cosumer behavior bring positive or negative influence to economic growth or economic recession to the country?

I shall attempt to apply behavioral economic theory to explain their cause and effect relationship why and hoe global economy growth or recession may be impacted by global consumer behavior change reasons ae blow:

I shall indicate travellingleisure and goods air plane transport industries example, since air planes are invented, it is a kind rapid air transport tool, it can help human to do both kinds of transport asrvice, one is goods transport and another is human transport . So, any individual or business goods can be delivered to another country offices or homes by air planes transport tools rapidly. SO, air planes can create more overseas purchase and sale business activities chance between different countries nowadays. Moreover, internet invention, it also increase more e-coomerce online purchase and sale business acitivies to global any one online buyer, he/she only needs to apply computer tool to click to the online seller webstore, when he /she likes the product, he/she can pay visa to buy the product from the onlin seller webstore at home conveniently.

Hence, e-commerce encourages global consumers to choose to buy any products from internet channel, it also brings global goods are needed to transport by air planes between different countries, e.g. one US online buyer makes purchase decision from onlin channel, then he chooses the product from Korean one online seller webstore. After he pays visa to the Korean online seller webstore , then the Korea seller will follow his US address to send the product to the US buyer's home after several days rapidly.

Hence, it explains that if future global consumers like to buy any products from any one country's onine sell webstore. Then, the product must need to be delivered to the online buyer's home. When the seller's product is not located to the online buyer's country warehouse. It needs to be delivered by air plane. When, global there are man consumers, their traditional visiting shops purchase habits are influenced to change online visiting webstores habits. Then, when their purchase habits are influenced to change by rapid, convenient, visa card payment online purchase method at home, time online purchase technological new payment channel method.

In future new online purchase trend development, it may influence future global traditional visiting shops consumption model to change visiting webstores consumption model. Consequently, consumers will choose to pay visa online purchase at home in preference. Also, it encourages visa card purchase , consequently, online purchase may influence these industries development, airlines goods transport service needs increase, it can increase new visa cards number to the frequent online channel e-buyer number. So, online consumption encourages global households save long time money in banks, because we can pay money by visa card payment after we buy any products from online. Global bank may have more money to save longer time from global households, long time money save , because we do not need to withdraw money to buy any expensive products, immediately, e.g. computer , television, furniture etc. When global households begin to accept online purchase method is better to compare visiting shop purchase method. So, future global airline goods transport and bank saving businesses these two industries may have positive impact by future global online buyers raising number.

Hence, when global consumers behaviors began to change online purchase , their online purchase activities may influence global banks can have long time saving money and airlines goods transport need increase rapidly. However, online purcahse activies will bring negative consumers emotion impact to some businesses, e.g. property rent business, because when the country has high population of consumers, they choose online purchases, they won't often vitis shops to choose any kind of products frequently, they only like to stay at home and turn on themselves home computers to find whether global whom sellers, they have webstores to let global consumers to buy their products from online channel. Due to the cuntry willl not have many consumers like to spend time to visit any shops in the country. It means that the country will have many shops are needed to be close, because there are less number peple visit the businessmen shops every day. It will cause property rent service providers can not increase rent income, even decrease rent income, when there are many businessmen close their shops and change onine webstores to replace actual shops. Hence, it seems that online buyers number increases, it may also brings positive impact to influence shop rent service income decreases to the property rent developers.

On global macro economic changing environment, online buyers number increases, it can encourage any kinds of products, they can sell more more easily. So, global product sale number may be influenced to increase rapidly, when global online purchase and sale transactions number increase, GDP on any kinds of product income may be influenced to increase . So, online buyers number increases, it must may bring positive impact to influence global trading GDP high growth, but global shops rent income property developers may be influenced to reduce, due to there are many shops may be caused to close in possible.

How travellers' leisure need change, it may influence travelling leisure service industry development? I shall attempt to explain how COVID 19 disease influences global travellers lesiure need change and airpine and travelling service providers, e.g. hotels, travelling agents, their leisure service needs change. Nowadys, COVID 19 disease has caused global many travellers feel fear to catch airplanes, because air planes all windows are needed to close, he/she has COVID disease, then he/she can bring any one passegner to get this kind of disease by air plane close window air environment. So, when globa many travellers feel afreaid to catch air planes, this kind of COVID 9 air contact disease, it can cause global travellers number has began to reduce, many of travelles began to reduce travelling times per year, even 0 time travel per year. Consequently, it will bring negative impact to global travelling industry development.

Firstly, COVID 19 disease influences global traveller individual travelling desire decreases, every traveller began to avoid to catch air planes to travel. So, any country;s airlines air planes flying times began to reduce, because it is no full seats booking to any airlinees. It means that airlinee must decrease income, alsoo they need to pay parking airplanes rent to any countries airports. So, fixed rent expenditure will need to pay, and many airlines began to dismiss the excess extra number of airline front service staffs, e.g. airport front service staffs, air plane check in /out staffs, even pilots number began also decreased.

So, airline unemployment ratio increases , it causes pilots, airlines service staffs need to change jobsm even some coutnries pilots , choose to do simple goods delivery jobs in supermarkets or securities. Also, COVID 19 disease influences hotels, travelling agents income began to reduce, because there are none many travellers need to live hotels, and they do not need travelling agents to help them to arrange any travelling journeys. So , COVID 19 disease influences many different countries travellers began choose any leisure activities to replace travel, because they feel afraid to get COVID 19 disease when they need to sit in closed window air plane environment.

This kind of disease can influence any one travller individual leisure choice began to change, such as they began to forgive travel siure activities, they will spend holiday to do other leisure activities in themselves countries , e.g. climbing mountain, swimming, running, playing table tennis, tennis etc. different outdoor sports. all of these leisure sports have same features, global any one leisure needer, he does not catch air plane to fo to another country to carry on playing these any one sport and he/she does not need to pay more price to enjoy these sports. Otherwise m travelling leisure activity, it must need any one leisure needer to spend much expenditure to enjoy this kind of leisure activity . So, it explains why many travellers beagan to choose to do any kinds of sports to replace spending money to enjoy travel leisure in their holidays,

On conclusion,m this COVID 19 disease had influenced global travel leisure businesses and travel related leisure service industries income and travellers number began to reduce and any countries GDP on travelling industry will have negative economic recession occurrence in this COVID 19 disease global envionment. Hence, it implies thaat consumers (travellers) behavior leisure activities need, it may influence global business activities increase or decrease , global economic growth or recession, they have close cause and effect relationship between consumer behavioral change and industries GDP changes in behavioral economic view.

Can economy effects students' academic performance

- Can student individual financial situation or economic environment influence individual learning performance ?

Why does student enrollment rise when the economy recession? When a strugging economy certainly forces extra pressure on young students seeking funds for loans and tuition cost, the enrollment rates for colleges continuous to rise. In fact, some experts theoritize that a poor economy environment actually helps a stimulate student enrollment. Whether it is the economy , new academic programs or better recruiting, community colleges are seeing an enrollment boom, when enrollment has been growing steadily , it may increase year institutions. To help prospective student interests when providing all current students with diverse support.

What the motivation had factors that are encouraging students to enroll, e.g. whether it is that the country 's young people feel the country begins have poor economy, so many of them choose to enroll schools to learn new knowledge, because scoial poor economy environment, it won't have many employers like to pay more salaries to employ new employees, consequencey, unemployment rate will rise, it causes students feel difficult to find jobs to do in general, even graduate students. So, it seems that economy recession may encourage students further study, because job supply is decreasing. so, it causes many young people choose to spend time to further study in order to wait economy recovery later. Then, they can prepare to seek any new jobs more easily when there are many employers like to increase employees number.

So, it explains that they have case and effect relationship between student enrollment number and the country's economy growth or recession or recovery, For example, when the country economy growth, in society, it will have many employers like to spend more salaries to employ new employees, because there are many people like to consume, when most of them have jobs to do and earn higher income. so, it seems that in society consumer individual increasing consumption attitude/desire that can help businesses grow, when businesses have more customers, they have effort to pay money to buy any things to use.

Businessmen ought need to increase employees number to help them to develop themselve businesses more successfully. So, it is economy growth period, moreover, many young people feel economy growth can create more employment chance in society. So, it encourages many students choose to forget to continue to pursue high level academic education, e.g. when the student had graduated undergraduate degree, due to he feels social economic environment is improved. So, employers are seeking new employees to help them to develop businesses. So, employment chance increases and salaries level will also rise. So, it encourages many undergraduate students do not want to pursue master degree. Because they believe that they can find jobs to do more easily in this time. So, it seems that the society's present economy suitation is either goos or worse, it can impact students to choose continue pursue higher learning stage or not. So, it explains that student individual learning desire and the social economy have close influential relationship.

● Why does economy scenarios can influence student learning behavior?

Why does economy scenarios can influence motivation and learning behavior on student achievement? Quality in higher education is not only determined by lecturers, it also depends on student individual learning desire, because if economy scenarios can influence the student learning desire to pursue continue learning or seek jobs in society. Then, quality in higher education won't be main factor to influence student individual learning in success or failure. If the student does not plan to continue to learn, even the school has good quality in higher education , it won't attract the student to choose to enrol to the school to continue learn easily. It is due to whether economy scenarios how influences the student decides to pursue or forget further study.

In fact, any countries must encounter or experience economic recession or economic growth or economic recovery period different social economic environment changes. It will bring negative or positive emotion impact to the country's every student learning attitude, in order to decide whether continue pursue learning is better or forget pursue learning is better. So, school fee whether is high or less, it is not main factor to influence student individual continue learn.

In macro economic view, the social's economic growth, or economic recession or economic recovery , any one of these economic scenarios change, it will bring positive or negative emotion impact to encourage the student either chooses to further learning pursue or forgive further learning pursue, in student further learning social behavioral economic view.

ON conlusion, on behavioral economic analytical theory, it explains our social macro economic environment new changes to be better or worse, it may bring indirect impact to influence the country's student individual learning desire or learning behavior either on pursue continue learning or forget continue learning in global societies. So, it also implies that whether the school's fee whether it is more or less, it is not main factor to influence student individual continue pursue to learn or not. If the student feels that movement, himself/herself country's social economic scenario is worse, or it is experiencing recession. The student will be influenced to choose continue to go to school to pursue further learning. So, worse economic environment or recession macro economic environment feeling, it may persuade any country's students trend to choose to pursue further study intention more than seeking jobs to work intention, because they feel social jobs provisin chances are influenced to reduce, and no many jobs to supply to them to choose, salaries will be reduced etc . these factors , they can caes the country will have many students make school enrollment choice more than seeking jobs choice. Hence, I believe that any country students school enrollment choices, they have close relationship to themselves country's economic scenario changes at the moment. Hence in behavioral economic view, it may explain why and how any country's economic environment can bring either positive or negative emotion influence to persuade or dissuade the student chooses to either continue further academic study or forgive continue further academic study. So, behavioral economy theory is one kind of new economy and psychological science. Psychologists can apply this theory to research and explain and conclude how and why our social economy change can impact students, consumers, households, businessmen believe in order to make rational decision to earn more economic benefit and avoid economic loss. Also, behavioral economy theory also may help psychologists and economists to predict how and why our societies will ought to be changed to be better ot worse by which kind of factors accurately. So, it may help government leaders or businesses organizations decision makers to do more accurate decisions or strategies to solve any challenges in success.

Can economy theory explains absolute consumer right behavior

What does consumer right behavior mean?

Economic theory is based on the assumption that investors and consumers are rational and very efficient machines. They make the best choices for themselves. Laboratory tests reveal that investors' behaviors are much more complicated relative to the behavior assumes in most economic theories. Hence, economic theories is used by economists, they try to explain economic phenomena, to interpret why and how the economy behaves and what is the best to solution, how to influence or solve these economic phenomean. In principle, the approach to economic theory is divided into positive and normative.

The most popular economic theories include; Analyses of different market structures have yields economic theories that dominate the study of microeconomics. IN general, economic theory is applied to market organizations. They are perfect competition, monololistic competition, olgopolu, imperfect competition.

So, in any business environment, business on abve four type of economic organizations, they may attempt to apply economic theory to complex consumers behavior. Consumer behavior theory is the study of have people make decisions when they purchase, helping businesses and marketers capitalise on these behaviors by predicting how and when a consumer will make a purchase in economic environment organizational view.

In fact, in societies any economic factors may influence consumer behavior. Economic factors that influence consumer behaviors are : personal income, family income, income expectation, savings, liquid asset of consumer. So, it seems that personal income of a person is determinant of consumer individual buying behavior.

Hence, the role theory says that much of what we buy is to fulfill to characteristics of a role we see ourselves as playing. This can help us understand consumer behavior because people are more likely to buy things for what they mean not for what they do. So, the theory is consumer realistic because of consumers focus on a modest let of important goods and services, they may able to achieve societies is close to the theoretical optimum in term over utility.

- How economic theory explains our social consumer behavior causes?

For example, one product brand and advertisement strategy, if the product can develop good attractive advertisement and famous brand. Its campaigns may be a real asset in economic view to better meet the needs of its customers and increases sales (socio-economic classification).

If act, instead of economic factor can influence consumer behavior, other factors may also influence they include psychological, social , cultural personal factors, e.g. social class, role and status, personal age, occupation, life style, personality, motivation, past purchase experience. All of these are the consumer individual psychological factor. So, economic environment changes, it may influence consumers, how to decide to buy the kind of products, but this economic factor, it can not control or derminate overall consumer behavior in the overall consumption mrket (country) , in maco economic vie , the micro economic view, psychology factor to the consumer, it can also dominate or control the consumer behavior, e.g. product choice. For example, one lawyer, he had good lawyer job and high income to support him to pay one time expenditure to buy a new car, so he does not pay instalement to the car seller to buy the new car. So, in behavioral economic view, he won't have economic pressure to buy the new car, he does not need to pay installment and interest to own the new car after one year. Hence, when he gathers information concerns the new car technology development, he spends time to compare the new car different brands, price new car dealr choice, purchase timing and amount, after purchase repair service behavior. He makes the evaluation of alternative to different brands of new cars. Although, brand (A) is new car, its price is more expensive to compare other kinds of cars, because it has good design, large size, more seats, steel quality for driving safety reasons. He has enough money economic effort to choose to buy this brand (A) new car. But, when he compares it to another brand (B) new car. Although, its present car price is cheaper, but it does not represent tht its stell quality is worse, or not more driving safety and he also knows that the brand (B) new car will have another new car model to promote to car market, after three months. Moreover, brand (B) new car seller can build famous car brand image to same to brand (A) new car by its advertisement channel.

Hence, it seems that it is one perfect competition (fair competition) new car market in this country. Any new car sallers can dominate or control their new car sale price freely. So, this country new car market competition is serious, because this high income lawyer spends time to compare the both brand (A) and (B) new cars. He will be influenced to choose to buy brand (B) new car by its advertisement. So, this lawyer car purchaser will not feel that friends believe him have high income to influence him to choose to buy the brand (A) new car. He only consider whether which brand (A) and (B) nee car price is more reasonable factor to influence him to make the final new car purchase decision. So, the brand (B) new car's advertisement had persuaded him to choose to buy (A) last invention new car after 3 months. He chooses to delay time to buy brand (B) 's new invention car after 3 months, because he does not need to drive one new car immediately.

Hence, it seems that economic theory factor won't be the main factor to influence the lawyer to buy the brand (A) new car immediately, althought he has high stable income job. His psychological factor also influences his new car brand choice decision, e.g. he will feel that whether it can represent he has high social status or class when friends know he had owned one high price of new car, whether a high price of new car must represent he has high income of lawyer occupation, so, it seems that this high income lawyer must not choose to buy the high price of new car. he must neeed time to gather or research information to evaluate whether which brand of new car is valid to choose to buy.

Consequently, economic theory must not explain absolute right consumer behavior, it also depends on other factor, e.g. behavioral economic psychological factor, to assist it to conclude more accurate judgement why and how the consumer does his/her final purchase decision. So, psychologic economic theory can apply psychology and economic theory to conclude more clear understanding how and why the consumer chooses to do his/her final purchase decision in nowadays consumption market.

Behavioral economy theory brings what advantages to our society

Why do we need behavioral economy to help us to solve social or business problem?

Whether what are the actual benefits , they may bring to influence our societies change better? I shall attempt to to explain above question. Economic is the social science that examines how individuals, businesses and entire societies manage scarce resources. Resources are by nature , limited. Only a finite amount of land exists, e.g. and people do not have unlimieted time to meet all of their needs and wants. So, if we can learn ho to apply behavioral economy theory to avoid resources waste, then our societies ought develop better.

Our society had changed from traditional economy to develop to nowadays knowledge economy. Traditional economy only produce and take what they need, so there is no waste or inefficiencies involved in produdig the goods required to survive as a society. However, traditional economy also have disadvantages, such as it isolates the people within that economt, large outside economies can win a traditional economy. It offers choices, these may be a lower overall quality of life, it creates specific health risk, unpredictability creates survival uncertainties.

Although, our societies had been experiencing knowledge economy, but it also have disadvantage, knowledge economy means that our societies or business organizations need to learn how ro use knowledge management to keep business growth or social developing. Knowledge management is a systematic approach to capturing and making use of a organization collective expertise to create value. The potential advantages of effective knowledge management are significant , but as with most processes, advantages of knowledge management or knowledge econmic society may include: Improved organizational or social productivities better and faster decision making, quicker problem solving, increased rate of innovation, supported employee/citizen growth and development within organizations or societies, sharing of specialiat expertise, better communication, improved business processes.

Hence if the organization or society can apply behavioral economic theory to learn knowledge management system , it can help the organization or society to develop better or more easier, e.g. create better products and services , develop better strategies, improve profitability or productivity, reuse existing skills and expertise, increase operational efficiency and staff productivity, recognise market trends early and gain on advantage over rivals make the most of organizations or social intellectual capital . Hence, it explains why when our organizations or societies can apply behavioral economy theory to learn how to apply knowledge management system to develop our organiztations or societies. Then, our societies or organizations will avoid to waste social resource organizational resource as well as achieve more productivities or service improvement, even gain profitability, it is the final aim of why our organizations or / and societies need to attempt to learn how to apply knowledge management system to achieve any objectives in behavioral economy view.

On conclusion, behavioral economic is the study of the effect that our societiesand organizations need to learn how psychological factors have on the economic decision making process of individuals. The importance of understanding behavioral economics for marketers is immeasurable as it follows for a better understanding of the human mind. So, behavioral economics plays a important role in our live and in the eocnomy. It helps governments and businesses learn on every day consumers activities and explains why we consume goods and services , the way we do, why we make certain choices, about ourselves or others and how we decide of action . Hence, behavioral economists need to examine each of these day -to -day choice resulting in progressive understanding of human behavior that combines both psychology and economy.

How do rules influence economic behavior?

Why are the rules of the economic system important? In our societies , our economic behavior occurs in a climate of formal and informal rules. There sulres often act as incentives and influenced the choices people make, people choose to do jobs taht do not keep them fit, and now they have to make more time to stay healthy. So, our societies are experiencing behavioral economic rules made in order to let every one need to adapt how to change and influence to our lives. it is one actual knowledge economic society or knowledge economic social living mode that we need to learn how to adapt to live. We need to learn how to apply knowledge of economic changing behavior. UNderstanding behavioral economic and psychology for social impact our businesses can bring products , sale growth more easily or our societies can be improved to our living quality better.

The relationship between behavioral economy and our society , it may explain that if the result of economic scarcity in a society occurrence, due to that productive resources are limited, therefore, people can not have all the goods and services, they want, a result, they must choose some things and give up others , like individuals, governments and societies , experience scarcity because human wats exceed with can be made from all available resources.

Behavioral economic is the study of psychology as it relates to the economic decision making processes of individuals and organizations. Behavioral economy theory uses psychological experimentation to develop theories about human decision making and has identified a range of biases as a result of the way people think and feel. BE is trying to change the way economists think about people's perception of value and expressed preferences.

However, in our societies, we need have three basic economic problems. Economic systems is as a type social system must confront and solve the three quantities of goods shall be produced, how much and which of alternative tools and services shall be produced, how shall goods be produced what technology a well as for whom are the goods , or services produced who benefts?

All of these are our daily economic problems any organizations (societies) had been changing. We need new social science behavioral economy theory to help use to solve any one of social economic individual problems, for example, when a particular incident becomes cognitively available, it is became of social influence. Individuals are specially averse to losses, but how do we know whether we are facing a loss or instead of a foregone gain ? What is the status from which losses are measured ? how might social influence reduces or increase people's willingness to sacrifice their material sale-interest for the sake of fairness?

All of these matter, applying behavioral economic theory may attempt to explain the reason why the consequency occurs. Also, when some countries governments can apply behavioral economy theory to help them to do reasonable strategic decision in order to avoid any one of these social negative events occur, such as organizational crime, discrimination, environmental hazards, or threats to national security before any one country government decides to implement any strategic action, they may apply behavioral economic theory to weigh whether their decision may bring socity to earn more benefit or more loss, for example, if the country government permits the oil manufacturing firm continues to research the possible oil manufacturing elements at the oceans. Whether their oil research behavior on the ocean , it will bring how serious environmental hazard to cause global oceans have many fishes die per day, how much percentage successful chance oil discovery on anywhere in the oceans. So, any country governments need to consider whether ocean land oil discovery chance is more important or reducing many fishes death number is more important when any country goverments continue to permit any one oil manufacturers continue to find oil land from oceans in order to manufacture more oil, during their ocean oil land manufacturing process, it may bring serious pollution to ocean water and causes many fishes drink the polluted oil water to be killed. For another exmaple, US government allows many local manfacturers set up factories in China, in order to let many US social manufacturers can pay cheap wages to employ China workers to help them to manufacture any products, e.g. mobiles, shoes, cloths, shirts, televisions etc. although US governmment can bring discrimination image to let China workers feel, they can have more job chance and to earn US manufacturer employers wages. In economic view, China can reduce workers unemployment ratio from US manufacturers' factories manufacture jobs chance. Also , US manufacturers can pay cheaper wages to Chinese workers to compare US domestic workers wages. But, US government neglects , it will also cause many US domestic factories manufacture workers had beed beginning to lose their factory manufacture jobs, because Chinese manfacture workers can replace them to do their Us social factory manufacture jobs more easily. Hence, in long term, US manfacturers choose to outsource local factory manufacture workers to them to do, it will cause US unemployed workers manufacture number increases., Hence , US government ought need to weigh long term high unemployment ratio social issue to US domestic factory manufacturing workers, whether US manufacturers cheap or low wages to Chinese factory manufacturing workers (low wage cost) is more important ot reducing US domestic factory manufacturing workers unemployed number social negative influence more important. If US government continue allows US manufacturers outsource domestic factory manufacturing workers to do, it must increase US local manufacturing workers unemployment number and it may cause US government needs to pay future more social welfare expenditure to these long time unemployment US manufacturing workers, even, social stealing crime may be influenced to increase . It implies that behavioral economy analysis can help our society to choose to make more reasonable decisions.

CHAPTER TWO

HOW AGRICULTURE FARMER WORKING BEHAVIOR INFLUENCES ECONOMY DEVELOPMENT

Introduction to farming industry development

Learning agricultural economic advantages

What is agricultural economic? What is farming? Why do we need to learn agricultural economy? Farming is an organized way to produce food., bio-energy and other non-food foods by cultivation. Agricultural economies deals with how to organize other non-foods; how the products are distributed, handled and consumed; and with the local and global impact this has on living conditions, societies, environment and economies. Also, farming and argicultural economic has close relationship.When global farming development can be kept the best, then it will bring every farmer has good income, even the country's economy will be also improved.

Farming can be defined as an organized way to grow crops and rear animals in order to provide food, bio-energy and other non-foods through cultivation with the purpose of selling the products, or using them in kind. Our definition of farming includes all kinds of animal farming and plant farming everywhere, irrespective

of location aims of production, methods of production, economy and society. It refers to all kinds of outdoor crop cultivation, plus greenhouse cultivation, and forms of animal food. We won't exclude fish farming. Farming activities include all kinds of form work that is conducted with or without the help of machinery and equipment, such as tractor driving control of automatic milking, field inspections, equipment repairs, digging ditches, mending fences, carrying feed and water for farm

animals, making budgets and discussion with agricultural advises. Finally, agriculture aovers a wider field than farming , for example in formulations , such as

agricultural production, agricultural sectors and politics.

Agriculture is whether a meeting between nature and human society? Whehter is necessary for human survival? Is it dependent on land, is ruled by weather, seasons and

biological rhythms, is both predictable and unpredictable, economizing with resources, is conducted by large numbers of farmers, and may be highly influenced by social and cultural factors? Why is agriculture both predictable and unpredictable? Because seasonality influences practical farming, agricultural business and food consumption. If the harvest fails, one generally has to wait for the right season before it is possible to start all cover again, for example, on grazing seasons. Seasonality thus characrerizes much of farm work and yearly rhythm in farming. So, the season may impacts supply and demand for agricultural products, and price levels on inputs as sowing seed, and outputs , such as grains and meats.Hence, farming's dependency on nature means that agriculture is both highly predictable and unpredictable. Days and seasons come and go, which gives farming a repetitive and foreseeable character. Both crop farming and livestock production are in ordinary weather patterns and seasons. Prolonged rainy seasons can delay seedinf and distrurb the entire growing season.

Why do farmers need to choose how to use degree of farming market orientation? Some kinds of farming are certainly much more frequent in some parts of the world trhan in others,for example, find both big commercial farms and poor smallholdings in Kenya, India, China and Braxil. There may also be homogenous farmung on plains where farmers have more in common with colleagues across border than with smallholders in other parts of the same country. So, China, INdia, Brazil and Kenya farmers need to choose where grow good taste food, fruit , vegetable in order to make wrong farming land investment loss.

What is food chain relationship? A food chain can be defined as a linear sequential structure that shows varios stages along the processes of production, handling and consumption of food. The food chain approach is widely applied, and a way to involve , such as the farmer, the transport sector and the consumer. It is also appliable to fibre, bio-energy and other non-food chains that are being produced in a agricultural sector. However, the chains for marketed foods is complex. On input supply hand, the purchased input resources that are put into the food chain. Among the input suppliers to farm production, such as fertilizer industries, seed companies, animal feed companies, farm machinery companies, agro-chemical industries,petrochemical companies and electricity suppliers. Energy and chemicals are also continuously required during later stages, which also use large amounts of inputs, such as packaging materials, transport and storage facilities. Then farmers are main the market oriented farm production of crops role and animal products, fibres, bio-energy and varying by-products form the basis for food chains and other agricultural chains role both.

The intermediate stages include larger or smaller parts of the total handling and final costs for agricultural product. SOme of these activities are frequently repeated along the chain, not least transport, repackaging and intermediate storeage. It includes these processes, such as post-harvest processes, storage , transport, distribution, wholesale, food processing, such as change and/or preserve foods, packaging and retailing. The final stage is consumption , or eating, it relates to consumer individual food purchase choice activities, such as the trip to the supermarket, storing in the household and cooking, and eventually alos some care with packaging and food waste.

However, waste is produced all along the chain, and is a by-products to foods. The distination between waste and by-products may be a some that to a great extent is decided by the ambition to reuse or recycle. Nonetheless, waste occurs, stored in landfills and/or emitted into air and water. Consequently, waste can cause air and water pollution to our natural environment. For example, HOng Kong city is not a good place to develop farming industry. The reasons may include: air and water is polluted seriously, the numebr of people living in urban areas had exceed the number of people in countryside in Hong Kong city, due to population had been increasing from Chinese emmigrants every day. Hence, HOng KOng';s agriculture development is worse and difficult to compare prior 1960. Moreover, HOng JOng has many people need to live, so many lands had been using to build houses, because HOng KOng is a small city, land shortage is serious. So, shortage of land supply and ships' gas emission and cars' fuels pollutes Hong KOng seas, rivers, and air. Hence, these HOng Kong
people's activities, manufacturers' pollution activites on manufacturing processes, shipping transport's oil emission activities , even air planes flying activities had influenced Hong KOng can not provide good natural environment to carry on farming activities in order to grow up its agricultural economic development again easily after 1960. Also, it means that Hong KOng's land used for permanent crops won't have possible to develop again. It is HOng KOng government's duty. It only considers housing, financial activities aspect, but it neglects to research how to continue to develop its farming activities in order to bring agricultural economic growth, such as before 1960's successful agricultural development on rural.

Why do we need to know where can provide enough livestosk food to eat and good climate environment farming land use? The reason is simple, global population is continue increasing, such as China, India. They are increasing many people , they feel needs to live in themselves countries, if they can not know how to find the best farming lands to grow food, vegetables , fruits
or let livestock to alive. Then, the future food shortage challenges may occur to cause these countries have many people die because global has no enough foods to supply to them to eat in possible. So, studies of farm animals around the world teach is to the most varied types of landscapes and places, such as windblown moorlands, muddy

backyards and enornous pigs or chickens, plants. SOme of kinds of animal farming are based on vast land areas, such as nomadism and large-scale rearing of sheep or cattle on low yielding pastures.

IN constrast, scientists find increasing numbers of plants with tens of thousands of pigs or chickens, to which the feed is transported from far away. So, seeking the best farming lands will be needed to any countries farmers in order to raise farming foods productive number more easily. The lands have enough water, none dry weater. Then, the land will be a good farming or harrested more easily. Farmers also need to know how to solve environmental problems to influence various kinds of livestock production.

They may include (1) how to directly connected with animals, such as emissions of greenhouse gases, such as carbon dioxide and methane from ruminants; emissions of nitrous oxide from animal manure; overgrazing, causing soil erosion and reduced biodiversity; leakage of nutrients from animal manure into water courses, high consumption of water, especially by high producing dairy cattles. (2) connected with feed production, it may include: Emissions of greenhouse, gases due to methods of cultivation; ;and degraduation due to eventual exploitation of forests and permanent pastures; problems due to use; overuse; of fertilizer and pesticides; water problems due to irrigation of feed crops, (3) connected with other parts of the food chain, it may include: Emissions from transportation, cooling, processing and packaging along the animal food chain.

Current trends in global livestock production need must increase. The reasons may include that the world has experienced large-scale increases in demand food of animal origin , when increased world population, increased per capita consumption of animal foods, increased livestock production need, partly on the basis of highly resource intensive methods of production, increased attention to the livestock sector's negative impact on climate change, increased attention to the livestock sector's negative impact on other environmental problems, increased attention to the value of animal
production for reducing poverty and generating cash income and developing smallholder farming needs.

Another learning agricultural economic reason, instead of solution to above farming land shortage and environment pollution influences difficult growing foods reason. The reason is learning how to increase agricultural production of non-foods. Agricultural non-food production includes all kinds of products that are obtained through farming for other purposes than to be eaten. Dealing with agricultural non-food production includes a plathre of different activites, such as : production of commodities, utilization of by-products, recycling of organic matter, various agricultural related service and extraaction of bio-energy.

Bearing in mind, that one-third of the global land area is agricultural land(plus another one-third of forest land), farming is involved in flows of energy and i ncontinuous growth of enormous quantities of organic substances in the form of vegetable and animal matter. This gives thew agricultural sector a unique position in the border land between agriculture, energy and other natural resources. IN this perspective, human may perceive the farmed landscape as an area for the production with more or less ambitious utilization of by-products and recycling of resources plus numerous other beneficial activities. For example, natural fibes from crop and other plants contribute to substantial parts of the entire agricultural non-food production. For another example, in cotton farming, connon lint is ususally the main purpose, with cotton seed as by-product , although both are highly valuable. Other plant fibes are of more typical by-product character. COir fibes from coconuts, for another example, are quite useful for mats and brushes, but hardly the primary motive for coconut production. IN addition, fibre crops generate straw and husks at early stages of the fibre chains and further along the chains other fibrous residues may be achieved. SOme of these may be used in animal husbandry, as building material or compested to be cycled back into the land. At the same time as some of the traditional use of fibres is replaced by plastics, new fields of application are being developed , such as mixtures between natural and synthetic fibes for industrial purposes.

However, cotton is globally traded and an important commodity in the world economy with regard to both the fibres and its valuable oil and protein rich cotton seed. IN addition, cotton is also important at regional and local levels, like many other plant fibres. According to FAOSTAT, the largeest amount of cotton lint was in 2009 produced by China, with India , in second place, US in third and Pakistan as number four. Taken together, the four leading cotton producing countries allounteed for much as 72 per cent of the total quantity.

On conclusion, following above issues , they explain that learning agricultural economy can also help any countries' non-food farming production farming industry, instead of food farming production development. Hence, it will be our future any countries and farmers duties to learn how to develop agriculture in order to make the best choice to achieve the maximum non-farming food or farming food production to bring global human living benefits.

- Farming economy researchs

Agricultural economics, study of the allocation, distribution, and utilization of the resources used, along with the commodities produced, by farming. Agricultural economics plays a role in the economics of development, for a continuous level of farm surplus is one of the wellsprings of technological and commercial growth.

Farmers have always had to worry about economics. At what price can they sell their produce? Will buying new dairy cows pay off in having more milk to sell? What's the going rate for farm labor? However, agricultural economics, meaning establishing general principles and scientific rules to answer such questions, didn't develop until the late 19th or early 20th century.While some economists focus on theory, the importance of agricultural economics is that it's an applied discipline, not just academic. Farmers need information that helps them stay afloat financially, and the various types of agricultural economics tackle the relevant issues. In general, one can say that when a large fraction of a country's population depends on agriculture for its livelihood, average incomes are low. That does not mean that a country is poor because most of its population is engaged in agriculture; it is closer to the truth to say that because a country is poor, most of its people must rely upon agriculture for a living.

In general, farmers and economists will like to resesrch these questions or concern these questions when farmers grow their farming business or farming economist research how farming industry brings our global economic influences, these questions may include: What are the production costs of agriculture? How can farmers manage them successfully? How can farmers use their land and their workforce most effectively? Do the costs of buying equipment outweigh the profits of greater mechanized efficiency? As demands change, such as the growing interest in organic produce, is it necessary or profitable for farmers to change what they grow or how they produce it? How can society balance the needs of farmers with those of hikers, dirt bikers and other outdoor-recreation enthusiasts? How do we balance the needs of farmers with the needs of the environment? What should government farm policy entail? etc. different questions. For example, if a family's income were to increase by 100 percent, the amount it would spend on food might increase by 60 percent; if formerly its expenditures on food had been 50 percent of its budget, after the increase they would amount to only 40 percent of its budget. It follows that as incomes increase, a smaller fraction of the total resources of society is required to produce the amount of food demanded by the population.

How farming industry develops ? That fact would have surprised most economists of the early 19th century, who feared that the limited supply of land in the populated areas of Europe would determine the continent's ability to feed its growing population. Their fear was based on the so-called law of diminishing returns: that under given conditions an increase in the amount of labour and capital applied to a fixed amount of land results in a less-than-proportional increase in the output of food. That principle is a valid one, but what the classical economists could not foresee was the extent to which the state of the arts and the methods of production would change. Some of the changes occurred in agriculture; others occurred in other sectors of the economy but had a major effect on the supply of food.

In looking back upon the history of the more developed countries, one can see that agriculture has played an important part in the process of their enrichment. For one thing, if development is to occur, agriculture must be able to produce a surplus of food to maintain the growing nonagricultural labour force. Since food is more essential for life than are the services provided by merchants or bankers or factories, an economy cannot shift to such activities unless food is available for barter or sale in sufficient quantities to support those engaged in them. Unless food can be obtained through international trade, a country does not normally develop industrially until its farm areas can supply its towns with food in exchange for the products of their factories.

Economic development also requires a growing labour force. In an agricultural country most of the workers needed must come from the rural population. Thus agriculture must not only supply a surplus of food for the towns, but it must also be able to produce the increased amount of food with a relatively smaller labour force. It may do so by substituting animal power for human power or by gradually introducing labour-saving machinery.

Agriculture may also be a source of the capital needed for industrial development to the extent that it provides a surplus that may be converted into the funds needed to purchase industrial equipment or to build roads and provide public services. For those reasons, a country seeking to develop its economy may be well advised to give a significant priority to agriculture. Experience in the developing countries has shown that agriculture can be made much more productive with the proper investment in irrigation systems, research, fertilizers, insecticides, and herbicides.

Like many economic disciplines, the agricultural economics definition stretches to a wide variety of fields and career paths. Agribusiness addresses issues in marketing, farm management, agricultural finance and trade. Policy analysts look at the effect of government agricultural policy on farms. Market researchers study market conditions to gauge the sales potential of different farm products. So, farming economic may include these aspects of research

1 Rural development and regional economics

2 Supply chain study and management

3 Natural resource economics, which studies how farmers can get the maximum use out of their land and other resources

4 Risk analysis

● Factors may bring risks to any farmers.

1 Time and Change external environment factor

Farming has always had an element of risk: One bad harvest or a crop blight can ruin a farm. However, the economics have changed over the centuries. At one time, increasing farm production was done entirely by expanding the amount of agricultural land: double the size of the farm, double the yields. Now, however, land is harder to come by, so farmers rely more on high-yield crops, machinery and the use of fertilizer. Another change is that governments in the 20th century became much more involved in controlling prices for produce. Agricultural prices fluctuate due to yield, supply and demand, so stabilizing prices and ensuring that farmers stay in business became a government priority.

2 Economic Factors Affecting Farming

Although farming is one of the world's oldest professions, modern farming is affected by uniquely modern economic factors. Farmers today compete in a complex economic environment where customers choose from produce grown all over the world and governments provide financial incentives for the production of certain crops rather than others. Although independently minded growers manage to create markets of their own through direct sales and other creative strategies, the majority of American farmers are still at the mercy of both economic factors and the weather.

Commodity Prices

The price of major commodity crops such as corn and soy depends of a variety of factors, such as investor speculation, weather and demand for these crops for both food and nonfood uses such as biofuels. Farmers who grow commodity crops earn or lose money based on the current rate that industrial buyers will pay for their output. In addition, commodity prices are affected by international economic factors, such as the weakness or strength of the dollar, because these farmers are competing with American farmers as well as with growers from all over the world.

Subsidies

The American government pays subsidies to farmers who grow commodity crops such as corn and soy because modern federal agricultural policy is based on the assumption that agricultural mass production benefits the economy by keeping food prices low. In theory, this policy provides farmers with a measure of economic stability, and provides consumers with affordable prices on the many processed food products made from these commodity crops. This policy encourages farmers to create an oversupply of a narrow range of crops because they make money for growing these foods regardless of current market conditions.

Labor and Immigration Laws

For better or for worse, mainstream agriculture depends on poorly paid labor that is often performed by migrant farmers, who are frequently living in the country illegally. The work pays so little that most naturally born citizens are unwilling to do it. If we are to continue buying agricultural produce at the prices to which we have grown accustomed, we must rely on workers who will work for the low wages that are customary in the field. Farming is affected by immigration laws that influence the availability of labor, as well as labor laws that allow or disallow subsistence agricultural wages.

What risks and opportunities corn or cotton farmers need to concern ? The cotton industry is huge, with cotton grown in dozens of countries around the world. Becoming a cotton farmer on a small scale is easier than starting a commercially viable farm that can compete with the enormous operations that already control the market. Cotton is a crop that requires lots of hot weather, so it is only viable in southern locations. Buy land that is suitable for growing cotton. corn farmer will need a location with a lot of hot, sunny weather and access to water. If a corn farmer is growing cotton as a hobby or for personal use, his farm doesn't need to be very large. If the corn farmer is attempting to make a living as a cotton farmer, he will need to profit from economies of scale, and will require at least 100 acres of land. This can be done on the job by working on a cotton farm and how operate the cotton plant, or more formally by attending an agricultural college and pursuing an advanced degree in agriculture. Learning by trial and error can be an expensive proposition in agriculture; the more the corn farmer learns in advance from the experience of others, the more likely the corn farmer is to avoid expensive mistakes. Plant the cotton farmer cotton seeds and provide them with all the requirements for them to thrive, including fertile soil, water and sunshine. Conventional cotton growing involves the use of large amounts of pesticides and herbicides. Decide if this the route what the cotton farmer wants to pursue, or if he wants to attempt to grow organic cotton. Growing organically is more labor-intensive, but the cotton farmer can sell his crop at a higher price. Develop a working relationship with suppliers and buyers. Agriculture is a competitive business, and any cotton farmers will need connections and a good reputation to sell their crop every year for a good price.

What are fish farming risks and opportunities ? Fish farming is a hot topic in some circles. Environmentalists are often critical of the impact fish farms can have on the environment, while advocates point out that they're a crucial source of high-quality protein. Wherever fish farmers stand on that debate, one of the big advantages of fish farming is that it's a fine entrepreneurial opportunity.

The Fundamental Problem which any fish farmers will be possible to encounter, they may include: Fish farming exists to address a fundamental problem, the demand for fish as a food source grows as the human population grows, and the number of fish available in the wild isn't keeping pace. Even in carefully managed wild fisheries, the combination of climate change, pollution and pressure from fishermen can produce unpredictable variations in the supply of fish. In a worst-case scenario, that can cause a fish population to crash, as Atlantic cod did in the 1970s and 1980s. In the long term, expecting conventional fisheries to continue to meet the world's needs with wild fish is as unrealistic as expecting a network of hunters to keep supermarket meat cases filled. Fish farming, or aquaculture as it's formally known, will need to make up the difference.

Fish farming risk

1 Keeps Fish Affordable

One of the basic principles of economics is that if demand is increasing and the supply is not, costs will go up. Over time, that trend could make fish unaffordable for all but the affluent. Bucking that trend is one of the biggest advantages of fish farming. By providing a steady, reliable, high-volume supply of fish, it helps the price remain manageable for most shoppers.

2 Reliable Supply and Wide Distribution

Having a reliable supply of fish is another advantage of aquaculture. The wild fishery fluctuates naturally, with catches rising or falling by the day, month or season. Fish farms turn out predictable harvests of fish at consistent sizes, making it easy for chefs, supermarkets, fishmongers and individual customers to plan their purchases. For restaurants and processors, this consistency means they can easily provide portions in standard sizes, too. Another advantage of fish farming is that it brings the supply of fish to where the consumers are. From open pens in inland lakes to tanks and ponds on dry land, fish farms can be set up almost anywhere there's a market. This cuts the financial and environmental cost of shipping and provides consumers with fresher fish. That's a win-win.

3 Consumer Health

Health authorities worldwide encourage more fish consumption, including the USDA's Dietary Guidelines for Americans, because it's a high-quality protein source that's low in saturated fat. Salmon has the added advantage of being especially high in omega-3 fatty acids, which promote heart health. Switching just a few meals per week from red meat to fish is not only healthier as a dietary choice, it's environmentally friendly as well: Fish farming is generally "greener" than meat production.

4 Preserves Wild Stocks

Another advantage of aquaculture is its potential to reduce the strain on wild fisheries and native fish stocks. The more fish farming meets our needs, the less incentive there is to purchase wild-caught fish. That in turn reduces the temptation to overfish and improves the likelihood that wild stocks can maintain a healthy population. Immature fish bred in captivity can even be used to re-establish species in places where they've been wiped out by overfishing.

However, one frequent criticism of fish farms is that they're not always efficient providers of dietary protein. Some operations rely on wild-caught "trash" fish or bait fish for much of their feed, meaning it's quite possible for the fish to consume more protein than they produce.

5 Risk to Wild Stocks

Unfortunately, fish farming also poses a risk to wild fish populations. Open-pen fish farms concentrate the creatures at unnaturally high levels, increasing waste and the risk of disease, just as many land-based hog and chicken farms do. This poses a threat to wild fish, which can be infected. Inland fresh-water systems can be just as harmful if they're located in a lake or river with its own wild species. Land-based systems that return used water to the local watershed also pose some risk. Escaped fish from these pens can become invasive, as fast-growing carp and tilapia do inland or farmed Atlantic salmon do on the West Coast.

6 Fish Farming as Entrepreneurial Opportunity

One additional advantage of fish farming is that it represents an opportunity from which entrepreneurs almost anywhere can benefit. Farms can be situated anywhere from open coastlines to a farmer's "back 40" to a shuttered factory in a Rust Belt city. Startup costs can be surprisingly low for a small operation, largely a matter of choosing the right species to cultivate and providing a suitable environment. Salmon, trout, catfish, tilapia, shrimp and crawfish are all common options. Some operators maximize their productivity through composite fish culture, which is raising a combination of compatible, noncompetitive species in the same bodies of water. This gives you more variety in your product line and more fish to sell at little additional cost.

● How economic Impact to fish and cotton farming industries

The social science of economics began as a branch of philosophy, but emerged as a separate discipline in the late 18th century after the publication of Adam Smith's landmark work, "The Wealth of Nations." Since then, economics has provided a scientific approach to understanding the ways in which families, firms and entire societies allocate resources to satisfy their needs and wants.

People live in a world of scarcity in which all resources—time, money, land and others—are finite. Because people do not have unlimited resources, they must allocate their time, money and other resources in a way that will achieve as many of their needs and wants as possible. For example, consumers want to obtain maximum value for their money, and businesses want to maximize profits subject to their existing capacity for production. Economics provides a systematic way to study production, consumption and resource allocation.

Throughout history, people have dealt with issues of resource allocation; often human survival depended on it. The concept of an economy did not develop until the Middle Ages, although markets and trade have existed since ancient times. Until the era of the Enlightenment in the 18th century, economics was not a discipline of its own, but a branch of philosophy, which also examined political, ethical and religious issues.Just as biologists and chemists apply scientific methods to understand questions involving biological and chemical phenomena, economists employ scientific methods, including hypothesis testing and quantitative analysis, to understand and explain economic phenomena. Why apartment rents are so much higher in New York City than in Austin, Texas; how government monetary policy will affect retail prices; what factors affect average wages in different countries—these and other questions involve economic phenomena. As a science, economics strives to provide answers and explanations.

Hence, economics plays an important role in the analysis and formulation of government policy. Just as consumers want maximum value for their money, politicians and taxpayers want to maximize the value of their taxes and other government resources at the lowest cost. Economists have an important voice in the policy arena, helping identify the types of policies that maximize benefits at the least cost to the public.As a scientific approach to policy, economics not only informs the debate over issues related to taxation, government spending and economic policies; it also applies to the full range of public policy issues, including health care, defense, education, energy and the environment.

Catfish Farming How Bring Profit

If one fish farmer or cotton farmer is looking for a decisive argument in favor of aquaculture, simple economics can provide one. The U.S. imports over 90 percent of its seafood, creating a yearly trade deficit that the USDA's Agricultural Research Service estimated at $14 billion as of January 2018. When you combine that economic impact with a fish farm's ability to fit in almost anywhere, the potential is clear: Fish or cotton farming can produce economic growth in places where jobs are sorely needed. Managing a fish or cotton farm sustainably can help reduce its disadvantages and increase its advantages. For conventional open-pen operators, for example, that can mean reducing the populations of fish or cotton in each pen to cut down on waste and reduce the need for medications. On land, fish or cotton farmers can opt for recirculating aquaculture systems that filter and reuse the same water constantly, isolating the farmed fish from local waterways and minimizing the risk that they'll escape and become invasive. An especially appealing option is aquaponics, a method of growing vegetable crops such as herbs, lettuce and tomatoes hydroponically with the same water that supports the fish. Waste from the fish fertilizes the plants, which in turn helps filter the water and keeps the fish healthy.

Aquaculture dates back thousands of years ago and is now a rapidly expanding business practice in the United States. Operating a catfish farm, for example, requires a precise and well-executed business plan. Farm operators must raise large amounts of capital to even begin a small fish-farming practice. There are, however, many benefits to fish farming over cattle or chicken farming, and savvy business considerations can help you how to profit in the world of farming catfish. For example, invest in a large farm. Large farms, on one hand, demand more acreage, thus costing more money. A farm costing $5,000 per acre multiplied by 90 acres equals $450,000 in the initial investment of the pond property alone. Building a large farm, however, allows you to sell more fish at one time — substantially increasing profit margins over smaller farms. Moreover, larger farms can export more easily to international markets — such as Asia — where fish is widely consumed. Design fish farm in a location with moderate temperatures and geography. Climates with excessive rain or snow can damage fish farming with flooding or freezing water. Choosing a geographical location away from areas where fault lines, tornadoes or hurricanes can result in annual natural disasters is also wise for the preservation of fish farm.Sell fishes in direct sales. Selling catfish direct to market eliminates the costs of unnecessary business entities raising the cost and taking a cut of the profits before the product reaches the consumer. Direct sales to a processing factory — which then sells directly to the public — reduce the need for dealing with grocery store chains or other costly business outlets. Using direct sales is a way to keep consumer prices down, maintain the freshness in fish and sell more of the product at one time.

● Pros and Cons of Biotechnology in Agriculture

If most people had to list the disadvantages of biotechnology, agricultural uses would rank high. Just look at how many foods proudly advertise as having no genetically modified ingredients. What are the advantages and disadvantages of biotechnology in agriculture?

Consider the pros of biotechnology, they may include:

Genetically engineering crops can make them resistant to disease and insect attacks. Inserting genes that make crops immune to herbicide allows farmers to eliminate weeds without hurting crops. There's less need to till the soil to kill weeds, which reduces erosion. Plants can produce toxic chemicals that kill off insect predators. Genetic engineering can make plants produce more food or improve their nutritional profile. Biotechnology can keep plant foods shelf-stable for longer periods.

Consider the cons of biotechnology they may include:

As farmers use herbicides more regularly, it accelerates the development of immunity in weeds. Genetically modified organisms are covered by patents. Farmers who replant seeds from a patented crop as they would with ordinary plants have faced lawsuits. Relying on GMOs reduces the natural genetic diversity found in agriculture. If, say, all corn or soybeans have the same genetic profile, there's a greater chance of some fungus or parasite wiping out the entire national crop. GMO seed is more expensive, though it can also lead to greater profits from a larger yield.

Risks of Biotechnology in Humans

Many people are uneasy about having products from GMOs in their food. Genetic engineering in human beings raises even more concern about the negative aspects of biotechnology. Monstrous experiments on humans have been a staple of horror movies, and for many people, the real thing is equally as troubling.

Many diseases stem from genetic problems, so treating them genetically can save or transform lives. This is effective if there's a single genetic issue that's easy to identify and treat. It's possible that eventually, we will be able to enhance human beings: stronger hearts, greater intelligence, more disease resistance. Much of our bodies and health aren't the product of single genes but complex interactions. It's entirely possible that in trying to improve ourselves, we'll create unwanted, disastrous side effects.

Some genetic diseases aren't as simple to treat as fixing one rogue gene. There are serious ethical issues when science experiments on humans. If we're altering genes to "improve" people, does that raise different ethical questions from altering genes to fix verifiable problems? Can we regulate human biotechnological treatments to gain benefits while restricting abuse?

All of above biotechnology technology whether it ought to apply to any agriculture industry to bring advantages and disadvantges, any farmers or farming economists or agricultural scientists must need to evaluate whether what future negative or positive influences human will face.

How developing countries develop farming industry

● How India land supply shortage may influence India farming industry economic development

We know how agriculture contributes to economic development and then how industry contributes towards development. However, the issue of choice of one sector over the other remains unresolved as far as economic policy is concerned. Industry which is, no doubt, important, will not progress unless agriculture is sound, stable, and progressive. Because of this interdependence these sectors are complementary, and not competitive. In the development of an underdeveloped economy, there is as such no conflict between agricultural and industrial development.

Hence, interdependence between agriculture and industry becomes strengthened through various linkages generated in these two sectors. The three most important linkages are : production linkages, demand linkages, and saving-investment linkages.Production linkages arise from the interdependence between agriculture and industry through the use of productive inputs. Agriculture draws some raw materials, like chemical fertilisers, pesticides, electric power, agricultural machinery and implements, etc., from the industry. Agriculture is also dependent on industry for the supply of materials for building up social and economic overheads in the agricultural sector. Further, many raw materials and inputs used in industrial production, e.g., cotton, jute, sugarcane, tobacco, etc., is supplied by the agricultural sector.

Demand linkages between the two sectors suggest that demand for one sector's product pulls demand for another sector in an upward direction. Urbanisation and industrialisation are synonymous. Under the impact of Green Revolution, agriculturists now experience rising rural incomes which has brought a change in the pattern of tastes and preferences of rural people. Increased rural income has resulted in an entry of industrial consumer goods, like TV, refrigerator, modem, car, footwear, refined sugar, edible oils, motorbikes, etc. In the urban areas, we see some sort of demand saturation of some of these products of consumer goods industries. The impact of rising urban incomes and industrialisation has a favourable impact on the demand for food, vegetables, fruits, various raw materials produced in the agricultural sector. It has been an article of faith in India that the demand stimulus for industrial expansion would likely come mainly from agriculture with low social and economic costs.

Finally, there is a savings-investment linkage between these two sectors. A self-reliant agriculture capable of exporting surplus food-grains helps in saving scarce foreign exchange resources of the country. Now these resources can be better utilised for importing capital goods and crucial raw materials needed for industrialisation effort. As agricultural production and productivity rises above the subsistence requirement, the volume of marketable surplus increases which provides sinews of industrialisation, particularly in the rural sector. Again, the rising volume of savings and capital formation consequent upon rising farm incomes give strong stimulus to demand for manufactured goods. Investment in one sector pulls investment of other sectors up thereby accelerating overall growth rate of the economy.

Similarly, the rise in non-farm incomes leads to an increase in the demand for various agricultural products. In the process, agricultural sector becomes diversified, modernised. Most importantly, the relative terms of trade between the two sectors affect the flow of resources from one to another sector. Terms of trade will improve for agricultural sector if over a period of time the prices of agricultural commodities move at a higher rate than the prices of manufactured articles. Thus, the terms of trade favouring agriculture results in an increased real income and hence, increased private saving and investment. The relative terms of trade also influence government saving and investment in these two sectors.If technological change is made in the primary sector there will be more surplus and, hence, more output in the industrial sector.

In the end, we must say a few words about the problem of inter-sectoral resource allocation. To begin with, it is almost impossible to make an optimum balance between these two sectors. In many of the developing countries, agriculture no longer enjoys a pride of place, for some obvious reasons. Neo-liberal era has seen the over-emphasis on the urban, industrial sector. That is why agricultural land is now being forcibly taken away for industrial development, infrastructural developments, and so on. Against this backdrop, farmers of these economies have been shifting their attention from the agricultural sector towards non- agricultural activities. How far these two sectors will complement each other, and to what degree, is an important issue. Indeed, the failure on the agriculture front is of tern attributed to faulty agricultural policy in many developing countries, including India. So, India is one good farming industry needing developing country example, any India fish and corn , furit , wheat, rice and meat farmers must need to concern how to use land natural resource for their farming development in order to avoid farming lands shorage challenge to influence India farming industry economic development.

- The Relationship between Economic Growth and Agricultural Growth To China

What is agricultural industry policy to future China ? China is number one in Agriculture. China ranks first in worldwide farm output, primarily producing rice, wheat, potatoes, tomato, sorghum, peanuts, tea, millet, barley, cotton, oilseed, corn and soybeans. The development of farming over the course of China's history has played a key role in supporting the growth of what is now the largest population in the world. Analysis of stone tools by Professor Liu Li and others has shown that hunter-gatherers 23,000–19,500 years ago ground wild plants with the same tools that would later be used for millet and rice.

What is China Farming method improvements ? Due to China's status as a developing country and its severe shortage of arable land, farming in China has always been very labor-intensive. However, throughout its history, various methods have been developed or imported that enabled greater farming production and efficiency. They also utilized the seed drill to help improve on row farming. For agricultural purposes the Chinese had invented the hydraulic-powered trip hammer by the 1st century BC. Although it found other purposes, its main function was to pound, decorticate, and polish grain that otherwise would have been done manually. The Chinese also innovated the square-pallet chain pump by the 1st century AD, powered by a waterwheel or oxen pulling on a system of mechanical wheels. Although the chain pump found use in public works of providing water for urban and palatial pipe systems, it was used largely to lift water from a lower to higher elevation in filling irrigation canals and channels for farmland.

Since 1994, the government has instituted a number of policy changes aimed at limiting grain importation and increasing economic stability. Among these policy changes was the artificial increase of grain prices above market levels. This has led to increased grain production, while placing the heavy burden of maintaining these prices on the government. In 1995, the "Governor's Grain Bag Responsibility System" was instituted, holding provincial governors responsible for balancing grain supply and demand and stabilizing grain prices in their provinces. Later, in 1997, the "Four Separations and One Perfection" program was implemented to relieve some of the monetary burdens placed on the government by its grain policy. As China continues to industrialize, vast swaths of agricultural land is being converted into industrial land. Farmers displaced by such urban expansion often become migrant labor for factories, but other farmers feel disenfranchised and cheated by the encroachment of industry and the growing disparity between urban and rural wealth and income.

The most recent innovation in Chinese agriculture is a push into organic agriculture. This rapid embrace of organic farming simultaneously serves multiple purposes, including food safety, health benefits, export opportunities, and, by providing price premiums for the produce of rural communities, the adoption of organics can help stem the migration of rural workers to the cities.In the mid-1990s China became a net importer of grain, since its unsustainable practises of groundwater mining has effectively removed considerable land from productive agricultural use. Due to China's status as a developing country and its severe shortage of arable land, farming in China has always been very labor-intensive. However, throughout its history, various methods have been developed or imported that enabled greater farming production and efficiency. They also utilized the seed drill to help improve on row farming.

However, China's agricultural productivity grew rapidly following the implementation of a series of economic reforms since 1978. Reforms led to more efficient resource allocation. China also began to disseminate new technologies (including improved seed varieties and animal breeds) and encourage mechanization. These "agricultural modernization" efforts laid a broad foundation for improved agricultural productivity. But evidence suggests that this growth may not continue into the future. With about 20 percent of the world's population, 6.5 percent of its land area, and rising living standards, China's ability to improve farm productivity will have a direct bearing on global food markets. China is already the leading importer of soybeans and cotton and has recently emerged as an importer of other major commodities, including corn, pork, wheat, and rice. A slowdown in productivity growth could bring further demand for imports.

During 1985-2007, China's agricultural output growth (in real terms) averaged 5.1 percent annually. Two developments underlie this growth: greater use of inputs and growth in what economists call "total factor productivity" (TFP), or the ability to produce more output from each unit of input. TFP growth contributed 2.7 percentage points to the growth in China's agricultural output while rising use of inputs contributed 2.4 percentage points. The mix of inputs changed as use of intermediate goods (including energy, pesticides, fertilizer, seed, feed, and other materials) grew 6.4 percent annually, offsetting declines in the use of labor and land. China's roughly equal reliance on increased input use and TFP contrasts with the recent experience of developed countries where TFP accounts for nearly all growth in agricultural output. For example, annual growth in U.S. agricultural TFP contributed 1.22 percentage points while input growth contributed 0.03 percentage points to output growth over 1985-2007.

Future China farming productivities may include below several aspects:

1 Crop distribution

Although China's agricultural output is the largest in the world, only 10% of its total land area can be cultivated. China's arable land, which represents 10% of the total arable land in the world, supports over 20% of the world's population.[23] Of this approximately 1.4 million square kilometers of arable land, only about 1.2% (116,580 square kilometers) permanently supports crops and 525,800 square kilometers are irrigated.[citation needed] The land is divided into approximately 200 million households, with an average land allocation of just 0.65 hectares, China is the leading producer of cotton, which is grown throughout, but especially in the areas of the North China Plain, the Yangtze river delta, the middle Yangtze valley, and the Xinjiang Uygur Autonomous Region. Other fiber crops include ramie, flax, jute, and hemp. Sericulture, the practice of silkworm raising, is also practiced in central and southern China.

2 Livestock

China has a large livestock population, with pigs and fowls being the most common. China's pig population and pork production mainly lie along the Yangtze River. In 2011, Sichuan province had 51 million pigs (11% of China's total supply).[30] In rural western China, sheep, goats, and camels are raised by nomadic herders.[31] In Tibet, yaks are raised as a source of food, fuel, and shelter. Cattle, water buffalo, horses, mules, and donkeys are also raised in China, and dairy has recently been encouraged by the government, even though approximately 92.3% of the adult population is affected by some level of lactose intolerance. As demand for gourmet foods grows, production of more exotic meats increases as well. Based on survey data from 684 Chinese turtle farms (less than half of the all 1,499 officially registered turtle farms in the year of the survey, 2002), they sold over 92,000 tons of turtles (around 128 million animals) per year; this is thought to correspond to the industrial total of over 300 million turtles per year.

Increased incomes and increased demand for meat, especially pork, has resulted in demand for improved breeds of livestock, breeding stock imported particularly from the United States. Some of these breeds are adapted to factory farming.

3 Fishing

China accounts for about one-third of the total fish production of the world. Aquaculture, the breeding of fish in ponds and lakes, accounts for more than half of its output. The principal aquaculture-producing regions are close to urban markets in the middle and lower Yangtze valley and the Zhu Jiang delta.

● What risks China will encounter to farming industry

All of China's regions have experienced strong growth in agricultural production since the mid-1980s fueled by both input and TFP growth, but the relative contribution of these two factors differs by region. Provinces with the most rapid TFP growth include a mix of coastal regions that led China's economic development and several western provinces. Most northeastern and northern provinces exhibited more input growth. Although the growing economy has pulled labor and land away from farming, the development of China's nonfarm sectors may have benefited farming by generating funds for investment in public infrastructure, science, and technology. Relaxed restrictions on foreign trade and investment may also have enhanced agricultural productivity by improving access to new technology and new markets.

However, the rapid growth in the past few decades may not have been sustained in recent years. Annual TFP growth peaked during 1996-2000 at 5.1 percent before slowing to 3.2 percent in 2000-2005. It then declined by 3.7 percent per year in 2005-07. The significance of this slowdown remains unclear. It may reflect a turning point in China's agricultural productivity growth, in which case gains from earlier reforms and technology transfers from developed countries have been exhausted. Alternatively, it may simply be the effect of transitory events such as animal disease epidemics or discrepancies in data. As urbanization draws more labor and land from agriculture and accelerates changes in food consumption, the capacity to reestablish positive agricultural TFP growth is important to China's future. So, China needs to concerns below several aspects to raise itself farming industry competitive position to global farming competitive market.

1) Finance is emerging as a major driver of sustainability.

Government policy and consumer preferences can certainly shift corporate behaviour, as tariffs on soy have shown. And most consumer-facing businesses are adapting to their customers' preferences for more sustainability.

2) Innovation will be part of any solution.

While the public sector has limited funding resources, private investment and capability could play an instrumental role in achieving sustainable agricultural development goals. But current levels are not enough to meet global food security challenges in the long term. Private investors remain reluctant to invest in sustainable agriculture because of the perceived uncertainties and high risks. Furthermore, conventional financing models have their limits, particularly in developing countries where most of the growth in food demand and production will come from. China need more innovative financing in which public and private sectors can work together, to create the necessary policy and investment environment for private finance in sustainable farming. China also should look at the renewable energy sector for new ideas, where public-private partnerships (PPPs) have successfully delivered mechanisms for pooling public and private financing and risk mitigation. Chinese people may not like change, but they like innovation. People don't like to give things up, but they like to have new options. Innovation is the answer. It is essential to change.

3) Success depends on collaboration. Bringing people on board is a must. To identify a solution is much easier than to implement it. In theory, everybody wants a more sustainable food system. But not everybody wants or is able to pay the price. That's why sustainable change requires us to bring on board all those who are affected. In order to achieve a sustainable food chain, farmers and producers may need further incentives. China's sizeable Grain for Green project offered grains, tax and other encouragements so that farmers would protect, instead of clear, their forested slopes. And agribusinesses will be wise to adopt the same principle. Sustainable farming will only be possible if farmers are on board.

4) Success requires solutions at scale and China is well-placed to deliver them.

The urgency of our biodiversity and climate crises means that we need to have solutions in place right now. And these solutions need to be at scale. The sustainability-linked loan mentioned above is not the first in the agricultural trading sector, but it is the largest so far. It demonstrates our intention to join hands with others in our industry and to contribute to sustainable growth in the global agriculture sector. That is part of the Chinese dream.

Hence, all of above technological innovation is needed to developed to China future farm industry, if it still hope to raise farming competitive position in global farming market.

- What factors influence US farming development

In farming economic view, in general, these factors will influence any countries farming industry developement. They may include: Human factors that influence agricultural use include: Population size leads to larger areas of cultivation and competitio for land. Farming techniques. Final destination of production. Globalisation . Agricultural policies. Environmental policies aim to protect the environment and guarantee safe, healthy food. Social and economic factors. These are human factors and include labour, capital, technology, markets and government (political). These are physical factors and include climate, relief and soil. Temperature (minimum 6°C for crops to grow) and rainfall (at least 250mm to 500mm) influence the types of crops that can be grown, e.g. hot, wet tropical areas favour rice, while cooler, drier areas favour wheat. Although farming is one of the world's oldest professions, modern farming is affected by uniquely modern economic factors. Farmers today compete in a complex economic environment where customers choose from produce grown all over the world and governments provide financial incentives for the production of certain crops rather than others. Such as US is one developed country, whether what are the main factors to influence its farming industry development. I shall indicate these main factors as below:

The history of agriculture in the United States covers the period from the first English settlers to the present day. In Colonial America, agriculture was the primary livelihood for 90% of the population, and most towns were shipping points for the export of agricultural products. Most farms were geared toward subsistence production for family use. The rapid growth of population and the expansion of the frontier opened up large numbers of new farms, and clearing the land was a major preoccupation of farmers. After 1800, cotton became the chief crop in southern plantations, and the chief American export. After 1840, industrialization and urbanization opened up lucrative domestic markets. The number of farms grew from 1.4 million in 1850, to 4.0 million in 1880, and 6.4 million in 1910; then started to fall, dropping to 5.6 million in 1950 and 2.2 million in 2008.

Nowadays, US farming productivities may include :

Arable farming , it means growing of cereals, vegetables and animal feeds. Flat relief; fertile well-drained soils; warm summers; rainfall – under 650mm (some in growing season); winter frosts to break up soil and kill pestsPhysical factors Flat relief; fertile well-drained soils; warm summers; rainfall – under 650mm (some in growing season); winter frosts to break up soil and kill pests as well as Human factors. Large market in south east; good transport networks; benefits from US government subsidies and intervention price, they can influence US arable farming success.

Dairying, Rearing of cattle for milk. Hill sheep farming, sheep rearing for meat .Physical factors, Gentle relief; fertile soils; high rainfall for grass growth; mild winters (over 6°C).Human factors. Access to large markets; milk subsidies up to the 1980s when quotas introduce, they can influence US dairying development success.

Hill sheep farming.Wool and Market gardening, growing fruit, vegetables and flowers. Physical factors, High, steep relief; thin infertile soils; high rainfall (over 1000mm); low temperatures unsuitable for crops. Human factors, Remote from large markets; limited labour; EU subsidies and grants, they may influence hill sheep farming success.

Market gardening includes Growing fruit, vegetables and flowers. Physical factors, Long hours of sunshine; most other factors are controlled. Human factors, Access to motorways and airports; large labour and capital input. They may influence marketing gardening success.

There are these main factors still influence US future agricultural industry development as below:

On Human Factors aspect, it may include: Labour: All farms need either human labour or machinery to do the work. Some farm types use very little labour, e.g. sheep farming. Others require a large labour force, e.g. rice farming in India. Market: This is the customer who buys farm produce. Farmers need to sell their crops and animals to make a profit. Perishable crops such as soft fruits fetch a high price, but need to be grown with a short travelling distance of the market. Finance: Profits are used to pay the wages and to re-invest in the farm, e.g. buying seeds, fertiliser, machinery and animals. This is known as feedback within the farming system. Tradition: Farmers may have always farmed in a certain way and be unwilling to change. Politics: Government may provide subsidies and loans to encourage new farming practices but they may also place limits on production to prevent food surpluses, e.g. quotas and set-aside in the European Union.

On Physical Factors aspect, it may include: Climate: Temperature – a minimum temperature of 6°C is needed for crops to grow. The growing season is the number of months the temperature is over 6°C. Different crops need a different growing season, e.g. wheat needs 90 days. Rainfall – all crops and animals need water. Relief: Temperatures decrease by 1>°C every 160 metres vertical height. Uplands are more exposed to wind and rain. Steep slopes also cause thin soils and limit the use of machinery. Lowland areas are more easily farmed. Soils: Crops grow best on deep, fertile, free-draining soils, e.g. the brown earths found in lowland Britain. Less fertile soils prone to water logging are best used for pastoral farming. Geography Aspect: The direction a slope faces. South-facing slopes are best for growing crops.

Hence, environment and human, e.g. farmers, government, farming scientists etc. both will be main factors to influence US future farming industry development.

Chapter 3

How farming influences developing and developed countries economic development

● How Agriculture Contributes to Economic Development ?

To explain why and how agriculture can influence economic development. We need to know whether agriculture role is important to our societies. Agriculture has always played a pivotal role in shaping the economy of countries. Since it fulfills the basic necessities of the people, all nations across the globe make special provision to improve the productivity. Even the ancient civilization has given it due importance. The agriculture sector not only provides food but also a means of employment to millions. It contributes to resolving sociopolitical issues and building a civilized society. Countries where the real capital income is less, more emphasis is given on developing the agricultural sector and its related industries since it can become the driving force to boost the economy. Whether under developing or developed, agriculture is still the basic occupation of the world.

I feel that role of agriculture may be explained as: With the discovery of agriculture, the hunter-gatherer community found a source for food, settling down at one place, and reduce hunting. The agricultural revolution changed the way the farming sector would impact the overall economy of a country. The agricultural development assisted greatly for industrialization in countries like U.S. and Japan as evident from the significant progress made by them. As a result, it became clear to the underdeveloped and developing countries that instead of putting limitations on a particular sector, the industrial and agricultural industries must co-exist for contributing to the development of the nation. The agricultural industry plays a big role in driving an economy being a major source of raw materials. It not increases the employment ratio, but also strengthens the purchasing power of the people. This sector can also help individuals for playing an instrumental role in country's foreign exports, and providing job opportunities for all types of skills. So, agriculture may create new jobs, e.g. supermarket, farming, fishing, restaurant, food wholeseller, food manufacture. Any related food activities industries may be influenced to creat any jobs changes by agricultural development.

Ways May Agriculture Boosts a Country's Economy, it may includes these several ways. Whether it is a developed country or a developing one, agriculture forms an important sector in improving GDP, which is important to determine the economic performance of a nation For the industries which are agro-based, it is the backbone of their products as major raw materials are obtained from the farm. The agricultural industry plays a significant role in boosting the national income in various ways such as:

1 Improving employment ratio

The agriculture sector and livestock industry are interlinked. Together, they create many job opportunities for the population. While the agriculture sector employs people for agricultural production, the livestock industry does it for producing and selling animal products. Since both these industries need to function through a chain of ancillary support such as warehouse and logistics, it helps in generating employment for the people.

2 Promotes infrastructure creation

When the focus is shifted towards development of agriculture, naturally, it boosts the small-scale industries situated in the vicinity of that area. As it involves a lot of operations, it would eventually mean the development of roads, storehouses, packaging units, and transportation services thus adding to the development of new infrastructure, when any countries food wholesalers need to deliver any foods to local or overseas by air planes, ships, lorries , railways etc. transport tools. So, it encourage non food direct relationship industries development in the world.

3 Helps to supply raw materials

Agriculture helps to produce raw materials that are required by other industries. Processing of these raw materials helps in manufacturing products for several uses. If the supply of materials is not as per the demand, then it can affect the entire supply chain thereby impacting the economyAs a result, the nation's economic turnover might take a hit thus adding to more expenses for the people.

4 Generates a source of foreign exchange for the country

Most of the primary products that are required in industries are obtained from the agricultural sector. For instance, the refined quality cotton dresses which you purchase from the mall get their basic material from the farm. When the raw material is available in abundance, the country can become a primary exporter of the products and generate a good income. As the international market is very dynamic and since the price of raw material is constantly fluctuating, the developing countries have now started focusing on the export of manufactured foods to increase the percentage of foreign income.

5 Bringing non -food primary sectors development chance

By providing food and raw material to non-agricultural sectors of the economy, by creating demand for goods produced in non-agricultural sectors, by the rural people on the strength of the purchasing power, earned by them on selling the marketable surplus, by providing investable surplus in the form of savings and taxes to be invested in non-agricultural sector, by earning valuable foreign exchange through the export of agricultural products,

On conclusion, the agricultural sector can assist to contribute significantly in generating capital income for a country in many ways. For example, when there is a surplus demand for the raw materials, it will, in turn, lead to the production of more goods supporting industrialization and increasing employment. Hence, when a country focuses on making advancements in the agricultural sector, it is, in turn, contributing to its own economic development by starting to address the problems at the root level. Giving significance to the issues at the base level can help to cut down the obstacles in the later stages, and also boost income for an economy.

● What is the main Role of Agriculture in Economic Development?

The agriculture sector is the backbone of an economy which provides the basic ingredients to mankind and now raw material for industrialisation. So, I believe that agriculture and industrialisation development must have direct relationship to bring both development. If the country's agriculture can develop better, then its industrialisation can also develop better. The reasons may include as below:

1. Contribution to National Income:

The lessons drawn from the economic history of many advanced countries tell us that agricultural prosperity contributed considerably in fostering economic advancement. It is correctly observed that, "The leading industrialized countries of today were once predominantly agricultural while the developing economies still have the dominance of agriculture and it largely contributes to the national income. In India, still 28% of national income comes from this sector.

2. Source of Food Supply:

Agriculture is the basic source of food supply of all the countries of the world—whether underdeveloped, developing or even developed. Due to heavy pressure of population in underdeveloped and developing countries and its rapid increase, the demand for food is increasing at a fast rate. If agriculture fails to meet the rising demand of food products, it is found to affect adversely the growth rate of the economy. Raising supply of food by agricultural sector has, therefore, great importance for economic growth of a country.

3. Pre-Requisite for Raw Material:

Agricultural advancement is necessary for improving the supply of raw materials for the agro-based industries especially in developing countries. The shortage of agricultural goods has its impact upon on industrial production and a consequent increase in the general price level. It will impede the growth of the country's economy. The flour mills, rice shellers, oil & dal mills, bread, meat, milk products sugar factories, wineries, jute mills, textile mills and numerous other industries are based on agricultural products.

4. Provision of Surplus:

The progress in agricultural sector provides surplus for increasing the exports of agricultural products. In the earlier stages of development, an increase in the exports earning is more desirable because of the greater strains on the foreign exchange situation needed for the financing of imports of basic and essential capital goods.

5. Shift of Manpower:

Initially, agriculture absorbs a large quantity of labour force. In India still about 62% labour is absorbed in this sector. Agricultural progress permits the shift of manpower from agricultural to non-agricultural sector. In the initial stages, the diversion of labour from agricultural to non-agricultural sector is more important from the point of view of economic development as it eases the burden of surplus labour force over the limited land. Thus, the release of surplus manpower from the agricultural sector is necessary for the progress of agricultural sector and for expanding the non-agricultural sector.

6. Creation of Infrastructure:

The development of agriculture requires roads, market yards, storage, transportation railways, postal services and many others for an infrastructure creating demand for industrial products and the development of commercial sector.

7. Relief from Shortage of Capital:

The development of agricultural sector has minimized the burden of several developed countries who were facing the shortage of foreign capital. If foreign capital is available with the 'strings' attached to it, it will create another significant problem. Agriculture sector requires less capital for its development thus it minimizes growth problem of foreign capital.

8. Helpful to Reduce Inequality:

In a country which is predominantly agricultural and overpopulated, there is greater inequality of income between the rural and urban areas of the country. To reduce this inequality of income, it is necessary to accord higher priority to agriculture. The prosperity of agriculture would raise the income of the majority of the rural population and thus the disparity in income may be reduced to a certain extent. Such as India and China developing countries , agricultural development must help to reduce their people income inequality.

9. Based on Democratic Notions:

If the agricultural sector does not grow at a faster rate, it may result in the growing discontentment amongst the masses which is never healthy for the smooth running of democratic governments. For economic development, it is necessary to minimize political as well as social tensions. In case the majority of the people have to be kindled with the hopes of prosperity, this can be attained with the help of agricultural progress. Thus development of agriculture sector is also relevant on political and social grounds.

10. Create Effective Demand:

The development of agricultural sector would tend to increase the purchasing power of agriculturists which will help the growth of the non-agricultural sector of the country. It will provide a market for increased production. In underdeveloped countries, it is well known that the majority of people depend upon agriculture and it is they who must be able to afford to consume the goods produced. Therefore, it will be helpful in stimulating the growth of the non- agricultural sector. Similarly improvement in the productivity of cash crops may pave the way for the promotion of exchange economy which may help the growth of non-agricultural sector. Purchase of industrial products such as pesticides, farm machinery etc. also provide boost to industrial dead out.

11. Helpful in prolonging Economic Depression:

During depression, industrial production can be stopped or reduced but agricultural production continues as it produces basic necessities of life. Thus it continues to create effective demand even during adverse conditions of the economy.

12. Source of Foreign Exchange for the Country:
Most of the developing countries of the world are exporters of primary products, such as India and China. These products contribute 60 to 70 per cent of their total export earning. Thus, the capacity to import capital goods and machinery for industrial development depends crucially on the export earning of the agriculture sector. If exports of agricultural goods fail to increase at a sufficiently high rate, these countries are forced to incur heavy deficit in the balance of payments resulting in a serious foreign exchange problem. However, primary goods face declining prices in international market and the prospects of increasing export earnings through them are limited. Due to this, large developing countries like India (having potentialities of industrial development) are trying to diversify their production structure and promote the exports of manufactured goods even though this requires the adoption of protective measures in the initial period of planning.

13. Contribution to Capital Formation:
Underdeveloped and developing countries need huge amount of capital for its economic development. In the initial stages of economic development, it is agriculture that constitutes a significant source of capital formation. Such as
(i) agricultural taxation,
(ii) export of agricultural products,
(iii) collection of agricultural products at low prices by the government and selling it at higher prices. This method is adopted by Russia and China,
(iv) labour in disguised unemployment, largely confined to agriculture, is viewed as a source of investible surplus,
(v) transfer of labour and capital from farm to non-farm activities etc.

14. Employment Opportunities for Rural People:
Agriculture provides employment opportunities for rural people on a large scale in underdeveloped and developing countries. It is an important source of livelihood. Generally, landless workers and marginal farmers are engaged in non-agricultural jobs like handicrafts, furniture, textiles, leather, metal work, processing industries, and in other service sectors. These rural units fulfill merely local demands. In India about 70.6% of total labour force depends upon agriculture. So, India and China many rural people have huge job chance , when themselve faming industry can be developed technological agricultural development in success.

15. Improving Rural Welfare:
It is time that rural economy depends on agriculture and allied occupations in an underdeveloped country. The rising agricultural surplus caused by increasing agricultural production and productivity tends to improve social welfare, particularly in rural areas. The living standard of rural masses rises and they start consuming nutritious diet including eggs, milk, ghee and fruits. They lead a comfortable life having all modern amenities—a better house, motor-cycle, radio, television and use of better clothes.

16. Extension of Market for Industrial Output:
As a result of agricultural progress, there will be extension of market for industrial products. Increase in agricultural productivity leads to increase in the income of rural population which is turn leads to more demand for industrial products, thus development of industrial sector. So, any agricultural productive machine, even artificial intelligent agricultural productive machine will be increased to any countries farmers' needs when they need to apply these farming machines to help them to raise crop productivities in short time , reducing workers numbers , reduces farming expenditures, short food delivery time. So, farming industrial tools invention is needed rapidly.

● The Influence of Agriculture On The Socio-Economic Development of Regions

How agriculture can influence to any countries‘ socio economic development of regions. For example, how China 's India's and US's rural regions can bring socio economic development of rural regions. The development of the field of agriculture has a positive impact on many people within the society. Rural and vulnerable groups and regions are influenced the most. Firstly, we must need to know whether what positive influences will bring to influence any countries' regions socio-economy, such as: The role of agriculture in food security. Population growth and demand for labor. The impact of agriculture in developing countries. Ecological challenges for the field of agriculture. All of these are main factors to impact any countries‘ regions socio economic development by agriculture development, when US, India and China countries can develop themselve agricultural industires of regions.

The majority of poor people and vulnerable societal groups live in rural regions. According to the study conducted by the US department of agriculture, poop people depend on agriculture when it comes to their livelihood. Therefore, it becomes quite obvious why agriculture plays such a crucial role in reducing poverty. Apart from providing the most vulnerable groups with food, it also gives them jobs. As a result of that, the rapid development of agriculture in rural areas has a huge impact on the cost of food for poor consumers. Once that cost is stabilized and the most vulnerable citizens can secure a job, their position in the society changes for the better. When they have a steady job, they are able to live a more comfortable life and enjoy more benefits our society can offer. Taking into consideration the fact that the field of agriculture is one of the very few options to get a steady job in rural areas, making sure this field is supported by the government should always be a top priority. However, when US, India and China decide the regions to develop themselve farming industry, these factors will influence their regions to develop agricultural industry success, such as: How to make farming more sustainable.How to deal with extreme weather conditions as well as how to improve the quality of soil on the regions.

However, if these countries' agricultural regions cannot come up with a more sustainable approach to agriculture, soon we will have no land to farm on. The latter is a very dire prospect which is the reason why it is time to get creative. For instance, urban framing is a great option. While rural areas remain focused on producing huge amounts of harvest (such as corn or wheat), people involved in urban farming projects can satisfy the need for fresh vegetables and greens in one part of the city. This way, both the consumers and the industry win.

There are numerous socio-cultural, economic, political, technological and infrastructural factors which also determine the agricultural land use, cropping patterns and agricultural processes. Of these factors, land tenancy, system of ownership, size of holdings, availability of labour and capital, religion, level of technological development, accessibility to the market, irrigation facilities, agricultural research and extension service, price incentives, government plans and international policies have a close impact on agricultural activities.

1. Land Tenancy:

Land tenure includes all forms of tenancy and also ownership in any form. Land tenancy and land tenure affect the agricultural operations and cropping patterns in many ways. The farmers and cultivators plan the agricultural activities and farm (fields) management keeping in mind their rights and possession duration on the land. In different communities of the world, the cultivators have different land tenancy rights. In the tribal societies of the shifting cultivators land belongs to the community and individuals are allowed only to grow crops along with other members of the community for a specific period. But among the sedentary farmers land belongs to individual farmers. In such societies it is believed that one who owns land he owns wealth.

The ownership and the length of time available for planning, development and management of arable land influence the decision making process of the cultivator. Depending on the nature of tenancy rights he decides the extent to which investment on land could be made. For example, if the cultivator is the sole owner of the land, he may install a tube well in his farm and may go for fencing and masonry irrigation channels. But a tenant farmer or a share-cropper will not go for the long term investment in the field as after a short period of occupancy he will have to vacate the land and the real owner may cultivate that piece of land either himself or may lease out to other cultivator. In fact, a farmer who has the right of ownership, he has the freedom to choose a system of production and investment which improves the quality of land and gives him increasing capacity to borrow money. The cropping patterns and farm management are also dependent on the duration of time for which the land is to remain under cultivation. For example, among the shifting cultivators (Jhumias of northeast India), the allotment of land to the cultivator is normally done for one or two years, depending on the fertility of the land.

The hilly terrain, the limited rights of the occupant and poor economic condition of the tillers hinder the development and efficient management of land. Since the land belongs to the community and not to the individuals, this type of land tenancy prevents the energetic, efficient and skilled individuals of the community to invest in the farm. Under such a system individuals are also unlikely to put much efforts or invest more money on the improvement of cultivated land as the field is allotted by the community for a short period. Under this type of land tenancy there is no incentive to individuals to improve the agricultural efficiency and productivity of the land. Contrary to this, a tenant having a lease for a longer period has considerable incentive to make his own improvements in drainage, irrigation channels, fencing and soil sustainability practices. Such leases are, however, rare. The tenancy system of short duration lease leads to insecurity for tenants. In India, the fear of landlords regaining control of farms has led to restrictions on long term letting. This has resulted into eleven months lease system. In the annual leasing system, however, very high rents are obtainable. In the short leasing system, it has been suggested that it enables a farmer to adopt his holding to his immediate needs but there is a strange temptation for a person who is working on the land only for one year to extract from the land as much as he can and put back the minimum. Consequently, the health of the soil due to unscientific rotation of crop is lost.

In India, at the time of independence (1947), there were two main tenure systems, i.e., the zamindari and the raiyatwari. These systems determined the relations between land on the one hand and the interested parties, the government, the owners and the cultivators, on the other. In the zamindari system, the land property rights were conferred upon persons who were avowedly non-cultivators but had sufficient influence in the region to collect land revenue from the cultivating peasantry. This was necessary at a time when the foreign government was not firmly established and direct control of land revenue and contact with the peasants was difficult. Owing to the zamindari tenure system, the real cultivators and tillers were exploited. They were, therefore, not interested in making investment in the land. Owner-cultivators who have a good deal of incentives to invest in land to improve the techniques of cultivation and to enhance productivity were discouraged. The tenant-cultivators in such a system face major disincentives like the fear of eviction, the insecurity of tenure, the rack-renting practice, the high rents and the inadequate surplus to invest.

In Southeast Asia, Latin America and parts of Southern Europe a system of land tenure known as 'metayage' is very widespread. In its simplest form it is a copartner ship between the owner who provides land, equipments, buildings, seeds, fertilizers and the metayer (cultivator) who provides labour and stock in return of a fixed share of the produce. The system sometimes involves pure sharecropping, i.e., there is no fixed rent, but the tenant cultivates the land and gives the owner a share, often 50 per cent of the agricultural produce.

In northern India, this system is known as 'Batai' This tenural system gives the tenant some protection from fluctuations in productions and crop prices and is usually preferable to fixed cash tenancies in which a tenant tends to fall progressively deeper into debts, whenever income from his crop falls below the outgoing rent. The traditional method of covering the deficit is by having recourse to a moneylender—a role used to be performed by the Jews in Europe, Greeks in the Middle East and the Bohras and Baniyas in India. In the rural areas of the developing countries, the moneylenders often charge exorbitant rates of interest and wield considerable power.

2. Size of Holdings and Fragmentation of Fields:

It is not only the land tenancy and the system of ownership which influence the agricultural and cropping patterns, the size of holdings and fragmentation of fields also have a close bearing on agricultural land use patterns and yields per unit area. In the densely populated areas of the developing countries the size of holdings is generally very small. The size of holding and the size of farm decide the degree of risk that a farm operator may bear. In general, larger the size of the farm, greater the capacity of the farmer to take the risk and vice versa. This, in turn, would affect the extent of specialization and also the nature of technology and equipment's (tractors, thrashers, harvesters, etc.) to be used.

In India, the average size of holding is very small. In fact, about 70 per cent of the total holdings are below one and a half hectares. The average standard size of holding that may give better agricultural returns cannot be maintained because of the fast growing rural population and the prevailing law of inheritance. The law of succession in the countries like India, Pakistan, Bangladesh and Sri Lanka results in the subdivision and fragmentation of holdings.

According to the law of inheritance in these countries, the property of the deceased is equally divided among the male heirs. Each son generally insists on having a share from each location and from each piece of land, resulting into further fragmentation of land. It is a wasteful and uneconomic method of land utilization in which improved agricultural practices cannot be adopted. The disadvantages of fragmentation of holdings are well known. It puts a large proportion of land outside the possibility of effective cultivation or economic development. The small fields are difficult to work with modern machinery and tractors etc.

n the opinion of agricultural economists, the fragmentation of holdings is a great obstacle and one of the major deterrents to economically viable cultivation. It results in wastage of land, labour and material inputs. It is responsible for increased overhead costs, including even the cost of production resulting in low returns from agriculture. The division of holdings may be socially justifiable but economically they are not viable.

3. Consolidation of Holdings and Operational Efficiency:

In order to overcome the disadvantages of fragmentation of holdings, consolidation of holdings has been done in many parts of the country. The advantages of consolidation of holdings are manifold. Important amongst them have been explained below. The fragmentation of holdings makes the efficient management and supervision of the farm operations difficult. It causes considerable waste of labour of the cultivator and his plough cattle. Land consolidation makes it necessary for him to look after the crops and put up a fence around the holding.

It also enables the farmer to construct a farm house on the holding and shed for his cattle and thus exercise efficient supervision and management. The use of tractors and machinery also becomes possible in the case of substantial holdings. All these advantages are reflected in inputs cost and increase in production. The area wasted in embankments and boundaries in scattered holdings is released for cultivation after land consolidation. The farmer can take effective steps in the areas where soil erosion is a problem. Moreover, it helps in the development of better road linkages. The consolidation of holdings would, however, be fruitless if the advantages derived from the operations were to disappear as a result of the acts contrary to the purpose of consolidation leading to fragmentation of the consolidated properties.

Apart from solving the problems of consolidation of holdings, there must be a size of farm below which its output is too small to maintain the family, at whatever is considered to be the reasonable standard of living. The experts agree that under the average agro climatic conditions in India a farm well above two hectares will be capable of reconciling the various minimal of income and employment. The solution of the problem may partly be found in the agricultural land ceiling. The basic idea of the agricultural land ceiling is to ration out land in such a way that above a certain maximum limit, the land is taken away from the present holders and is distributed to landless or small holders according to some priorities. The objectives of ceiling strategy are to increase agricultural productivity of arable lands with a much more equitable income and power distribution and with a new structure suited for technological changes.

Since independence, in India, a number of steps have been taken to make structural changes in the agrarian societies and land reforms. The Kumarappa Committee, also known as the Congress Committee of Agrarian Reforms, recommended comprehensive measures for land distribution, creation of basic holdings, tenancy reforms, organization of small cooperative reforms and minimum agricultural wages. But so powerful was the lobby of the big and middle class peasants that the recommendations were shelved. The enthusiasm for land ceiling is much greater now, but it is doubtful whether the results will be encouraging. As a matter of fact, land reform is costly and has profound social consequences, but what is socially just may not be economically efficient or politically tenable.

4. Labour:

The availability of labour is also a major constraint in the agricultural land use and cropping patterns of a region. Labour represents all human services other than decision making and capital. The availability of labour, its quantity and quality at the periods of peak labour demand have great influence on decision making process of the farmer. The different crops and agrarian systems vary in their total labour requirements. The labour inputs vary considerably round the year for most of the agricultural enterprises with the result that many farmers employ a mixed system of production in order to keep their labour fully employed. Even then, in many parts of India, seasonal unemployment remains on most of the holdings, while during the peak periods of crop sowing (rice, wheat, sugarcane, vegetables and potatoes) and harvesting, there occurs acute shortage of labour which influences the sowing and harvesting operations and thereby affect the decision of a farmer whether to grow or not a crop.

Many of the cultivators of western Uttar Pradesh (Saharanpur and Muzaffarnagar districts) have given up the cultivation of rice owing to the non-avail- ability of workers at the times of transplantation and harvesting. The farmers of Punjab are increasingly dependent on Bihari labourers for the harvest of their wheat and rice crops. In many of the developed countries like the United States, Germany, Japan and U K, and in some tracts of the developing countries like the plains of the Punjab and Haryana in India, the rapid loss of farm labour is becoming a matter of great concern.

There are two basic reasons for the decline of agricultural labour, especially in the developed countries, such as US. Firstly, the industrialized nations offer alternative and financially attractive employment. Secondly, there are greater leisure opportunities for the industrial workers. In India, China developing countries, very few job opportunities occur outside agriculture which lead to unemployment of agricultural landless labour and small size farmers. Thus, the availability of labour has a direct impact in the labour intensive cropping patterns and its importance is much felt in the plantation estates and the subsistence paddy farming typology.

5. Redicing Capital And Artificial intelligent Mechanization and Equipment need:

Capital subscribes definite limitations to the selection of crops. Agricultural inputs like the livestock, irrigation, seeds, fertilizers, insecticides, pesticides, feeding stuffs, labour, purchase of land, machinery, carts, vehicles, various agricultural equipment's, buildings, fuel and power, sprays, veterinary services and repairs and maintenance require capital. All the farmers make their decisions on the basis of capital to invest.

The traditional way of cultivation is giving way to the market oriented crops which need more capital for getting higher returns. In the underdeveloped countries, moneylender is still the main source of finance in the remote rural areas and he advances money to the farmers at a high rate of interest with the intention of exploitation. Moreover, the permanent investment in agricultural system like plantation (tea, coffee, rubber) put a great restriction on the selection of alternative cropping patterns.

The development of irrigation facilities without capital is not possible. The role of irrigation in the areas of erratic rainfall, arid and semiarid regions is quite significant. Its importance has substantially increased after the adoption of High Yielding Varieties(HYV) in the developing countries. Irrigation not only enhances the yields of crops, it also helps in the intensification and horizontal expansion of agriculture. The development of irrigation which is one of the primary bases of agriculture needs enormous amount of capital. So, new agricultural machines, such as robotic will increase needs to any countries farmers.

The technological changes including the use of modern hand tools, animals drawn implements, tractors, thrashers and more economic patterns of farm management play a vital role in the selection of crops grown and decision making at the farm level. These changes help in improving the crop yields.

The improvements occur partly from the use of more effective equipment but also, because mechanization makes it possible to carry out farming operations more quickly and at the precise time calculated to maximize outputs. In the plains of the Punjab and western Uttar Pradesh, for example, the increasing substitution of tractors for bullocks has greatly shortened the time; the farmer has to spent on the ploughing and sowing of the kharif and rabi crops. This enables the farmers to cultivate their fallow land before it becomes infested with weeds in the summer season—a practice which was not feasible when oxen drawn plough was used. The result was a substantial diminution of weeds and increased cereal crop yields. More far-reaching is the impact of rice planting, and harvesting machines in Japan and China, where traditional methods entail the putting in of every single seedling of rice by hand at an immense cost and back-breaking toil.

In China, simple machines, constructed mostly of bamboo, wood and a few metal parts, have been in use since 1958. The machines, under normal conditions, do twenty times the amount of work of a hand planter, thus greatly shortening the time needed to plant the rice crop. The deployment of such machines is especially important for areas with two or more than two crops a year. The improved tools and farm implements can change appreciably the cropping patterns, cropping intensity and crop combinations resulting into high agricultural returns. In fact, tractors have largely transformed the agricultural landscape of the Punjab and Haryana in India.

6. Transportation Facilities:

Transportation facilities also have a direct bearing on the cropping patterns of a region. Better transport linkages are advantageous because of the economies in farm labour and storage costs which they make possible. These savings in turn help to make it economic for farmers to buy fertilizers and better equipment's. Better transport also makes it possible for farmers to put their less accessible land to more productive use.

In areas inadequately served by the modern means of transportation, the surplus produce is often damaged either by adverse weather or by rats, pests and diseases. In the hilly states of northeast India (Meghalaya, Mizoram, Nagaland, Manipur, Arunachal Pradesh) costly crops like ginger, pineapple and banana are grown in surplus quantities but the poor means of transportation and inadequate road linkages deprive the cultivators of most of the profits. Contrary to this, in the United States, the truck farming is done at distant places from the big cities and markets as the farmer is able to supply his perishable crops (vegetables, flowers and fruits) to the distant markets within a short period of time at a reasonable rate of transportation.

7. Marketing Facilities:

The accessibility to the market is a major consideration in the decision making of the farmer. The intensity of agriculture and the production of crops decline as the location of cultivation gets away from the marketing centres. This is particularly noticeable when a bulky but low value crop has to be transported to the market. If it takes much time to send the produce, especially at the peak time, to the market when the farmer could have been profitably employed in other activities. The marketing system also influences the decision making of the farmer. In most of the countries the agricultural commodity markets are controlled by the buyers rather than sellers.

The farmers, however, can influence the market by storing their products on the farms or in cold storages until prices are remunerative. But since the number of buyers is lesser than the number of sellers and the cultivator is not financially well off to store the crop, the bargaining position of the farmer remains weak. The fluctuations in prices of agricultural produce many a times compel the farmers to change the cropping patterns.

Thus, the size of market may be an important factor because a market may encourage transport and handling innovations together with economic scale. Wheat has a great international market because it is convenient to handle even though it is a bulky commodity. Great Britain which imports about 8 million tonnes (metric tonnes) of wheat and other cereals has encouraged the development of special carrying ships, the opening of new water routes, such as the Hudson Bay from the Canadian wheat lands and the construction of new railway systems in the country.

8. Government Policies:

The agricultural land use and cropping patterns are also influenced by the government policies. The fluctuations in the price of sugarcane, wheat, oilseeds and legumes provide impetus or disincentives to the cultivators to grow these crops. Under certain political conditions, the government may stop the farmers to grow certain crops.

In the socialist countries like Russia, Romania, Bulgaria, Albania, Cuba, etc., the combination of crops, their rotation, a real strength and mode of disposal are completely controlled by the governments. In developing countries, like India, the government announces the price of various cereals and cash crops well in advance so that the farmers may devote their agricultural lands to different suitable cereal and other money fetching crops.

Apart from the domestic policies, the governments enter into international agreements to supply certain agricultural commodities to each other in order to maintain the balance of trade. The British government imports a substantial quantity of dairy products from New Zealand and Australia. Canada and Argentina export wheat while Cuba, Indonesia and India are the exporters of sugar. These international agreements have a close bearing on the cropping patterns of different countries.

9. Religion:

The religion of the cultivators has also influenced the agricultural activities in the different parts of the world. Each of the major religions has certain taboos and the use of certain agricultural commodities is prohibited in each of them. The Khasis and Lushais of Meghalaya and Mizoram are not interested in dairying as milk and milk products are taboo in their society. Piggery is prohibited among the Muslims, Hindus hate slaughtering, while Sikhs never go for the cultivation of tobacco.

The productive and adequately irrigated loamy tracts of western Haryana (including Bhiwani, Hissar, Mohindergarh, and Sirsa districts) are ideally suited for the cultivation of sunflower. It is a short duration highly remunerative cash crop which matures in only 60 days. For the last two decades, the farmers in these districts were obtaining two sunflower crops in a year in between the kharif and rabi crops. Unfortunately, the population of Neelgai (an antelope) has multiplied in this region significantly. This antelope which is being considered as sacred cow relishes the plant of sunflower and prefers to stay in or around its fields. The Neelgai menace has forced the cultivators of Haryana to give up sunflower cultivation. It is one of the unique examples in which the wild animals have influenced the cropping pattern significantly and the progressive farmers of Haryana are being deprived of a highly remunerative cash crop. Keeping into mind the religious sentiments of the Hindu farmers and the importance of sunflower as a cash crop (oilseed), the government should evolve a suitable strategy to check the fast growth of Neelgai population, failure to which the process of agricultural development in the region may be adversely affected.

In brief, the socioeconomic and politico cultural factors, especially land tenancy, landownership, size of holdings, fragmentation of fields, availability of labour, capital, accessibility to the market, storage facilities, government policies, international agreements and religion of the cultivators substantially influence the agricultural patterns and agricultural land use of a region.

How tea farming industry influences developing countries growth

- Which aspects will influence GDP growth

Agriculture accounts for 46.3 percent of the nation's Gross domestic Product (GDP), 83.9 percent of exports, and 80% of the labour force.The biggest countries in agriculture are leaders in production of wheat, rice, pulses etc. The top agricultural nations are China. India, USA. Indonesia etc.o research why and how farming development can influence GDP growth. China has the largest GDP in the world. It produced $25.3 trillion in 2018. But its GDP per capita was only $18,120 because it has four times the number of people as the United States. So, to research how agricultural development can bring GDP growth rapidly . We need research on these several aspects how US apply technology to innovate farming productivities skills:

On Agricultural Baseline aspect

USDA (United States Department of Agriculture Economic Research Service) Agricultural Projections report provides longrun projections for the farm sector for the next 10 years. These annual projections cover agricultural commodities, agricultural trade, and aggregate indicators of the sector, such as farm income. USDA's long-term agricultural projections provide a scenario for the farm sector for the next 10 years. Projections cover agricultural commodities, agricultural trade, and aggregate indicators of the sector such as farm income. The projections identify major forces and uncertainties affecting future agricultural markets; prospects for global long-term economic growth, consumption, and trade; and future price trends, trade flows, and U.S. exports of major farm commodities.

ERS economists participate in the long-term projections analysis and lead the preparation of the USDA long-term projections report. Other USDA offices and agencies involved in the long-term agricultural projections process include the World Agricultural Outlook Board, the Farm Programs and Conservation Business Center, the Foreign Agricultural Service, the Office of the Chief Economist, the Office of Budget and Program Analysis, the Risk Management Agency, the Agricultural Marketing Service, the Natural Resources Conservation Service, and the National Institute of Food and Agriculture.

James Hansen and Erik Dohlman (2020) reported that ERS provides three annual outputs covering agricultural baseline projections as below:

The Agricultural Baseline Projections Report, released in February each year, provides projections for the farm sector for the next 10 years. See the most recent report USDA Agricultural Projections to 2029.

The Agricultural Baseline Database provides 10-year projections from USDA's annual long-term projections report, which is published in February each year. The database covers projections for major field crops (corn, sorghum, barley, oats, wheat, rice, soybeans, and upland cotton) and livestock (beef, pork, poultry and eggs, and dairy), starting with the February 2000 report.

International Baseline Projections data indicate supply, demand, and trade for major agricultural commodities for selected countries. These projections provide foreign country detail supporting the annual USDA agricultural baseline, which provides longrun, 10-year projections.

So, in long term, US will develop high technological agricultural industry to different projects. It will influence US GDP growth in rapid speed in the future.

Reference

James Hansen and Erik Dohlman, Agricultural Baseline Projections. Source: https://www.ers.usda.gov/topics/farm-economy/agricultural-baseline, February 18, 2020

On Agricultural Research and Productivity Aspect

Advances in agricultural productivity have led to abundant and affordable food and fiber throughout most of the developed world. Public and private agricultural research has been the foundation and basis for much of this growth and development. ERS data, research, and analyses quantify agricultural productivity improvements and the sources of improvement, in the U.S. and globally. A major focus is on developing indices of productivity growth that accurately reflect changes in the quality and mix of both inputs and outputs in the agricultural production process.

Keith Fuglie el. (Jan 2020) reported that ERS-compiled statistics (see the ERS data product, Agricultural Research Funding in the Public and Private Sectors) show that since about 1980, growth rates in public R&D in the United States have been generally slow. Levels of private investment have generally been higher, but with greater variation. In the early 2000s, public and private agricultural research investments began to diverge more rapidly. Real (inflation-adjusted) spending for private agricultural and food R&D nearly doubled between 2003 and 2013, while real public R&D spending fell. By 2010, private R&D for agricultural inputs alone surpassed the public level for all research.

ERS research finds that growth rates in public R&D in high-income countries as a group have also slowed, see Agricultural Research Investment and Policy Reform in High-Income Countries (ERR-249, May 2018). For high-income countries as a group, public agricultural research expenditures (adjusted for inflation) grew rapidly after 1960. However, growth slowed markedly in recent decades and has now turned negative. In constant 2011 dollars, public agricultural R&D spending in these countries grew from $3.9 billion in 1960 to a peak of $18.6 billion in 2009, before declining to $17.5 billion by 2013 (the latest year with complete data). This decline in public R&D spending marked the first sustained fall in agricultural R&D investment by these countries in 50 years, and was most pronounced in the United States and Southern Europe. The United States continues to lead among high-income countries in public agricultural R&D spending, but the U.S. share of the total declined from 35 percent in 1960 to less than 25 percent by 2013. See also the May 2018 Amber Waves article, Agricultural Research in High-Income Countries Faces New Challenges as Public Funding Stalls. Also see the ERS data product, International Agricultural Productivity.

To estimate the likely impacts of public research and development (R&D) funding choices on productivity growth, ERS projected future productivity growth with alternative public R&D investment scenarios. This analysis found that declines in public R&D have a more pronounced effects in the longrun than in the short-term. Even if public R&D investment recovers, future productivity growth (in terms of total factor productivity) would take some time to resume due to the lag between research investment and application. See the September 2015 Amber Waves feature, U.S. Agricultural Productivity Growth: The Past, Challenges, and the Future for more information.

Models and data decompose the sources of growth in global agricultural output. Globally, productivity growth accounts for a rising share of the increase in agricultural production, easing pressure on natural resources to supply the rising demand for food and agricultural commodities (see the ERS data product, International Agricultural Productivity, Growth in Global Agricultural Productivity: An Update (Amber Waves magazine, November 2013), and Accelerating Productivity Growth Offsets Decline in Resource Expansion in Global Agriculture (Amber Waves, September 2010).

Thus, On Agricultural Research and Productivity Aspect, US such as one developed country , it will achieve different kinds of agricultural technological innovation methods or techniques in order to raise itelf country's agricultural productivities number rapidly. Then, US GDP growth speed will be possible to increase rapidly .

Reference

Keith Fuglie, Sun Ling Wang, and Eric Njuki , Agricultural Research and Productivity .https://www.ers.usda.gov/topics/farm-economy/agricultural-research-and-productivity,January 13, 2020

Productivity Is the Major Driver of U.S. Farm Sector's Economic Growth. According to the latest statistics, Paul Heisey and Keith Fuglie (2018) they indicated , the level of U.S. farm output nearly tripled between 1948 and 2017, growing at an average annual rate of 1.53 percent. USDA's Economic Research Service (ERS) researchers attribute this growth mainly to productivity advancement.

To monitor the performance of the U.S. farm sector, ERS develops productivity statistics along with price and quantity estimates of 10 output sub-categories (such as meat animals, dairy, and food grains) and 12 input sub-categories (such as hired labor, durable equipment, and pesticides). ERS's agricultural productivity statistics are based on a broad productivity measure that reflects all inputs, called total factor productivity (TFP). Annual TFP growth is the difference between the growth of aggregate agricultural output and the growth of aggregate inputs used on farms under the control of farmers.

Reference

Paul Heisey and Keith Fuglie, Agricultural Research Investment and Policy Reform in High- Income Countries , https://www.ers.usda.gov/amber-waves/2020/july/productivity-is-the-major-driver-of-us-farm-sector-s-economic-growthby , ERS, May 2018

- How does the tea agriculture sector affect the Malawi economy?

Tea is the most popular drink in the world after water – an estimated 70,000 cups are drunk every second. Yet tea farmers and workers struggle to get a fair deal. This can have a very real and human cost. One in four children in Kenya's tea and coffee-growing regions are malnourished, leading to stunted growth. One in 10 children in the tea-growing regions of Malawi die before their fifth birthday.Tea is produced on large plantations or estates and picked by employed workers. It is also grown on small plots of land by smallholder farmers who sell their freshly-plucked green leaf to plantations or tea factories for processing into black tea.

In Africa, the average smallholder's farm is less than half the size of a football pitch. Tea farmers face the challenge of low and fluctuating prices for the green leaf they sell, and a lack of power in a tea supply chain dominated by large companies. On tea estates, the challenges for workers vary depending on the origin. Workers may face low wages, long working hours and a difficult relationship with estate management. Often it is the management they depend on for basic needs such as housing, healthcare, access to water and even education for their children.

Kenya's agricultural sector directly influences overall economic performance through its contribution to GDP. Periods of high economic growth rates have been synonymous with increased agricultural growth. The tea sector is a dominant sector and the coffee sector has started to pick up following a decline in the recent past. Malawi is one owning the natural environment to grow tea country. In 2019, Malawi's economic growth is projected to reach 4.4%, increasing over the medium term to 5.0 - 5.5%. Growth in 2019 is buoyed by a good harvest overall, despite the impact Cyclone Idai. Solid agricultural growth is likely to support agro-processing and households' disposable incomes, which should, in turn, drive the service sector.

Malawai

Population live in rural areas. Tea is one of the country's most important industries and main export crops. Tea is Malawi's biggest employer, with 50,000 people working in the sector. While these jobs pay above the national average, tea workers remain poor. The 16,500 small-scale tea farmers in Malawi also find it challenging to make a decent income and provide for their families. Poor diets are a fundamental issue in Malawi, and malnutrition is one of the reasons why one in ten children in tea-growing regions don't live past the age of five.

However, Malawi is highly vulnerable to climate change, which affects where and how tea can be grown. The impact of deforestation in the country has been significant, causing flash floods and limiting firewood for the rural population. Both small farmer organisations owned and governed by the farmers themselves and tea plantations that comply with strict Fairtrade Standards for hired labour can become Fairtrade certified. Fairtrade Standards for tea include an origin-specific Fairtrade Minimum Price, which acts as a safety net against the unpredictable market. Standards also include payment of the additional Fairtrade Premium of US$ 0.50/kg black tea, for producers to invest as they see fit. Examples include putting resources into better farming so they can earn more money for their crops, or it could be for education, clean water and clinics for the community. 392,700 farmers and workers across 11 countries are involved in Fairtrade tea production. 10,700 tonnes of tea was sold as Fairtrade in 2017. This means certified farmers and workers earned €5.3 million in Fairtrade Premium in 2017. On plantations, workers invest almost half of their Premium in community services such as housing, education and healthcare. However, Fairtrade certified organisations sell only around 7 percent of their tea on Fairtrade terms – this means they don't benefit from being certified to the extent that they could. So, natural good environment can help Malawi to grow any kinds of tea in order to raise different kinds of tea taste to supply to export to different countries tea markets in order to satisfy tea drinkers' drinking need seriously. So, tea industry will be Malawi's main agricultural income source ,even it can compete to any other tea export competitors and it can also create many tea growing and tea manufacture job chances to many tea workers in Malawi. Consequently, Malawai's tea export will help it to raise GDP growth rapidly.

CHAPTER THREE

LEARNING ORGANIZAIONAL BEHAVIOR AND ECONOMIC GROWTH RELATION

Factors causes China achieves future new world factory manufacturing leader position

I shall indicate below factors may cause China becomes future global new world factory manufacturing leader position reasons as below:

New economy demand and supply theory

predicts China stable income person consumer purchase behavior

China Stable income person consumer purchase behavior

1.0 Behavioral economic method predicts stable basic income consumer individual spending behavior

Can apply demand and supply theory predict that the consequences of a stable basic income consumer's consumption behavior? It may be significantly different than the ones are predicted by the standard economic model if more realistic assumptions of human consumption behavioral prediction success.

DEMAND AND SUPPLY THEORY assumes that consumer will compare whether whose benefits are more than costs after they buy the product or consume the service. I assume the consumer is only the who have stable basic income source consumer target. This stable basic income target consumers who will evaluate or feel they will earn more benefits than costs to every product in their consumption process, after they will make final decision to choose to buy the product to use or consume the service. Otherwise, if they feel they won't earn more benefits after they buy the product or consume the service in the consumption process. Then, they won't choose to buy the product to use or consume the service. In behavioral economic view point, it indicates their consumption behaviors are depend on comparing the product or the service whether it can satisfy their desire benefits and their desire benefits to the product or service must be more than their consumption cost.

There are four points to apply behavioral economic method to predict each stable basic income individual income spending. They include: motivation, conspicuous consumption, social preferences and crowding theory.

Each stable basic income consumer individual spending amount will be different and it is represent that every high stable basic income consumer must decide to consume any high cost services or buy high cost products to use. Although some economic teachers assume general high income people will accept to spend more expenditures for enjoyment or buy high cost of products to satisfy basic high level necessary expenditures. But, applying behavioral economic analysis, it is not absolute true, some low income people also accept to spend more to buy high cost of products or increasing spending expenditures for enjoyment for their basic necessary expenditures.

The field of behavioral economic can be fined as a combination of economics and psychology that tries to capture human behavior in a more realistic. Understanding each consumer individual consumption behavior, we need to know how who does each decision to influence each consumption choice. Consequently, analysis reaches the conclusion. Every high or low level stable basic income consumer individual behavioral consumption that the microeconomic consequences of a stable basic income of individal consumer target consumption group could be efficiency enhancing, but at the same time incentives about positional concerns could lead to wasteful and inefficient spending to the stable low basic income consumer target group.

How to apply demand and supply theory to predict the stable basic income target consumer group's consumption behavior ?

What is basic income mean? A basic income is an income paid by a political community to all its members on an individual basis, without means test or work requirement. How to apply behavioral economic method to contribute to the basic income consumption prediction?

I assume high income tax is charged to one high income tax payee , it will influence the high income tax payee individual consumption desires to be fallen, also extrinsic incentives will effort and intrinsic motivation and how the labor market change these variables under and big changes predicting, how income security changes social consumption preferences, e.g. how a big change affects the overall level of status -seeking behavior and this effect with income inequality to influence consumer individual consumption attitude or habit.

How can behavioral economic methods predict consumer's consumption decision, in special the stable basic income consumer target group? In any consumption decisions are involving risk and uncertainty, the standard economic model usually assumes that decisions are based on final condition, regardless of the changes are caused by the results of a consumer's decision.

An alterative mode of how consumers make decision and judgement under risk and uncertainty. This situation is often occurred in consumption market.In behavioral economic view point, it explains how consumer's consumption, however, which excludes the stable basic income earn factor can influence the stable basic income earn target consumer group decides to make final consumption decision to compare to the non-stable basic income earn target consumer group. The reasons include as below:

(1) Consumers evaluate decisions over gains and losses with repect to some natural reference point, when they feel need to consume, which is assumed to be judgement about a sequence of outcomes are based on changes in wealth, rather than whether how much absolute basic income earn to influence whose consumption desires.

(2) Thus, behavioral economic theory assumes the consumer is the low level of income group in society, but when who feels that he is still gains more than losses when who decides to buy the expensive product or consumes the expensive service. Then, the low level of income consumer who will accept to buy the expensive product or consume the service easily. Due to whose gains feeling is more than losses feeling, when who buys the product or consumes the service.

(3) Behavioral economic theory also assumes the taxpayer will pay high income tax in this year. The, even the high income taxpayer can earn high basic income, but due to whom needs to pay high income tax in this year. Then, he/she will reduce much spending, even he/she reduces spending on cheap products or cheap service consumption for enjoyment. This is the taxpayer's economic decision to influence whose consumption behavior, due to the high income tax expenditure factor influences whose consumption behavior to change to be reduced spending expenditures in this year.

How to apply division of labor and surplus of value of labour theory to predict labor market changing behavior ?

Instead of applying behavioral economic method to predict every consumer individual consumption effort. Behavioral economic method can be also be applied to predict every country's labor market changing behavior. Particularly, how salary clerical workers or low wage labor workers should move from one type of job to another based on these factors. They include as below:

Their intrinsic motivation and how their levels of effort would change after this movement, investigates the effects of income security on social perferences in labor market changing behavior, and how cooperation in social contribution is affected when income security is guaranteed, how to predict the role of positional externalities on conspicuous consumption and how would change the incentive to influence consumption. So, it seems that general labor market job changing behaviors will not influenced by external economic environment better or worse changing factor, or salary changing factor etc. different environmental condition changing factors influence to employees' job changing. Generally, employee's job changing behavior is more influenced to persuade who changes job by himself/herself intrinsic motivation negative emotion influence mainly.

How to apply motivation crowding theory to predict labor productivity? One of the main challenges of economic theory is to find what are the optimal incentives that increase productivity of labors. The standing point is usually extrinsic incentive be it is form of monetary compensations for high effort or fine for low effort.

It is a kind method of reward or punishment to increase or decrease number of productivity to every labor. But it can only raise short term number of productivity in possible and it can not guarantee high quality of productivity. So if one employer wants a labor to do more of an activity or with a higher quality, consider paying the labor for working hard on punishing whom if for providing a low level effort.

This idea is that people do not like to work, and therefore they used some sort of compensation for doing a specific activity, and that the more they are paid the harder, they will work. So, payment better compensation is only beneficial to encourage labors to do one specific task or activity in short term. This method can not be suitable to rise long term beneficial productivity and high level quality of production or excellent performance in long term and it can only keep in short term raising productivity and high level quality of production or excellent perofrmance benefits.

Consider paying the labor for working hard on punishing whom if for providing a low level effort. This idea is that people do not like to work, and therefore they used some sort of compensation for doing a specific activity, and that the more they are paid the harder they will work. So, payment better compensation is only beneficial to encourage labors to do one specific task or activity in short term. This method can not be suitable to raise long them beneficial productivity and high quality of products.

However, economists would argue that, is a labor has high intrinsic motivative to perform a task, who will provide a high level of effort without compensation by himself/herself but an even higher level of effort of whom is compensated. If a labor does not have any intrinsic motivation to perform a task or an activity, who will provide no effort or a low effort of whom. There is no compensation, but who will increase this level of effort of an extrinsic incentive is implemented.

Hence, in behavioral economic view point, the labor individual high level effort is a main psychological factor to influence whose productivity to be raised or the qualities of products to be raised, when the products are manufactured by the high level effort labor. It means that high compensation is not the good method to encourage labor productivity or raise quality. Otherwise, how to influence the one low level of effort of labor to change to be one high level of effort labor. It is the best psychological method to influence the labor to raise productivity and quality and service performance to any products or services in manufacturing process or service process for any organizations in long term beneficial possible.

How can apply behavioral economy method raises basic stable income consumer consumption desire

Economists aim to develop models of human behavior and interactions in consumption markets. But consumers behave in complex ways, such as how to predict consumers to make rational decisions in consumption processes. Moreover, self-consumption control and motivation can vary significantly across different individual consumer.
In order to build useful consumption prediction models, economists make simplifying assumptions, aims to predict how to raise stable basic income consumer target group consumption more success. However, behavioral economy method is one kind of accurate consumption prediction method. It can be applied to predict economic decison-making to every consumer consumption choice more accurate raising whose consumption desire?

I shall indicate how to apply different behavioral economy methods to raise stable basic stable income target consumer group consumption desire in these different consumption situation (consumption environment) aspects as below:

1. Stable basic stable income consumer group consumption great or small amount desire

The consumption of products and services is a fundamental part of consumer's welfare. Basically, every one who has stable basic stable income, who will like to consume any products and services. Even, consumption great or small amount desire won't be depended on whether the person whose income is more or less. It means low income level of people will still like to consume great amount to buy expensive products or consume expensive services, because consumption is human's part of life and basic needs.

This stable basic income people will like to consume, because they have stable income source when they do not worry about unemployment occurrence to cause them have no enough money to support their lifes. Otherwise, non-stable basic stable income people won't like to consume because they feel they have no stable basic income source to support their lifes and they will worry about unemployment occurrence any time. Hence, stable basic income people will have more consumption desire to compare non-stable basic stable income people in any countries usually. Behavioral economic method indicates they feel their economic benefits will be loss if they planned to buy any products or consume any services easily. So, they prefer to save money in bank more than consumption.

Demand systems and micro-economic

Why stable basic income people will like to consume? Because who have more demand, a demand system shows the level of consumer demand for different products and services: e.g. one basic stable income person may refer to the demand for clothes, another the demand for food etc.

How the demand for that particular product varies with the prices and demographic factor will influence who to accept consumption. Such as stable basic income people who will not consider to decide to buy the cloth to wear or the food to eat if who feel the cloth or food price is even more expensive to compare other kind of cloth or food. Otherwise, non-stable basic income people who will consider to decide to buy the cloth to wear or the food to eat if they feel that they still have enough cloths to wear or enough food to eat at homes , even these food or cloth price are less expensive to compare others. Because they feel they lack stable income effort to support them to consume. Hence, basic stable income factor can influence the consumer's consumption decision.

2. Life-cycle advertisement method can influence consumer individual consumption behaviors to be increased

Consumer behavior makes strong assumptions about the informational and computational bases of consumer behavior. Generally, consumer behavior is reasonably characterized as the maximization of expected lifetime utility subject to budget constraint and conditional on the available information.

Generally, consumers prefer to buy any discounted products or it is reasonable that consumers accept to buy many attractions to persuade them to buy any kinds of bargain discount products. Hence, low bargain discount product is one good behavioral economic principle to encourage or persuade or attract any consumers to increase consumption. What is behavioral life-cycle model? This model explains consumer behavior can be persuaded to buy any discounted products by advertisement, e.g. television, radio, newspapers, magazine etc. promotion channels. Because frequent advertisement promotion method can let any consumers often remember the product's brand, discounted price, style, colour and image from advertisement content.

So, advertisement can be one part of consumer behavioral life-cycle. For example, when the television audiences often watch TV. Hence, when the brand of product advertisement often makes fun image and discounted message to let TV audiences to remember this brand of product, when they are watching TV. Then, it has possible to persuade any potential consumers to choose to buy this brand of any products or consume this brand of any services, due to its advertisement of discounted sale message is very attractive to every one to let this advertisement audience's attention to remember this brand of products or services are selling or serving in market at this moment. So, it is advertisement image behavior influences audiences to buy the brand's any products attractively and persuasively.

3. Raising electricity consumption from electricity user individual habit

For electricity use market case example, how to analyze people's behavior in consuming electricity using a behavioral economic framework ? Electricity consumption is modeled by the means of consumer's individual useful habit, electricity price, consumer satisfaction level, willingness to invest in new technologies, social interactions, and marketing strategies by the power utility. Because electricity is necessary to every home or electric vehicle users needs or businessmens' office etc. different needs every day.

Power companies supply electricity to a region's homes and industries. However, electricity needs modernization of power system companies expect to increase price. Due to competitive factor, such as other fuel resource choices, outdated kind of energy electricity supply, and renewable fuel energy source competition.

Hence, applying behavioral economic concept, I assume electricity consumers will compare to electricity and other kinds of energy choices to weigh up the costs and benefits of all alternatives, aiming to maximize their benefits, before making a decision to choose to use electricity for their house electricity demand or electric vehicle or shop or factory manufacturing etc. function of different aspects of electricity users.

For example, electricity business clients, they aim to reduce cost, such as energy expenditure, when they use any energy to manufacture their products in factories. If they feel electricity is expensive price to compare other kinds of energy power supply. When, they feel that they can not earn much beneficial advantages to use electricity to produce their products. Otherwise, if they feel other any kinds of energy supply can replace electricity to give more benefits to compare electricity energy. Then, many business electricity users will change to use other kinds of energies to consume to replace electricity power.

However, electricity can have competitive ability in electric vehicles market, if many drivers feel environment protection is more important to compare vehicles will be popular to be drived, due to many drivers don't want air pollution. They will like gas vehicles. Hence, the main attribute from the consumer side is one their habit electricity consumption behaviors, satisfaction level, energy efficient interaction with the power utility.

Consequently how to predict electricity consumer's demand. The important factor is how to let electricity users to feel power companies are changing a reasonable level to compare other similar energy supply products. When electricity users feel electricity which can bring more benefits to compare other kinds of energy products. Then, in energy supply market, if the demanding number of electricity consumers can increase more than other kinds of energy demanding number. Then, it is right time to raise electricity price to charge electricity consumers. Hence, how to persuade electricity consumers to feel that they can have more benefits to compare other kinds of energy products. It is the main successful factor to electricity power supply companies.

1.1 Consumer confidence is as a predictor of consumption spending

Behavioral economists believe it has link between confidence and economic decisions to cause consumers to choose spending, if the consumer has confidence to believe the product is worth to use, then who will accept to buy the product to use.

Concentrated on the conceptualization of confidence and its role in mode in theories of consumption. It also concerns on whether the confidence indicators contain any information beyond economic fundamentals. The concern is whether confidence can be explained by current and past value of variables, such as income, unemployment, inflation or consumption or in other way.

Whether confidence measures have any statistical significance in predicting economic outcomes once information from the above variables is used. Economic variable factor will also influence consumer confidence to decide consumption spending, e.g. real consumption expenditures (income, wealth or interest rate).

Finally, it will identify under which circumstances confidence indicates can be a good predictor of household consumption. Hence, survey is one good measurement method to predict whether how much every household has confidence to spend to consume the brand of products to use. Why is survey a good confidence consumption measurement prediction to every household in every country?

The reasons include survey can gather every household consumption habit historicial data to evaluate whether every survey person has how much confidence to consume the brand of products. Which in most cases correspond to periods where there are large changes in household survey indicators, liking during financial crises or geopolitical tensions to measure or predict whether the country's future good or bad economic condition factor will influence every household consumption desire in the year.

This modelling approach assumes that there is a certain (inknown) in confidence index changes beyond which confidence starts impacting consumption behaviors. So, sample household surveys can show the contribution of confidence in explaining consumption expenditures increases when household survey indicators feature large changes. So that confidence indicators can have some increasing predictive power during the survey investigation period in the year.

Other view point, surveys have been concerned on whether the confidence indicators contain any information beyond economic fundaments. The conern is whether confidence can be explained by current and past values of variables, such as income, unemployment, inflation or consumption or the other way. Whether confidence measures have any statistical significance in predicting economic outcomes once information from different external variable factors to influence the survey household group.

What is confidence in consumption survey ?

Confidence in consumption. For example, to measure whether how much degree of strong fluctations in the economy, such as recessions and recoveries will influence the country's household confident consumption in the year.

The surveys consumers' questions usually concern on major expenditures and changes in the respondant's financial situation, focus on job availability and current business conditions etc. questions. It is then possible that about consumer confidence depending on the relative performance of the variables that may be more relevant balances, with respect to the factors that determine unemployment and other labor market related issues. It aims to investigate whether those any one of variable factors will influence consumers general loss confident consumption desire in this year.

What is a confidence indicator ?

A confidence indicator is considered as an explanatory variable for consumption together with standard variables used on predicting consumption expenditure. However, the natural real personal consumption expenditure is unexpected and unpredicted easily.

In conclusion, consumption expenditure depends the consumer individual confidence. If the consumer has much confidence to feel this year economic change will be better and he/she is easily to find job, then he/she will accept consumption easily in this year. It seems financial wealth and unemployment etc. economic factors will influence every household consumption desire. So, survey is one kind of good psychological consumption predicton method to predict consumption spending for any country in the year. I recommend manufacturers may choose to apply survey method to attempt to enquire sample survey people to gather data to predict whether what degree of consumption desire to them and find solution methods to solve low degree of consumption desire challenge.

1.2 How to apply behavioral economy methods to influence employee individual psychology to achieve raise productivity of long term incentive intention?

Increasing salary is short term incentive productivity method

Behavioral economy assumes labors will choose to do beneficial behaviors to themselves when they feel their work behaviors can earn more benefits to themselves more than their employers in the organizations. Otherwise, if they feel their work behaviors can earn more benefits to their employers more than themselves. Then, they won't choose to do their work behaviors, e.g. rasing productivities or work hard. Due to they feel work hard or raise productivities behaviors that only give more benefits to their employers more themselves.

Whether does cheap product price incenitve consumption desire to influence effective consumption behavior? Whether is monetary increasing salary payment incentive labors might be willing to work on task? I feel raising labours' productivities is similar to raise incentive consumption, which both have similar point, such as increasing salary payment or cheap product price is the main factor to influence incentive consumption or raising productivities. Hence, it seems monetary factor is not the main effort to encourage labors to work hard.

In labor's behavioral economic view point, for example, if a employer pays a employee more doing a task, who might be less willing to work on it, who might be less productive given whose efforts and who may enjoy the task less. If you want your employees to save more for retirement. You may want to give them fewer investment options. If you want them to engage more in a task, you might want offer them an additional alternative, instead of increasing salary to that task. Thus, increasing salary is not the onl method to encourage productivities of incentives.

How to improve the design of incentive structures to encourage productivities in any organizations?

Any monetary incentive can only encourage productivities in short term. It can not only encourage productivities in long term in any organizations. It is similar to cheap or discount product price can only attractive consumers to buy the product in short term, it can not attract consumers to choose to buy the product in long term, it prefers to have more options to encourage labors to incentive productivities, e.g. investing good beneficial retirement plans. Suggesting that employees do not have free disposal of their investment options. These standard inventives seem irrelevant raising salary monetary factor, they can be quite effective in inducing labors to take particular actions to incentive productivities in long term. Due to when they can hard work, then they have more beneficial retirement plans or investing plans for their retirement. It means when they can achieve the most effective or efficient productivities to the employer for long term. It will give better retirement benefits and investment benefits to the better or even the best performance of employees. Otherwise, the worst performance employees won't earn good retirement benefits and investment benefits, when their employers feel their perform very poor in the organizatons in long term.

Hence, increasing salary level method is not one successful long term incentive method to persuade every employee to raise productivities or encourage excellent performance optional method. Increasing salary level is only similar to reduce product price and it is only short term encouragement to consumption or productivities method.
In conclusion, extrinsic monetary factor can not incentive labor's raising productivities more than every employee themselves intrinsic motivation to raise productivities as excellent performance in any organizations. Thus, organizations need to let employees to feel that they can give long term economic benefits to encourage their intrinsic motivation effort to be raised their productivities or performance more effective or efficient in order to achieve long term both win-win economic benefits to employees and employers both.

Building employees and managers kindly co-operational relationship method

If you are an economist, your employer has no without any financial incentive to encourage your economic research tasks in your organizaton. It is equally difficult to vertify that such activity will contribute to your growth of human capital and increased productivity in research or teaching.

The standard model, which explains employee's effort only through the way (determined by productivity), is therefore incomplete. In particular, it doesn't consider that incentives to work do not have to be monetary in other words, that there are other things besides the disutility of labor (Kamenica, 2012) and section 1.3 have.

Why will short term wage increasing method only influence short term labor supply to raise productivies? The effect of reference rasing wage can be most easily identified on short term labor supply to raise productivities. For US, New York city taxi drivers case, they have to decide every day for low long they are going to offer their services, given the day-to-day variable ability of demand they face (peaking during bad weather and/or when big conferences and public events are taking place in the city).

In the standard model, houes worked should grow with any growth in demand for New York taxi drivers' services. (one day's earning will have only a negligible income effect in the longer run). And yet actual cabbies work less on a demand heavy day. One of possible explanations suggests that New York city taxi drivers expect a certain income, they have set themselves a specific target income, who expect to achieve every day. During low demand for their taxi services, then they work longer hours to reach the target, when during peak demand, theit referential income is achieved quickly and they only work short hours. Elasticity of hours worked with respect to their earnings is therefore negative (Lamerer, Babcock, Loewenstein, & Thaler, 1997).

However, taxi driver is either one self employment business or one taxi company employment driving service occupation. It is similar to other kinds of service jobs in societies. Servicing employees, such as waiters, salepeople, securities, customer services, bus drivers etc. different kinds of service occupations. They are not similar to manufacturing occupation to be applied how many amount of piece of products production to evaluate their productivitie efforts. Thus these any one of service job nature is depended on their service performance to clients to feel their service performances are excellent to compare general service performance effort of service employees.

Considerably, respectly, I assume that if these service employees' managers can build kindly working environment, e.g. manager individual attitude and behavior can let their employees to feel happy to work together in their teams. Then, the managers' kindly as enthusiatic behaviors or attitudes will let every employee more positive encouragement of service attitude to serve their clients in their teams. Then, the client complaining number will be possible reduced, even none of any complains. Hence, building kindly relationship between managers and employees will raise excellent service performance to any orgnization's service nature employees.

Can bonus method encourage service performance to be raised ?

In service job nature of bonus method can also raise employees' overall productivities or service performance. For example, when employees got a provisional bonus before the start of the workweek, but were warned that they would lose it on payday,unless they achieve the productivities or excellent service performance norm, they worked more productivites or let many clients to satisfy their service performance. Hence, managers can achieve bonus plan to compensate any excellent productivity or excellent services to them. Then, they can let clients to feel their service performance more satisfactory than employees of a control group who were merely given the standard promise to receive a bonus upon achieving the norm.

The effort was relatively small, however, productivity grew 1%. Interestingly, the effect of a loss was stronger when eholw teams were rewarded this way, social pressure came to bear on the less productivity team members. When the team members won't earn any bonus. So, long-term productivity gains were achieved through bonuses paid by excellent performance compensation method to compare to low service performance employees receiving no bonuses at all.

Economic views of human motivation nature

There are only two main types of economic actors and by making simplifying assumptions about how these types of actors behave and interact. The two basic sets of actors in this mdel are firms, which are assumed in this model are firms, which are assumed to maximize their profits from producing and selling products and services, households, which are assumed to maximize their utility (or satisfaction) from consuming products and services.

It seems any employees will choose to do behaviors to achieve to earn much benefits from their organizations. The models of economic behaviors that consider consider employees' choice of goals, the actions they take to achieve these goals and the limitatons and influences that affect their choices and actions.

For university students choose which universities to study case, suppose that any college enrollment students are deciding which courses to study. Thus, it implies that if the university can provid many different kinds of suitable or right courses to any college enrollment students to choose to study. It means that if the university can provide many different kinds of courses to enrollment students to choose to study. Then, it will have much chance to attract enrollment students to choose this university to study. It's competition can be raised by many courses choice factor. but, in fact, it is not absolute right, although the university can provide many courses to provide to enrollment students to choose to study. But, it is not guarantee to represent it must attract many students to enroll this university to study.

For example, suppose that college enrollment students are deciding which courses to choose to study. Although, it has right course to prepare to these enrollment students to choose to study. But, they see a summary of evaluations from hundreds of other students indicating that a certain course is very good in this university. Then, suppose that they match a video interview of just one student to give a negative review of this university of the course. Even when students were told in advance that such a negative review was worse to this university of the course. They tended to be more influenced by the negative review than the summary of hundreds of evaluations, even although such behavior seems irratonal. Hence, although many right courses choice has much chance to attract students to enroll this university to study. But, if its bad educational quality from this course from negative review factor, which will influence the enrollment students number to be reduced.

It implies that students will compare this university's the cource educatonal quality whether is better or worse to compare other universities' similar course educational quality, even this university's this course fee whether is reasonable in educational market. This is cost and beneficial comparison behavioral economy principle to all enrollment students before they decide to choose which universities.

Hence, this case implies that universities how to train teachers' teaching skills to let students to feel that they can learn new knowledge from their teaching staffs absolutely. It means how to raise education training skills to raise teachers' teaching performance. It is very important factor to influence the university's teaching development success. So, many courses choice is not important factor to attract many students to enroll the university. Otherwise, although the university can not provide many courses to let students to enroll, but it's teachers can provide excellent teaching service to teach whose students. This is important factor to attract many students to choose to enroll this university to study.

1.3 Under-level productive efficiency and low- consumption desire behavioral economic influences

In behavioral economic influence view point, I feel that under-level productive efficiency is the represent low production number to the manufacturer as well as low-consumption desire is not represent less consumers demands or customers lose confidence to the product.

On the one hand, I shall apply behavioral economic method to analyze why inder productive efficiency is not represent low production number influence. Otherwise, I feel under-productive efficiency will have possible to increase production number after the manufacturer can review what factor(s) to influence under-productive efficiency.

I shall give reasons to explain as below:

As Jim, P. & Brendan. M. (2013) indicated who had ever been experiencing failure to do their businesses. Although, they had lost a million dollars, but they felt that they can be tought to learn undiscovered knowledge to know how to do their businesses successful by their wrong judgement and decision learning experience. They explained that " in ll risk taking, speculation, business ventures, entrepreneurial activities, it is the loss side on which you must focus first. This is even true for gambling, the gambler determines how much he's willing to bet, and loss, before the game is played. He doesn't wait for the game to end and then let the croupier or dealer assign his wager for him. How do you determine the downside, and how do you control or minimize it? With objective decision making and a plan that has as its starting point the stop-loss parameters".

Hence, it explains any business will have under-level productive efficiencies and low consumption desire business risk. However, to any any one entrepreneur, who needs to know it is one game between the himself/herself and whose clients. They also need to know with objective decision making and a plan that has as its starting point.

Hence, I assume that if the entrepreneur has wrong decision to cause under-level productive efficiency, it is possible that, due to there is no enough employee number to manufacture the product or many employees are not skillful to manufacture all product in normal time or many employees are lazy etc. different factors to cause under-level productivies. However, when they discover their productivities are very low to compare similar competitors their employees' productivities and efficiencies. Then, they can attempt to find what factor(s) to cause low productivities and loe efficiencies. it is possible that any one among of these factors case. They include many employees' lazy to influence low productivities or there is no enough employee number or many employees are not skillful to manufacture their products in production process.

Hence, wrong decision or plan is not represent failure.

Otherwise, it can give chance to let the entrepreneur to lern whether what the factor(s) is (are) to cause low productivities and low efficiencies in whose product manufacturing process. As I feel that under-level productive efficiency is not represent low production number. Because I assume that if one worker lacks enough skills and manufacturing experiences to manufacture the product, but who can spend less time to manufacture the product and whose spending manufacturing time is same to the another owning enough skillful worker's time to do the product. Hence, I believe that the product quality from the low-skillful worker's manufacturing skill, it's quality will be worse to compare to the product quality from the high skillful worker's manufacturing skill. Hence, if the low skillful worker needs to spend much time to produce the product, but the product quality can be same to the high skillful worker's product quality. It means that it is sure because the low skillful worker has no excellent skill to compare to the high skillful worker to produce the product. Hence, his manufacturing spending time must be longer than the high skillful worker's time. It implies that the low skillful worker spends less time to raies high production number, but his product must be poor quality to sell. Then, his fast and efficient manufacturing speed that is not achieve economic beneficial to the organization's manufacturing process, e.g. less electricity spends to manufacture the product. Otherwise, the low skillful worker's fast and efficient manufacturing speed of behavior will raise the organization's cost in manufacturing process because consumers would not like to choose to buy any low quality product when they can choose which similar products to compare which one has the best quality and cheap price to buy. Hence, efficient production is not the main factor to influence the business's success. Otherwise, good quality of the product factor is more important to compare it to influence the business's success.

On the other hand, I shall apply behavioral economic theory to analyze why low-consumption desire is not represent consumer demand lose to the business. As Jim. P. & Brendan. M. (20130 also identified " rather than looking for success to follow, who explained the formula for failure to avoid. As an Wang, founder of Wang laboratories said " it is my belief that there are no secret to success." The formula for failure is not lack of knowledge, brains, skills or hard work and it's not lack of luck, it's personalizing losses, especially of preceded by a string of wins or profits. It's refusing to acknowledge and accept the reality of a loss when it starts to occur because to so so would reflect negatively on you."

Thus, as whose feeling to explain why low-consumption desire is not represent less consumers demands or customers lose confidence to the product. The reasons include the causes of low-consumption desire are possible due to worse economic environment factor influences consumption desire to be reduced. It is not due to whether the product price is too high or quality is worse to compare others. Hence, as Jim & Brendan indicated the formula for business failure is not lack of knowledge, brains, skills or hard work and it's not lack of luck. It's not lack of luck. It's personalizing losses, means its reflecting to knowledge and accept the reality of a loss when it starts to occur. As it is applied to explain why low-consumption desire is not represent less consumers demands or customers lose confidence to the product. It's possible that external economic environment changing worse factor to cause the business personalizing losses, it is not reflect who lacks knowledge, skill, hard work factors to cause failure. Hence, ho to predict when and how and why economic environment changes worse will be important factor to predict when and how and why consumption behavioral changes to cause business's success.

Reference

Camerer, C.F. Babrocks, Loewenstein, G., & Thaler, R. (1997). Labor supply of New York city candrivers: One day of a time. The Quacterly Jounrnal of economics, 112 (2), 407-441. doi: 10.1162/003355399555244.

How do you view the outlook for consumer confidence in your key markets next year? Source from :
http://www.Just-food.com Confidence survey, Nov.
2015

Jim. P. & Brendan. M. (2013) . What I learned losing a million dollars, p.160. Colimbia University, Columbia business school press, New York, US.

Kamenica, E. (2012). Behavioral economics and psychology of incentives. Annual review of economics, 4 (1), 427-452. doi: 10.1146/annurev-economics-080511-110909.

Maselli, 2012 Technology driven job polarization in
EU , 2000-2010. % change in labor supply
skilled/upgrade (ISCED) and labor demand for
skills/tasks (ISOD).

Ethnographic research

ethnographic method measures

China stable income consumer purchase desire

How can ethnographic research predict consumer emotion ?-Applying video recording method to predict consumer behavior

Critically assess the role of ethnographic research as a means of learning More about buyer behavior. To critically assess whether the role of ethnographic research as a means of learning more about buyer behavior. I shall indicate what the marketers who use general methods to learn more about buyer behavior to compare to ethnographic research difference. In general, marketers learn buyer behavior who shall follow the simplified stages in the buyer decision process , such as the beginning is from need recognition to information search to evaluate to decision to the end of post purchase evaluation stage. Hence, the any buyers behavior shall be cycle stage to decide whether who shall repeat to choose to buy the company's product or use it's service if who feel the product or service had achieved their satisfaction after who spent. The marketers shall use questionnaires or marketing researches to enquire consumers to gather their ideas to analysis to get evaluation to assess whether how whose companies need to produce what kinds of new products style, design, color, price level and sale channels to achieve the most suitable marketing strategy to raise their sale competition. Otherwise, the role of ethnographic search is one different method to learn more about buyer behavior. In general, companies shall not need to arrange questionnaires to enquire participants to fill to answer questions to gather data to carry on evaluation and which do not need to follow the simplified stages to assess target client groups purchase decision process to carry on the sale and post purchase evaluation cycle to evaluate whether what are their product criteria or weaknesses which need to improve to raise their sale competition in their market. I think ethnographic research can get closer to the truth about consumer behavior. On behalf of companies' clients, which can seek to uncover hidden truths about the way their clients' lead their lives, by paying volunteers to be followed for days on end, being filmed and having their every more recorded. Companies will pay their target householder participant group to carry on an observational survey by digital cameras to be filmed record at home. One essential feature of ethnographic research is that it must not have any predetermined agenda. There is little value in undertaking this type of research if the mind set of the researcher is expecting to see preconceived phenomena, it is the unexpected that is often of most interest, and which is so difficult to pick up through more structured forms of survey. In fact, participants in a survey may feel self conscious when who are being filmed, and the more interesting insights are likely to be observed when participants are feeling relaxed and off their guard .It is not just what people actually do that can be interesting, but what they almost do, and the body language used when members of the household are discussing an issue. It can take several hours of filming to yield just a few moments of true insights into participants' true attitudes and behavior.

One example of the company's ethnographic research in action was provided by a project commissioned by the footwear brand Dr Martens. It wanted to understand how young people used fashion brands in their every lives . Why for example, did some brands, such as Nike trainers or baseball caps become popular in youth culture? The researchers identified groups of young people around the world who responded to Dr Martens' target market. In return for a payment, volunteers were followed for several days and their daily routines filmed with a handheld digital camera. In total, 180 hours of captured film was edited to just one hour of highlights showing the key drivers of youth culture which are relevant to the Dr Martens brand. It seemed that young people preferred fashions that allowed them to customize an item of clothing and in some way take ownership of it. The research drew the conclusion that iconic fashion items for young people had to have a distinctive label or style that made their wearers stand out as part of a tribe. Hence, ethnographic research seems to help this company to know why the young clients choose to buy other brand sport shoes, it is possible that they the other brands sport shoes' color or design can be accepted more to than to buy Dr Marten brand's sport shoes when they wear different style of clothing. Hence, it can use digital camera to observe the worldwide choice of paying target youth volunteers whose daily individual behaviors at homes to get the more actual evidence to evaluate what factors influence youth clients choose to buy other brands of sport shoes. Otherwise, if it use structured questionnaire surveys to enquire youth clients , it is possible that who can not give their feedbacks honestly.

Otherwise, observable youth people whose daily activities can help this company to know it is possible that their design and color of clothing are one factor to influence their choice to buy preferable brands of sport shoes to wear if who felt the brand of sport shoe was suitable to wear to influence their clothing to be felt more smart in appearance. However, I suggest companies to avoid to tell householders what the research project is about, until it is over. That way, the chances of participants deliberately playing to the camera can be reduced. Hence, ethnographic researcher ought not tell to participants why who needs to record their daily activities at home till to the end of observable survey finishing due to it is possible that the participants will not perform their actual behaviors if who knew the researcher's observable intention. However, if marketers need to understand how whose companies clients actually make purchase decisions to their products, who shall use structured questionnaire surveys for collecting large scale factual data, but it will have major weaknesses when companies can not understand individual's attitude. Complex sets of factors that influence their buying decisions can only rarely be captured by a questionnaire.

Qualitative approaches such as those using focus groups can get closer to the truth, but participants often still find themselves inhibited from telling the full story to the companies to know.

Ethnography is one of many approaches that can be found within social research. Ethnography was a descriptive account of a community or culture. Ethnography usually involves the researcher participating in people's daily lives for an extended

period of time, watching what happens, listening to what is said, and/or asking questions through informal and formal interviews collecting documents. In more detailed terms, ethnographic work usually has most of the following features: People actions are studied in every contexts rather than under conditions created by the researcher, such as in experimental setups or highly structured interview situations as well as data are gathered from a range of sources including documentary evidence of various kinds, but participant observation and/or relatively informal conversations are usually the main ones as well as data collection is for the most past relatively unstructured in two senses and it doesn't involve following through detailed research design at the start and the categories that are used for interpreting what people say or do are not built into the data collection process through the use of observation schedules or questionnaire to analysis.

Generally, fairly small scale, perhaps a single setting or group of people. This is a facilitate in depth study and the analysis of data involves interpretation of the meanings, functions and consequences of human actions and how these are implicated in local and perhaps also wider contexts what are produced for the most part are verbal descriptions, explanations and theories and statistical analysis play a subordinate role at most. How ethnography can learn more about buyer behavior. It means collection of data to pursue an answers to these questions more effectively and to test these against evidence. Collecting data in natural settings, in other words in those that have not been specially set up for research purposes (such as experiments or formal interviews). Where participant observation is involved the researcher must have some role in the studied and this will usually have to be done at least through implicit and probably also through explicit, negotiation with people.

How video recording method predict consumer behavior:

The methodological model for social research is physical science conceived in terms of the logic of the experiment. Ethnography was sometimes dismissed as quite inappropriate to social science on the grounds that the data and findings it produces are subjective. Hence, ethnographic research is the role to learn more about buyer behavior through marketers may have been listening more to consumers (e.g. through qualitative research), efforts have almost always been directed at controlling consumers; ranges of products or services pre determined by producers have been pushed through with little real involvement of consumers in the process at a time in which consumers are ever more aware of what is being done to marketers. Ethnographic field research involves the study of groups and people as who go about every day lives. There has two distinct activities. First, the ethnographer enter into a social setting and gets to know the people involved in it; who participates in the daily routines; develops ongoing relations with the people in it and observes all the approach. But second the ethnographer writes down in regular systematic ways what who observes and learns when participating in the daily rounds of life of others. Thus, the researcher creates an accumulating written record of these observations and experiences. These two interconnected activities comprise the core of ethnographic search: firsthand participation in some initially unfamiliar

social world and the production of written accounts of that world by drawing upon such participation. Hence, ethnographers are committed to get close to the activities and everyday people.

Getting close minimally requires physical and social proximity to the daily rounds of people's lives and activities, the field researcher must be able to take up positions in the midst of the key sites and scenes of other's lives in order observe and understand whom. In learning about others through active participation in their lives and activities. Finally, close continuing participation in the lives of others encourages appreciation of social life as ongoing processes. Through participation the field researcher sees how people do uncertainty and confusion, how meaning is through talk and collective action, how understandings change over time.

Consumer behavior refers to the behavior that consumers display in searching for purchasing, using, evaluating and disposing of products and services that who expect will satisfy their needs and it's behaviors that are directly involved in the action of obtaining, consuming and spending products/services, including the decision processes that precede and follow these actions. The knowledge of consumer behavior helps the marketer to understand how consumer think, feel and select from alternative like products, brands and the like and how the consumers' buying behaviors are influenced by their environment, the reference groups, family and salespersons. Most of the factors are uncontrollable and beyond the controls of marketers, but who have to be considered when trying to understand the complex behavior of the consumers. Consumers buying cycle processes involved when individuals or groups select, purchase, use or dispose of products or services or ideas or experiences to satisfy needs and desires.

In the marketing context, the term consumer refers not only to the act of purchase itself, but also to patterns of aggregate buying which include pre-purchase and post purchase activities.

Pre-purchase activity might consist of the growing awareness of a need or wants and a search for and evaluate of information about the products and brands that might satisfy it. Post purchase activities include the evaluation of the purchased item in use and the reduction of any anxiety which accompanies the purchase of expensive and infrequently bought items. The various factors include lifestyles and its impact on the consumer behavior.

On the first hand, ethnographic research can learn more about buyer behavior as below: ethnographic research described the dominant, positivistic consumer perspectives and methodological and analytical overview of the traditional perspectives. There are two factors mainly influencing the consumers for decision making. Risk aversion and innovativeness. Risk aversion is a measure of how much consumers need to be certain and sure of what who are purchasing. Highly risk adverse consumers need to be very certain about what who are buying. Whereas less risk adverse consumers on tolerate some risk and uncertainty in their purchasing. The second variable, innovativeness is a global measure which captures the degree to which consumers are willing to take chances and experiment with new ways of doing things. Hence, ethnographic research can learn whether the buyer's shopping motivation is abound with which various measures of individual characteristics, e.g. innovative, variety seeking etc. different factors to the buyer behavior.

On the second hand, perception is a mental process, whereby an individual selects data or information from the environment organizes it and then draws significance or meaning from it. Perceived fit is an attitudinal measure of how appropriate a certain channel of distribution is for a specific product. Consumer's perception of the fit between a service/product and channel is very influential in determining whether who will consider using that channel for a specific service. In fact, perceived fit was found to be more important than consumer's preference for the distribution method or service. Product quality and packaging and brand awareness familiarity with a channel is a measure of the general experience who have with purchasing products through special channels , e.g. internets, newspapers advertisement factors let consumers to decide to choose to buy or not buy the specific product. Shopping motives are defined as consumer's wants and needs as who relate to outlets at which to shop. Two groups of motives, functions and non functional have been proposed with time, place and possession needs and refer to rational aspects of

channel choice. The functional motives included convenience, price comparison. Otherwise, the non functional motives entailed recreation and it related to social and emotional reasons. Hence, ethnographic research can assess whether the product or service is the functional motive or non functional motive to cause the buyer's choice.

On the third hand, economic theory holds that of largely rational and conscious economic calculations. Thus, the individual buyer seeks to spend whose income on those products that will deliver the most utility (satisfaction) according to his tastes and relative prices. It aimed to simplify assumptions and examine the effects of changes in single variables (e.g. price) holding all other variables constant. (e.g. low price of product is the higher the sales. The identified the impact of price differentials on consumers' brand preferences; changes in produces on demand variations; changes in price on demand sensitivity and scarcity on consumer choice behavior amongst many others. The consumer behavioral perspective in contrast to the economic view which underscores the importance of internal processes in consumer decision making, the behavioral perspective emphasizes the role of external environmental factors in the process of learning, when which it is argued causes behavior. The behavioral perspective therefore focuses on external environmental, such as advertisement that stimulate consumer response through learning. Consumers must be exposed to information, e.g. advertisement of it is to influence their behavior. Hence, ethnographic research can assess whether the product/service is consumer behavioral perspective or behavioral perspective to cause the buyer's choice.

On the fourth hand, consumers were suggest that high involvement with a product results in an extended problem followed by an information search, alternative evaluation, purchase and post purchase activities. The process is aided by an active information processing sequence involving exposure, attention, comprehension, acceptance and retention. The choice is determined by the outcome of the information process aided decision sequence may have satisfying or dissatisfying outcomes. Consumer's motivation and intention and that unpredictable factors (such as non availability brand or insufficient funds) may result in modification of the actual choice made by a consumer. This model assumes that observed consumer behavior is preceded by intrapersonal psychological states and events (attitude intention-purchase sequence). Hence, the events are as outputs of the processing of information, taking for granted that consumers seek and use information as part of their rational problem solving and decision making processes. Hence, ethnographic research can learn why the buyer doesn't choose to buy the product whether it is unpredictable or predictable psychological factors.

On the fifth hand, personality perspective means some purchases have more personal relevance than others. When this partly reflects on factors, such as price, it also bears on the way in which some products enhance the consumer's self concept , e.g. possessions are considered to reflect on a consumer's image of whom. Personality in general is understood as a concept. Personality has also been understood as the unique way in which traits, attitudes, when individuals might not always be uniform and predictable in their patterns of choice in different situations, it might be possible to make sense of and to forecast the general reactions of broadly defined groups and classes of purchasers.

It is the concept of consumer general behavioral response patterns that forms the basis for marketing's personality based segmentation strategies. The possibility of using measures of personality to guide marketing action, for example in segmenting markets , tailoring new brands of innovative consumers and repositioning mature brands has encouraged a large volume of research. Attitude itself is a learning experience and can lead to a change in attitudes before buyers enter the buying process. Thus, attitudes don't automatically guarantee all types of behavior. They are really the product of social forces interacting with the individual's unique temperament and abilities and social influences are not all of the behavioral variations in people. Two individuals subject to the same influences are not likely to have identical attitudes, although those attitudes will probably more points than those of two and cognition. Affect refers to the way a consumer feel about an attitude object, behavior involves the person's intentions to do something with regard to an attitude object and finally cognition refers to the beliefs a consumer has about an attitude object. Thus, ethnographic research can learn whether it is from external social factors more or internal personality factors more to cause the buyer's choice. The theory of cognitive information processing , attitudes are formed in the order of beliefs, affect and behavior. Attitudes based on behavioral learning follow the beliefs, behaviors and affect sequence and finally attitudes formed based on the experiential hierarchy follow the affect, behavior and beliefs route. A consumer who is highly involved with a product / service category and who perceives a high level of product/service differentiation between alternatives will follow the cognitive hierarchy (beliefs affect behavior). From the ethnographic research marketers perspective the sequence of attitude formation is from a communication point of views from a strategic point of view, such as it has proved useful in specifying the different elements that work together to influence buyers' evaluations of attitudes ; products or services may be composed of many attributes or qualities, some of which may be more important than others to particular people. So consumer's decision is to act on whose attitude is affected by other factors, such as whether it is felt other factors, such as whether it is felt that buying a product/ service would be met with approval by friends and family. The complexity of attitudes is underscored by multi attribute attitude models, in which sets of beliefs and evaluations are identified and combined to predict an overall attitude.

On the final hand, the situational influence perspective, a situation is defined by factors over and above the characteristics of a person and product or service. For example, situational affects may be behavioral (e.g.

entertaining friends), experiential or perceptual (e.g. being depressed or being pressed for time). According to the behavioral influence perspective of low involvement decision situation, consumer decision making is a learned response to environmental cues, as when a person decided to buy something on impulse that is prompted as a surprise special in a store.

According to this approach, then ethnographic research marketers must concentrate on assessing the characteristics of the environment, such as the physical surroundings and product/service placement, that influence members of that target market. For example, point of purchase (such as product/ service samples) are particularly useful in inducing impulse purchases. Ethnographic research marketers focus on measuring consumers‘ effective responses to products or services and develop offerings that elicit appropriate subjective reactions and employ effective symbolism. Situational effects can also be perceptive, e.g. there could be a number of ways in which mood can influence purchase decisions. For example, stress can impact information processing and problem solving abilities. In addition, time poverty can impact buying decisions. An individual's priorities determine whose time style. According, consumer buying change is not something which consumers do for themselves, rather it is a result of something that is done to them by some internal ,e.g. trait or external ,e.g. environment force over which they have little or no control. Thus, ethnographic research can assess what is the situational influence factors to cause the buyer to choose to buy the product or consume the service. In conclusion, conditions of competition are changing rapidly today and companies need strategies to react to those changes promptly to raise competition. Due to technological developments, physical differences of products/ services have decreased. Differentiation should be on the meanings products/ services bear instead of on their physical features and a successful brand differentiation can be possible by building personality. Hence, understanding consumer behaviors are related to marketing natures in the product sale or service provision to every marketer who needs to considerate to win whose competitors.

Discuss the ethical issues that are raised by ethnographic research.

Consumer research has been important to the development of marketing theory and practice. Consumers are seldom, if ever, involved in the research design and analysis processes which raises issues that go beyond ethics. Particularly, problematic when participant observation is employed , as little is and little could be addressed by research guidelines and codes of ethics relevant to marketing research. Some of the relevant ethical issues to participant observation that arise from the lack of the consumer in the research process as well as the potential issues that may be involved in participatory research designs, the shortcomings of the available ethnographic marketing research guidelines and codes of ethics as for as participant observation is concerned. Some argument regards the real time and nature of ethical circumstances at the field where the ethnographic researcher must often respond to unexpected situations immediately.

Why ethical ways of thinking it is important to recognize that are raised by ethnographic research.

It is possible that the issues of power that can arise ethnographic research as well as it is from the consequences of simply doing
research , even if the intentions are good and it is from the fact that ethnographic research marketers' knowledge system is necessarily linked to other forms of structural power (e.g. gender, race, development, the system). The ethnographic research marketers whose emotional and power issues present in ethnographic research relationships are also acknowledged to influence ethnographic results, and this is where the key issues of using research participants for data collection comes in. Ethnographic research designs that objectify and don't include research participants in the conceptualization of the research study through to data analysis have been widely criticized by ethnographic researchers and these issues must be considered within the scope of the ethics of care.

Researchers (ethnographers) need have moral responsibilities toward research, included informed consent, confidentiality, reliability and validity. In sum, ethical guidelines and codes of conduct can be beneficial in alerting consumer researchers of ethical ways of conducting research. However, participants needed rules to be aided by researchers‘ own ethical reasoning in the field. The ethnographic researchers need to highlight the importance of constant negotiation of participation in the different stages of research, how participants may not be willing (due to lack of time or even personal circumstances) to help ethnographic researchers in the data analysis process and how researchers' own deadlines and academic constraints may get in the way of the idealized research process of involvement between ethnographic research participants and researchers are well to their discussed topic. In general, ethnographic researchers need to know what who need to understand about ethics, such as harm, consent, data protection etc. recap of ethical approval what it is and what ethnographic researchers need to do and what further sources of information and support need. In ethic principles, ethnographic research should be designed, reviewed and undertaken to ensure integrity and quality. Participants must normally be informed fully about the purpose, methods and intends possible uses of research, what their participation entails and what risks, the confidentiality must be respected research participants must take part voluntarily, harm to research participants must be avoided in all instances and the independence of research must be clear and any conflicts to interest or partiality must be explicit and increasing stakeholder demands. The mature of the ethical consumer is educated, middle class or over emotional to decide what kind products who needs to buy and how many numbers are enough to buy. For example, with the environment dropping out of media attention, ethic provided new moral ground and campaigns or opening of a chain of ethical supermarkets, ethical image became a desirable commodity for the big retailers. Some ethical customers need to satisfy with fair trade marked products to buy from the ethical supermarkets. How morality may play a significant role in the performance of buyers' actions. It is concerned specifically with how rules, responsibilities and values centering on right or wrong influence the character of consumption.

The idea that morality (ethicality) can have a considerable impact upon the consumption. Hence, I think business moral performance is needed to satisfy every buyer's decision of consumption and it is linked to the ethnographic research growing literature on ethical consumer behavior. Within psychology, for instance, morality can be seen as a process of cognitive learning where systematic punishment and reward help to educate individuals of their actions. Whether consumption is informed by at least some of the available moral perspectives to some of the available moral perspectives, so it caused ethical issues that are raised by ethnographic research. Ethical consumption is concerned with predicting market behavior, it included some kind of relationship between the attitudes, values and behaviors of a defined ethical consumer group. For example, ethnographic researchers have been interested in the effects of environmental concern on environmentally friendly consumer behavior. Depending on how ethical consumption is defined, it recognizes alternative forms of what are essentially moral values, attitudes and buyer individual behavior. Consumer behavior has been changed by external elements, such as economy, technology, cultures, religion etc. factors. It would be unfortunate to be great importance for an understanding of ethical consumption issues.

In conclusion, consumption behavior is the art of need for desire to, it could be thought of as directly influenced by certain core values held as sacred within society. For example, ethical buyer behavior may concerns about animal protection, environmental protection, human protection etc. life rights issue. Facts, knowledge and truth about morality in consumption are seen as being raised by ethnographic research. According, the relationship between morality and consumers behavior could be better through of as the products of a continued process of political, social, technological and religious re-organization of life. For example, capabilities of new digital , microchip technology enhanced many consumers with the delights of efficient, task-saving, small and shiny products. Simultaneously, and not unrelated turbo-charges cars, mobile phones, cock tail parties etc. high technological products are arguably reflected power, success and good living to influence buyer behavior ethically daily in our society. Hence, I believe ethical issues that are needed to consider by ethnographic research.

Discuss possible alternative approaches by which marketers may learn more about youth culture.

Market based trading -selling, buying and consuming has existed in our society. Human action and interaction and behaving in different roles in exchange markets and various trading situations which is a typical of consumers and market trading interplays of several actors in economic, societal and cultural contexts as well as consumer behavior and consumer culture and consumption which have close relationship. Individual youth consumer or a group of youth consumers who is described as humanistic economics where people, their values and culture are primarily analyzed. In general, research on brands and organizational issues of the marketing function defined the questions of how to sell more products or provide more services to speed up the general level of consumption in order to better the economic situation of a firm or a nation. Basically, individual youth buyer seeks to speed whose income on those

products/services what will deliver the most utility, typically satisfaction, according to whose tastes and budget. In economic, consumer behavior is identified with rational decision making. Decisions are automatically translated into purchasing and consuming, The price and income constraints are generally accepted factors in an economic analysis of
consumer behavior. Consequently, consumers are seen as rational actors that purposefully optimize the production of their utility.

Sociological and macro and cultural perspective which focuses on consuming , emphasizes on emotions, multicultural new consumers aspects, cultural studies and the meaning of culture for consumer research surfaced also in the late 1980 years. For example, consumption symbolism, different aspects to property and possessions, political consumption, research and cultures and subcultures. In consumer studies can be traced to the mid 1990 years, when consumer culture was recognized as a distinct cultural entity. Consumption was seen as a society activity which above all others, unities economy and culture. The one alternative approach is that learning more about youth culture, there is a clear common sense about its influence on social youth consumption changes, and the importance of its analysis in order to understand modern youth consumption. For example, marketers may learn more how to make youth to cause excessive consumption nowadays. The influence of the means of mass communication and oriented medias has contributed to send promotion messages to different youth audiences, e.g. from children and teen ages to youths. To see themselves in real conditions why who need to buy products or need services before beyond their possibilities have been planned to buy electronics, cars and even a house etc. products.

The another alternative approach is that marketers may also learn what are youth consumer modern culture how to make them, such as symbol status and power how become habituated to consume familiar products/ services able to reinforce familiar image in youth cultural different target groups. The final alternative approach is that culture is sociological influence on client's needs, it is based on the individual's physiological and psychological needs, such as food choice. Maslow recognized that once individual have satisfied these basic physiological needs, such as foods and drinks, who may seek to satisfy social needs by cultural influence, for example, the need to have meaningful interaction with peers. More complex still, western cultures see increasing numbers of people seeking to satisfy essentially internal needs for self satisfaction, products therefore satisfy increasing complex needs. Moreover, food is no longer seen as a basic necessary to be purchased and cooked for self consumption with growing prosperity, youth people have sought to satisfy social needs by eating out with friend or family. Youth peoples' satisfaction of such social needs may influences on their foods sating basic needs. Hence, if the youth clients had afford to go to restaurant to eat more expensive and good taste foods. The high class food culture can change the youth client's food necessity to influence whose food choice.

A young child is often considered society unacceptable, so such youth behavior is socialized out before the child reaches adulthood. The faculty cultural influences a child's perception of the world and the family cultural influences lasts into adulthood. For example of this effect on buying processes can be found in youth adults selection of a particular brand breakfast cereal because it is the one that who were brought up with youth individuals are surrounded by peer group/or reference groups with act as a guide for youth consumption of behavior peer groups can be primary and direct to influence their youth culture (e.g. colleagues at work and school), popular movie actors can secondary and indirect to influence to their youth culture (e.g. guideline or behavior provided by popular movie actors or media figures) ; youth individuals culture can also
identify with a social class and the values of this class can influence youth behavior, e.g. school culture or working class. However, culture in its widest sense influences youth buying behavior and deference to suppliers can differ significantly between different countries' youth culture to choose to sell their products or provide their services to the countries' youth markets. Youth needs are also influenced by the situation in which youth currently find themselves in their countries. The subjects of age and socio-economic status can have profound effects on youth buying behavior at different youth age market segmentation, such as youth client groups can divided to any companies to concentrate on selling, e.g. between 20 ages to 40 ages or between 10 ages to 20 ages etc. different age groups.

In conclusion, marketer may learn more about youth culture from different countries‘ family life cycle stages of change which have sought to take account of their increasing complexity to influence to estimate the countries’ youth buyer numbers. The family relationships can include single parent family, married parent family, no children family youth buyer groups of family life cycle youth buyer changing numbers in marketers‘ target countries. Due to all different countries family life cycle youth buyer numbers can indicate the countries’ youth individual needs changing numbers and the target countries‘ youth buyer numbers are likely to change their purchase tastes and needs as youth culture goes through life. Hence, marketers can measure the target countries youth age segmentation estimate numbers to decide how many products or how much services to supply to them to satisfy their needs accurately.

Quantitative and qualitative method
measures stable income consumer
purchase desire

Marketing research methods -applying survey or questionnaire methods to predict consumer behavior

Critically evaluate the relative merits of quantitative and qualitative approaches to data collection for a large retailer.

The marketing research process needs to follow these steps: defining the problem and research objectives, developing the research plan, collecting the data, analyzing the data, then presenting the findings.

In general, the specific marketing research major activities include: Research into customer needs and expectation and a variety of qualitative techniques are used to study the often complex sets of expectations that customers have with respect to a purchase. For example, when buying a personal computer, what are customers’ expectation with respect to reliability, after -sales support, design etc? Customer satisfaction surveys indicate customer areas of satisfaction or dissatisfaction; how spending money on various forms of communication, such as advertising, sales promotion, and public relations; researching similar industry studies about competitors in completely unrelated business sectors how to improve own marketing effectiveness; researching key client studies about number of customers how to make special efforts to ensure that these customers are satisfied with its standards of service and prices; researching into intermediaries, such as agents dealers are close to consumers to gather information about consumers‘ needs and expectation. For example in relation to reliability, delivery times and after sales services; researching front line employees their attitude towards the company and researching environmental scanning changing on trends to influence the company development in the future. Structure of market research includes spending on market research, types of market research and potential problem. Market research means researching the the immediate competitive environment of the marketplace, including customers, competitors, suppliers, distributors and retailer. Otherwise, marketing research includes all the above and companies and their strategies and markets of whose products sale or services provision and the wider environment within which operates (e.g. political, social, economic etc factor influences). Hence, marketing research means the systematic design, collection, analysis and reporting of data and finding relevant to a specific marketing situation facing the organization. In general, the ten most common market research activities for a large retailer data collection, include determination of market characteristics, measurement of market potential, market share analysis, sales analysis, studies of business trends, short range forecasting, competitive product studies, long range forecasting, pricing studies and testing existing products.

The reasons why a large retailer needs to conduct that research in new product development include the product must appeal to the customer, timely market research can help the large retailer to predict its client’s needs/wants, market research tends to point out success and failure before its product is launched for real and it can save its money and time. A large retailer’s market research can be sources by either primary or secondary or both and it can use either qualitative or quantitative or both methodologies and it can achieve objectives either exploratory or descriptive or causal experimental.

The primary source is collection of data specifically for the problem or project in hand and the secondary source is based on data previously collected for purposes other than the research in hand. e.g. published articles, governments etc.

On the quantitative benefits hand, it is cheaper to sample
size ; probabilities in depth motivations and feelings, it allows managers to observe real client reaction to the issue, e.g. comments and associations regard a new product fresh from the laboratory. It often used precursor to quantitative research, it can give the research department a low cost and timely sense of which issues in quantitative research. Quantitative research is designed to gather information from statistically representative samples of target population. The sample size is related to the size of the total population being studied, the variability within it, and the degree of statistically reliability required, balanced against time and cost constraints. It includes these skilful analyses such as below:

Correlation analysis means two phenomena are associated with each other. For example, whether change in household income is associated with the amount that a household spends on eating out of or firm's advertising expenditure on a product and sale revenue for it's relationship. Regression analysis means to use to build a model of causes (independent variables), which lead to an effect (the dependent variable). Companies shall use a historical database to test models that are assessed for the amount of variance in the dataset that they explain. Analysis of variance is used to test hypotheses about differences between two or more means. It is widely used in experimental frameworks where the researcher wished to examine the effects of two or more treatments on customers.

Conjoint analysis can provide valuable information for market segmentation, new product development, forecasting and pricing decisions and it can analyze the real life trade off that shoppers make when evaluating a range of features that are present in a range of product. Cluster analysis is frequently used in segmentation studies, but does not provide the marketer with a unique solutions.

Neural network analysis splits a dataset into a training set and a testing set. However, quantitative analysis techniques can suffer from a number of weakness , such as sampling error, measurement error, significant estimation of sample population error, inappropriate estimation of population may be validated statistical tests and inappropriate interpretation of results can highly subjective.

On the qualitative merits hand, large retailer can get merits, such as many sample size and questions and information per respondent and much application of questioner's skill, analyst's skill and type of analysis. Qualitative techniques essentially seek to recreate the listening ear and interpretative mind that so many entrepreneurs use so well. Qualitative marketing research involves the exploration and interpretation of the perceptions and behavior of small samples of individuals and the study of the motivators behind observed actions. It can be highly focused, exploring in depth, for example, the attitudes that buyers have towards particular brand names. The techniques used to encourage respondents to speak and behave honestly. However, it is difficult to assess the validity of qualitative research techniques, and the tests for significance that are available for most quantitative techniques are largely lacking for qualitative techniques.

The quantitative and qualitative approaches to data collection for a large retailer its merits can achieve objective is either by exploratory, it means preliminary data needed to develop an idea further, e.g. outline concepts, gather insights, formulate hypotheses; it is either by descriptive, it means to describe an element of an ideas precisely, e.g. who is the target market, how large is it, how will it develops ; it is either by causal, it means to test a cause and effect relationship, e.g. price elasticity is by experiment. Moreover, the quantitative and qualitative approaches to data collection can help a large retailer to find methods how to solve problems to raise competition confidently. In the beginning, of the market research process step, it needs to define the problem and objectives, such as it needs to distinguish between it's research type needed, e.g. exploratory descriptive or causal . Then, it needs to develop the research plan, such as deciding on budget, data sources, research approaches and instruments, sampling plan and contact methods. Next, it needs to collect information, such as information is collected according to the plan. Following step, it needs to analyze the information , such as statistical manipulation of the data collected, e.g. regression or subjective analysis of focus group. Final step, it needs to present the findings, such as overall conclusion to be presented rather than statistical methodologies.

Data collection gathers for a large retailer, it can gather syndicated data from householders, it is gathered either by psychographics and lifestyle, advertising, evaluation etc. styles of surveys and use panels or both sources. Primary data is originated by a researcher for the specific purpose of addressing the problem at hand, the collection of primary data involves all six steps of the marketing research process as well as secondary data has already been collected for purposes other than the problem at hand. These data can be located quickly and inexpensively. The intention to uses of secondary data for a large retailer, it aims to identify the problem and better defines the problem, develops an approach to the problem, formulates an appropriates research design, for example by identifying the key variables, answers certain research questions and test some hypotheses and interprets primary data more insightfully.

On qualitative merits to secondary data collection for a large retailer. The criteria aspect, this data collection method can give merits of response rate, quality and analysis data, sampling technique and size, questionnaire design, fieldwork benefits to a large retailer, so it's data should be reliable, valid to the problem; on error and errors in approach, research design, sampling , data collection and analysis and reporting, so it can assess accuracy by comparing data from different sources. On currency aspect, this data collection method can assess time lag between collection and publication, frequency of updates, so census data are updated by syndicated large retailer; on objective aspect, secondary data collection method can help large retailer to judge whether the data collected were needed to used for which parts of market strategies benefits for consumer research, so the objective determines the relevance of data; on nature aspect, this data collection method can define key variables, units of measurement, categories used, relationships examined, so it can reconfigure the data to increase a large retailer market strategies benefits usefulness and on dependability aspect, this data collection method provides expertise, credibility, reputation and trustworthiness of the source, so it's data should be obtained from an original source to raise market research benefits to a large retailer. Hence, internal secondary data collection can help large retailer department project to store project to analyze sales by product line, by major department, e.g. men's wear, by specific stores by geographical region, by cash versus credit purchased, sales in specific time periods, by size of purchase and trends in many of these classifications were also examined.

Secondary data collection can include demographic data, which is type of individual household level data available from consumers, such as identification, e.g. name, address, telephone , sex, marital status, age, income, occupation etc. as well as psychographic lifestyle data, such as consumer personal interest. Hence, a large retailer can get this quantitative and qualitative data to judge whether who is segmentation target to compete in its business market. For example, market research demands cooperation and trust between the client commissioning a study and the company carrying it out.

The reputation that a market research agency has built for itself is particularly important where qualitative research is involved as well as qualitative research techniques are utilizing quasi quantitative technique in order to enhance their credibility.

In conclusion, large retailers are reliance on customer's view due to many experienced larger retailers are relying more on interactive development with lead clients. Because traditional market research for truly innovative new products have frequently proved misleading. Hence, quantitative and qualitative approaches must need to use to gather to assess how to achieve marketing strategies timely and objectively and relevant to win whose competitors nowadays.

Discuss the limitation of statistically based consumer databases of the type discussed here. Do qualitative approaches based on small groups offer any advantages?

Any large retailers need to follow this process to use marketing information system to gather data from consumer databases. First step, which need to gather data either from internal data or external data source or both. The internal data includes enquires, orders, customer complaints etc. as well as the external data is from customer panels, intermediaries etc. Next step, the marketing information system will carry on processes as data collection and analyzing internal data. Final step, the marketing information system will produce outcomes, such as input to decision support system and data for decision makers to evaluate and storage of data in a data warehouse outcomes. A large retailer can collect consumer data computerized database, from online bibliographic database or from internet numeric databases, full text database or offline directory databases, special purpose databases. Hence, computerized published external secondary sources can help large retailers to identify individuals or organizations to collect specific data, for example, consultants and consulting organization directory, directory of market research reports, studies and surveys and research services directory and gather indices to help in locating information on a particular topic in several different publications. Hence, large retailer can collect classification of computerized databases include bibliographic databases are composed of citations to articles, numeric databases contain numerical and statistical information , full -text databases contain the complete text of the source documents comprising the database, directory databases provide information on individuals or organizations and services and special purpose database provide specialized information. Hence, large retailer can get syndicated service to collect and sell common pools of data of known commercial value designed to serve a number of clients and syndicated sources can be classified based on the unit of measurement (households/consumers) and institutions two groups. Syndicated services of householders/ consumers include surveys, data collection is from psychographic and lifestyles, general and advertising evaluation as well as it also include panels data collection is from purchase and media of volume tracking data and scanner diary panels as well as it also include electronic scanner services is from scanner diary panels with cable television.

Potential problems to limitation with market research of statistically based customer data bases include, small groups do not know when and how to do research from database and problems exist with research buyers and suppliers and it needs frequent techniques and small groups exist problems with traditional market research effort. On limitation of when and how not to conduct market research issue, it includes lack of resources, closed mindset, poor timing arrangement in marketplace, research results are not actionable, late timing is process, unclear objectives and cost outweighs benefits limitation. On the lack of resources occasion issue, if quantitative research is needed, it is not worth doing unless a statistically significant sample can be used, On the research results, small groups' clients are difficult to get psychographic data from statistically based consumer databases to analyze to carry on market research. On the closed mindset limitation issue, when research is used as a preconceived idea. The statistically based consumer databases needs long time to gather data to analyze to carry on marketing research in its process. It cause poor timing to give clients to find marketing research result, if the client wants to know whether who ought to invest to develop the new product to promote to the marketing to sell from statistically based consumer database in the short time.

On cost outweighs benefits limitation, the statistically based consumer databases expected value of the information gathering time and resources spending cost should outweigh the cost of gathering the data from normal marketing research method.

On the limitation of problems with research statistically based customer databases , qualitative limitations include narrow concept of research, unrealistic view of timeframe, as well as variable quality of market researchers and it is possible that market researchers have not own sufficient technical to apply statistically based customer data bases. For example, market researchers will feel difficult to find facts from statistically customer data bases and who will spend much time to define research result from finding.

The qualitative approaches based on small groups offer any

advantages from statistically marketing research customer databases only, but small groups can not offer any advantages from statistically market research customer databases. The reason is due to market research is about determining the characteristics of a market, for example, in terms of its size, requirements, growth rate, market segments and competitor positioning. Otherwise, marketing research is broader and is about researching the whole of a company's marketing activities. In most organizations, such search would probably include monitoring the effectiveness of its advertising, intermediates, and pricing position. Hence, small groups need to focus on marketing researching its company's internal marketing activities, such as pricing strategy, advertising method. Due to small groups are not large organizations, which did not focus on market research to external marketing environment, such as growth rate, market segment etc influences. However, statistically based customer databases also have these qualitative approaches to small groups offer advantages include, easy of completion, realism, comprehensive, per-testing, questioner training, respondent motivation, repetition, cultural issues, bias in formulation and sensitivity of question etc. qualitative approaches.

China future digital product market development

The effects that I expect the development of interactive electronic media to have on retailer's collection of marketing research information from consumers. Limited use of market research indicated formal market analyses

continue to be
useful for extending product lines, but they are often misleading when applied to radical innovations. Problems, with traditional market research has allowed prominent product failures and wrong predictions; markets are increasingly becoming micro-segmented, e.g. sports shoes aimed at fashion conscious women specifically for aerobic, so mass market research becomes correspondingly irrelevant; it is helpful for improvements, but traditional market research method is less for radical innovations and is less for more accurate targeting. Thus, I expect the development of interactive electronic media effects to have on retailers collection of marketing research in formation from consumers. It may be advantageous to analyze continue to be useful for expanding product lines in the most short time and it will not mislead to businessmen when who applied this electronic media on retailers collection of marketing research method to get radical innovations accurately. For example, predicting whether who are major targeting segments for the sport shoe company to sell in the short time accurately, such as between 10 ages and 30 ages young male client group or young female client group or between 31 ages to 50 ages adult male client group or adult female client group.

On the evaluating internet resources for retailer's collection of marketing research legal hand, it needs to indicate the content of a resource must be reflective. If there is change, the resource must promptly reflect that change; if a law has been amended, any discussion on the web must reflect the law as amended. Otherwise, the internet resource is not qualified for citation in legal marketing research; research specialization and achievement, institutional and professional affiliation, medium of communication, e.g. professional journal and publishers are all useful criteria to evaluate credibility; questions to ask include: Is it a reviewed articles? Is it a law review journal? And does the author exhibit critical assessment of a resource? ; Copyrighted work means that an individual or an institution could claim ownership, responsibility and liability for the resource. It also publication and therefore users may have to comply with the principle of fair value; resources with citations journalistic ones. Researchers should therefore accord higher preference to resources with citations; many web resources disappear with the resources who contain. For instance, an electronically published law report must not only be current but also be continuous for it to be a dependable source for consultation, it is important to examine whether a resource reflects the attributed of misinformation half truths prejudice; a marketing researcher needs resources that can be connected to individual retailer or company's resources. In general, online market researchers know that search engineers vary in how who select ranking of results. With the advent of search engine optimization and the role of online marketing search engines, results are impacted by things other than returning results that are customized to rank higher sponsored links, with the page owner paying advertising dollars to get their site ranked higher. General search engines can be helpful when getting started or determining the scope of a particular question. Search engines like Google, Yahoo can be powerful tools. It is good practice to not rely on only one general search engine. General research engines, like Google, also have power helpful in narrowing large search results.

An old librarian advertisement page is that customers can have something quick, cheap and accurate but who can only pick two out three. Therefore, choosing the top two most important factors will help consumers decide between conducting an open web marketing search and using specialized commercial databases. However, law firm librarians need to play important roles in helping their firms and staff members locate, manage and use internet resources efficiently and cost effectively and who need to understand not only the needs of their firms and clients, but also the specific types of information available online as well as offline to meet clients' unique needs and who also need to help business firms grow and strength their client services by taking advantage of the rich information online. For instance, law librarians need to lead the form in creating the best and most comprehensive combination of knowledge and information re-sources, including capturing and preserving reliable free and low cost internet resources, that accommodates the firm's budget and user needs, maintain the firm's intranet, further enabling cost effective online legal research, promote free and low cost online resources and research techniques, whenever, feasible to help attorneys and staffs improve research efficiency and cost effectiveness, manage electronic subscriptions which now generally account for a large annual spending than books and newsletters, educate users and conduct training sessions on online research skills, provide tailored content for individual users or groups to facilitate intelligent filtering of the abundance of available information online, provide guideline on the usefulness and reliability of legal resources, guide attorneys as well as consumers in finding information from the internet efficiently.

On evaluating internet research surveys marketing research hand, there have advantages of internet research surveys, rather than mailing a paper survey, a respondent can be given a hyperlink to a web site containing the survey or in an email survey, a questionnaire is sent to a respondent via electronic mail, possibly as an attachment . Electronic media survey is as an alternative to conventional survey modes , e.g. the telephone, mail and face to face interviewing. For example, a web survey can relatively simply incorporate multi-media graphics and sound into the survey instrument, automatic branching and real time randomization of survey questions and/or answers into self administered web surveys. However, unlike when phone and mail surveys were first introduced, concerned exist about whether these internet based surveys are scientifically valid and how they are the best conducted. Because internet can offer possibility of multimedia and interactive surveys containing audio and video, convenience samples to respondents email address. As a result, quick polls and other types of entertainment surveys have become increasingly popular and widespread on the web marketing research.

On the web marketing based surveys had particular three of benefit assumptions to attract companies to choose to do marketing research: (a) internet based surveys are much cheaper to conduct, (b) internet based surveys are faster, (c) when combined with other survey modes, internet based surveys yield higher response rates than conventional survey modes by themselves. In general, companies shall consider the following key characteristics of surveys choices: Response rate, timeliness, data quality and cost .

(Adrian, P. 2012) indicated that in response rate hand, web surveys respondents that can or will answer via the web may not be sufficiently large to compare mail surveys possibly. However, a company AT& T employees surveys experiment indicated to report a 63% response rate via email (63 returned not of 100 sent by email) compared to a 38% response rate for postal mail (14 returned out of 40 sent by mail). Interestingly, it indicated the response rates to the fast that, at the time, At& T employees received a lot of corporate paper junk mail yet over the internal email system, they received little to no electronic junk mail. I expect the development of interactive electronic media market research survey can achieve responses from a convenience sample might be useful in developing research hypotheses. Responses from convenience samples might also be useful for identifying issues, defining ranges of alternatives or collecting other sorts of non inferential data.

On timeliness hand, survey timeliness is increasingly stressed. The length of time it takes to field a survey is a function of the contact, response and follow up modes. the relevant measure is not average response time, but maximum response time (or perhaps some large percentage of the response time distribution) since survey analysis generally does not begin until all of the responses are in. However, simply concluding that internet based surveys are faster than mail surveys ignores the reality that the total amount of time for survey fielding time is more than just the survey response time. A complete comparison must take into account the mode of contact and how long that process will take and the made of follow up allowing for multiple follow up contact periods. For example, if email address of respondents are unavailable and a probability sample is desired than respondents may have to be contacted by mail. In this case a web survey only saves time for the return delivery of the completed questionnaire and not for the contact and follow up, so that the resulting time savings may only be a fraction of the total survey fielding time. For example, a internet survey company, knowledge networks has indicated that to achieve 70 to 80 % response rates they must leave a survey in the field for about 10 days. This period comprises one workweek with two weekends because they find that most respondents complete their surveys on the weekend (Adrian, P. 2012).

In conclusion, the delivery time of an internet based survey is faster than the delivery of a survey by mail, it does not necessarily follow that the increased delivery speed will translate into a significantly shorter survey fielding period. Two points are relevant: dramatic possible for specialized populations and even for populations in which all electronic surveys are possible.

On the quality hand, the primary purpose of a survey is to gather information about a population , the information is useless unless it is accurate and representative of the population. When survey error is commonly characterized in terms of the precision of statistical estimated, a good survey designing seeks to reduce all types of errors, including coverage, sampling, non response and measurement errors. Data quality includes unit and item non response, honesty of responses , particularly for questions of a sensitive nature, completeness of responses particularly for open ended questions and quality of data transcription into an electronic format for analysis of requires by the survey made. Data quality is usually measured by the number of respondents with missing items or the questions, longer answered are usually considered more informative and of higher quality email surveys may incur a higher percentage of items missing than mail surveys. Other quality issues for internet based surveys resulting from some sort of sampling errors are generally the same as for conventional surveys. However, such accuracy may be misleading if non response biases are not accounted for and researchers need to carefully consider the trade offs between smaller samples that allow for careful non response follow up and larger samples with less or no follow up. Web surveys can be programmed to conduct input validation as a logical check of the respondent's answers.These types of checks improve data quality and subsequently save time in the preparation of the analysis file. This will eliminate errors and from the respondent's point of view, simplify the process of taking the survey.

On cost hand, designing a survey fundamentally involves making trade off between the quality and quantity of data and cost. For smaller research surveys that are not subsidized in any way, a major component of total survey cost is frequently the researcher's time for survey design and subsequent data analysis. The labour cost of the personnel who actually execute the survey. It depends on the size of the survey and the complexity of the design either researcher labour cost, survey personnel labour costs or a combination of the two will likely dominate the survey budget.When lower costs are often of the benefits, of internet based surveys, Couper et al. (1999) found no cost benefit in email compared to postal mail surveys in their work. In a large and comprehensive survey effort of different government agencies. Couper et al. compared an all email survey (contract, response and follow up) versus an all mail survey. They found that evaluating and testing the email software took over 150 hours almost 4 times as much as they budgeted.

For the mail survey, costs for printing and posting were $1.6 per reply and data editing and entry cost about $1.81 . For the mail survey , managing the email cost $1.74 per completed case. In addition, they handled over 900 toll free call of a technical nature when the printing and mailing costs were eliminated for the email survey. Couper et al.(1999) found that the cost of evaluating and testing the email software, additional post collection processing and the cost of maintaining a toll free phone line which was largely dedicated to responding to technical questions related to the email surveys offset any savings. For example, email survey was designed so that respondents would use the reply function of their email program so the resulting replies could be automatically read into a database upon receipt.

I expect web marketing based surveys can reduce errors to avoid to mislead companies to find the wrong marketing strategy to compare paper surveys from every time of individual group customer questionnaires researches from internet. Moreover, I also expect web marketing based surveys can reduce cost to compare paper surveys from every time of group customer questionnaires researches from internet. In conclusion, I expect the development of interactive electronic media to have on retailers collection of marketing research information from consumers, the internet companies need to consider the electronic surveys response rate and time and quality and cost and legal responsibilities issues to let any companies to use their electronic media to carry on marketing research from customers to feel more satisfactory to compare to traditional questionnaires market research media if internet companies still hoped business companies still chose to use whose service to do marketing research in the future.

New economic social development causes China is as the world factory

How has China achieved an export boom and why it can become world factory? Is it high population the main factor

to help China to become world factory? I will attempt explain as below:

IN lase decade, China is only one farming developed country, its agriculture is its main GDP income source.

But, when it enters new economic development, its industry had been developed to replace its traditional agricultural development in furture new economic society. China's export boom has been accompanies by huge inflows of FDI since its

opening up in the lare 1970s. As CHina became the third largest exporting nation ($594 billion) in the world in 2004 from the thirty-second ($18 billion) in 1978. HOw does FDI affect CHina's export performance?

IN fact, China's exports mainly through labor-intensive processes and component specialization within vertically integrated international
industries, inaddition to export through converting import-substituting industriesl, exports thtough converting import-substituting
industries, exports of local raw material processing. So, FDI enhances exports as well through spillover effects on local firm's exporting activities(domonstration effects, linkages, and diffusion of technology). Moreover, FI helped in improving CHina's export commodity structure
through expanding exports in manufacturers and high and new-technological products. Hence, it seems that high population growth is not the main factor to cause China can develop its manufacturing industry in success. It ought be its manufacturing technological improvement factor to help it can develop its domestic manufacture industry, even it can assist foreign investors to choose China's factory labours to help US, UK, Germany, France etc. different western businessmen to manufacture their products.

ON the other hand, China's cheap labour is another factor to help it become world factory. For example, one US factory labour needs to
pay US$20 minimum wage per hour to help US any factories to manufacture their products. Otherwise, China's labours are only needed to pay US$10 minimum per hour to help US any factories to manufacture their products. So, China's cheap labour wage factor may be another important factor to persuade any foreign countries product manufacturers to choose China's labours to replace their local labours.

ON the other hand, China's duty-free processing trade factor may be the critical role to excite its export business, also it can assist its manufactory factory needs raise, because China's export and import activities increase, so it can bring China' labor needs to help it to manufacture any kinds of products to local manufacturers and overseas manufactories. Then it will assist China's factory labours number increasing need indirectly.

The duty-free processing trade in China has two varients in practice: processing imported materials into exports and processing
imported components into exports. The first one referred to as processing materials, takes place under a contract in which a foreign firm (usually located in Hong Kong) ships
materials to domestic factories, which usually play a fairly passive role in such contracts. The domestic factories , often township or village enterprises, account for bulk (86 percent in 1995) of this type of processing trade (Naughton, 1996).

As a new form of economic trade development to China, the processing trade has increased rapidly in China during the past 30 years from agricultural industry development
stage. The share of exports under processing trade in total exports rose from 18% in 1996, to 47 % in 1992, and to 55 % in 2004. The share of imports in total imports went up from 16 % to 41% , at least two factos contribute to the rapidly growing processing trade. First factor may be the export-oriented FDI strategy adopted by the China government encourages foreign firms (mainly from Hong Kong and Taiwan) to engage in processing trade. China has this competitive strength point is that along with China's cheap resources (e.g. labour and land)
, a variety of incentive policies also play a role in attracting large inflows of foreign investment to exporting production. Another factor considers to the classication method of processing trade. Due to growing globalization and international specialization of labor, more exports involve imported foreign contents, rather than
traditional exports that have complete domestic contents only.

Hoever, I believe that China's world factory development can succeed, instead of cheap labour and raw material, free-duty export and import trade and foreign investors increasing
number factors, its manufactory technology improvement may be one main factor to influence China can continue to keep the world factory leader position in this new economic development
environment. I shall attempt to explain as below:

Is Technology improvement the main factor to assist China becomes world factory ?

The Chinese economy thrives as a manufacturing powerhouse and the nation's products seem to be everywhere. The majority of tags, labels, and stickers on a variety of goods proclaim they are "Made in China." Because of this, it's understandable Western consumers might wonder, "Why is everything made in China?"

Some may think the ubiquity of Chinese products is due to the abundance of cheap Chinese labor that brings down the production costs, but there is much more to it than that. In addition to its low labor costs, China has become known as "the world's factory" because of its strong business ecosystem, lack of regulatory compliance, low taxes and duties, and competitive currency practices. Here we review each of these key factors.

Some may think the ubiquity of Chinese products is due to the abundance of cheap Chinese labor that brings down the production costs, but there is much more to it than that. In addition to its low labor costs, China has become known as "the world's factory" because of its strong business ecosystem, lack of regulatory compliance, low taxes and duties, and competitive currency practices. Here we review each of these key factors.

Given the abundance of Chinese products in the marketplace, it's understandable consumers might wonder why so many goods are made in China. One of the reasons companies manufacture their products in China is because of the abundance of lower-wage workers available in the country.

China's business ecosystem of networked suppliers, component manufacturers, and distributors has evolved to make it a more efficient and cost-effective place to manufacture products. While Western manufacturers comply with various health, safety, employment, and environmental regulations, Chinese manufacturers generally operate under a much more permissive regulatory environment.China has been accused of artificially depressing the value of its currency in order to keep the price of its goods lower than those produced by U.S. competitors.

Lower Wages factor

China is home to approximately 1.39 billion people, which makes it the most populous country in the world. The law of supply and demand tells us that since the supply of workers is greater than the demand for low-wage workers, wages stay low.

Moreover, the majority of Chinese were rural and lower-middle-class or poor until the late 20th century when internal migration turned the country's rural-urban distribution upside-down. These immigrants to industrial cities are willing to work many shifts for low wages.China doesn't follow (not strictly at least) laws related to child labor or minimum wages, which are more widely observed in the West.However, this situation seems to be changing and more provinces report they have increased their minimum wages in response to increases in the cost of living.

Business Ecosystem factor

Industrial production does not take place in isolation, but rather relies on networks of suppliers, component manufacturers, distributors, government agencies, and customers who are all involved in the process of production through competition and cooperation. The business ecosystem in China has evolved quite a lot in the last 30 years.

For example, Shenzhen, a city bordering Hong Kong in the southeast, has evolved as a hub for the electronics industry. It has cultivated an ecosystem to support the manufacturing supply chain, including component manufacturers, low-cost workers, a technical workforce, assembly suppliers, and customers.

American companies like Apple Inc. (AAPL) take advantage of China's supply chain efficiencies to keep costs low and margins high. Foxconn Technology Group (a Taiwan-based manufacturer of electronics) has multiple suppliers and manufacturers of components that are at nearby locations. For many companies, it's economically unfeasible to take the components to the U.S. to assemble the final product.

Lower Compliance factotor

Manufacturers in the West are expected to comply with certain basic guidelines with regards to child labor, involuntary labor,
health and safety norms, wage laws, and protection of the environment. Chinese factories are known for not following most of these laws and guidelines.Historically, Chinese factories have employed child labor, have had long shift hours, and have not provided the workers with compensation insurance.

Some factories even have policies where the workers are paid once a year, a strategy to keep them from quitting before the year is out.Faced with mounting criticism, the Chinese government has claimed to institute reforms that protect workers‘ rights and provide for fairer compensation. However, compliance with the rules in many industries is low and change has been slow. Additionally, environmental protection laws are routinely ignored, enabling Chinese factories to cut down on waste management costs.

Taxes and Duties factor

The export tax rebate policy was initiated in 1985 by China as a way to boost the competitiveness of its exports by abolishing double taxation on exported goods. Exported goods were subject to zero percent value-added tax (VAT),
meaning they enjoyed a VAT exemption or rebate policy.7? Additionally, consumer products from China were exempted from any import taxes. These lower tax rates helped to keep the cost of production low, enabling the country to attract investors and companies looking to produce low-cost goods.
For recently China and U.S. Tariffs example, In July 2018, the U.S. announced China-specific tariffs, targeting 818 imported Chinese products valued at $34 billion.8? This was the first of many rounds of tariffs imposed by both countries, resulting in $550 billion of U.S. tariffs applied to Chinese goods and $185 billion of Chinese tariffs applied to U.S. goods, as of Feb. 2020.9?10? Over time its expected Americans will feel the impact of these tariffs in the form of an increased cost of goods, while the Chinese economy is expected to experience a slowdown.

Currency factor

China has been accused of artificially depressing the value of the yuan to provide an edge for its exports against similar goods produced by U.S. competitors. China keeps a check on the appreciation of yuan by buying dollars and selling yuan.
The yuan was estimated to be undervalued by 30% against the dollar in late 2005.11? In 2017, the yuan appreciated 8% against the dollar, a
move that experts say came about after President Trump threatened to label China a currency manipulator.
However, this trend reversed and the yuan weakened against the dollar beginning in June 2018 when the U.S. imposed tariffs on Chinese goods. On Aug. 8, 2019, China's central bank lowered the yuan to 7.0205 per dollar, the weakest level since April 2008.13? The weaker yuan makes Chinese exports more attractive and is seen as China's response to its trade war with the U.S.

Although, above these factors can assist China become nowadays , even future world factory leader. However, manufacturing technology improvement factor is still the main factor to help it can continue to keep world factory manufacturing leader position. Beucause nowadays, any western development countries own high technological manufactuturing skill, e.g. robot. Robot can help any factories to raise productive efficiency and productive numbers in short time. So, any westen countries manufacturers may choose to apply robots to help them to manufacture bulk products in short time. They do not need to employee China's labours to help them to manufacture any kinds of products. Because labour productive speed and time must be slower than robot. If China can not have high manufacturing technology to satisfy western manufacturers' product efficient productivites neeeds, I believe that China's cheap labor and resource will not attract them to choose China labours to help them to manufacture any kinds of products in the future very easily.

Does China's robotic technology can help China to continue to become future world manufacturing factor leader? Under the Chinese government's “Made in China 2025” industrial master plan, the number of industrial automatons operating
in the country would expand tenfold to 1.8 million units by 2025, when up to 70 per cent of the robots used in China

would
be made in the country, from half in 2020, and 30 per cent now.

It's an ambitious, multibillion-dollar pursuit. Sitting on the western bank of the Pearl River, with Guangzhou city to the north and Shenzhen to its east, Foshan is at the heart of southern China's manufacturing industry.

Guangdong province is China's largest regional economy, accounting for 10.4 per cent of the country's 2016 gross domestic product, and 11.4 per cent of the industrial base, according to the statistics bureau.

"China is the factory of the world, and there are millions of manufacturers that still depend on traditional labour-intensive methods," said Ren Yutong, executive president of the Guangdong Robotics Association, a government think tank. "If the country wants to maintain its top spot as a global exporter, each Chinese manufacturer has to start replacing humans with robots due to skyrocketing labour costs and the ageing population. [China] has already started running out of workers."The number of domestically made industrial robots sold in China rose 58 per cent last year to 141,000 units, according to government statistics.

Because of China's outsized workforce, the density of automation usage lags other countries: 68 robots per 10,000 industrial workers, compared with 631 bots for every 10,000 manufacturing staff in South Korea, the global leader in automation.

Singapore, Germany and Japan all have higher densities of automation than China.China wants to more than double that usage density to 150 for every 10,000 workers by 2020. To do so would require massive amounts of government help.The Guangdong provincial government offered 943 billion yuan in subsidies between 2015 and 2018 to help local manufacturers automate. Further up north in Zhejiang province, local authorities have set aside 800 billion yuan to spur 36,000 enterprises to make a similar switch by 2020.

So, it seems that China government had planned one long term robotic manufactory development plan. It aims to help China to continue to develop to become to global manufacturing factory, or robotic (AI) manufactory factory. Because China government knows that if it hopes any western counties manufacturers can continue to choose China labors to help them to manufacture any kinds of products. It must need have advanced manufacturing technology to persuade them to replace their domestic manufacturing technology. Moreover, it discovered that western countries manufactuers had begun to apply robots to help them to manufacture any kinds of products. So, if China still choose the traditional labour manufacturing method, it does not follow western countries to research how to apply robots to help itself countries manufacturers, even foreign manufacturers to manufacture themselves products. Then China's cheap labour and resources and free -duty trade advantages will not bring attractive influential effort to persuade any one western country's manufacturer to choose its labours to help them to manufacture theis products more easily. It means that China government need to encourage itself manufactuers to teach their labours to learn advanced manufacturing skills how to apply robots to cooperate to them to manufacture any kinds of products rapidly together. So, when many China factories' labours can know how to control robots to manufacture any kinds of products proficiently. Then, they can become robotic proficient manufacturing workers to prepare to help any western countries manufactuers to manufacture themselves products more proficiently. It is one only way to help China can continue to become global world factory.

Consequently, it explains why China needs have manufacturing technological improvement in order to help it can continue become future global world manufacturing factory. It is one important technological factor to influence China's world factory industry development in new economic
society.

reference

Naughton , Barry (1996). " China's emergence and prospects as a trading nation," Brookings papers on economic activity, 2, 273-344.

New economic society influences human right marginal social cost and benefit social analysis need

When our societies had been experiencing new economt societies, many people only concern on materialisam enjoyment aspect. Then,many stealing crimes, violences crimes number may increase in our societies. Is it right time to any countries policy decision makers need to spend time to evaluate whether their policies can bring marginal socical benefits or marginal social cost more? Because if the policy decision maker's policy is not effective, it can not reduce social crime rate and social marginal cost will also increases consequently.

Economics provides a way to analyze the decision-making processes of work in social situations. Economists can also help when a social scientist wants to know the consequences of a country deciding to try a murder a case as a capital case in which the outcome may be the death penalty, when an international non-profit organization concerns what occurs in one of its target areas, when a travel considers the incidence of terrorism in a specific area.

However, each of these events relates to the decision makes themselves, the costs and benefits they face, and outcomes of those decisions. This process is called cost to benefit analysis. So, it explains that why it has relationship between economis and human rights, when one organization or individual neesds to make any decisions which concern human right area absolutely. Hence, human right economic economic may be explained by economists of human rights that economics is one way to analyze the choices being made in each area of human rights and indicates either positive or negative incentives that can be used in policy-making to affect those choices.

However, human rights studies and economics are social sciences that study interactions within society. ON the other side, an economist must gain an understanding of the specific human rights topic in order to have an accurate perspective about the types of decisions, costs and benefits that exist within that area. So, economists are need to be train to step into an unfamiliar field will have more career and life opportunities as well as more tools to change the world.

Human rights may include those issues, such as freedom and equity, right to be recognition as a person before a court of law, freedom from discrimination before the law within each human right, violation, there are monetary and non-monetaty costs. When a country district attornoy makes the decision to try a care as a captial crime, the country is liable for the cost of the capital case. So, each of the violations of human rights is the choices, based in part on costs to the decision maker.

Marginal cost is the cost of last unit produced or chosen in economic theory. IN human right marginal cost economic theory explanation aspect, for example, the number of times a person is convicted of a relatively minor illegal offence can add up to equal a relatively serious illegal offence, usually pubishable by imprisonment. Consequently, the more times the person is caught, the less chance , he will have to get a good job and bad things will be needed for survival in a community. The person decides to steal, the marginal cost increases. So, in society, the number of times food stolen increases, than the social marginal cost of stealing food will also increases. So, our society needs to concern how to bring social net benefits of human rights violation, it means that when the number of times food stolen reduces, then the society will bring marginal benefit of reducing stealing food.

Hence, it is social decison-making maker individual duty to learn even when the stolen item is food. If theft is increasing in an area, policy-makers may look for incentives, which are positive or negative motivations used to modify behavior in order to avoid the stealing of food crime number increases. Increasing the penalty to theft or finding net ways to catch someone stealing increases the cost of someone choosing whether to steal foods. It is a good method to reduce social stealing food crimes occur. Also, costs to society increase in terms of increased needs for physical and mental health care, legal service, child care, housing counseling, violence prevention. If the society has many family violent crimes number increases. It will bring direct intangible cost (non- monetary value), such as pain and suffering, emotional loss of a loved one through a violent death, as well as indirect intangible costs, monetary cost may be unmeasured. These costs to the victim include lacks of self esteem, learned helpnesses, health problem, drud and alcholol abuse, depression etc.

socical cost raising problem.

Hence, in any countries decision makers ought consider how to reducing social marginal cost raising problem, due to family violence, stealing crimes number increases. For example, whether the country increases migrant number to increase in labor demand in itself labor supply market. It is one attractive

way or not. If the country permits many migrants immigrate to itself country, then it may influence the country itself native workforce job seekers feel difficult to find suitable jobs to do suddenly. Although, it will bring positive social benefit to employers when they may have enough labours to supply to them to work, but it mayalso bring negative socical costs, when many migrants immigration may raise the labour competition to itself local job seekers. So, any country's leaders must need to spend time to analyze whether migrants may help itself country to increase labor supply or raising job competition to itself country local job seekers or raising local unemlpyment ratio effect.

ON conclusion, future our society needs consider whether our policy can bring effect to real reduce social marginal costs more or raise social marginal benefits more when we need to implement any social decision in order to avoid social cost raises effect. It is our future new economic society will encounter marginal social cost raising occurrence challenges as well as our social policy decision makers need to spend time to research how to solve the social challenges and compare and evaluate its marginal cost and benefit relationship to them to our future societies' any social needs.

Environment Economy-Pollution and illness influences consumer behavior

How the economic consequences of outdoor air pollution influences consumer behaviors ? Air pollution can increase number of respiratory and cardiovas cular diseases. How they can impact economic growth, e.g. on human health, mortality and morbidity and agriculture aspects ? Whether when this diseases are caused from outdoor air pollution, why it can influence consumer behavior or brings negative consumpton emotion?

The macroeconomic costs of these impacts of outdoor air pollution that are linked to economic activity, and it raises welfare costs related to activity morality and pain and suffering from illness to consumers. For example, market costs are those that are associated with biophysical impacts that directly affect economic activity, e.g. lower crop yields affect agricultural production . Non market costs may also include the monetised welfare costs of morality (premature deaths) , and of the disutility of illness (pain and suffering).

Raising emissions reflect the assumptions on economic growth with increasing GDP and energy demand, especially in fast growing economies, such as the high population countries, India and China. These large changes are due to the increase in the demand for agricultural products and energy (include transport and power generation). For continuousing increase in energy demand to China and India car drivers, when they need to drive their cars to go to anywhere often. The higher emission will bring serious pollution. The environment protecting householders will decrease to use emissions from energy demand for, with reflects technology improvement in energy efficiency, the use of cleaner fuels, and biomass in open fire to cleaner energy sources including LPG, ethanol or enhanced cooking stoves. Hence, when many people get the diseases from air pollution. It will increase the medical (healthcare) cost to governments or when government needs to give welfare assistance to patients.

The three different market impacts of air pollution may include: reduced labor productivity, increased health expenditures and crop yield losses. They may reduce the GDP pollution feedback on the economy. At the global level, the consequences of labor productivity and health expenditure may impact to market cost increases,because increases expenditure to labor productivity, health expenditure and value added generated in agriculture from low productivity changes in crop yields.

What is the welfare costs of mortality and illness ? It is possible to attribute a cost to non-market impacts, such as the premature deaths and the costs of pain and suffering from illness . The welfares cost of the premature deaths caused by air pollution are calculated using the value of a statistical life to any one. Large costs can also associated with the pain and suffering from illness. So, pollution causes diseases to bring welfare cost increases, they include hospital living day to every patient when he is caused illnesses from air pollution. Moreover, it will impact government pollution expenditure to raise welfare cost to assist the low income level pollution illness patients' hospital living welfacre cost when they need to live long days in hospitals.

How does air pollutin impact on consumer automobile choices ? Air pollution levels can bring negatively affect the sales of fuel inefficient cars to China or India car drivers. They will choose to buy electronic cars to drive to replace fuel cars, because electronic cars only need to charge battery and it can reduce air pollution. When China or India their big city people's income level is rising, they will have more money to buy electronic cars to drive to reduce air pollution. Moreover, they believe that electronic cars can have better car quality and reduced air pollution need to charge battery fuel efficiency to compare fuel cars, when they need to often drive cars on roads. Som electronic cars demand will be the preference choice battery fuel efficiency or green driving tools to compare general fuel cars to satisfy China and India car purchasers when they are living in serious air pollution environment cities.

When the high environment protection awareness car buyers number is increasing in the countries, environment protection awareness will influence their car choice decison on which car to buy , when they are living in more heavily polluted cities tend to buy less fuel-inefficient cars. So, the electronic cars number need will increase in China and India both car market, because these two countries have similar characteristics, they have high population and gardens and farms number is less and there are many people are living in cities and many people are high income level , they usually have one car at least. So, they must feel cities are serious polluted by their diving behaviors. So, their environment protection awareness are ususally higher to compare other countries , they have less cities. So high air pollution to cities can excite the environment protection awareness to China and India car purchasers as well as they will prefer to choose to buy electronic cars to replace fuel cars to drive in possible, because they do not hope to live a high car dirty cities to cause their poor health when they have high income level. Also, it implies that it has direct relationship between China and India cities have high income level people number increases and air pollution level increases and electronic car demand number increases and fuel car demand number decreases in China and India car market in micro economic China and India electronic car and fuel car demand and supply market.

I assume that each China and India car consumer makes a relatively fuel or electronic car choice among possible car transmissions, between the option of buying no car and buy car or between the option of buying electronic car and fuel car. However, air pollution will be one major factor to influence China and India car purchase demand number on electronic and fuel car supply number. If china and India's air pollution can reduce, then car purchase number will increase, as well as the fuel car demand number will also increase ,because China and India have many cities are polluted serious. It can influence car purchase buyers how to decide car choice to make car or no car purchase decision, even purchase either fuel car or electronic car decison.

● How consumer decisions are impacted on environment?

Environmental impacts may occur on households, when they need to buy food, mobility, house, household goods and appliances for home use in household consumer behavior view. It can bring direct impacts, that occue because of the use of householder products and services during householders are staying at home. When householders feel need to raise living quality, they will considerate how they use services and related household products. When minimizing the use of natural resources and toxic materials as well as the emissions of waste and pollutants over the life cycle of the service or household product, e.g. using electricity or fuel time at home, cooling time and bathing time at home activities. So, for on householder who has high environment protection awareness and energy protection awareness, he will reduce long time to use electricity or fuel use time for cooking, bathing, watching television, listening radio time activities at homes, because he does not hope energy waste and protect air fresh at homes.

So, consumption is concerned by environment factors, such as demographics, technology, income and prices, psychological, social , cultural environments, e.g. consumers economic behavior is influenced by habt, routines, conventions etc. different environment factors influence. So, economic assumptions of rational and regular behavior is based on long-established principles, such as utility maximization. For example, when one country is encountering serious air or water pollution, then consumers will spend long time to search any data (marketing research activities) when they need to make purchase decision on pollution environment as well as pollution environment is dependent on (e.g. attitude, intention to the consumers).

Because when pollution environment will influence consumption behavior, such as behavioral and experimental economic to consumers. It implies on pollution environment's psychological assumptions on individual consumption motives, such as on the role of mental habits, loss confidence. So, consumers usually feel to spend long time to make purchase choice or decison on pollution environment, exaggerated optimism, expectatons, avoiding miscalculation,short-sightedness more enjoyment etc. psychological factors. When they need to make purchase decision on pollution environment, e.g. when one car consumer will need to make choice to buy one car, when he is living in China city, city is polluted serious. So, he will need to spend long time to gather any car model and brand and quality and fuel quality air polluted level to achieve to choose to buy the most clean fuel and the most least air polluton car to avoid to cause air polluton when he is driving the car in the China's city. So, air pollution way causes the China environment protection awareness car consumers to spend long time to gather any less use fuel car information to avoid to cause air pollution when he needs often to drive the car on the city roads in the China cities. Hence , air pollution may cause the China car purchasers feel need to spend more time to gather car information in order to decide whether he ought to buy one car or no car purchase choice on the air pollution environment. So, the car must use less fuel to avoid air pollution easily when he drives the car on the China's cities' roads.

Reference

Dimson, Marsh & Staunton, London Business School (2005) In The Global Investment Returns Year Book, ABN Amro.

Fiscal Policy And Long Term Growth, International Monetary Fund, IMF policy papers, Washington, D.C. Available from April, 2015, http://www.imf.org/external/pp/ppindex.aspx.

How artificial intelligence impacts energy
consumers using behaviours

Nowadays, many countries began to educate citizens who have responsibilities to use energy at homes or offices or public places or any indoor environments in avoiding to do energy wastage behaviours or misuse energy wastge attitudes as well as teaching them have responsibilities to protect their earth's natural environment to reduce air, water pollution in order to void rising temperature to bring globl warm challenge to influence our quality of life to be poor, even facing death threat, due to our natural environment is damaged and polluted by our energy wastage behaviours.

In fact, I feel the energy wastage eduction is not one efficient or effective method to persuade every energy consumers, such as householders, office workers, factories workers, any entertainment places workers or enjoyers, such as cinema service staffs, shopping center staffs etc. entertainment places to reduce to use any electricity for light or any entertainment aims to consider themselves working environment or entertainment environment to satisfy, e.g. cinema movie to satisfy customers' needs. For example, private vehicle drivers, public transportation tool drivers, householder energy users, businessmen energy users who still only consider themselves passengers comfortable aims, e.g. spending much electricity often to turn on light in buses, taxi, cars, trams, trains, underground trains in morning or afternoon time. So, these public transportation tools are popular to waste electricity because they expect their passengers to feel comfortable in summer , so they will often turn on air conditioners to keep colder in summer or turn on warmers to keep warmer in winnter all the transportation working hours. So, these drivers are doing energy wastage behaviours. Moreover, these private car drivers only expect to feel comfortable , so they will open air conditioners to keep colder in summer when they are driving cars, even they are stopping cars on the road. So, they are also waste energy.

Hence, they will be negligent to consider how to use energy in efficient attitudes or energy saving behaviors in order to avoid energy shortage challenge occurrence. However, since (AI) technology began be popular to be accepted to use by human. (AI) scientists began to carry on researching how to apply (AI) technologies, e.g. big data gathering , robotics to assist human to adapt or learn to use any kinds of energy in efficient and no wastage attitudes or using behaviours habitually.

I shall explain how to apply (AI) technology to assist human to adapt to use energy in order to avoid to do energy wastage behaviours easily to every energy users as below:

In consumer psychological view point, the behaviours of individuals can have a standard rational choice model, in which people, such as energy users objectively weigh up the costs and benefits of investing time and money into " greening" their homes or offices or any working places or entertainment places or transportation tools being more energy efficiently. So, the social, cognitive and behavioural factors are important in explaining why many energy users, such as householders, vehicles owners or public transportation tool drivers, office workers, businessmen who are neglient to avoid to spend much excessive energy to drive their vehicles on the roads , to turn on lights in offices or any working environment or entertainment places or at homes all days. When they feel that they need more enjoyment, raising productivity, raising service performance to satisfy customers' needs. So, when they weigh economic benefits and cost. They will choose to use more energy to achieve their profit growth or customer number growth or improving quality of life intentions.

Hence, it also explain why education method is not effective to achieve energy saving aim for every energy users, e.g. it has no reward to compensate to their losses, when they choose to reduce energy consumption to cause that they have economic losses. So, it seems any country's government or schools energy saving education method which won't achieve the best energy saving consequency nowadays.

Why does (AI) influence energy users to reduce and use more energy in order to achieve their energy -saving habitual impact easily than education method? I shall explain as below:

(AI) technology can be one auto-manual tool to help householders to protect their homes to be more green environment and be more energy efficient. For example, householders can install (AI) auto-energy efficient measurement tool to record whether they will spend how much money for energy . e.g. electricity , gas consumption at home every day. So, they can know whether they will pay how much money for electricity or gas fee. (AI) auto-energy efficient measurement tool can also change householders‘ energy consumption behaviours to save more electricity or gas when they discover that the day' electricity or gas using number is excessive to cause they will be pay more extra electricity or gas expenditure on the day. Then, they will find whether why or how or what reasons cause them to spend excessive electricity or gas energy at homes, then they will change their energy wastage behaviours to save energy more easily. So, their energy -saving behaviours are influenced by the (AI) auto-energy efficient measurement tool's daily electricity or gas using record at homes.

So, (AI) auto energy efficient measurement tool can help householders to save energy and money when they need to use electricity or gas energy at homes. But making the kind of improvements that have these effects is not always simple, they usually require some planning, time to prepare to adapt how to do avoiding energy wastage behaviours at home habitually . So, (AI) auto-energy efficient measurement tools can focuse on what householders might be able to do and further encourage the uptake of energy efficiently measures as well as it might be able to motivates householders to act through restructuring existing incentives and using collective rewards.

When, they discover that the (AI) auto energy efficient measurement tool shows either electricity energy or gas energy or both using energy number is excessive too much to compare the normal energy using number on the day suddenly. Then , they will attempt to find what reasons influence their energy spending number is excessive on the day, in order to change their energy using behaviours or habits and they will be more acceptable to adapt to do energy saving behaviours because they can earn energy expenditure saving rewrd and money saving reward in order to avoid further the excessive energy using number to be increased to pay more electricity or gas energy expenditure , due to they often do unnecessary energy using habitual behaviours at homes.

Hence, (AI) auto-efficient energy measurement tool will have much effort to persuade householders to choose to do energy saving behaviours habitually at homes, due to it can provide the more acceptable number concerns their daily electricity and gas energy using record at homes to let them to know how and why their energy expenditure changes to spend more suddenly in order to let they can understand the reasons why and how cause their needs to pay extra excessive energy expenditure at homes.

The main important reward is that the householders can be encouraged to measure their energy using number and find the reasons why and how their energy using behaviours cause their extra excessive energy using number on the day. Then, they can find what the factors are to cause their electricity or gas energy using number to be increased suddenly on the day and change their energy using behviours to avoid the energy using number to be continus increased in order to avoid to pay extra excessive electricity or gas fees on the month immedicately.

6.1 How to apply (AI) technology to improve energy efficiency and better climate change and the security of energy supply as well a resource efficiency?

Increasing energy efficiency involves using a reduced quantity of energy to achieve the same or improved product, process or sevice. It is generally measured in a physical unit as the ratio between energy output and energy input. Similarly, resource efficiency refers to the ability to use a reduced quantity or volume of resources to produce the same or an improved service or product and it is measured as the ratio betweenn useful material output and material input, both measured in physical terms (Dahlstrom and Ekins, 2005).

Hence, if it was only (AI) technology can increase energy efficiency or reduce resource effifiency to improve service performance. Then, it will reduce energy wastage. So, it bring this question: How to apply (AI) tool to reduce resource consumptin indentified by analysis of historical resource efficiency?

It presents an historial analysis that seems have relationship between energy and resource efficiency improvements and resource consumption across a number of different sectors of activity, including iron, and steel production, electricity generation from coal, oil and natural gas and motor vehicle travel.

So, future(AI) technology needs to fight social and behavioural barriers to energy efficiency in the housing sector. If future (AI) technology can improve energy efficiency for home renovations and it can consider the social factors. It is a qualitative investigation technology of the decision making process guiding to teach householders hoe to use overall energy was reduced by the householders‘ house renovation. It will also bring another question: How can (AI) technology can help householders to do decision making to reduce overall energy consumption by householders' houses renovation, such as reducing energy using when the householder needs to renovate whose house's design, e.g. extensions and additional bedrooms or bathrooms . So, future (AI) technology can be needed to help low income householders to increae energy efficiency and reduce energy consumption when their homes need to renovate whose houses‘ design ,e.g. extensions and additinal bedrooms or bathrooms or bookrooms or children toy rooms at hoomes.

Due to low income householders were concerned about energy consumption for environment and economic reasons, upfront costs rather than life-cycle costs were considered more important when the low income householders need to renovate to extend extra bedrooms, bathrooms, studyrooms to buy extra electronic appliances to install them in these rooms to use. Then, they will be concerned energy awareness how will be more consume when the low income householders choose to renovate their homes design to extend more rooms to feel more comfortable, or large size, but they also need to consume or use more electrciity or gas energy for extra electronic appliances in these rooms possible as the same time.

Hence, future (AI) technology needs to assist these low income householders how to reduce or avoid to ue extra more energy, when they renovate their homes' designs to cause to need to buy extra more electric appliances to use more electricity or gas energy at homes. Moreover, future (AI) technology ought have effort to help any countries‘ buildings to be efficient energy saving buildings to be efficient energy saving buildings to help householders to use less energy to live in their builsing efficiently. When the country's overall buildings can use energy efficiently , it won't only bring energy saving benefits, even it can bring the country's economic cost to be reduced , due to any building' energy efficient using high technological method. So, future (AI) energy saving technology will concentrate on how to help any buildings to use energy efficiently , in order to achieve energy -saving efficient buildings to let the householders and office energy users to either live or work in energy -saving efficient buildings to avoid energy wastage aim.

Hence, future (AI) energy -saving technology needs to focus on how changing energy users‘ energy wastage behaviours to energy -saving behaviours. How to apply (AI) energy-saving technology to assist energy users change their behaviours to spend unnecessary excessive energy to use habitually daily.

I recommend that future (AI) robotic cans be such as energy-saving machines to help any factory workers to cooperate to work to achieve efficient energy -saving aim, but they can also raise productivities. So, factory robotic are as learning tools, allowing factory energy users (factory workers) to teach themselves how to use less energy to achieve the productivity won't be decreased intention. So, when the robotics and factory workers work in the factory environment together. The robotics can give feedback to let these factory workers how to cooperate to use lesser energy to work efficiently in factories.

Other information and advice achieving better understanding and control of energy use in factory. So, future factory robotic machine men are such as teachers teach students in classrooms or trainers provide training to train trainee in factories. It means that robotics and factory workers can learn how to understand to do every working steps to avoid to spend extra excessive energy , but they can also raise productivities as the same time in factories.

So , future (AI) robotics will be demanded to invent to be one energy-saving machines to assist factory workers to use lesser energy to manufacture any products in manufacturing process, but they can also have productivity and efficiencies won't be reduced in the efficient team work method. So, every factory robotic machine mman is needed to be designed to own the advanced manufacturing technological skills or manufacturing methods to assist the factory workers to manufacture the kind of products in team work together in order to shorten time and using the most efficient manufacturing methods to achieve and produce the best quality products and the highest productivity in energy-saving working environment in factories. For example, when every team watch factory's factory workers who need to operte with ten workers per team in the watch manufacturing factory. One robotic machine with ten workers per team will need to raise to manufacture at least fifty watchs number per hour to compare only ten workers per team can manufacture the maximum fifty watchs number per house, when the robotic machine participates to every team to work together.

The robotic machine must need to help them to use lesser time and electricity energy to manufacture more than fifty watches number pe hour in order to achieve long tem energy saving and time saving and efficient raising productive economic benefits to the watch manufacturing company. Hence, the watch factory's every watching manufacturing robotic machines can encourage the watch manufacturing firm to choose to use them to assist every team watch manufacturing workers to work in order to achieve high efficient productivities, high quality of watch manufacturing, reducing every watch manufacturing , reducing every watch manufacturing time and the important intention is energy -sving efficient benefit to reduce to spend more extra excessive electricity for long term expenditure.

So, in the future , every robotic machine will need have these benefits to satisfy manufacturers' every -saving needs in their participative manufacturing process in order to achieve energy expenditure to reduce for long term economic benefits to persuade them to use these energy-saving efficient robotics in factory attractively.

● Is the low income and rising price of modern fuels both factors best to influence Nigeria householders choose to use energy efficiently?

Firstly, for Nigeria householders energy consumption habit at homes example, it is richly with natural resources, modern energy resources which provide many householders with biomass (mostly firewood) and some other householders modern energy sources, such as kevosene, liquefied, petroleum, gas and electricity for their use. So, it is one country which can manufacture to provide energy for itself to use. It doesn't need to depend on other countries to import any kinds of energy to householders to buy to use at homes. But, it has social challenge, the poverty problem in Nigeria goes beyond low income, savings and growth rate, due to its low level of education, poor governamce, high level of unemployment factors influence.

It is important to know how Nigeria householders meet their basic energy needs between poverty and energy can bde described in terms of quality and quantity of energy used. Generally, most poor householders use biomass fuels because of affordability and they (householders) do not have energy equipment (such as, gas cookers, electric cookers etc.) . So, it seems Nigeria householders won't demand their living quality to be improved. It implies that they will use any kinds of energy efficiently at homes, e.g. gas, electricity, due to they find themselves in energy poverty. Although, this country has enough nature resources to manufacture energy to provide to householders to use, but due to many people are low income group, so they won't spend too much expenditure to buy much energy to use at homes. So, the rising prices of modern fuels, such as liquefied, petroleum , gas (LPG) and electricity and their erratic supply have made many householders revert to the use of traditional fuel, such as firewood and charcoal.

It brings this questions: Is the low income and rising price of modern fuels both factors best to influence Nigeria householders choose to use energy efficiently?

The hypothes is predicated on the economic theory of consumer behavior. However, when income increases, householders not only consume more of the same goods, they also need higher quality . So, it applies economic theory to householder's energy consumption behavior at home. It explains why low living standards induce greater dependence on firewood and other biomass fuels owing to a combination of income and substitution effects, such as Nigeria low income household energy home users case. it explains why Nigeria householders can accept to use firewood and charaval traditional energy to replace liquefied, petroleum , gas (LPG) and electricity modern energy . So, economic theory explains the Nigeria household energy users why they can accept to use traditional energy to replace modern energy and their energy useful or consumption behaviors are efficient at homes. Although, Nigeria has enough natural resource to manufacture modern energy to supply to householders to use at homes. But, due to these modern energy products prices are raised to the price level of householders who can not accept. it causes to Nigeria householders only choose to buy the cheap biomass, firewoods to replace high price of modern energy products to use at home often. So, they can accept their quality of living to be fallen down. So, expensive modern energy product price is one factor to influence some countries' householders to choose to buy cheap traditional poor quality of nature energy, e.g. firewood or biomass, to use at homes. Hence, they can raise energy efficiency to use when they choose to use traditional nature energy to replace modern nature energy at homes.

● Does season factor influence New Zealand householders' energy consumption behaviors at homes

Secondly, for New Zealand householders energy consumption habits at homes , for example, their living quality needs are general comfortable need feeling. Their countries' houses of space heating was found to average 34% of total housholder energy use. The relation to space heating includes low indirect temperature are associated with persistent under-heating , whether some space heating sources tend to be higher or lower in winter indoor temperature than others and winter indoor temperatures are compared to international benchmarks and established healthy temperature ranges. So, New Zealand occupant's perceptions of winter indoor temperature conditions are presented and explored in relation to heating patterns and household energy consumption. So, it seems that NZ winter temperature is low. Moreover, it will influence householders need to turn on heaters to keep more warmer feeling indoor. Then, they will use more electricity energy. In special, if the householders' houses spaces are large sizes . Hence, their heaters need long time to keep whole houses' areas or spaces or rooms temperature to be rised up in order to let they do not feel very cold in winter. So, NZ's winter extreme cold weather will influence householders' energy use or consumption to be increased in winter.

The electricity efficiency to every NZ householder is very high in winter to compare spring, summer, autumn seasons. Hence, if NZ electricity suppliers expected to forecast electricity consumption more accurate in NZ. In order to ease the life for both electric net designers and electricity suppliers, it was decided to find out, how the NZ weather conditions and every householder's house space size factors to influence the power consumption to NZ householders. If there is a clear trend observed , then this relation can be used for power consumption forecasts to NZ householders.

Why does NZ weather condition factor and householder's house space size factor can predict householders' electricity consumption at homes. Due to geographic location on the global the lowest south sets specific conditions for weather, such as NZ's south island geographic location is near to south ocean in our earth. It is a country where average annual temperatures are well between 10 degree to below 10 degree at NZ south island special geographic location to near to the sourth ocean in our earth at the same time.

However, large part of mankind is living in the conditions where there are four different seasons in NZ geographic location, dark winter, which is cold and snowy, spring with rising temperature and high precipitation, sunny , dry and rather hot summer, and windy and wet autumn. These conditions lead to different patterns in electric appliances use in NZ householders, in special, in NZ south island householders. If trends in electric energy use have substantial correlation with weather conditions, this can help NZ electric energy suppliers and producers to forecast electricity consumption and thus organize and manage production of electric energy.

Consequently, it will lead to much more stability in energy supply to NZ every householder. For example, when the NZ energy supplier gathers data concerns every householder's house space size data, e.g. the house has how many sleeping rooms, toilets, bath rooms, eating rooms and reading rooms number, even the house has how many family members are living in every NZ geographical location. Then if it can follow different location of NZ houses spaces sizes whether they are large or small space size as well as whethe every house has how many family members are living to evaluate whether how much electricity efficiency can satisfy their comfortable living needs in winter. Then, it can evaluate whether they will use how much electricity efficiency for their needs in different seasons. If in winter, many householders are living in the large space size house in the geographic location. Then, it is possible that the geographic location is householders will use much electricity efficiency and where geographic location hosueholders who will be possible to pay the most highest electricity fee to compare the other geographic location of small space size of house householders. Hence, weather factor is the most influential to change NZ householders ' electricity energy consumption behaviors at homes.

● Urbanization level and income per capita both tangible factors as well as temperature (weather variation factor) will have close relationship to influence China householder energy consumption or useful needs at home every day
For China householder energy consumption habit example, what factors can determine to impact this country's householders energy useful behavior at homes? Can the impacts of these factors be quntified? What are China householder energy consumption trends and characteristics? I shall explan as below:
I believe the influential factors include these three aspects to China householder energy users: Income per capita, urbanization level an annual average temperature (weather). These factors will influence any China householder energy useful or consumption behavior at homes.
Temperature (weather variation factor) is intangible from eastern region to western region of Chin, variances largely depend upon economic level and the provincial level. So, some regions were warmer and cooler temperature will influence the regional China householder how to use electricity. In addition, th influence of urbanization level varies according to income level as well as the urbanization level has more significant impact on the structure and efficiency of China householder energy consumption thatn on its quantity. So, the urbanization level and income per capita both tangible factors will have close relationship to influence China householder energy consumption or useful needs at home every day. Moreover, these two tangible factors (urbanization level and income per capita both factors) have the more influential to impact China any one of household family energy consumption or useful habit to compare temperature factor at home. Because temperature can only influence than to choose to turn on heaters to keep more cooler in summer or turn on air conditions (fans) to keep more warmer in winter.
The electricity energy needs for these equopment tools which will be influenced less. Otherwise, the urbanization level and income per family householder how to choose to spend more or less electricity or gas etc. energy at homes. Because in behavioral economy view point, when individual householder has more income and the urban in the China geographic location is lising many high income and high household families memebrs to every house. Then, the urbanization household energy household enery useful or consumption level will be raised. Such as China household electricity users case, e.g. large cities have many high income and many houses have more than four families members to live on one house together. Then, the electricity or gas energy efficiency will be influenced to rise. The city urbanization and per capita income level is high to these large cities have high to income population, who are living in these cities in China.
Moreover, the impact of lifestyle on energy use mainly reflects types and purposes of fuels are chosen by different China households factor which will influence the urbanization level of energy choice use. China is a country with typical binary economics and social diversity and these is significant difference in the consumption pattern between urban and rural regions. Urban residents consume high-quality energy, such as electricity, natural gas , heating power, solar energy and gasoline. For rural residents, usually use coal, and bismass energy because they are cheaper price energy products which requires much time and labor and are heavy indoor pollutants . The difference in energy consumption pattern between urban and rural China residents is closely related related to living of quality needs, building structure, e.g. steel or stone etc. different materials, manufacture, easily access clean and effective feels through the electric grid, natural gas network and district heating systems.
Therefore, it explains why urbanization level is as an integrated variable reflecting social progress situation to

influence urban and rural regions, such as large cities , small cities and rural countryside regions' household energy consumption or useful behaviors which have differnet kinds of fuel useful demands and energy efficiencies qualify and quantity demand, or needs at homes. Consequently, it explains, urbanization level and income per captia level both factors are more influential to China household energy consumption at home to compare temperature (weather , seasonal) factor.

● Employment rates or gross domestic product macro economic variation factor, residential space size factor, and the government's implementation of energy labeling schemes provide significant impacts on Taiwan residential electricity consumption .

For Taiwan householder electricity consumption characteristics in the residential sector, which has different factors and pattern to compare China householder electricity householder electricity consumption habit at home. Although, they are the same Asia country. I shall explain these reasons as below:

For Taiwan electricity householder factors influence their energy useful or consumption behaviors at homes. The main factors can influence their electricity energy useful patterns include: employment rates or gross domestic product macro economic variation factor, residential space size factor, and the government's implementation of energy labeling schemes provide significant impacts on Taiwan residential electricity consumption . However, the impacts of electricity raising price and the energy supply reducing shortage efficiency standards do not significant to influence the Taiwan residential electricity consumption behavior at sources.

It means that it won't influence Taiwan householders to use electricity or gas or any kinds of energy number to be reduced, even the Taiwan government energy suppliers sudden raise, any kinds of energy price and reduce to supply energy to satisfy Taiwan householders daily essential needs at homes.

In fact, Taiwan had improved gross domestic product (GDP) and it had raised employment rates recently. So, many Taiwanese has jobs to work, due to Taiwan economy had improved to be better. So, growth had also raised. The economy improvement causes many Taiwanese had enough jobs to work, due to new businesses are set up. Many consumers excit any kinds of businesses are invested to Taiwan from overseas or local investors. So, consumption is grown, the electricity consuming applicances are selected, as the household consumer focus grousp number if also influenced to be increased. So, Taiwan economy had improved to be better, it will encourage many electricity consuming applicances products are encouraged to excited to be selected to seel in Taiwan. Due to many different kinds of electricity consuming appliances are supplied to attract Taiwanese to choose to buy to bring to their homes for cooking, boiling water, or keeping rooms to be cooler or warmer temperature confortable feeling intention in winter or summer seasons. So, these electricity consuming appliances, e.g. rice cookers, heaters, air conditions, fans, bathing gas heaters etc. different home electricity consuming appliances will be increased to supply to satisfy Taiwan householders' needs. When they decide to buy any news electricity consuming applicances to bring to homes to use.

● Environment scientists' education message how to influence Greece householders home energy consumption behaviors from primary energy to change secondary energy

Finally , I shall indicate Greece, this western which will influence this country's householders have desires to do household energy conservation patterns or conservation energy consumption behaviors or energy conservation activities at homes. I shall explain the social economic variable, such as consumers' income and family size variation factor which can influence the different Greece family household members differences towards energy conservation preferences. IN addition, the variable, such as environmental information feedback and consciousness of energy problems are characteristics of the energy saver consumer.

Why and how can environmental pollution , environmental protection, energy conservation information message can influence Greece householders to choose to do energy use consumption conservation or less energy useful behaviors at homes. It is one interesting energy efficient use behaviors , due to Greece householders are influenced by energy conservation or environmental protection message.

In fact, scientists agree overconsumption of natural resources is a major threat to oue lives in earth. Environmental problems like greenhouse effect, ozone layer depletion, and acid rain effect are not any more problems of a specific region or environmental problem. Also, economic theory is indicated that in order to gain comfort and time

households are becoming excessive energy users, neglecting the environmental impact of their choices.
Environment scientists bring these environment pollution message to influence Greeks (Greece householders) to change their energy consumption behaviors at homes. The environment scientists' message indicate that we are facing global warmth and natural resource and energy shortage challenges. Due to our Earth have limited natural resource numbers to supply to us to manufacture energy, but global population has been increasing every year. Thus, it is possible that we have energy shortage crisis. Also, manufactures are spending too much energy to waste to manufacture any products, the energy will cause air or water pollution in manufacturing process or drivers are driving their vehicles to pollute air on the roads.
Hence, environment scientists' message influence Greece householders began to consider these questions concern to reduce fossil fuel energy. Why do we need to Safety in using fuel and handle gas leaks? Why do we feel town gas smell? How is electricity located at electric station far away from town area? How to solve problems caused by the use of fossil fuels? How to reduce the use of fossil fuels?
Greece householders consider to solve the problems, the best way is to reduce thir used of fossil fuel. This helps prevent fossil fuels form being used up too quickly. Also, it helps them to reduce environmental problems because fewer pollutants are given out when less fossil fuels are used. Can human help to reduce the use of fossil fuels? Fossil fuels are mainly in power station. Although they use some fossil fuels for our gas cooker and car, it won't make much difference if I use less. Fossil fuel is not used renew primary energy. Most of energy Greece householders use come from fossil fuels, for example, the electricity we use is generated in power stations by burning fossil fuels. The buses they ride use diesel oil. Therefore, they can help reduce the use of fossil fuels by saving energy in Greece daily lives.

The actions that Greece householders can take such as: setting the air-conditioner to a higher temperature, walking instead of using lift, taking a short shower instead of a bath. This reduces the use of the hot water and thus the energy needed to heat the water. Thus, many people can help a lot to reduce our use of fossil fuels to avoid fossil fuel shortage risk occurrence.

Greeks (Greece householders) had been beginning to conern that they will face energy shortage challenge if they can not adopt more energy conservation actions. Because the Greece government began to bring negative environmental pollution and energy shortage challenge message if they often waste to use any kinds of energy, e.g. electricity , gas excessive number efficiency at homes. Then, they will be possible to fac energy shortage and environmental pollution challenge to their country in future one day. So, this energy shortage and environment pollution message has bring predictive negative worries to influence many Greece householder energy home users choose to reduce to avoid the waste of any kinds of energy use at homes.
So, their reducing energy use actions that had encouraged them to cause habits to avoid to waste excess energy to do any non essential electric appliances useful or consumption activities at homes often. Moreover, the environment protection and energy conservation message has changed many Greece householder to make decision and activities to change their lifestyle to b low living quality from high living quality. So, the environment protection and energy conservation message factor has much influential to change Greece household energy users' daily energy conservation or less energy use consumption activities at homes.
Greeks feel greenhouse energy can be environmental protection enegy. A greenhouse can trap heat in the sunlight and keeps the air inside the greenhouse warm enough for plants to grow. The glass roof and walls of a greenhouse let in sunlight but prevent heat from escape, this makes the greenhouse warm inside. Similarly, some gases in the Earth's atmosphere can trap heat from the sun and keep the Earth warm. This is called the greenhouse effect. The gases energy that can trap heat from the sun are called greenhouse gases. It is future one kind of potential primary energy to reduce environmental pollution new energy products for human consuming. So, environmental protection message influence them to consume greenhouse enegy at homes.
So, environment scientists' environment pollution message had influence Greece householders concern to apply seconday energy (environment protection) to replace electricity energy to use at home. They will change energy to use at home. The scientists' messages have more influential Greece householders energy change consumption behaviors at homes. The messages are as below:
There are different forms of energy, e.g. light, heat, sound, wind, water, electrical kinetic, chemical and potential

energy. Some form energy is primary energy and it can not renew to use, e.g. light, sound, wind, water, fossil fuel etc. Some form energy is secondary energy and it can renew to use in possible, e.g. nuclear, electric charge battery etc. Why does human need to concern how to manufacture secondary energy? Because it is possible that our natural resource will be consumed all, thus we will face primary energy shortage risk. If human can invent any new form of man-made secondary energy to renew to use in order to avoid primary energy shortage to supply to use to use, then human won't only depend on our Earth natural resource energy supply numbers. We can invent any new secondary energy to renew to use again either replaces primary energy or instead of primary energy limit number supply.

What is energy change? For television energy change power case. Firstly, electrical energy changes to television power to be used by television itself, then it changes to light power, next it changes to light power. How to choose fuel form to use? Due to energy can change to different form of powers to supply different form of power advantages to supply to human to use, so it is possible that we can also invent any secondary man made renew used energy to change different form powers to supply us to use, e.g. nuclear energy changes to light or sound or heat form of powers ; electrical charge batteries changes to light or sound or heat form powers to satisfy our daily life needs.

The environment scientists' energy consumption education influence Greece householders concern how to change to use secondary energy to replace primary energy at homes as below:

For primary natural resource fuel energy example, different fuel has different feature, e.g. easy to burn, safe to use, gives out a lot of energy, inexpensive, produces little air pollution, easy to transport and store. How can we use in different channels, such as heating food, hot pat, driving vehicles.

For example, although coal is not expensive to cause electricity energy for past transportation tool, e.g. traditional coal energy train or our daily home cooking, but it has negative influence to environment air pollution. Hence, we ought to follow the primary natural resource energy's feature to decide how to apply what aspects of our life needs.

For example, if the country's people hope to reduce pollution when who use any kind of energy, e.g. US , Europe energy markets. The energy entrepreneur ought concentrate on manufacturing the kind of energy which can reduce environment pollution to be the least level to supply the country people to use, e.g. electric charge battery supplies to these countries' drivers to drive their vehicles on the roads, wind energy or water energy to manufacture electricity power supply to reduce air or water pollution ; or if the country people hope to buy the inexpensive energy to use, even the energy's quality and performance is worse, e.g. China, India, Hong Kong markets. The energy entrepreneur ought concentrate on manufacturing the lowest cost and enough supply of natural resource to manufacture the kind of energy to sell cheap price to these countries to use, e.g. China, Africa can accept to use e.g. gas, coal, fuel energy to use to compare developed countries people, e.g. UK, US; or if the countries people who hope to use energy which can easy to transport and store, e.g. light coal. The energy entrepreneur can choose to concentrate on manufacturing much coal to supply to the countries people to use, e.g. China, Arica Thus, to choose to manufacture which kinds of energy supply to the countries market people to use, the energy entrepreneur how decides to manufacture which kind of energy, it depends on which kinds of fuel advantages of the countries people most concerning.

What is energy meaning? It is defined a dynamic quality, it is a fundamental entity of nature that is transferred between parts of a system in the production of physical change within the system, and it is usually regarded as the capacity for doing work, and it is usable power (such as heat or electricity) or the resources for producing such power.

Why does secondary energy own investment worth? Because the different forms of primary natural resource energy will have supply shortage crisis, such as natural resources coal, gas, solar, wind, water, geothermal, biomass(organic material) etc. However, human can attempt to explore any undiscovered Earth or Space resource to manufacture any kinds of secondary energies, e.g. nuclear energy, electric recharge battery energy to supply to electric vehicle or space robots transportation tools to use or satisfy our daily life needs in future one day. So any kind of undiscovered secondary man-made renewed used energy resources have potential commercial worth to any energy entrepreneurs, it is possible that they can replace traditional primary energy to supply to human to use for our different aspects of life needs. In the future, the secondary energy demand will increase, when primary energy supply number has decreased form natural exploration. So, it will cause the effect of any demand of secondary energy product to be raised and prices to be increased in possible. Due to global population has been growing up, considerably China and India both countries populations have been increasing rapidly. Scientists predict there are more than 1.2 billion people worldwide will lack access to electricity, and more than 2.5 billion still use wood, charcoal to cook and heat in the future when primary energy has no enough number to supply to us to use. Hence, the fact that demand is this much greater than supply to make energy a prime market for further growth.

Although, secondary energy will have much investment worth, but energy like all other investments will carry risks. The internal and external risk factors include such as: policy is always changing to prohibit which do energy trading more easily between the energy exporting and importing countries, the secondary energy manufacturer itself own abilities to invent and to manufacture any kinds of secondary energy, improved technology can quickly make an technology obsolete, geopolitical rifts can happen overnight, the country's energy consumer (user)'s preferable choice to use which either kinds of secondary energy or secondary energy. So, it seems that (man-made) renewed used secondary energy industry can provide above-average returns, but it can also bring high risk commercial investment.

Traditionally, energy supply companies will apply those methods to operate energy providing businesses. For Shell,. Exxon examples, which had own gas stations, explore and drill for gas on their own. Other companies specialize in a part of the energy market, e.g. leasing oil rigs for example, or operating a pipeline. Energy supplying companies can choose to manufacture any kinds of energy to supply, e.g. trade oil, gas, coal, uranium, electricity etc. Any energy price and supply is demanded on the countries energy users' which kinds of energy most choice need or certain energy commodities to be chose to use popularly. For example, if US most people prefer to use secondary man-made renew used energy more than primary energy. Then, US energy manufacturers ought concentrate on manufacturing much different kinds of secondary man-made renew used energy to prepare to supply to its domestic US market in order to raise secondary energy price to sell in its country. So, the energy manufacturer's energy manufacturing choice, it is depend on which the country's people prefer to use which kinds of energy for their daily life needs.

However, scientists predict secondary energy market will have large market share, due to primary energy will have shortage to explore to supply in our earth and future energy consumers(users) prefer to choose to use more efficiency, less energy consumption, none environment pollution cause, cost effectiveness, renew to use of any kinds of energy. For example, the electricity recharge battery secondary man-made renew used energy is one kind of reducing air pollution power to push any electric battery vehicles to be driven to compare gas energy during drivers are driving their cars on the roads. They can reduce noise and air pollution and drivers can drive safely, who only need to buy one electric recharge battery to recharge in any electric recharge battery stations on streets when the electric recharge battery has no enough power to push their cars and they need to recharge their electric recharge battery drive when they had driven between one to two days. Due to primary energy, e.g. fuel , gas, the kinds of primary energies will have shortage to supply to global drivers to drive their traditional cars. Thus, the electric recharge battery or any undiscovered secondary energy will be future driving market needs. So, man-made renew used secondary energy, e.g. biofuel, hydro-electric, nuclear, will be one kind of efficient, clean, less pollution cause, cost-effective of energy to supply to our global vehicle market, even any other undiscovered new markets. Supposing they are popular to be used for electric vehicle market globally in future one day, then their prices will be decreased and constructed to average car requires up to 1,700 gallons of oil. Also supposing that making average computer requires more than ten times or weight to fossil fuels, every calories of food eaten in the US requires roughly then calories of fossil fuels. Hence, cheap energy will be one successful factor to influence future potential energy consumer (user) individual choice needs. Conversely, ion good economic times, people are more willing to travel, to buy products, and all of which success demand and low process for energy.

In the future, secondary energy will be the best choice to food production market. The modern food production system is essentially a success of changing fossil fuels into food. So, raising energy prices are almost higher food costs and even shortage for fossil fuels energy. If one day, one kind of discovered secondary man-made renew used energy can supply to any restaurants or homes to be used to cook at the cheap price, then the profit is very high for this kind of food production energy. Thus, future food production secondary energy consumption market is large and because the primary energy inputs for agriculture are higher than the energy outputs of the food. However, future secondary man-made renew used energy for food production system is only one part of whole energy consumer in food industry. The food production is related to whole food consumption market which includes: household cooking energy market, agriculture or vegetable, rice, fruit etc. foods farming machines energy market, food manufacturing factories market, food machine package market, transportation food delivery market, supermarket or fruit/food sale stores market. They must need any energy inputs to achieve the food production or food transportation or warehouse / stores electricity supply or cooking energy needs. Hence, these food suppliers relate to any whole food factory manufacturers, food retailers, food wholesalers, farmers and home/restaurant cookers, all of them must need to use energy to carry on their food producing or food cooking or food transportation activities every day in overall food industry. Thus, it seems that undiscovered any second energy demand will be increased, when the primary energy supply number is decreasing. Also, when people can accept to use secondary energy to replace primary energy to be used for any cooking, transporting food, manufacturing food, food retail stores or warehouse food delivery energy need activities. Then, the secondary energy price will be fall down to attract many food energy consumers.

Nowadays, the food industry energy may includes primary nature resource gas energy or electricity energy for house house families or restaurants cooking needs, food delivering lorry drivers driving needs usually. If future second man made renew used energy is invented successful popular to be used, e.g. hydrogen, electric recharged battery energy for electric vehicles or restaurant/home families cooking needs or food factories machine maufacturing energy needs. Then, the seconday energy will have possible to replace primary energy to be food industry energy market.

Wiley, composition services graphics indicated that global primary energy consumption had been increasing 30 billion tons from 1830 year to 510 billion tons in 2010 year as well as global population size had been increasing from 70 billion 1830 yeat to 510 billion in 2010 year. Thus, it seems that global primary energy consumption will be needed largely after 2010 year. If future global nature resource primary energy is explored full number and it had not enough energy number to supply global human to use. Then, it will being many people feel uncomfortable and inconvenient,e.g. Some countries won't have enough energy to supply transportion tools to be driven, some homes and restaurants won't have enough energy to supply to cook to eat or to provide restaurant clients to eat etc. daily activies, due to human's much activities which are needs energy supply. Thus, it seems that global primary energy comsumption will be needed largely after 2010 year.

Wiley, composition services graphics also explianed that why the primary energy consumption demand can be needed to achieve the same level to the global population size increasing in 2010 year. The graph showed these reasons why cause the same level of global population size and global primary energy consumpion demand which may include: The graph showed that after a nation is developed, its per-person energy use hegins to level off. In North Ameruca and Europe, where energy demand has remained flat, or fallen dightly, in each of the past few years. But the 1.3 billion people on those two continents are far outweighted by the 5 billion people in Asia and Africa, e.g. Chinese and Indian. who currently have more energy need to comapre average per man to North America and Europe per man, ensuring that overall energy demand will rise for years to come.

Wiley, composition services graphics also predicted that the growth in primary energy demand. China will have 4,500 million tons in 2035 year. India will have 3,000 million tons in 2035 year. Other developing Asia will have 2,000 million tons in 2035 year. Russia will have 1,500 million tons in 2035, Middle East will have 1,300 million tons in 2035, other rest of world will have 1,000 million tons in 2035. Hence, it implied that China will be the largest primary energy need country in the future.

China will be future the primary potential energy consumer market. The primary energy includes water, coal, wind, fossil oil, gas ,solar, geothermal energy, biomass (organiz material) etc. different natural resource primary energy. Otherwise, US, UK, Europe will be secondary energy potential need market. For example, electrical recharge battery energy will be raised demand to supply to any future new design electrical charge battery vehicles in US, Europe, UK markets.

Due to US, Europe, UK people concern environment protection, so they will invent many electric charge battery vehicles to consume electrical charge battery to replace polluted gas energy to avoid air pollution when the drivers are driving cars on themselve countries' roads. For example, second man-made renew used nuclear energy can be applied to rockets to pusch them to leave our earth to fly to other space far away and consuming nuclear energy will be cost efficient, and nuclear energy saving will be more when nuclear to spend long time to be used in any long time space journey. Hence, nuclear energy and electric charge battery secondary energy will be popular to be applied to vehicles and rockets energy needs in US, Europe, potential marketss, even our daily energy needs in global second energy market.

Who are your energy business's competitors (peers)? How do they compare? How have your energy business company performed cyclically? How to choose to manufacture to sell which kinds of primary or secondary energy product(s), either manufactures only primary energy product(s) or manufactures only secondary energy products or both? Which countries do you plan to sell your energy product?

Illustration by Wilsey, composition services graphiss showed that these natural resources to energy product the world's electricity percentage, such as below:

41% of coal, 5% of oil, 21% of gas, 13% of nuclear, 16% of Hydro, 3% other renewable secondary man-made energy. Hence, coal will be future the major natural resource to produce electricity. The energy entrepreneur ought attempt to explore any coal resources, when who choose to supply electricity power to consumers for future energy consumption country markets.

Wiley, composition services also predicted that the expectation is that North America coal will supply the expectation is that North America coal will supply Asian demand, Us export terminals have a total capacity of 173 million tommes output. China will drive 16% of the nations total output. China will drive the sea-born demand for coal over for the forcessable future. Chinese energy consumption will grow more than 12 % between 1980 and 2009 years. Though, China heads global demand, India is growing faster in terms of coal imports. Much of the global coal demand will be supplied by Indonesia and Australia. Colombia, Russia, South Africa and Mongolia are also players in global export coal energy resources.

Hence, environment scientists' education messages influence Greece householders believe that secondary energy will be one kind of new energy product to replace traditional primary energy product for human energy consumption market global needs. Hence, it is right time any energy entrepreneur needs to research how to explore any undiscovered man-made renew used secondary energy products to avoid primary energy shortage crisis occurrence. Greece householders will be the highest population number to choose secondary energy to replace primary energy to use at homes. it means that environment scientists had changed Greece householders' energy consumption behaviors at homes.

In conclusion, different countries will have different factors influence how the country's householders energy consumption behavioral changes. Hence, it seems that any country's householders' energy use of consumption behaviors will be possible influenced by extermal environment factors influence. Also, every country's energy providers can attempt to find whether the country has what kinds of unique factors to influence its householders' energy consumption efficiency to increase or decrease in order to find the methods to solve the energy efficiency demand reducing challenges successfully.

Explaining how organizational strategy solving problem

Economy theory solves business problem, manager can use economics to strategize and solve a variety of business problems. Is it bossible? In fact, the basic problem of an economy ca be solved either by the decisions of the government or by the market through interactions of buyers and sellers. How to judge whether it is one good economic theory? A good theory is simple enough to be understood, when complex enough to capture the key features of the object or situation being studied. Somethimes economists use the term model instead of theory. For example, the most common four economic theories may include: Since the 1930 s, four macroeconomic theories have been proposed: Keynesian economics, monetarism, the new classical economics and supply-side economics . All of these theories are based, in varying degree. So, applied economics solves economic problems may be by solved by providing informaton on how people, businesses and governments behave.

However, business economics is a field in applied economics which uses econoic theory and quantitative methods to analyze business. Business economics focused on the economic issues and problems related to business organizations. Business economics also covers most of the problems that a manager or an establishment faces for example, price theory, on the other hand, helps the firm in understanding how prices are determined under different consumer emotion or external economic environment etc. factors. Moreover, business economics and quantitative methods also applies economic theory to the study of organizations. for example, the principal-ahent problem has become a standard factor in political science and economics, basic economic theory explains how and why that when demand exceeds supply, producers tend to raise price, or public choice theory how and why affect economic output, due to global economic outlook is significant trade uncertainty.

So, economists explore how individuals and businesses can help secure a healthy environment, when they attempt to find the most right economic theories to help businesses to solve their business problems. In general, it makes use of statistical and analytical tools to assess economic theories in solving practical business problems. For example, rapid devaluation solutions can be applied to solve economic crisis, fiscal occurrence in the 1930 s. It helps to stimulate demand and creates jobs to solve social unemplyment challenge in 1930s. This will provide some relief to businesses and tax cut increases disposable income in 1930s global economic fiscal crisis occurrence. For anther exmaple, the gig economy is enabled by technology, such as robotic productive tool invention, it can help factories to raise efficiency to manufacture as well as reduces labors number. So, effective economic theory may help managers to solve any organizational problems easily.

In general, the main economic problems may include: What to produce in which quantities? How to produce? For whom to produce? How efficiency are the resources being utilized? Is the economy growth? So, economic problems are the science that studies human behavior in relationship with ends and scarce means that have alternative uses. In other way, it deals with the problem of choice, economic problems asserts that an economy's finite resources are insufficient to satisfy all human wants and needs. Hence, it brings this question: What causes economic problems? It may be explained that goods and services . All economic problems that satisfy human wants and produced with the help of resources, such as land, labour, capital, and enterprise. These resources are scarce when wants are unlimited, due to scarcity ot these resources, an economy can not produce all that goods and services as required by its citizens. It implies that the fundamental economic problem is the issue of scarcity but unlimited wants, to decide what goods and services need to be produced, how to make the best used of limited or scarce. For example, the global economy will be adversely affected by the COVID-19 pandemic with short term global growth projections. The crisis highlights the need for urgent action to COVID-19 health and it will influence global economic recession. Global economy can not recover to grow up in short term. So, COVID-19 pandemic disease can cause global economic problem in short term because it influences global travellers number reduces or their travelling leisure desire reduces, visiting restaurants to eat desire reduces. Then organizations began to reduce staffs number because customers number decreases. Consequently, global economic recession is influenced to occur by COVID-19 pandemic disease. So, sometimes some unpredicted extermal environmental factor may influence any countries occur economy recession in prior, even global economic recession later, such as COVID-19 pandemic disease cause.

Hence, global economists began to consider how to apply different economic theories methods to solve unpredicted economic problems in order to prevent global serious economic recession occurrence.

Engagement (Building good organizational culture) Strategy solves Hill Wood Medical Centre organization international different culture difficult cooperation problem

- How and why can engagement strategy solve medical organizational departments difficult culture cooperate problem ?

Organizational cultures and subcultures will influence Hill wood Medical Centre organizational performance and commitments. The subcultures may take precedence over the organizational culture for individual employees and thus gain their commitment. Hill wood medical centre can therefore focus on the relationships of both organizational culture and subcultures to satisfy staffs need to serve patients in happy work environment. Organizational culture includes leadership style and job satisfactory measurement. Hence, employees' commitment was examined in relation to the level of consent to and conflict with managerial strategy. Although, managerial strategy is not the same as leadership, the attributes and skills required in leadership could be seen as an essential part of managerial strategy. Organization culture(s) has (have) a causal modelling approach to examine the determinants of organizational commitment and labour turnover. Organization culture(s) can include a variety of variables , e.g. age, pre-employment expectations, perceived job characteristics and the consideration of leadership style, which all influence organizational commitment indirectly via effects on job satisfaction. I supposed that Hill Wood Medical Centre existed relationship of organizational culture and subcultures to influence staffs feel satisfactory and commitment. Also of interest is the relationship of these variables with leadership style, job satisfaction and subject characteristics, such as age, level of education to its staffs in this hospital.

In Hill Wood Medical Centre organization, its organizational culture was the hospital cultures and subcultures which refer to the culture of the wards or work units or operation rooms to every department staff commitments refer to nurses team and medical service chief medical officer team and surgeons team and administrative department etc their different departments' individual staff's commitments. There is a culture relationship between this medical centre organization commitments and it was measured with administration department and operating rooms and wards department etc different departments' subcultures as well as surgeons and nurses and doctors and administration staffs etc different teams' subcultures. More specifically, it is expected that such as Hill Wood Medical Centre organizational culture could be more supportive and innovative to its different departments, such as wards and surgeons operating rooms and administrative office etc different departments subcultures.

Thus, I believe there is a strong relationship between this medical centre organizational cultures and subcultures and commitment and characteristics of this organizational overall culture, such as corporate values and beliefs commitments and performance to Hill Wood Medical Centre organization. However, I think this medical centre's bureaucratic work practices organizational cultures often result in negative employee commitment due to its supportive work

environment could not result in greater commitment and involvement among employees. For example, these different departments needed to met Sharon Lawson, administrator of Hill Wood Medical Centre to discuss how to solve their departments problems in their meetings in that day, but Sharon Lawson could not had any suggestions in these meeting in that day. It seemed that this medical centre had negative culture and subcultures to get negative results due to who needed to spend time to wait Sharon to meet them and the administrator could not give any suggestions to solve their department problems on that day. Such as Holly from state health department told Sharon the general inspection needed to be improved, e.g. kitchen needed cleanliness and inspectors felt this medical centre needed to allow patients access to drug supplies, but this state health department representative had requested inspection before six months and Helen controller asked Sharon about the new computer hardware who requested six months ago and Helen told Sharon who needed it now for billing efficiency to office use, but Sharon decided to make request to board for computer hardware purchase next meeting and some surgeons were drunk to work in operating rooms, who caused danger to patient's life to cause some patients complained these surgeons, but Sharon did not solve whose complaints at that day immediately and medical staffs were discussing why the medical centre had not purchased one upgraded piece of standard diagnostic equipment used in body scanning $700,000 cost, but Sharon had not enquired whose reasons clearly to decide to buy the equipment next year, but doctors did not understand why Sharon could not purchased this year. Then the nurses agreed to give Sharon a week to investigate the situation

and attempted to resolve it and a meeting was scheduled for next week to review the situation.

Finally the medical centre's attorney needed to wait for twenty minutes to discuss about what steps were to be taken to solve with surgeons, Dr Chambers who was complained about drunk wine work in surgeon operating rooms issue, but Sharon had no more time to meet whom to discuss on that day. Hence, it seemed that this medical centre had not good culture and subcultures in its organization, such as Sharon had not enough time arrangement to meet them to discuss their departments' problems on the same day. It seemed that Hill Wood Medical Centre had no good organizational culture and subcultures to cause staffs conflicts and administration department also wasted much time to handle departments' meetings only. If Hill Wood Medical centre culture and subcultures could be changes, such as every department could attempt to discuss how to solve their problems before who met the administrator . Then I believe that who could give reasons or ideas to support their view point to persuade Sharon made final decision to shorten their meeting time. Hence, this medical centre seemed that it's subcultures and culture were negative.

I supposed that it's nurses team subcultures tended to identify more cooperation closely with different teams, such as surgeons operating rooms team, doctors team, wards team etc departments to compare the administration department. It meant nurses teams' subcultures needed often exhibit greater loyalty and commitment to these departments in the Hill wood Medical Centre organization. Thus, it seemed that it needed better subcultures in nurses teams to share different departments‘ job to reduce staffs conflicts to serve patients satisfactory. However, Hill Wood Medical Centre organizational culture and subcultures could influence staffs' job satisfaction and commitment positively or negatively due to this medical centre cultural variables could influence their feelings , such as the amount of reward, flexibility of work schedule and balance of work and home life etc. Hence, Hill Wood Medical Centre culture could cause those intrinsic factors to influence every units staffs‘ feelings of job satisfaction. In relation to educational level and organizational commitment, it seemed that educational level was negatively relative to this Hill Wood Medical centre, such as it could permit surgeons were drunk to work in operating rooms often, it was danger to every patient life during surgeons were drunk to work . Hill Wood Medical Centre overall culture was from low to top level communication channel and bureaucratic work organizational culture was often in negative employee commitment, such as all departments needed to wait the administrator to arrange meeting time to solve their departments problems in the same day. However, much decisions could not get solutions from the administrator.

It seemed that this Hill Wood Medical Centre's bureaucratic organization cultures and subcultures caused Sharon had arranged more meetings on that day to influence who had not enough time to do their departments' duties on that day efficiently due to who only concentrated on handling meetings issues on that day. I think Sharon Lawson who did not know how to arrange what kinds of job duties and meetings which were more important which ought to handle on that day or what kinds of job duties and meetings which were not more important to handle on the same day. Hence, who could not get any discussion result in these meetings on that day due to Sharon, administrator had not enough time to negotiate their departments to solve problems successfully in meetings. In conclusion, this medical centre organizational cultures and subcultures seemed that which were not positive to staffs‘ commitments and job satisfaction. Such as its different departments needed to spend much time to wait administrator to arrange meetings to discuss their problems, but who did not make any decisions in their meetings. The administrator would influence different departments overall work efficiency and effectiveness to be poor. So, it ought need to change its organization culture and subcultures to raise its different departments' efficiency and effectiveness as soon as possible.

- suggestion engagement strategy influences to medical centre departments‘ staffs build kindly culture efficient cooperative method

Describe the culture or cultures at Hill wood Medical Centre ? Are these subcultures ?

How would you recommend that Sharon administrator measure effectiveness at Hill wood Medical Centre?

The medical centre performance effective evaluation meant to measure whether the degree to its overall organization was improving or deteriorating. The measurement combines quantitative and qualitative analysis and efficiency trend to get the degree of effective result. On the quantitative analyses measurement, e.g. medical errors occurrence rates ; patients medical treatment health rates. On the qualitative analysis measurement, e.g.acquiring executives who communicated a culture of quality through personal supportive polities and investment of resources, such as the degree of diagnostic equipments effectiveness, the degree of staff quality improvement and the degree of health information technological effectiveness and the degree of every patient's service satisfaction etc. Performance measurement effectiveness is well established throughout medical and health care industry, of which include the core areas of finance, operations, clinical care and information technology services as below:

Finance is an organization often measures the efficiency of its accounts receivable, i.e. timely collection of payment for services rendered, such as this Hill Wood medical centre can collect how much payment for services from patients per week and it earns how much profit or loss per week. Operating is an organization needs the lengths of time to take for a patient to receive an appointment in the practice or measures individual patient whose satisfaction with the care received, such as the satisfactory degree of Hill Wood Medical Centre every patient how who feel to every doctor, physician, surgeon and nurse whose service performance and personal attitude to whom.

Clinical care is an organization measures how often care is delivered in accordance with evidence based guidelines or how effective that care is in improving every patient outcome, such as whether Hill Wood medical centre had how many doctor and surgeon and physician and nurse numbers who could treat every patient to be health to satisfy who don't feel sick or hurt again after who left this hospital. Information technology is an organization widely integrated into health care settings to support for performance measurement, such as whether Hill Wood medical centre needed to buy how many diagnostic equipments to use to body scanning for surgeons or needed to buy how many computers to office to use to achieve the best performance.

This Hill Wood medical centre needed these processes to measure its quantified numbers to a health care service provided to on behalf of or by a patient that was needed on scientific evidence of efficiency or effectiveness, so it could quantify a specific system, e.g. getting a test done or a service performed and it's outcome could measure to quantify every patient's health status resulting from its nurses and doctors and surgeons and physicians whose health care. Thus, in the clinical area, Hill Wood medical centre could measure every patient outcome to compare to every care standard, such as every patient's test value to measure effectiveness. Measurement effectiveness is central to the concept of this Hill Wood medical centre quality improvement, it provides a
mean to define what medical centres or hospitals actually do and to compare that with the original targets in order to identify opportunities for improvement. On clinical care and operational measure aspect:

Hill Wood medical centre ought to establish standardized and systematic procedures for problem solving to able to test and implement major practice changes. Such as clinical guidelines or care maps for specific conditions or procedures, department specific quality plans with short and long term goals, improved educational and training materials for clinical staff error reduction, hand washing and infection prevention, education materials for patients regarding full prevention, information technology that reduced medication errors and improved data collection etc these changes. To decide whether how much change criteria it ought need to change it's measurement effectiveness was depending on the nature of the change and the rate of acceptance and adoption of staff. It aimed to resistance to change in culture from surgeons and physicians and nurses and doctors; measured how much limited resources were available to use or maintain quality related equipment investment, such as office equipments or operational rooms diagnostic equipments of numbers as well as whether how to make the patient complaint numbers to be reduced to achieve zero tolerance to any staffs as well as whether departmental quality plans could achieve special goals effectiveness measurement as well as whether training could be achieve continuous quality improvement to staffs measure
effectiveness as well as organizational structure change could be raised staffs service performance efficiently, such as whether creation was needed on service quality and addition staff and responsibilities were needed for quality improvement
as well as whether patient care redesign and more training was needed for aides and multi disciplinary leadership teams change. Establishing organizational culture and subcultures of service quality measurement effectiveness aspect as below:

. Setting how long time to achieve short term and long term attainable goals and celebrated successes to individual staff and individual units involved in reaching their goals.

. Keeping the individual unit staff involved in problem identification and problem solving time spending. It aimed to raise everyone to feel much valuing expecting all to participate
to solve any problems in the most shorten time.

On finance and information technology measure effective aspect:

Effective organizational culture and subculture change could encourage every unit leader and peers to be patient, but recognized that changing took time and continuing to keep quality improvement to measure whether it needed how much time to balance quality and financial goals and considering investments, such as how many equipment numbers were needed to buy to provide to office and operational room units to use to raise office productive efficiency and effectiveness as well as operational rooms service efficiency and effectiveness to measure to achieve quality improvement from a short and long term perspective to this Hill Wood medical centre. It aimed to evaluate whether new policies were bringing equipment into operating rooms or office to use was needed or was not needed

. I recommend Sharon, administrator needed to indicate these qualitative performance effectiveness measurement questions included:

.What barriers did this medical centre face in implementing the strategies or achieving success?

.Did it overcome those obstacles and if so, how?

In conclusion, to measure effectiveness of this medical centre whether how it could achieve quality improvement for success. I recommend Sharon, administrator needed to consider what should be the indicators to include implementation of aggressive quality targets for performance indicators as well as how to decide tightening of recruitment and standards and enhanced respect for all staffs in enhancement of quality improvement processes to shorten time to solve problems in

efficient manner and hoped to decide new investments in quality related information technology combined with the number of staffs input numbers efficiently and effectively.

Thus, the four core areas of performance measurement was one quality improvement models of high performing effective measurement to Hill Wood Medical Centre.

What do you think some of the effectiveness criteria might be?

I think some outcomes of effectiveness criteria to this Hill Wood medical centre, it might be the practice changes appeared to have resulted in improved outcomes for patients. In

addition to major improvements in the combination quality measures which based on morality, morbidity and complication rates, such as below:

Process/ operations effectiveness criteria: faster receipt of test result, faster patient flow, easier and more efficient data sharing and recording, fewer medication errors. So, I think it could measure the doctors and nurses and surgeons and physicians who serve to every patient's performance whether what effectiveness criteria to these staffs from their every serving patients' satisfactory level. Health related effectiveness criteria: calculate the reductions in morality rates, e.g. the surgeon reducing numbers were drunk to work in operational rooms every month and the patient health numbers every month.

Work environment and reputation effectiveness criteria: increase in patients satisfaction and staff satisfaction numbers and morale improved status numbers every month in this medical centre. If it could increase the numbers of patients satisfaction and staff satisfaction and morale improved

status numbers, it would have greater ability to improve service quality to surgeons and doctors and nurses in this medical centre.

Bottom line effectiveness criteria: the effective measurement of decreasing or increasing costs per medical centre units and length of stay for certain conditions and increased or decreased patients admission numbers and market share numbers every month. I think it lacked enough equipments for office to use and diagnostic equipments numbers were needed to be upgraded to use in body scanning because the departments leaders needed to met to Sharon, administrator to permit to buy those equipments urgently. It seemed this medical centre service effectiveness criteria would be poor due to there was not enough equipments to provide to these units to use possibly. Hence, if this medical centre could raised the quantitative and qualitative effectiveness criteria as above, it would change positive outcomes to motivate these units doctors, surgeons, nurses, physicians and administrative individual team leaders and their colleagues to strengthen the service quality improvement process to this Hill Wood medical centre. However, I think this Hill Wood medical centre performance was poor from the above

effectiveness criteria analysis. Performance must be defined in relative to explicit goals reflecting the values of various stakeholders.

On conclusion, when the international medical center can have one excellent engagement (good organizational culture) strategy, it can solve international medical staffs whose cooperative challenges more easily. This medical centre internal stakeholders were such as patients, doctors, nurses, surgeons, physicians etc and external stakeholders were patients, debtors, banks, Government shareholders etc. This medical centre performance might be defined according to the achievement of specific targets of either clinic to patient services or internal departmental operations. Targets might relate to traditional hospital functions, such as health treatment, care and rehabilitation as well as administration, ambulatory patient delivered services and health care networks. Following this medical centre evidences which indicated the poor performance of effectiveness criteria, such as Sharon, administrator lacked enough time to meet some department leaders to help them to solve problems successfully on that day, so it caused who needed to make another meetings to discuss their problems again. It seemed the administrator wasted their time to do other important duties on that day efficiently and effectively. I think Sharon, administrator was not one effective administrator in this medical centre. If who could not change whose management attitude to co-operate with other department managers(leaders), then who could cause poor subcultures to different departments to build to this medical centre overall organization culture and who also influenced other department performed ineffective and inefficient results due to Sharon, administrator who did not know how to arrange time to meet them everyone efficiently.

In conclusion, I think if this medical centre hoped to reduce doctors and nurses and surgeons and physicians and administrations etc staffs frequently conflict and maximized work effectiveness of its departments. Sharon administrator had responsibility to change whose personal work attitude to adapt their subcultures to co-operate with different departments. Otherwise, this medical centre would not be maximize effectiveness and would increase staffs conflicts to cause staff turnover numbers to be increased seriously.

England NHS public hospital patient price structure of marketing strategy

1. What do you understand by the concept of a pricing model? Critically discuss their relevance to a public sector service ,such as the NHS.

A price model reflects the fact that companies can generate revenue through a variety of combination of the basic price and prices charged for optional additional items. Some price models may be sustainable by giving away a product at very low price initially, but then charge higher prices for essential items that are needed to make the product function. Sometimes, the dominant pricing model in a market is challenged by a new entrant, with the result that consumers' expectations are changed. The price model can occur in perfectly competitive market or non perfectly competitive market. A perfectly competitive market characteristics include there are many producers supplying the market, each with similar cost structures and each producing an identical product. No single supplier on its own influence the market price because it is not monopoly, water and electricity is managed by government to control the public utility company which can not charge high fee to every householder user at the reasonable price ; both buyers and sellers are free to enter or leave the market and there are no barriers to entry or exit and there is a ready of information for buyers and sellers, for example about competing alternatives, e.g. oil products and stock markets where shares are bought and sold are exist in perfectly competitive market. In perfectly competitive markets, firms are price taker and their ability to set prices is limited by the level of demand and supply within the market they serve. If the total demand go up, all other things being equal, the going rate of prices in the market for their product will rise. Likewise, if there is a drop in total supply for whatever reason (e.g. because of bad weather, there will be further pressure for prices in the market to rise. The final price paid in the market will reflect the balance between supply side and demand side factors.

The model of perfect competition presented the forces of competition may be ideal for consumers because the tendency of market forces to minimize prices and/or maximize firms' outputs. But in such markets, suppliers are forced to be price takers rather than price makers. in a perfectly competitive market, firms are unable to use marketing strategies to affect the price at which they sell. At a higher price, buyers will immediately substitute identical products from other suppliers. Lower prices would be unsustainable in an industry where all firms had similar cost structures. Otherwise, an non perfectly competitive market, firms are able to use marketing strategies to affect the price at which they sell. Such as UK medical service market , private hospitals and public hospitals and clinics which can raise their service fee to their patients to follow their patients demand due to their doctors and nurses service performance, medicines quality and price and patient beds supplies factors to influence their service charges to their patients in UK. Hence, NHS needs to provide different and excellent medical service to its patients to make them to feel it's service is better to other private hospitals and clinics if it wanted to apply price model to its car parking or hospital phone system service charge to its patients because it is a public sector medical service organization. It ought not charge extra service fee to its patients in its hospitals. If it charged extra service fee, such as car parking and hospital phone system service which are same or higher or lower than other private hospitals or clinic , which need to ensure which medicine quality, doctors and nurses performance which are better than private hospitals and clinics and its patient beds need have enough supply to any patients when who feel need to sleep in its hospital. Because NHS image is a non profit medical organization to any UK poor patients, who choose NHS medical service are due to its medical service charge is cheaper than private hospitals and clinics and who feel it can provide free car parking and free hospital phone system service.

A market is defined here need not be a physical location where exchange takes place (as happens in retail and wholesale grocery markets). A market in the economist's sense refers to all individuals and firms who wish either to buy or sell a specific product. A market is defined in terms of products or service and geographic description, so the UK soft drinks market refers to all individuals in the UK who seek to buy soft drinks and the suppliers to that market. The UK medical service market structure can describe as the number of consumers, such as patients and medical providers , such as private hospitals and public hospital , such as NHS (National health service) and clinics; the barriers that exist to prevent new private hospitals or clinics or public assistance hospitals from entering the UK medical service market (or prevent UK patients do not prefer to choose NHS medical service); the extent to which the supply medical services is concentrated in the UK small number patients normally and the degree of collusion that occurs between patients and/or private or public hospitals or clinics medical service providers in the UK medical market. Governments often seek to regulate the prices of key products and service, such as electricity and telephones and public hospitals medical services, so it is important to understand how firms can reconcile the sometimes conflicting approaches of market forces and regulation, such as NHS public sector medical service in United Kingdom. Of course, if NHS public sector medical service planned to charge some non major service fees, such as car parking and hospital phone calling service to its patients and hospital visitors and staffs which are same to private hospitals, it needs to consider pricing model should never be seen as an isolated element of hospital's marketing decision making. It needed to consider its service performance of its doctors and nurses, its social responsibility of public medical service image whether it is better or worse than private hospitals that it had created and NHS 's distribution strategy whether it's patient beds supply numbers are enough to patients and whether it's medicine quality and supplies and prices which are reasonable to compare to private hospitals or clinics in this medical service market in United Kingdom. Private business organization with a broad range if products or services are often price different with their portfolio in quite different ways. They may have developed a price model, which describes the way that it uses pricing of its portfolio to maximize its overall revenue. Hence, one product or service may be charged at a very low price, on the assumption that it can raise higher price if many clients choose to buy its product or consume its service. In some sectors, a number of different pricing models co-exist. For example, in the emerging multi-channel television broadcasting market, some channels are provided free of charge to users, but make revenue from selling advertising space, when others charge to users, either on a monthly/annual basis or a pay to view basis. The idea of a pricing model is familiar to private sector organizations, but do they have a role to play in the public sector? In the UK, pricing models are increasingly being discussed and developed for services which have previously been considered a vital service and available freely to all.

Adrian, P.(2012) showed that the National Health Service (NHS) has a long and proud tradition of providing health service to all, according to an individual's need, paid for out of general taxation, according to individuals' means. Pricing has historically had very little role to play in the NHS. However, from the mid-1990 year, individual NHS trusts began exploiting charges for ancillary services as a means of boosting their revenue. One of the first targets for charging was users of hospitals' car parks. Trusts argued that providing car parks was not central to the mission of NHS trusts, and conveniently, government was encouraging more people to use public transport and leave their cars at home. Critics argued that patients were essentially captive and public transport was not a realistic alternative for most people. However, it showed that at one hospital in London, a patient who attended A&E on the advice of her GP, was charged UK$3.75 for the first two hours' use of the hospital car park and UK$7.5 thereafter. She was ten minutes over the two hour period and therefore had to pay higher charge. She also questioned the fact that charges were reduced to UK$1 per hour after 6:00 PM, when many hospital departments were closed. For private sector service, a lower evening price, when there is not much demand from customers, and plenty of spare capacity, it quite common. But is it right that a hospital should only charges lower prices at the not busy time when much of the hospital itself is closed? If lower prices are designed to stimulate additional demand, it this a realistic prospect when many hospital departments are only available between 9:00 AM to 5:00 PM? Another source of revenue exploited by many hospital trusts from the use of bedside telephones by patients. Many trusts entered agreements with private telephone service providers which allowed incoming and outgoing patient calls only through the officially appointed system, which used a premium rate number.

A proportion of the revenue was retained by the hospital. Conveniently, hospital trusts pointed to evidence that mobile phones could harm sensitive medical equipment , and therefore used this to eliminate competitive pressure from patients' mobile phones, forcing them to use the hospital's own telephone system. The ethic of hospital telephone pricing was challenged by the House of Commons Health Select Committee, which accused some trusts of using excessively outgoing call, adding to patients' costs, and boosting hospital revenue. It cited a hospital in Essex where people wishing to telephone patients were being charges 49p per minute at peak time and 39p off peak. By comparison , a typical household rate for a long distance phone call was around 7p in the peak and 2p in the off peak. The select committee also expressed doubts about whether a ban on mobile phones in hospitals was actually a result of possible interference with medical equipment and recommend visitors should be able to use mobile phone within certain areas of hospitals. So, it seems that UK private hospitals patients phone calling service fee is below than householder phone calling service fee and it is not every patient must need to use phone when who stays in hospital as well as the visitors should able to use mobile phones and who should not use hospital phones within certain areas of hospital, who will not interference with medial equipment. Otherwise, by banning mobile phones, had private hospitals been more concerned about creating a monopoly environment for pricing their telephone service, than any possible risk to their equipment? However, I think National health service (NHS) which is one public government assistant hospital, it can not be same to private hospital to charge unreasonable car parking fee or hospital phone service fee to its patients, due to these ancillary services is not hospital main income source and it is one non profit hospital, it needs to provide the fair and non expensive medial charges to its poor patient segment because who are not rich, so who will prefer to choose NHS medical service to compare to choose private hospital services in United Kingdom.

National health service (NHS) is a privatization, fragmentation and market competition of health care provision supposedly to cut costs and improve the efficiency of the health service in England. The NHS was set up in 1948 year to be a free and accessible care, publicly owned and funded sector service in England. NHS needs to consider to redefine its relationship with health service, limiting the quality and quantity of care it can expect to receive, how it access that care, who is delivering if and even how it is paid for. The result will be poorer, fragmented services with larger differences in quality and access. Services/treatments will cost more and the public will increasingly have to pay for aspects of its care that used to be free at the time of treatment. Traditionally privatization has been through the sale of public assets and services to private owners through the mass sale of shares, e.g. the sale of telecoms, railways, energy or water services. These companies than own the services and are able to make profits from them like any other are able private businesses. In the NHS until now, this model of privatization is taking place through a combination of the reduction of the role of government in regulating health provision, the transfer of services to the private sector through commissioning from any qualified providers, such as independent sector treatment care centers, outsourcing of parts of services to the private sector, the creation of market mechanisms for the distribution of funding within the NHS (e.g. commissioning, payment by results mechanisms, the purchaser-provider split and so called patient choice policies). The use of private finance initiatives that use private money to build new buildings and infrastructure and then the state has to pay, the creation of foundation trusts that are run much more like private businesses and have the ability to raise funding through private patients that pay for services, allowing services to become not for profit organizations, such as social enterprises, cooperatives or mutual and thus leave public ownership, limiting access to certain services previously provided by the NHS. Provided healthcare tends to cost more. It requires a large bureaucracy to operate, with huge transaction costs that come with contracts, billing and litigation. In general, as the proportion of private spending on health care rises, so does the overall cost.

The creation of healthcare market can also impact upon the continuity of care people receive. There is always the threat that the private sectors or other providers who take on a service that doesn't secure the expected financial returns may cut losses and withdraw from the provision of that service. NHS is under increasing financial pressure. For example, surgery like hip and knee replacements are more expensive areas of care, the results cause the loss of training opportunities for junior doctors expenditure spending and other health professionals as ever large shares of routine surgery and medical procedures are diverted away from the NHS. Centers for research and medical innovations are also threatened. This can lead to service being out. NHS hospitals will therefore fail financially and be pushed into greater debt. This could lead to hospital mergers, closure or the private sector coming in to run the service on profit making contracts. NHS will bring poor health care service if it will not increase its service charge price to patients. The poor service will be caused, such as permanent damage may have been inflicted on patients with serious conditions due to the lack of follow up care after treatments. In a second worrying example dangerous delays affected the patients of a privatized out of hours. A competitive market system leads to greater rationing and gradually drives patients to take on more responsibility for funding their own care. It seems this already in the privatization of long term care and dentistry. Patients may soon have to top up the cost of their hospital care in the same way that many already do for community health services. The concern is that the NHS will provide a less comprehensive range of treatments. For the private sector, the aim is to make a profit from every contracts, which is not the same as providing the best service . For example, Southern Cross, where the need to make profit lead to the rapid closure of care homes, leaving old people with no home. Hospital people with learning disabilities and challenging behavior were subject to physical and psychological abuse. Privatization will lead to fragmentation of the health services. This is a process on a commercial footing and redesigning the system along market lives. With different organizations delivering different service in different locations, it is also likely to lead a new health service with some area receiving much better care than others, hardest, leading to greater health inequalities. Fragmentation of services leads to worse clinical outcomes as staff have less opportunity to work in a fully integrated dynamic multi disciplinary team. Patients with complex needs can be particularly considerable.

The impact of privatization on current NHS staff, who are transferred from NHS employment to non NHS organizations would be changed terms and conditions at the time of transfer. These terms and conditions could be changes at some time in the future, staff would no longer be covered by the national negotiating arrangement in the NHS, meaning they would not be entitled to any future pay uplifts or agreed charges to the change terms and conditions of service . If staff moved from this employer to another outsourced community service, who would lose their entitlement to access the NHS pension scheme and would be treated as new staff rather then former NHS staff, the new service provider could argue that the service who will be providing is so different that they will not be requiring staff to transfer. Those staff will than be made redundant. In conclusion, NHS is one public medical service non profit organization. It's pricing model ought be public service price model, such as no price discrimination and non competitor based pricing aim. It may be difficult or undesirable to implement a straightforward price-value relationship with individual of public services for a number of reasons: Such as NHS public sector medical service pricing can be actively used as a means of social policy, subsidized prices are often used to favor particular patient segment groups, such as car parking fee charges to visitors or hospital staffs only as well as hospital phone system service charges to visitors only or prescription medical service charges favor the very ill and unemployed patients and low income patients and students patients.

2. What factors should influence the level of charges at an NHS car park?

Principles for fair hospital car parking, such as NHS is important because its car park service represents the hospital reputation. Charging for car parking is often necessary, but needs to be fair, providing a travel plan for users of all types of transport, controlling parking fairly, with concession for those whose health conditions or work commitments mean they have to park frequently or at anti social hours, showing car park and transport costs and how charges are invested, thinking about the environment and how transport can reduce the NHS 's impact , being open and involve patients and the public. It is important to get car parking and transport policy and it is communication, right to ensure fair access, good patient and staff experience and to protect hospital organization , such as NHS reputation. Clinical and social changes as car ownership to patients, staff and visitors to hospital sites has increased. For services with rural or urban , as public transport infrastructure is less convenient and reliable . When for specialist treatment, some patients need to travel greater distance and modern hospitals have often been located on the edge of population centres.

Car parking is also a factor in patient's experience of using healthcare. When much progress has been achieves to improve the patient environment inside the hospital, including cleanliness and new buildings, patients frequently report dissatisfaction with transport and parking arrangement. Visitors concerns both cost of car parking and also the availability of space for people with an essential need, illustrating the competing demands that managers need to balance. Patient experience is an important objective for hospitals; poor experiences can undermine confidence in clinical quality and stress can be worsened by poor transport and parking policies. Car parking can have a major impact on the local and national reputation of the NHS hospital . As patient choice increases, reputation and loyalty will be key drivers for provider's commercial sustainability. It seems car parking is one important factor to influence patients who choose hospital more than location/ transport/ easy to get to/ reputation of consultants factors. Ensuring that patients can access hospital when they need to is an important part of healthcare delivery. Many patients who need to travel to hospital by car, either because of mobility or illness, a lock of alternatives or through choice. However, providing a car park is not the only component of a travel plan. Access to healthcare should be considered in terms of service planning, decisions on location of services, building design, access routes and the other transport modes. One of the factor of the current changes to the way that NHS hospital services are delivered is that healthcare should be localized where possible. In many cases, people who used to have to travel to hospital are being treated in community health centers. The NHS hospital can also ensure services are accessible. Most notably, ease of access has recently been improved by reducing waiting times and by enabling patients to choose and book their appointment at a time and location that is convenient to them. Another of factor is whether NHS hospital had or had not ran a bus service from a nearby park and ride car park that runs every 15 minutes. The service has proved popular and is now run by the UK country council.

The hospital is been to extend the shuttle service to the other three park and ride car parks which serve the city. The other factor influences NHS hospital charge includes the control parking fairly with concessions for those whose health conditions or work commitments mean they have to park frequently or at anti-social ours. In order to ensure that those patients who really need to access hospital by car are able to NHS often need to ensure that car parking space is available on site. Space is usually constrained, NHS hospital is in city or town center with high land costs and planning constraints. Charging some patients, visitors and staff to park can manage demand for space when ensuring that those who really need to park are able to access services. Where charging is required to manage demand, the overriding principle should be to ensure that where possible those patients who have the greatest need to park are prioritized. Where managing demand is a reason for charging for car parking, there may be scope for varying rates for different times of the day and the week, for example, increasing charges for non essential users in peak hours but applying a minimal charge at night when there is less reason to ration space. As well as prioritizing car access for those with greatest needs restrictions on car parking may also be required to deter non hospital traffic, particularly where NHS hospital is located in controlled parking zones, near shopping centers or other facilities that might need to illegitimate required use of NHS hospital grounds. In these cases , NHS hospital may be required to be charge the same as local car parks to avoid abuse by non visitors. However, alternative arrangement could also be explored, including day permits for people with appointment. NHS car parking fair policies should need to be fair application. This is often a cause of concern for patients and visitors.

Concessionary schemes and season tickets should be well publicized and available, since a patient may not known in advance low frequently who will need to attend a clinic in the next month. Penalty charges, or towing away should only be applied extreme circumstances with a presumption of good faith that no patient or visitor chooses to stay in hospital longer than necessary and may how on arrival how long who will have to wait for treatment. Running a car park can be expensive. These are maintenance, security, insurance and running costs and the NHS hospital has to pay for the space the car park uses. Costs are particularly high where land prices are high or there is increased risk of crime. At the same time, patients and the public rightly don't expect healthcare to suffer to pay for parking.

The transport costs of non car owners are not subsidized by the NHS budgets to provide subsidized free car parks . To make car parking fee would be to penalize those using public transport. Therefore, fair charging is often the most sensible answer to adopt these two demands. Climate charge and pollution and congestion factor also have health impacts. Reducing car dependency is also a public health objective in order to reduce traffic accidents and increase physical activity.

These NHS organizations have a number of environmental and health reasons to seek to encourage people to use other modes of transport. Parking charge together with the expansion of alternative bus an cycling options to encourage a modal shift from cars to alternative transport. Patients , visitors and staff need to be made aware of these aims. NHS hospital can achieve a travel plan to develop to its car parking with the aim of during a period of busy time reducing single occupancy car journeys by 15% over three years, ensuring tat patients and visitors do not have to search for a space for more than ten minutes at peak times, encouraging the number of direct bus routes to the site to increase reducing staff parking spaces per employee by 10% as staff numbers grow. Car parking charges were introduced as part of the plan with certain categories of staff on exempted from charges (night and weekend staff, disabled staff, volunteers, car sharers and tenants of residential accommodation. From an environmental perspective, NHS travel plan supposed to reduce numbers of cars arriving at the site and the numbers of bus car raise. It aims to improve bus services to cause air pollution at the busy car parking period and cycle parking spaces and improved cycle facilities have encouraged staff to commute by bike. Additionally, a park and ride scheme aims to reduce car traffic of the NHS hospital in the busy time.

Moreover, it is absolutely wrong to charge cancer patients regardless of income, for unavoidable parking costs. From a staff point of view, NHS hospital car parking is an indirect tax on healthcare. However, most unions also support the aim of reducing car usage, as long as policies are fair. Because NHS hospital needs to develop transport policies for patients requiring regular cancer treatment. This approach has potentially negative publicity into a positive image to public. These ought be free parking for the duration of a cancer patient treatment or as often as is needed. So, price structure strategy will be needed to this UK hospital to solve nowadays challenge.

- Outsourcing service Strategy solves Unversity cost raising challenges

If you are studying at a university or college, critically reflect on the pricing strategy that it has adopted for ancillary services.

The development of a costing and pricing strategy will provide an university staff with greater access to price information, thereby providing a more accessible platform from which to base negotiations with commercial organizations. As prices will be informed by cost, the university will be seeking to apply pricing strategies that maximize university as opposed to maximizing income. In fact, any universities is education industry which is different to common businesses which provide service or product to raise price when client numbers are increasing easily. Due to if an university which planed to increase school fee to charge students, which needed have unique courses to attract students to choose to study and its lecturers educational experiences and education methods needed to make student to raise learning interest and feel the courses are useful to choose to study the university subjects, so who shall compare the university subjects to other universities subjects, then to evaluate their school fees and lectures educational experiences and qualifications to decide whether who ought to choose the university or another university to study. So, I believe that the university can not raise its school fee easily if it has no more confident its subjects and lecturers which can make students to study to feel more satisfactory till to graduate. Otherwise, it will reduce student admission numbers if it still increase school fees, due to it has not researched what the subject contents are students who like to learn. Hence, any universities can't increase its school fee easily.

However, university ancillary services have primary paths to reduce internal cost to raise competitive advantages, such as services differentiation, low internal cost or internal span structural advantage. I shall recommend these price strategy to adopt to reflect some university ancillary service (non major) service. The pursuit of a service differentiation strategy to an university advantages. The university needs truly understanding its unique core service (value) and then focusing resources on its ancillary services. An implicit part of having a focused price strategy is not only defining what the university is going to invest in, but is also clearly articulating what the university is no going to do. For example, if the university investigated its students did not like to eat some foods taste, which ought to change some foods taste which could satisfy its students eating needs in its university canteens. Even the university could charge cheaper student parking fee to compare outside public car parks when they park their cars in university parks from the morning to afternoon studying busy time. It could only permit students to park their cars in its students private car parks. Hence, university staffs and visitors could not permit to drive whose cars to park in university private student car parks, so university staffs could park whose cars in university staffs car parks as well as visitors could park whose cars in university visitors car parks. However, who also needed to pay cheaper parking fee to compare outside public car parks to buy car park tickets to park their cars in university staffs and visitors both car parks in any limited time. Even, the university book shop could sell lower second hand books and new books prices to compare other private book shops to attract students to choose to buy studying books from university bookshops. However, if the university tried to pursue too many areas of service differentiation, which was likely to invest too broadly and thus reduced the return on investment for previous capital possibly because it needed time to research whether which aspects of it needed to change to adopted students tastes to satisfy their needs, then it needed time to change its services and it also needed time to evaluate whether it's changed services which can satisfy its students demand to make decision to raise its service prices. Hence, it ought concentrate on changing one aspect of ancillary service to ensure it's changing was right to adopt students' taste to attempt to raise service price. Then, it could attempt to evaluate whether what ancillary services which needed to change to achieve price raising possibility. University recognizes that focusing on the core is hard to do, given the history and culture of university. But the worst case scenario for an university is to be relatively expensive and completely undifferentiated. Whether will who pay high school fee per year to go to an university that is completely undistinguished on any ancillary service?

An university looks to areas where which can make cuts and achieves efficiencies, an university should start farthest from the core of teaching and research ancillary services. Cutting from the outside in and building from the inside out. Growth in programs and research, increasing faculty and student demands and increasingly compliance requirements have all contributed to the growth of administrative costs. The reasons are often very legitimate. But as new programs are added, old programs often are closed down in some university ancillary services, e.g. unimportant administration internal service . The resulting breadth of campus activities creates too much complex it for staffs to manage with any efficiencies of scale in university. Units don't trust one another or the center to provide ancillary services. Data center management is a good example of fragmentation on campus. At the university, the central information technology group managed fewer than half of the servers on campus in its data center. For the servers located in the colleges, fewer than half were managed by college information technology groups, the rest were considered hidden at the department or faculty level. Despite the internet data and security risk of having too many unmanaged serves on campus in the university's central information technology department. In similar cases, outsourcing data centers would be a good solution. Third party data centers could provide more solutions, higher levels of securing, greater flexibility in capacity and lower cost than internal solution. Redundancy, an university is an many other campuses, it was managed at the department level, there were no product standards and each department negotiated its own vendor contracts. A sample of purchase order showed that the same item was being bought for as much as e.g. 36% more in some departments than in others. By centralizing end, standardizing more if its procurement to expect to save more expenditure. An university hierarchy, most campuses have too many middle managers. Before it reorganized , an university has average spans of control (the number of employment). Campuses engage to save cost. An university campuses engage in too many activities that require to broad a skill set to effectively deliver in house. Take information technology application management for example, not only does it need to support classrooms and research needs across a diverse set of disciplines (history, music, law, engineering, biomedical science etc. different subjects), it also has to cover functions (finance, human resource, research, administration, student registrar, libraries and student services etc. functions). It weren't enough, information technology also has to serve industries beyond the core academics, including bookstores, retail food, debt cards, total museums, publishing houses. A single IT group would have a hard time managing all it that well, given the expertise required, leading to either poor service delivery, sub scale and costly delivery.

Outsourcing more of non core activities would reduce campus complexity and cost. Third party provides have greater scale capability and skill because the outsourced service is their core business, enabling them to deliver the same or better service at a lower cost. In order to reduce aministrative costs without diminishing service and perhaps even enhancing it's campuses will need to subscale operations by creating shared service or outsourcing improve processes by eliminating low value work and automating much. Better manage university assets to whether it is real estate, physical assets or intellectual property, a number of activities where partnership with third party providers would allow for financial relief and improved performance. Hence, an university can also invest its intellectual property to build its build to raise its market value for long term to raise its sale price for long term.

In conclusion, an university can attempt to use these two kinds of price strategies to adopt to reflect to its ancillary services. Such as the first is competitors price strategy, the university can set its students and visitors and staffs car parking fee by examining what its competitors such as, it's close public car parks are charging their car parking fee services whether they are similar in terms of the university car parking service characteristics fee to satisfy its parking car users' needs as well as the university can set its canteens meals price by examining what its competitors, such as it's close private outside restaurants meals price whether they are similar or different taste and low meal price to attract students or staffs or visitors to choose to eat their meals . The another is demand based pricing strategy, the students are prepared to pay represents the upper limit book numbers to the university's every year studying books. Such as the university book shops can decide every years different subject second hand or new teaching books price to follow the students demand. For example, if the subject second hand or new teaching books supply numbers is less than the student demand numbers, the university can raise the subject books sale price. Otherwise, if the subject second hand or new teaching books supply numbers is more than the student demand numbers, the university needs to reduce the subject books sale price, even it needs to reduce their prices to be lower than outside other private book shops marketing price to sell in the year. Hence, it seems that any universities can adapt price strategy to reflect to their services or products prices.

● Outsoucing service strategy can help this university to solve staff management challenge.

When you are one university entrepreneur how you manage university leaders to raise excellent management performance. Frances Workman could own those above personal trait leadership characteristics to do this Willard University president job successfully. For example, Frances workman has been president of Willard University for less than two years. Frances had been an excellent speaker and used every opportunity to speak to citizen groups as well as who also worked hard to build good relationship with the major politicians and business leaders and who managed to maintain favourable relationship with most. Frances had proved to own a trait leader's personality ability, such as intelligence and verbal fluency, self confidence and interpersonal skill. Frances was an achievement drive leader, such as France could lobbied legislature and the Willard Universitycoordinating board for a larger share of higher education budget dollars. In the result, Frances could build favourable image to efforts to increase funding for Willard University within two years, as well as Frances president, could build a positive image to people and let them to build a positive image to people and let them to build a positive image of Willard University . The results of whose efforts included an increase in enrolment of more in the last year.

This occurred when most other colleges enrolments were also decreasing as well as $2 million dollars outside funds were donated to Willard University and faculty morale was higher in the first year. Hence, Frances could judge and adapt and dominance and was tolerance for stress to deal new issue to achieve this Willard University aim successfully within two years. It proved that Frances owned trait leadership style. However, Frances was seemed to be employee centre leadership style president, it meant a behavioural leadership style that emphasised employees' personal needs and the development of interpersonal relationships and a employee centre leader frequently delegated decision making authority and responsibility to others and provided a supportive environment, encouraging interpersonal communication. For example, Frances president, concentrated on handling external matters and who delegated the responsibility for daily internal operations to whose three major vice presidents. Hence, Frances could build concentrate on building positive image to public people and let them to build a positive image of Willard University. Finally,Frances could help Willard University to increase student enrolment numbers of

more in the last year and $2 million outside funds were donated to Willard University and faculty morale was higher in the first year. Otherwise, this occurred when most other college enrolments were also decreasing. Thus, it proved Frances Workman leadership skill was successfully. Secondly, based on information provided, Alvin Thomas was lack trait theory of leadership style personal characteristics, who was not such as self esteem and dominance, whose ability was not such as intelligence and non verbal fluency, non judgement, non adaptability, non enthusiasm, non achievement drive, lack self confidence , non tolerance for stress and non interpersonal skill. Hence, Alvin Thomas lacked trait leadership style to do Eastern State University president successfully. For example, Alvin Thomas had been president as Eastern State University about three years, who was not as popular externally as Frances and who was not a particularly effective speaker. Hence, it proved Alvin Thomas was not a verbal fluency and lack interpersonal
skill president.

suggestion of solvable method:

Based on the information provides, describe France's and AI's leadership styles.

Leadership means the process of providing general direction and influencing individuals or groups to achieve goals. Formal leader can be formally designated by the organization or informal leader can provide leadership without such formal designation. Leader needs to lead group, team and social processes can directly or indirectly affect behaviour in organizations. The behaviour of leader has positive effects to link between leadership and organizational performance and who needs have developed a vision as well as specific goals to whose organization. Leadership styles (traits) that have been identified as important include flexibility and creativity, especially because of the importance of innovation to leader whose organization. Firstly, based on information provided, France's was belonged to trait theory of leadership style, trait leadership style includes those personality characteristics, leader was such as self esteem and dominance; leader's ability was such as intelligence and verbal fluency, judgement, adaptability, enthusiasm, achievement drive, self confidence, tolerance for stress and interpersonal skill. Frances Workman could own those above personal trait leadership characteristics to do this Willard University president job successfully. For example, Frances workman has been president of Willard University for less than two years. Frances had been an excellent speaker and used every opportunity to speak to citizen groups as well as who also worked hard to build good relationship with the major politicians and business leaders and who managed to maintain favourable relationship with most. Frances had proved to own a trait leader's personality ability, such as intelligence and verbal fluency, self confidence and interpersonal skill. Frances was an achievement drive leader, such as France could lobbied legislature and the Willard Universitycoordinating board for a larger share of higher education budget dollars. In the result, Frances could build favourable image to efforts to increase funding for Willard University within two years, as well as Frances president, could build a positive image to people and let them to build a positive image to people and let them to build a positive image of Willard University . The results of whose efforts included an increase in enrolment of more in the last year. This occurred when most other colleges enrolments were also decreasing as well as $2 million dollars outside funds were donated to Willard University and faculty morale was higher in the first year. Hence, Frances could judge and adapt and dominance and was tolerance for stress to deal new issue to achieve this Willard University aim successfully within two years. It proved that Frances owned trait leadership style. However, Frances was seemed to be employee centre leadership style president, it meant a behavioural leadership style that emphasised employees' personal needs and the development of interpersonal relationships and a employee centre leader frequently delegated decision making authority and responsibility to others and provided a supportive environment, encouraging interpersonal communication. For example, Frances president, concentrated on handling external matters and who delegated the responsibility for daily internal operations to whose three major vice presidents. Hence, Frances could build concentrate on building positive image to public people and let them to build a positive image of Willard University. Finally,Frances could help Willard University to increase student enrolment numbers of more in the last year and $2 million outside funds were donated to Willard University and faculty morale was higher in the first year. Otherwise, this occurred when most other college enrolments were also decreasing. Thus, it proved Frances Workman leadership skill was successfully. Secondly, based on information provided, Alvin Thomas was lack trait theory of leadership style personal characteristics, who was not such as self esteem and dominance, whose ability was not such as intelligence and non verbal fluency, non judgement, non adaptability, non enthusiasm, non achievement drive, lack self confidence , non tolerance for stress and non interpersonal skill. Hence, Alvin Thomas lacked trait leadership style to do Eastern State University president successfully. For example, Alvin Thomas had been president as Eastern State University about three years, who was not as popular externally as Frances and who was not a particularly effective speaker. Hence, it proved Alvin Thomas was not a verbal fluency and lack interpersonal skill president.

A path goal leadership theory focuses on several types of leader behaviour and situation factors as well as Directive leadership behaviour is characterized by implementing guideline, providing information on what is expected, setting definite performance standards and ensuring individuals follow the rules. Participative leadership behaviour is characterized by sharing information, consulting with those whose who are led and emphasizing group decision making. However, Alvin Thomas was seemed to be job centre leadership style president, it emphasises employer tasks and the methods used to accomplish them. A job centre leader supervises individuals closely , provides instructions, checks frequently on performance and sometimes behaves in a punitive manner toward them. For example, who did not spend much time dealing with the external affairs of the University, who delegated much of that responsibility to one vice president. Hence, who spent much of whose time working on the internal operation of the University and less of whose time working on the external affairs. Although, who delegated much of responsibility to one vice president to assist who to do external affairs, but Eastern State University's a large number of students still without adequate faulty and it was not involved in externally funded research as well as although, who spent much time dealing with the internal operation of the University and who was committed to develop a quality University, but who did not change the administrative structure of the University within three years. He seemed to lack leadership skill. For example, who planned to give responsibility to one vice president and who had high performance expectation to them, set ambitious, goals and reviewed every significant decision made in the University and replying heavily on whose vice president to implement them effectively and who developed planning system and maintained good relations with University board. Hence, who often needed to supervise whose every vice presidents to deal external affairs closely and provided instructions, checked frequently on their every performance within those three years. But, Eastern State University student enrolment numbers declined slightly by almost 300 students and Eastern State University record was removed from American association of University professors, externally funded research had increased by approximately by $2 million dollars during the previous year, even faculty morale was declining and most faculty members did not believe who had an important voice in the administration of the University. However, who spent much of his time working on the internal operation of the University, but faculty morale was declining and most faculty members did not believe who had an important voice in the administration of the University as well as who could not lead to the one vice president and who also could not provide instructions and checked whose performance how to deal external affairs correctly. Hence, it implied that whose leadership skill was not successful within these three years.

What are the important factors that the leaders of Willard and Eastern must consider in order to be effective?

The important factors that the leaders of Willard University and Eastern State University must consider in order to be effective as below:

Outsoucing service strategy can help this university to solve staff management challenge. The Eastern State University president, Alvin Thomas both were as their organizations' chief executive officers who were very important given the substantial influence design Universities strategies and overseeing Universities' implementation to lead their vice presidents to deal internal or external affairs efficiently and effectively. Frances Workman and Alvin Thomas both presidents needed to develop a vision for their Universities' units or groups led, who also needed to manage Universities limited resources under their direction to include financial capital, but especially human capital, e.g. vice president and administrator position numbers and who also needed to build valuable interpersonal relationships (social capital) with University staffs and good University images (goodwill) to let current and future students and parents to fell those two Universities goodwill existed in global education market. Hence, both Willard

University and Eastern State University both presidents needed to provide effective leadership that could enhance associates productivity, e.g. Improving lecturers' teaching methods and skills and improving office administrators and service staffs whose service performance to manage human capital well and built and maintained relationships both with whose Universities' different organizations(departments) with internal associates and other leaders ,e.g. vice presidents and externally with alliance partners and colleges and universities.Those two university presidents ought need to criticize if their universities didn't meet their goals or their university teams have a losing reason. Hence, these two university presidents needed to revise their performance to find why their universities could not achieve their goals and they needed to discuss any meetings to attempt to find any solutions from university boards every year. These two university presidents (leaders) needed to provide direction and to influence all universities staffs during who begun to do their new jobs and during who were doing their new jobs, who needed to attempt to do these activities effectively, e.g. providing useful information (guidelines) to assist vice presidents how to carry on dealing their external and internal affairs, resolving conflicts, motivating followers, anticipating problems, developing mutual respect among groups (university departments)members and coordinating groups (departments) activities and efforts. It aimed to revise what presidents do activities were not effective and then they could know what activities who needed to change to discuss with vice presidents to find solutions more effectively.These two university presidents also needed to build leader member relations, it meant the degree to which a leader was respected and was accepted as a leader and had friendly interpersonal relations. If these two presidents could build friendly interpersonal relations to their colleges, such as vice presidents, administrators etc senior staffs. It would increase these staffs confidence and assistance to these two presidents further the years. Thus, if these two universities' presidents could attempt to change their management attitude to their colleagues (staffs), special senior position staffs, then I believed that they could lead their universities' different teams (departments) to work more effectively.

In fact, not all people in positions that call for leader behaviour, e.g. management positions. A manager who follows rules and fails to provide direction to and support for whose associates is not acting as a leader.The measuring the effectiveness of leaders factors include productivity, job satisfaction, absenteeism, turnover rates of staffs being led. Thus, the presidents of these two universities needed to consider how to lead whose staffs to work effectively in order to achieve their universities' aim every year. Otherwise, these two presidents would be only a manager role who only followed universities' rules to work, but who did not provided direction to and supported to their associates effectively. Hence, who would not acting as a leader role. Any leaders who need have leadership traits characteristics include that driver refers to the amount ambition; leadership motivation refers to a person's desire to lead and influence others; assuming responsibility; leaders with honesty are truthful what they say and what they do; leaders must be confident in their actions and showing that confidence to other; leaders who posses a high degree of intelligence are better able to process complex information and deal with changing environments and these two presidents(leaders) of this two universities needed to prepare management knowledge of the domain in which who were engaged allows who to make better decisions and prepared to anticipate future their universities internal and external issues and understood the implications of their colleges, e.g. vice president actions easily.

Compare and contrast France's and AI's effectiveness as leaders of their respective Universities .

In fact, Willard University president Frances Workman ,whose leadership was more effective than Eastern State University president Alvin Thomas performance. The reasons were that Frances had worked in Willard University for less than two year, who could deal external issues and internal structure of the organization, administrative component effectively. For example, Frances had started a new alumni club to help finance academic needs, such as new library facilities and higher salaries for faculty and staff successfully. In addition, who lobbies legislative and the university coordinating board for a larger share of higher education budget dollars. In the result, her favourable image to efforts to increase funding for Willard University. Frances could concentrate on handling external matters and who delegated the responsibility for internal operations to her three major vice presidents.However, before Frances arrival, this university had several presidents, but none of whom could manage university's internal affairs effectively. Due to the lack of leadership resulted in low faculty morale, which affected student enrolment to cause university had a poor public image. Otherwise, after Frances arrival, who could build a positive image to people and let them to build a positive image of Willard University. The results of whose efforts include an increase in enrolment of more in the last year. This occurred when other colleges enrolments were also decreasing. Hence, Willard University had a serious competition to it's competitors and $2 million dollars outside funds were donated to Willard University and faculty morale were higher in the first year. Otherwise, another Eastern State university, had Alvin Thomas as president who had been president about three years longer than France's working period and who was not as popular externally as Frances, who was not a particularly effective speaker and did not spend much time dealing with the external affairs of the university, who delegated much of that responsibility to one vice president, who did work with external groups but in a quieter may than Frances did and who spent much of his time working on the internal operation of the university. However, who led this university poorly and the Eastern State University had these problems which included a large number of students without adequate faculty; it was not involved in externally funded research. Although, who was committed to develop a quality university, but who did not change the internal operational administrative structure of this university from his one vice president successfully. In fact, State University still had more students than Willard University, but its student enrolment declined slightly by almost 300 students after Alvin Thomas started to manage this university. Although, Alvin Thomas had high performance expectations to staffs, set ambitious goals and reviewed every significant decision made in the university and replying heavily on whose one vice president to implement them effectively and who developed planning system and maintained good relations with university board. However, State University record was removed from American association of university professors, although, externally funded research had increased by approximately $2 million dollars only during whose three years working periods; but faculty morale was declining and most faculty members did not believe who had an important voice in the administration of the university. Hence, Alvin Thomas who could not lead faculty staffs built confidence to continue to serve this university and who could not raise public had confident its lecturers whose educational quality and performance.

What did each do well?

The Willard University president, Frances Workman who performed more well to compare another Eastern State University president, Alvin Thomas as below:

France had performed as an excellent speaker and used every opportunity to speak to citizen groups as well as who also worked hard to build good relationship with the major politicians and business leaders and who managed to maintain favourable relationship with most. Hence, who could build favourable image to efforts to increase funding for Willard University within two years. Frances knew whose strengths, so who concentrated on handling external matters and who delegated the responsibility for daily internal operations to whose three major vice presidents.

In conclusion, who was an effective leader to lead three vice presidents and the student numbers were also increasing largely and Willard University and faculty morale was higher in the first year during Frances had worked in the university within two years.

The Eastern State University president, Alvin Thomas could not perform well within three years. Although,who did not spend much time dealing with the external affairs of the university and who delegated much of that responsibility to one vice president to deal external affairs, so who could spend much of whose time working on the internal operations and less of whose time working on external affairs. However, Eastern State University's a large number of students still without adequate faculty and it was not involved in externally funded research and who did not change the administrative structure during Alvin had worked in the university three years. In the result, student enrolment numbers declined slightly by almost 300 students and university record was removed from American association of university professors, even faculty morale was declining and most faculty numbers did not believe who had an important voice in the administration of the university. Hence, who only knew how to delegate to give responsibility to only one vice president to deal internal operations and who concentrated on dealing external affairs alone. However, externally funded research had increased by approximately by $2 million dollars during the previous year. In conclusion, Alvin Thomas could not lead whose teams to deal external affairs and internal operations effectively to compare to Frances Workman, who only helped university to give funded research $2 million amount increased, but who could not build good university image and raised department administration efficiency effectively within these three year.

What could each have done to be more effective?

I should recommend these methods to raise these both university presidents Alvin and Frances whose leadership who each could have done to be more effectively. It would be divided internal operations and external affairs two aspects:

On the dealing external affairs hand, they needed have clear external marketing and communication strategic plan. It aimed to create marketing, communication and branding strategies that maximize demand for these two universities' degree course programs to persuade many external parties (donors) to donate more to support them. First, they could oversee the editorial direction, design and production of all publications, universities web properties, social media initiatives, advertising and media with a goal of creating dynamic and engaging materials that reflected the key brand attributed of these both universities.Second, they needed to lead crisis and issues management planning and rapid response messaging to deal strategic counsel on reputation and issues management to senior leadership.

Third, they needed set strategy for marketing, communication, advertising and promotions to ensure that all messages from their universities were accurate, consistent and presented a image and they needed to built partner with university leaderships to generate innovative ideas and solutions to engage donors. Fourth, they needed to oversee the development and execution of their strategies for their universities' interactive and social media programs and supervised the development and deployment of web/social media sites aimed at enhancing their universities' brands and reputation as well as they needed to lead a diverse team of web producers, graphic designers, project managers, marketing and editorial writers, media specialists to provide mentorship to staffs both in terms of departmental strategies. Aimed to increase donation chances and student numbers for long term.Fifth, they needed to cultivate strong working relationships with staff faculty and students across their universities and they also needed to raise the value of the Willard University and Eastern State University and effective studying market to present whose universities' history (stories) to know.They could attempt to use these communication medias (channels), social media e.g. university magazines, radio or television advertisements and other forms of digital communication. Proven success at developing and implementing online and social media strategies to enhance visibility and engagement and loyalty.The most important, their vice presidents also needed to appreciate for their universities' history, achievement and aspirations of Willard and Eastern State Universities and the ability to effectively articulate whose presidents' vision to diverse external audiences as well as who also needed to have ability to synthesize complex information and produced marketing and communication materials that addressed a wide variety of goals and objectives as well as they also needed to have excellent judgement and creative problems and solving skills including negotiation and conflict resolution as well as who also needed have confidence to project credibility to the media and other strategic stakeholders.Moreover, these two university presidents needed to prepare enough resources to provide, e.g. strategies, media communication channel, excellent leadership skill and effective human resources. The, these two presidents(leaders) could have more ability to attempt to perform more effective for their job duties.

These two universities presidents' fundraising responsibilities were creation and communication of a vision for their universities. Thus, they should temper whose ideas and goals to match the overall fundraising potential of their universities. The fund donors wanted to know about their presidents' vision and their universities; strategic direction along with the resources their universities needed to get.

Conversations between these presidents and prospective major donors and who would focus on what the donors wanted whose gift to accomplish. It is important to listen to the donors rather than drive hard. Fundraising included not only such factors as having a clear vision for these two universities and strategic priorities that would be reason with prospective donors and afforded sufficient fundraising potential, but also possessing a professional staff with the expertise and budget to get job along and a commitment was from the president of their time and energy to lead the campaign to successful completion. Seeking external fundraising counsel was often very useful to these two universities. Hence, these two presidents should also recognize that the long term nature of donor relationships was that who existed between the donor and their universities, not with these two presidents personally due to these presidents, academic deans, faculty members and professional fundraising staffs were agents role acting on behalf of their universities. On the dealing internal operational affairs hand, If these two university presidents were going to spend most of their time leading, then who needed to recruit others to do the managing. They needed to put together a group of managers to every university departments, e.g. administration, marketing and communication, finance and accounting ,student service, education etc departments. It aimed to let every department had a manager (leader) to lead their teams to adopt every department sudden changing in any time. After appointed these staffs, they must be delegated to deal as much of the problem solving. Moreover, their universities‘ committee chairing also needed to be delegated to avoid to deal extra internal operations with detail and caused to have too little time to perform the key function of setting the target and motivating people for their main duties. To lead change successfully, these both university presidents needed an effective decision making structure that could respond rapidly to internal and external affairs and pressures. It meant making the decision making structures needed to become less hierarchal and complex. Many changes were failure because the vision and the strategies were not adequately communicated to the staffs to get whose commitment and support to achieve organizational success effectively.They also needed effective communication strategy for their universities, normal methods of communication,internal newspapers, meetings with deans and heads of universities which were all important. Moreover, they also needed to visit other universities and departments regularly, held informal meetings with small groups of senior staffs, recruits and other natural groupings.These two universities also needed to considerate how to evaluate staff performance to compensate them to feel fairly.The new systems of appraisal method, including 360 degree assessment for senior management and promotion which together linked the work of individuals much more directly to their key university objectives also be needed to be achieve. So, these two universities needed to appraise individuals and units and vice presidents were needed to motivate by recognising and rewarding achievement and who were not compensated not only by praise and status but also by money and these two universities also needed to allocate resources which would always be scare to units and to individuals on a performance related basis.Assuming to these two universities academic were responsible for academic affairs when their presidents and administration practiced a centralized management of all resources and planning decision, it meant that their universities' departments needed to share and allocate their duties clearly. So, new ways were needed to facilitate this process of change possible and to avoid the risk.

The introduction of a supportive evaluation system, aiming at identifying not only areas of excellence, but critical situations as well, in order to get possible solutions for their whole universities‘ departments as well as the introduction of a new goal oriented approach in administration and the linkage of the expansion of the administrative staffs to goals.I suggested that their universities' organizations of the administrative structure needed a clear definition of functions and responsibilities to match the newly focussed objectives and general development plans, such as there would be no faculties, but quite large academic departments whose heads would report to vice presidents directly. Hence, university heads needed to change their duties, as the vice president was responsible for academic affairs and external relations as well as the chef executives (presidents) was responsible for finance, human resources and other internal management activities. For example, one of the largest tasks was to devise a combined programme of undergraduate and postgraduate courses.It was also necessary to plan and implemented new administration systems for finance, human resources, student records, libraries, computer systems websites etc. It meant that these would be in overlap of some services and staffs. It was decided that the new reorganizations would have two heads for an interim periodand to follow a process, e.g. offering job sharing or alternative jobs to staffs displaced. It aimed to reduce their universities‘ expenditures. They then had to be challenged to consider realistically what the new department should become, what was needed to make that new vision become reality and what might need to realise the vision and ensured it made an impact externally. The reason of this new vision needed to be considered immediately was that it provided a structure, a focus to planning and stopped development where staffs were focus on the negative aspects of change. There was a range of internal and external relationships that had to be managed reorganization. If the department was viewed as the internal structures, their universities themselves presented a whole range of relationships for the department to negotiate. Then there were the further external alliances and partnership outside their universities that needed to be developed.

In conclusion, if these two universities presidents could reorganize their universities' internal departments operational structure and built clear goals and objectives to let internal departments to know as well as who could change personal attitude and found consultants to assist them to promote their image to let public had more confidence to their universities' education and courses quality. Then, their donations and student enrolment numbers would be caused to increase further possibly.

Building effective organizational international communication strategy solves broadcasting television department cooperation challenge

- upward communication strategy solves
broadcasting television department
communication challenge

When you are one television company entrepreneur, how you manage your television film and movie teams work efficiently. KBTZ was a large television station in United States. It was one of the largest revenue producers in its entertainment market and employed more than 180 staffs and it was as the local television leader in the use of sophisticated electronic equipment. The station's physical plant was planned to accommodate the new equipment and to boost its image at the leader in the entertainment market. However, its organization development caused much problems to need to solve.

On the one hand, due to external pressure to cause organization change, such as entertainment market competition needed to have high technological new equipment to purchase to provide to different departments to use, e.g. cameras, films etc. equipment. Hence, different department staffs needed to learn how to use these equipment to raise productive performance quality. On the other hand, due to internal pressure to cause organizational change, such as reducing aspiration performance factor was caused poorly in KNTZ organization, which meant gaps was occurred between what an individual, unit or organization wanted to achieve and what it was actually achieving in KTZ organization. Due to KBTZ television station's operational department ,engineering department, programming department, sales department, news department etc. departments which every department individual staff, work group, division or overall KBTZ organization was not meeting its own expectations to adopt KBTZ new organization changes as well as television programming needed new productive tactics to change new strategies and processes often caused follow poor performing individual staffs, units and KBTZ whole organization, which might reduce aspiration levels instead of making changes sufficient to increase performance. Because KBTZ large television station often compared itself with other television stations in the entertainment industry , when comparisons with similar others suggested that better performance was possible. However, KBTZ staffs could not adopt organizational change development suddenly, so it caused many different departments felt difficult co-operation together in KBTZ television station organization. In fact, American television station entertainment industry was encountered by life cycle forces, it meant the natural and predictable pressures that built as to KBTZ television station organization grew and that KBTZ television station must hope to continue growing.

Hence, KBTZ television station was at elaboration stage, it meant KBTZ needed for balance, focused on efficiency and innovation, formal procedures existed and empowered low level
managers and associates in its organization if KBTZ still wanted to keep its large television station position in United States. However, KBTZ 's large television station's physical plant planned to accommodate the new advances equipment to provide different departments staffs to use and to boost its image as the leader in the United States entertainment market. It would cause its staffs feel difficult to adapt to adjust efficient and effective co-operation between departments due to it's planning change caused a process involving deliberate efforts to move KBTZ television station within its organization undesirable state to a new and more desirable state during KBTZ 's organization development was carrying on. Hence, due to its organization development change it would cause these basic problems at KBTZ organization as below:

suggestion of solvable method:

As I was the KBTZ consultant to meet with Valerie Diaz, president and general manager, who explained the key problem as:

The first problem was the high stress to which KBTZ 's manager and associates who felt about time deadlines in television problem, e.g. when it's precisely six o'clock , KBTZ news department staffs must be on the air with the news. All of the news material, local reporting, news, interviews must be processed, edited and ready to go

at six o'clock. This news department staffs felt difficult, due to who could not have any half prepared material extended deadlines to cause lose the KBTZ 's audiences. This situation caused a great deal of conflict and turnover increased, such as a number of well qualified and motivated employees were leaving KBTZ television station. The news department's employee turnover was about 35% which was too high as well as KBTZ also had trouble hiring qualified people who fit their culture and
these new qualified staffs feel difficult to co-operate with KBTZ staffs to cause conflict. It seemed to be team conflict problem.

The second problem was that business manager felt difficult to manage different departments, due to who previously worked in sales and in the general manager's office, but who lacked management training and this was whose first managerial position to help in managing whose departments.
It seemed to be personal difficult management problem.

The third problem seemed the news department and business office and programming department indicated who felt the new director who lacked leadership ability to manage any departments, such as new department managers and associates felt extreme dissatisfaction with the department head, new director who had very negative attitudes toward their overall work environment , new director lacked leadership ability to let news department managers and associates communicate easily. Moreover, news department associates also complained of very low reward, including pay, promotion opportunities and managerial praise and who also complained of constant criticism, which was the only form of managerial feedback on performance. Hence, it implied the new director did not attempt to solve any departments staffs difficulties to adopt new organization change to cause their dissatisfaction and conflict and complaints occurrence to whom. It seemed to be new director personal leadership problem and news departments staffs team communication and individual dissatisfaction problems.

The fourth problem was operations department manager who complained another departments, such as news department staffs, who were confused all of the time and engineering groups, staffs were lazy and who did like cooperation to influence operational department performed ineffectively, due to these groups needed to co-operate to work together. So operations manager suggested me (KBTZ 's consultant) dismissed chief engineer and shaped up (reorganized) the news groups and the engineers groups . It seemed to be difficult co-operation occurred between operations department and engineering and news both departments problem.

The fifth problem was chief engineers who complained the unreasonableness of certain people in other departments. For example, the difficulty indicated that whose team engineers could not immediately repair some malfunctioning equipment in their area and it could take several hours just to determine the cause of the failure. It seemed that engineer department lacked enough engineers and equipment were provided to them to work from operational department . It caused team conflict problem.

The sixth problem was the program director complained the station was missing a lot of opportunities in other areas, e.g. news and sales, the chief engineer was incompetent and operations managers were difficult to motivate low level managers to make any decisions or took any responsibilities . It seemed the program director who felt dissatisfactory to other departments personal performance problem.

The seventh problem was the promotion manger who expected a little training to provide in how to deal with people, innovation and communication problems. It seemed that promotion manager felt difficult to adopt new organization change problem.

The eighth problem was sales department representatives complained who ought to increase salaries due to whose good sale performance. It seemed that sales representatives'
dissatisfactory problem. Finally, the business office and programming department also made one survey to indicate individuals in these departments to have generally positive attitude, such as job satisfaction, but who had two important negative attitude in whose working environment. In general, these low and middle level staffs whose negative attitude of task environment major problem indicated who thought that whose department heads and the general manager could handle downward communication better , it meant that the middle and low level staffs felt the top level managers lacked effective communication to them as well as these were several comments about being underpaid relative to other station employees.

Although, the survey indicated the managers and associates whose high satisfaction, but who also believed that the negative factors led them to be poorly motivated. Such as some low and middle level associates reported that who were not sure who was top level immediate manager , since both the assignments editor and the assistant news director gave them assignments. It seemed that who lacked communication between departments to influence who did not know who had actual authority to give job to them to do.

It would cause difficult to co-operation to finish every job between department. If the assignments needed to finish urgently, who would influence any news, entertainment programmes could not been finished before the time deadlines. It seemed to be team communication problem. The another problem was that, some low and middle level associates also reported that creativity (thought to be important in the jobs) was discouraged by the director's highly authority management and structured styled as well as new director personal work attitude was not good style. It seemed that this new director had unsuitable personal management skill to lead this KBTZ different departments to follow whose guidelines to finish their jobs daily, to cause these departments ' staffs felt dissatisfactory to this new director's personal work attitude . It seemed that this was new director's personal management attitude problem. Moreover, this business office and programming department's survey also indicated these departments existed these problems in KBTZ television station organization.

Firstly, although most of operation department associates were satisfied with their jobs and reported pride in their departments and only some associates felt satisfactory about their operations department manager (head). All other some associates tended to feel overworked (reported a 74 hours workweek) and thought the department head expected too much and who also thought who were underpaid relative to their task demands and criticized managerial feedbacks on their performance and the department head never prised position performance and who only regarded them for poor performance and who also reported concern over the conflict with engineering group , but who believed operations and engineering department conflict, whose departments' leaders (managers) should be resolved. It seemed that this operations departments manager could not manage some departments staffs to work in normal hours to cause them to feel unhappy to work and they also felt underpayment and unreasonable feedback on the performance problem. Anyway, the engineering department many associates were very dissatisfied with whose jobs and who had conflict to operational department and who also believed engineering department head did not support them and who lacked department meetings to receive feedback on their performance from the chief engineer. It seemed that this engineering department's chief engineer who performed more poor to compare to operations department manager to cause
many associates felt dissatisfactory to him. Otherwise, the survey indicated that only promotion department associates had positive attitudes and their job satisfaction were high and everyone viewed their task environment positively and who had only few negative attitudes were primarily directed toward the ineffectiveness of the news department . It seemed that promotion department had none any problems, so its associates could criticize the another news department ineffectiveness result confidently.

Finally, the sales department's colleagues could not responded to the survey to indicate whether what kinds of problems who felt .Due to sale department head was the KBTZ television station manager's son family relationship , so who could not respond to complete this survey whether whose feelings to this sales department manager was satisfactory or was not satisfactory to him, it would cause who lost their job if who responded whose actual feelings to me (consultant) to know at that day possibly.

Which organization development techniques should I consider using and why?

As I was KBTZ television station consultant, I should apply these organization development techniques to solve this company problems. Organizational development techniques included relationship techniques, such as T-group training,
team building, survey as well as structural technique, such as management by objective and supplemental organizational processes. The news department problem, such as high stress to this department managers and associates. It was respect to time deadlines in television problem. The department's staffs must be on the air with the news. All of the news material , local reporting , news , interviews must be processed, edited and ready to go at six o'clock. So, this news department staffs often worried about extended deadlines or who only half prepared material

or who lost the audience, it caused conflict and a number of well qualified and motivated employees would leave this KBTZ television station organization and KBTZ also felt trouble hiring new qualified people could adapt KBTZ organization's culture to help KBTZ organization to raise competition in this USA entertainment market. On the other hand, due to news department staffs who were confused all of the time, so it also caused operations department manager who felt difficult co-operation with to cause operations department and news department would be often conflicts about news department extended time deadline issue. Even, program department director also complained the station was missing a lot of opportunities in other areas, e.g. news and sales. I should use organization development technology, relationship technique T-group training to solve this news and operation departments cooperation problem, which meant news department would implement group exercises in which individual focused on their action, how others perceived their actions and how others generally reacted to them, so participants often learnt about unintended. Hence, this news department managers and associates who could divided several groups, it aimed to focus on their individual action, e.g. local reporting group, news report group, interviews group, news material preparing group. So, these every group members (staffs) who could perceived whose individual group action and reacted to another group individual member action, such as news material preparing group individual member could focus on gathering news material preparing job duties, then who could gave news material to news report group individual member to prepare to analyse materials to prepare to report.

Another interviews group individual to prepare how much time needed and what places should be choose and who to be interviewed to prepare every day different news to let audience to watch six o'clock news programs in television every day. Then, who could gave local reporting group individual member to analyze their every individual interviewing
record to produce every local reporting.

Thus, T-group training benefit was that participants, such as KBTZ news department's material group individual member, local reporting group individual member, news production group individual member, interviewed group individual member who could often learnt about why unintended negative consequences were caused of certain types of any group individual member's behaviour to cause to extend time deadlines or to cause only extend time deadlines or to cause only half prepared material due to very few time was enough to prepare precisely at six o' clock to ready to go before this news department all groups must be processed to edit. Hence, group member which needed to finish whose identified group job, e.g. interview group members who only needed to focus on carry on training how to make date and time appointment to meet individual in the beginning to till to how to prepare what kinds of interview questions would enquire and every interview was planned which needed how long time to finish. Hence, such as interview group individual member could review whose every interview progress to aim to achieve to shorten time to perform the better news programs quality to provide to television audients to watch at everyday six o'clock news time. Hence, the news department's every group member could give chance to enquire survey feedback from every team leader (manager) to review their everyday news job to investigate whether whose group performance would cause unintended negative consequences to influence other group performance to be poor, such as investigating the day's news extended causing was due to the day interview group's individual member who could not organize overall interview procedure to arrange time to finish effectively or other group's individual member to cause. Hence, relationship technique T-group training method could review whether which group(s) to cause the day news extended deadlines or found whether which group(s) caused overall team which could not prepare all material to finish the day news watching at six o'clock . It was one fair method to measure whether which group staffs were qualified people or whether which group staffs were not qualified people to co-operate in this news department.

Other problem was about business department head, business manager seemed that who lacked management training to prepare to do this position, such as who previously worked to do this position, such as who previously worked in sales and in the general manager's office only. Hence, who must need to provide training to prepare to know how to manage KBTZ 's television station organization different departments, such as news department, sales department, operations department, engineering department, program department, promotion department efficiently. As I was KBTZ 's consultant , I felt KBTZ could provide relationship technique of survey method to assist whom. If every departments could get survey, then this business manager could obtain enough dates to meet all units to discuss problems easily. Then, when who collected all departments' problems from this survey, KBTZ could use structural technique of management by objectives method to assist him (business manager), it meant a management process in which individuals (different group members) negotiated whose group daily task objectives, such as engineer group member could negotiate how much equipment who needed to repair urgently and how many equipment who could repair and gave reasons why who could not repair some equipment in that day. All departments might have task objectives to measure whose every group members performance to revise what factors caused whose performance to be poor in order to correct

to achieve every department's group member could raise work efficiently. Thus, this management process needed spend much time to revise every department's group individual negotiate task. For example, the business manager needed to meet engineering group leader (chief engineer) and members(engineers and technicians) to discuss whether how many equipment who needed to repair and whether how many equipment who needed to repair and whether how many equipment who felt who had no much time to repair this week, then next week, this business manager would enquire these engineers to revise whether what reasons occurred to cause who could not repair all machines last week.

As this engineer department individual member technician who had negotiated task objectives to let whose chief engineer and engineering manager to know whether who felt that who could finish task to repair how many machines every week, then they could meet to attempt to explain what factors caused them could not repair all equipment further week. Hence, this business manager could used the same management by objectives structural technique method, such as every department individual member needed to negotiate task objective to finish every week, then who needed to meet whose department manager to revise what factors influenced their work efficiency, e.g. news department material group could meet to discuss task objective about how much time and how many staffs who needed to prepare to gather any related material to report this week ; interview group could meet to discuss task objective about how much time and how many staffs who needed to prepare to organize any effective interview procedure to prepare individual interview this week ; news edited group could meet to discuss task objective about how much time and how many staffs who needed to be edit for daily news this week. Thus, this business manager could know all department's every group individual task objectives per week clearly, then who could meet them to attempt to find whether what factors which caused any department's group individual member who could not achieve whose last week objectives efficiently and effectively.

The new director seemed have unsuitable personal management style to lead whose different departments to work together to cause their dissatisfaction to him in this KBTZ television station organization. For example, the news department felt this new director lacked leadership ability to led news department managers and associates communicate easily. Moreover, news department associates also complained of very low reward, including pay, promotion opportunities and managerial praise and who also complained of constant criticism , which was the only form of managerial feedback on performance. Hence, it implied the new director did not attempt to solve any departments staffs difficulties to adopt new organization development change to cause their dissatisfaction and conflicts and complaints occurrence to whom. I should suggest this new director as a leader who needed to find method to help different department leader(manager) to lead whose associates to feel this KBTZ organization must earn more beyond the past by providing a rationale for change currently and let them to feel guilt and poor anxiety about this KBTZ organization chose not to change and create a sense of psychological safety to them to concern the change, such as news department associates who complain of low reward, including low promotion opportunities and managerial praise and who also complained of constant criticism feedback on performance.

It seemed that who would also complain about low reward, low promotion opportunities and managerial praise and unfair feedback on performance to this new director , even who had good personal managerial style to lead all departments to work. A reason was why these departments, such as news department colleagues complained as above issues because who felt the new director could not adopt to work due to KBTZ sudden change to cause who should be de-commit and dissatisfactory form the status. Hence, this new director needed to let who to know KBTZ organization would cause poor anxiety and guilt to them in the future if KBTZ organization did not change at this moment as well as this new director might create of psychological discomfort to these departments to let them to know that organization would loss from its television competitions, even it would dismiss who if KBTZ television station should not choose to change at this moment, such as the negative outcomes would be made and KBTZ 's managers and associates would suffer if changes were not made. Moreover, this business manager also needed to remind every department members that as well as who also needed to downward members to know this who individual would need to change to adopt this new organization change culture to every department in large meetings. Even, this new director also needed to let every department manager (leader) to know how this change process needed to carry on and every department manager also needed to implement evaluation systems to track every department's group individual expected behaviours and work performance whether whose work were more efficiently or whose work were not more efficiently during this KBTZ organization was carrying on changing at the same time. Hence, every department manager could create efficient reward systems that reinforce every department's group individual's expected behaviours and who could also ensure that whether the hiring and promotion systems which could support all departments colleagues new demands. Especially, news departments felt low reward dissatisfaction. Hence, it could measure whether who ought to raise reward or who ought not to raise reward of their work performance to evaluate more efficiently and effectively. In conclusion, this KBTZ organization leader (new director) ought attempt to let all departments staffs to know why it needed to change organization style and what would be the disadvantages to any departments colleagues if it decided not change at this moment. Then, I believed that department staffs complaints would be reduced and who would feel more fair to pay reward after who knew how who needed to do whose task to adopt this employer to feel satisfactory.

- film producing entrepreneur downward communincation strategy solves team cooperation challenge

When you are one film producing entrepreneur, how you manage your actor teams to work efficiently. Helen Reardon is the producer and director of the film, Going North, based on a novel, the best seller list for 16 months and who is considered to be one of the best directors in Hollywood, who already has two Academy Awards to whose credit and many hit motion pictures.Tom Nesson is a promising young actor, his most recent film, the western express was well received on the box office. Because his current popularity, who was chosen to play the leading male part in Going North film.The next days, Tom won't work in about 10 minutes later, who explained that the makeup people were show in getting his makeup on. No one questioned this, any who began where who had staff off yesterday. However, Helen dissatisfied Tom's performance to play his role action during this movie was carrying on.Hence, who had argued. In result, Helen enquired president in the studio executive offices to demand who either dismissed Tom Nesson, actor or dismissed who self.

The studio executive did not want to lose either Helen, producer and director of film or Tom actor or both. Neither had a history of being difficult to work with. They were not sure what was causing the problem. This movie seemed to be causing all kinds of problems. e.g. strike and the disagreements between wardrobe and set design. They obviously needed to examine all of the circumstances involved to the making of the film. I supposed to use these communication networks to give reasons why causing problem between Helen and Tom. Communication occurs at several different levels and the communication that occurs among individuals or groups of individuals. This is referred to as interpersonal communication.

Networks serve various purposes in organizations and which can used to regulate behaviour, promote innovation, integrate activities and inform and instruct group members. Network also differ in the extent to which who are centralized or decentralized. In centralized networks, all communications pass through a central point or points, so that each member of the network communicates with only a small number of others.Traditional organizational hierarchies, where subordinates communicate to their boss who are centralized networks and all units must communicate with a central headquarter, which then simultaneously coordinates all the units. In decentralized networks, many people or units can communicate with many others.

However, wheel and Y networks are more effective in accomplishing simple tasks and these structures promote efficiency, speed and accuracy by channelling communication through a central person as well as the circle and all

meeting; and the actor, Tom and the producer and director, Helen and executive presidents can spend time to discuss how to solve their conflict in their meeting. This movie firm executive presidents can arrange meeting to discuss with makeup department's staffs how to either increase makeup department staff salaries to let them to accept to do overtime job or it could choose to employ more right numbers staff to reduce makeup department staffs overtime or it could adopted makeup department staffs' any opinions in order to reduce their overtime.

In conclusion, of this movie firm management could have downward communication to spend some time to discuss how to solve every teams' conflicts together immediately , I believe that their conflicts would solve immediately.

Fair compensation strategy solves factory workers and baseball players cooperation challenge

I shall assume fair compensation strategy can be applied to schools. When one school students need to cooperate to finish one assignment. Although school students do not need salary to compensate their performance for finishing the assignment when they need to cooperate to do the assignment together. But, school assignment result will be such as one salary compensation to pay to this assignment MBA team. So, the work hard student must earn higher assignment mark result to compare the poor student.

In this university MBA A-team students team, the dimensions of diversity were responsible for the conflict were as the different groups of these five students should be treated equally that rewards should be based on merit (university project result) and decision maker (team leader) should be blind to the sex or ethnicity of MBA students to arrange their different roles and job duties to carry on doing this business plan project in their university. Hence, workplace diversity management can apply to this university MBA students diversity management. Workplace equal employment opportunity is similar to this university MBA A-team five students equal roles and duties opportunity as well as workplace organization decision maker is similar to this university .MBA A-team students team leader who needs to decide either employees or MBA A-team student team

members to pay attention to characteristics like sex or ethnicity to determine if who affect employment consequences or to arrange university MBA A-team five student members every role and duty to finish this business plan project. In workplace, every employer needs special actions , such as hiring the ethnic minority candidate when applicants appear to have equal qualifications, are considered appropriate requirements to remedy the effects of past discrimination and thus attain equal opportunity.

Thus, this university ought feel that it was such one employer, it needed to help A-team to choose one MBA student for A-team leader from whose prior working experiences and qualification. Then, it needed to give reasons to these other four A-team student members to explain why it felt this MBA student was the best right applicant for their A-team leader. University professor Bowell group advisor might give probation period to this student leader if this A-team four members complaint this team leader who could not serve in the executive function to assign and oversee everyone's work and gave the presentation at end of project. Then , professor Bowell this team advisor might suggest them to select another new leader, so this A-team would not be disbanded easily. As this university selects the right applicant for every position. It needs committee to assist its selection processing. If the dean determines that the committee lacks diversity , it can be reconstituted by including persons from other departments or even other universities. The search committee chair must review information from candidates to ensure that minority and female and male applicants are in the pool.The dean's office reviews applications of diverse candidates of none of them appears among the search committee's choices of candidates to be interviewed, the committee must provide an explanation. Finally, the university team advisor ought be similar to an employer who needs to choose who are the top student candidates (employees) to make A-team (job offer) from their educational background, working experiences. It aims to reduce dimensions of diversity were responsible for the conflict.

Describe which barriers to effectively managing diversity were present in this situation?

Diversity can be defined as a characteristic of a group of people where differences exist on one or more relevant dimensions such as gender. First, faults can be present in situations characterized by diversity. Faults occur when two or more dimensions of diversity are correlated. For example, if all /most of the young people on a cross-functional task force represent marketing when all/most of the older individuals represent product engineering, then a fault is said exist. Faults merge multiple identifies (e.g. young and marketing focused) to produce barriers to effective collaborations within a group. Research on this phenomenon is relatively new, but has produced findings suggestion poor group outcomes. It can be applied to this A-team university team members conflict what barriers are to effectively managing diversity were present in this situation.

The barriers to effectively managing diversity were present in this situation , it is possible that this A-team group members who have different educational and working backgrounds to cause barriers to effectively managing diversity in this situation. For example, Rebecca is a young marketing manager for a large and high end Italian fashion company. She hopes this university MBA course can help her to be promoted to an executive position as well as Aran is 52 year old founder and CEO of an management consultant firm. He hopes this university MBA course can help him to retire from his consulting firm earlier and become an in house information system consultant to a large multinational firm. When she knew Aran promoted him to be this A-team leader because he had the most experience and he should serve in the executive function. Thus, he would assign and oversee every member's work and he would also give the presentation at the end of this project. Although, Aran have more confident to give reasons why he is the best person choice to be this team leader to manage every member and he also give useful suggestion that Cameron, an internet entrepreneur who heads his own small but successful company who will be in charge of analyzing the financial feasibility of their project, developing the marketing plan, and evaluating the technical operations and the other members need to assist him. However, Aran is one managing consultant and Rebecca is one young marketing manager. Aran's educational and working experience is related to information system, but Rebecca educational and working experience is related to marketing field. Thus they have different expertise and skill. Rebecca feels that she has marketing field experience and she is younger than Aran. So, she have more ability than Aran to attempt to do a team leader to manage this A-team members how to produce marketing plan and report and presentation effectively. In conclusion, because these five students have different educational and working experience in their expertise field, so they feel themselves has ability to attempt to be team leader or attempt to do their job duties who prefer to choose by themselves. It will cause difficulty to any one team leader to manage diversity in this A-team members effectively and successfully.

- Factors cause electronic assemblies factory workers team poor performance

When you one electronic assemblies factory entrepreneur, how you manage your workers team work efficiently. The best ways evaluate to measure what factors are seemed to be influencing this company electronic assemblies products manufactory factory workers team performance.

The First factor, we need to know what kind of methods which can be used to measure team performance, then, we can follow these measurement methods to judge what factors are seemed to be influencing this team performance more actually. Effectiveness and efficiency are the best ways to evaluate team performance. Efficiency is oriented towards successful input transformation into outputs. Effectiveness measures how outputs interact with the economic and social environment and it is being used to reflect overall performance of the team. This company electronic assemblies products manufactory factory team of workers could be evaluated team performance in terms of effectiveness. It's main focus is to achieve team's mission, goals and vision, such as whether how many workers could attempt to finish to wire eight assemblies an hour to meet their one client, Pacific electronic company to know how many assemblies of numbers had been finished to wire currently in order to meet whose Pacific electronic company client shipping schedule or not. At the same time, which value these electronic assembly workers whose performance in terms of their efficiency which relates to the optimal use of resources to achieve the desired output, such as whether how many worker numbers and machine tool numbers would be needed to provide to wire assembly numbers to finish in order to meet whose Pacific electronic company client shipping schedule or not. However, this team performance would have this question ,such as whether there was a difference if this team was effective yet inefficient. Hence, this team would face unprecedented challenges (factors) which were seemed to be influencing team performance. The first factor was such as, it's client Pacific electronic company needed shorten time to finish wire assemblies which was the main factor to influence performance, such as this team workers would feel difficult to increase to wire eight assemblies an hour from three assemblies an hour, so who would feel anxiety to meet the shipping schedule to finish whose job and quality of assemblies production could not be satisfied to Pacific electronic company client possibly.

The second factor was such as, this company factory and office team management structural relationship. Usually, high team performance has strong upper management and human resource standards which had been set in place. Because of high team performance expectation, right staffs were being hired to fulfil the positions in order to employees were well aware of the performance measurement and the importance achieve the excellence in their duties. Due to a high degree level of employee involvement needed to be in the team production process, the entity was awarded with staffs commitment which reduced rotation level and the cost associated with the hiring and training process. Hence, employees who were devoted to the team were well aware of necessary knowledge and skill and experience to create unique solutions for clients. Training can be an essential tool for maintaining and improving the productivity of staffs and relevance of skill. The ongoing shortages of labour and skill, the company should be taking action to reduce the impact of staffs scarcity by training staffs who already had employed.

Development opportunities were provided to motivate staffs by providing them with skill and knowledge enrichment . At the same time, a better skilled, more motivated workforce would help boost competitiveness, improved productivity and increased profit margin. Moreover, this company lacked good team communication relationship, such as Bill, factory team supervisor who only knew whose same workers of team, such as some of workers Dennis and Steve and Jack who would feel difficult because whose workers were supposed to wire three assemblies an hour normally with five years, but who were supposed to do eight assemblies an hour to sudden meet one client, Pacific electronic company client schedule to finish confidently as well as who would feel dissatisfactory, due to whose wages did not increase much more to pay for performance to the optimal compensation currently and these workers lacked enough training to face this sudden change to face this client's demand. Thus, it was possible that to influence whose team performance to be poor due to who could not adapt this sudden change from this client's demand. Due to Bill, electronic factory supervisor had not communicate to face to face to contact to enquire whose workers whether what reasons to cause who would feel difficulties if who needed to increase to finish wire assemblies and attempted to find solved methods due to sudden clients' demand. Hence, Bill could not have knowledge and skill to judge whether the reasons were either the numbers of workers or machines were not enough or both to cause that they would feel difficulties to increase their speed and effort to finish up to eight wire assemblies of numbers to meet this clients' current schedule sudden change demand at this moment.

The third factor was whether this company had effective strategic approaches to this team. A high team performance which maintains five major approaches: They include strategy, customers, leadership, processes and structure , values and beliefs. Strategic approach takes the team to a higher plan of maturity with a vision where the entity is going; customer approach strives for loyalty; leadership approach is associated with management knowledge to transfer the strategy to employees (teams) level and which will have a direct impact on their behaviour and beliefs and teams' processes and structure and high performance team will strive for implementing innovative policies to support team strategy; the last model is value and belief which translates into team ability to implement the strategy. In fact, this team lacked effective strategic approaches, such as Mr Martin, office manager did not told Bill, electronic factory team supervisor how to lead whose team to a higher plan to maturity with a vision where the entity was going, such as team lacked training or team lacked enough numbers of worker and machine to provide to increase to produce up to eight wire assemblies of numbers to meet this client's schedule shorten change demand to cause this team lacked evaluation to measure every worker individual effort to judge whether who ought have effort to already to finish more wire assemblies of numbers and who ought increase their wages due to they had more effort to raise more productivity to produce eight assemblies or more numbers. Hence, it caused the effort workers did not like to increase the productivity to meet this client sudden change easily due to who felt unfair treatment to compare the other less effort workers in this team.

However, the Pacific electronic company client would lose confidence to Mr Martin office manager if who could not accept Dave, shop of supervisor suggestion either to add some more incentive bonus to these workers to raise whose productivity or providing training or providing more machine and worker numbers to attempt to assist current workers ability to meet the client's schedule. Otherwise, it would cause this client did not choose to find its help next time again. The important factor was whether this factory supervisor and shop supervisor and office manager who had effective communication to predict how to solve any sudden clients' order change trouble between of them. However, I think that, Bill factory supervisor lacked effective leadership to whose workers team in this factory, such as it seemed that some workers; Dennis, Steve and Jack who responded to Bill factory supervisor who felt difficulties to wire eight assemblies an hour suddenly. In fact, some of them had confidence to finish who told lie to Bill because Bill, factory supervisor could not be a good leader to know how to lead whose team to wire assemblies efficiently and effectively daily. Thus, Bill's leadership would have a direct impact on team workers behaviour and team performance poorly if Bill could not change whose leadership skill and who needed to facilitate workers team performance rather than to direct the team, due to who was a formal leader to their team. The company lacked value and belief with translated into team ability to implement the strategy, such as Mr Martin, office manager could not communicate with Dave, shop of supervisor and Bill, factory of supervisor by face to face contact to discuss whether how who could raise to produce wire assemblies of numbers during any clients' sudden shorten schedule occurrence before, so it caused this factory workers team had not more confident to increase to produce more eight wire assemblies of numbers one hour due to this clients' schedule sudden shorten change. Otherwise, if who could often to discuss to suggest any methods to raise these factory team productivity, this factory leader, Bill would have enough time to plan already how to lead whose factory team workers to co-operate to raise productivity efficiency and effectively in this shorten schedule.

suggestion method:

Identify the team norms and goals. Are they compatible with organizational objective?

● What factors seem to be influencing team performance?

I felt that some of this electronic company factory team norms and goals are compatible with organizational objectives in some situations, but some of whose team norms and goals are not compatible with organizational objective in some situation. Norms mean rules or standards that regulate the team's behaviour and providing direction and are part of the team's mental model. When individual team members violate team norms, some type of punishment is usually applied. Although, norms allow teams be function smoothly, who can sometimes be harmful to team members. It is important that teams develop norms that both foster team productivity and performance and promote the welfare of individual members. This company goal was that it's factory team needed to finish identified wire assemblies of numbers to satisfy every business clients to meet whose identified schedules individually. Hence, Bill, the electronic factory team supervisor who needed to follow Dave, shop of supervisor's instruction to inform whose workers team to finish all wire assemblies of numbers to meet every business client's identified schedule on or before due date. Thus, Bill , factory team supervisor needed to give team norms to let whose team of workers to know whose factory's rules or standards that regulated whose workers teams individually behaviour and providing direction to let them to know when (what the client schedule date was) and what the wire assemblies of numbers the team which must need to finish to deliver to whose clients by shipping. Hence, this factory's rules and standards regulation could be one part to this factory team's mental models on this aspect to achieve this factory workers team norms were compatible with this organizational objective.

Although, the factory workers team norms allowed them to function smoothly, but Bill, factory supervisor could sometimes be harmful to the factory workers team to influence whether

the factory workers team productivity and performance standards level of those wire assemblies of products quality, such as Bill, factory supervisor informed to those factory workers team to increase to produce eight wire assemblies of numbers one hour for normal three wire assemblies of numbers one hour suddenly. It was caused these workers felt anxious whether who should be dismissed if who could not attempt to produce eight wire assemblies of numbers one hour from Bill, factory supervisor demand. It seemed that the factory workers team norms and goals were not compatible with this company organizational objectives because this company organizational objective was needed workers finished to produce three wire assemblies of numbers to deliver to every client before schedule due date. It was depended on the situation of the factory whether it had enough time and machine and skilful worker numbers to supply to finish the identified wire assemblies of numbers to every client identified schedule individually. Otherwise,

currently, on this situation, it seemed that this factory lacked enough worker and machine numbers and enough time and training to those old(current workers), it caused who felt difficult that every worker needed to finish to produce eight wire eight assemblies of numbers minimum per hour to meet this Pacific electronic company client's identified schedule change suddenly. It also seemed that this company current organizational objective was not same to its prior (past) organizational objective, such as every team worker needed to finish to produce three wire assemblies of numbers minimum per hour before to meet this Pacific electronic company client's
identified schedule change suddenly. It was given more difficult to let this factory team every worker to attempt to finish to produce eight wire assemblies of numbers minimum per hour to meet this current Pacific electronic company client's sudden schedule change. Hence, in this situation, I should feel this factory team norms and goals were not compatible with their company's past organizational objective for this Pacific electronic company's earliest past three wire assemblies of numbers of every worker individual production demand in the identified schedule. In this situation, this Pacific electronic company client's wire assemblies of production numbers needed to be changed which caused this company factory team expectation schedule and wire assemblies of production numbers, such as every worker needed to produce eight wire assemblies minimum per hour of numbers of it's production goals and should be changed, but this factory team norms and production goals was still same to this Pacific electronic company client's earliest production numbers, such as every worker needed to produce three wire assemblies of numbers per hour. It meant that who needed have more time and worker and machine numbers to assist them to finish to produce if some workers had no enough effort to produce eight assemblies of numbers per hour to finish to meet this client's identified schedule change, otherwise, who needed to extend time to finish this client's production numbers schedule if none of them could produce eight wire assemblies of numbers at minimum one hour. This, this factory team norms and goals seemed that who were not compatible with organizational client's current objective to every worker needed to increase to produce eight wire assemblies of numbers per hour to finish to meet this Pacific electronic company client prior (not changed) schedule possible. Otherwise, these current factory workers could increase to finish eight wire assemblies of numbers to meet this client's current schedule goals. If this factory team some workers could finish eight or even more wire assemblies of numbers of numbers per hour individually. Thus, this team productivity could still achieve this client's expectation goals to finish to meet on or before schedule. It implied that this team norms and goals was compatible with organizational current objective due to client's expectation wire assemblies of overall increasing numbers had been finished to meet schedule from this factory team overall productivity together. Thus, it caused why this factory team norms and goals would be compatible with organizational team objective of finishing enough wire assemblies of overall numbers to meet this client's schedule date goals possibly or this factory team norms and goals would not be compatible with organization team objective of not finishing enough wire assemblies of overall numbers to meet this client's schedule date goals possibly.

How does the team function to meet individual needs?

This company, Steve and Jack were electronic wire assemblies products factory manufactory workers (members) among of this factory team, who had worked in this factory team five years. Bill was this company factory supervisor, who needed to supervise this workers team to help every business client to finish every electronic wire assemblies of products order to meet whose identified schedule, then delivered to them by shipping channel. Hence, if Bill, factory supervisor
who could not lead whose workers team to co-operate to produce the identified electronic wire assemblies of products of numbers to finish to meet the individual business client's identified schedule before due date to deliver to them by shipping. It would cause that this company and the and the client would feel this company Mr Martin, office manager and Dave, shop of supervisor could not achieve their service agreement to finish electronic wire assemblies identifies numbers to deliver to them before schedule due date. The result would cause this company lost this client, even this company would accept guilty from this client's complaint. Hence, Bill, factory supervisor needed to lead whose workers team to work efficiently to achieve whose job responsibility to finish every individual business client identified good quality and non damaged of electronic wire assemblies of products of numbers to deliver to them by shipping before schedule due date.

In fact, this factory workers team was combined (co-operated) by every individual worker. Hence, if Bill, factory supervisor expected whose factory team could have good productivity and efficiency, who must individual needs. Otherwise, if some workers did not like to work hard, who would cause this team to delay to finish the identified electronic wire assemblies of numbers to deliver to the individual business client before the schedule due date. Hence, if ill, factory supervisor could
satisfy every individual worker needs, then Bill could lead this team to perform more effectively and efficiently. If this factory work could be done by individual without any need for teamwork was not necessary in this factory. I supposed that this factory needed different workers worked in different steps to cooperate to finish every electronic wire assembly product. The reason was possible that because the employer felt every worker could be more proficient to practise to finish the identified step to co-operate to work together in one team, thus every worker could be raised productivity and efficiency in team, it could get more benefits than individual worker did all steps to finish every electronic wire assembly product alone in this factory. However, as the number of this factory team workers increased, the need for cooperation also increased. As some point, the effort of Bill, factory supervisor who managed the factory team who would outweigh the benefit of having more workers and this factory team performance would began to decline. Hence, if this factory team of worker numbers increased suddenly.

Although, every business client's electronic wire assemblies of products individual order finishing time would be reduced possibly, but it seemed that Bill, factory supervisor would feel more difficult to spend more time to lead this team to manage every individual worker who how to co-operate to work more efficiency and who should also feel difficult to satisfy individual worker needs if this team increased many worker numbers sudden seriously. Hence, this factory team overall performance of efficiency and effectiveness would begin to decline for long term due to this factory team increased many worker numbers suddenly to cause every individual worker felt that who could not satisfy more needs than before. Team structure means of coordinating formal team efforts. Leaders are appointed and work rules and procedures are detailed and job descriptions specify individual task responsibilities. It is necessary to coordinate the efforts of individuals assigned to the different tasks. Otherwise, tasks may not be performed in the correct sequence and employees may duplicate their efforts or work against each other. It seemed that this factory workers team which electronic wire assembling steps could be similar to bank loan department and collection department steps. If one individual worker who had much effort to finish whose wire assembling job step more quick to compare another less effort worker individual wire assembling job step. It seemed that the much effort worker could have much time to attempt to help the another less effort worker to finish whose step. Hence, it was possible that this factory team function could compare every individual worker's effort whether who could had more effort and time to help other worker to finish whose wire assembly job step during the less effort worker could not finish whose wire assembling step quickly. Thus, this factory team function could evaluate whether who individual worker had more effort and much time to attempt to help another less effort individual worker to finish their wire assembling job step for every individual client. It implied that these much effort individual workers who had needs to pay to optimal compensation more than the less effort individual workers for whose better performance in the factory team. It was possible that the piece pay rate compensation was not suitable to these more effort
individual worker to satisfy whose individual needs to accept in the team because who could increase return to multi tasking, in which the same workers did both easy to observe tasks, such as wire assembling production of every step and hard to observe tasks, such as process improvement of wire assembling production of every step and producing exact wire assembling quantities of output (no more and no less). I suggest this factory ought change piece rate compensation to time rate compensation and gain sharing payment method to the more effort individual worker productivity , the individual more effort worker who could receive time rate compensation plus a usually small amount bonus linked to the productivity of the establishment to this factory team during who could increase return to multi tasking to assist whom to finish the another job step of less effort worker's wire assembling job duty for any individual client's wire assembling products delivering order before schedule due date.

I supposed that this factory team function adopted transfer lines in which individual worker was transferred between stations either by machines or by a moving conveyor assembly line. In either case, time rates compensation were more advantages than piece rates compensation due to it was more fair to the every more effort individual worker if who could finish whose wire assembling individual step before schedule due date and who had more time to assist another less effort worker to help who to finish whose wire assembly step immediately. In result, these every individual workers could raise this team efficiency to help this factory team to finish the identified wire assembly numbers to deliver to any client by shipping before the schedule due date normally. Bill, factory supervisor and Dave shop of supervisor who both could obtain high effort from this factory workers on observable tasks by noticing where the wire assembly inventory piles up between stations, without incurring the costs of piece rates. I supposed that the wire assembling products required operations on different machines, performed in different orders setting up fixed paths for work to travel would have made low effort in production more observable, but would have made the wire assembling production process very inflexible. Therefore, Bill, factory supervisor needed put each individual worker in charge of a machine that could do several jobs. (each with a negotiated rat) and encouraged this team workers to do each job quickly via piece rates. Since there was recurring demand for each wire assembling product for a long time, management did not have to negotiate new piece rates very often. I suggested that Bill, factory supervisor should design the observable tasks , e.g. the step of wire assembling production to be done by one group of factory workers and the unobservable making improvement to the step of wire assembling production, fixing problems to be done by another group with a different compensation scheme and observable and unobservable tasks were separated in this factory team. Thus, wire assembly production workers focused on producing output and were paid to piece rate. Quality was the responsibility of other departments workers, such as inspectors, who identified defective parts and engineers , who attempted to design less defect wire assembly products and processes, these all individual workers who every was paid time rates. All else equal, the low rates compensation was paid to less effort individual worker per piece and the higher rates and bonus compensation was paid to high effort individual worker per time rate to finish every individual business client's order. Finally, this factory team function could give synergy to achieve an effect of the total output of this factory team is greater than the combined outputs of individual worker working alone. In conclusion, this factory team function could use time rates and bonus compensation method to pay to the individual more effort every worker to let who to feel this employer was more fair to every individual worker performance. The more effort workers ought have more reasonable compensation to compare the less effort workers in this factory team.

- If I was Dave, shop supervisor, what team concepts should I apply? why?

If I was Dave, shop supervisor, I should apply these team concepts to this electronic factory wire assembling team. When, managers assign associates to teams, who often make three common assumptions, which can lead to mistakes; such as, who assume that a large team size always better and who assume that everyone knows how or is suited to work in a team and who assume that people who are similar to each other will work better together and so they can co-operate happily. Group means two or more interdependent individuals who influence one another through social interaction. Thus, if I was Dave, shop supervisor, I and my shop staffs would be one group. Bill, factory supervisor and factory team workers who would be another group factory workers team ; Mr Martin, office manager and office staffs would be another group top managers team. Our company needed these three groups communicate and co-operate to work together to deliver message between about of us about every individual business client's wire assembly product numbers demand and schedule due date to ensure when every client's order could confirm to finish to deliver to the client by shipping factory supervisor and whose workers was a team because this team had two or more workers with work roles that required them to be interdependent who operated within a large social system, as our factory performing tasks, such as every individual worker needed to produce every part of wire assembling in different stage relevant to our organization's mission , such as finishing the indicated wire assembling numbers to meet individual client's schedule to deliver to whom by shipping with consequences that affected others inside, such as Bill, factory supervisor and others outside, such as Dave, shop supervisor and Mr Martin , office manager of our organization, such as company and Bill, factory supervisor had membership that was identified to these on factory team and those not on the team, such as Dave, shop supervisor and sellers teams as well as Mr Martin, office manager and office administration teams. Effective team performance can be more difficult to achieve when team members belong to difficult identify groups or when their identification with these groups conflicts with the goals and objectives of the team, such as these factory some workers who felt difficult to raise to produce eight wire assembling from these wire assemblies in this factory team, but Mr Martin, office manager needed Dave, shop supervisor to notify to Bill, factory supervisor to let whose factory workers every one to know whether who could raise productivity to this eight numbers and who could not, then who decided whether how to solve that Pacific electronic company client could not receive wire assemblies of identified number before schedule due date by shipping. In fact, Dan shop supervisor would had conflict, with Mr Martin, office manager who explained workers felt wages were less, so who would not worked hard to raise effort to produce more wire assemblies, but Mr Martin , office manager disagreed whose suggestion and who enforced Dan, factory supervisor to enquire whether these factory workers who could do eight wire assemblies possibly, it would cause some workers felt anxious to be dismiss if who could not finish this numbers. This, these group conflicts caused non effective team performance with the factory group goals and the shop group goals and management group goals which were more different. If I was Dave, shop supervisor of this electronic company, I would apply management team concept to my shop group because I believed we were both the senior level shop manager and office manager who needed to coordinate the activities of our respective units, e.g. shop top management teams and office top management teams as well as Mr Martin, office management group . Otherwise, Bill, factory supervisor would be production team because workers who needed to supervise whose factory workers group to produce tangible products, such as identified wire assemblies of numbers to meet every individual client's schedule due date.

A final consideration in Dave, shop supervising team effectiveness is whether a supervising team is needed to perform the work at all or whether the work is best performed by Dave, shop supervisor individually. I this case, it would have been better to have individual separately, Dave, shop supervising team effectiveness is measured on knowledge criteria, affective criteria and outcome criteria. Knowledge criteria reflected the degree to which Dave, shop supervisor individually increased its performance capability . Affective criteria addressed the question of whether Dave, shop supervisor individually had a fulfilling and satisfying to supervise shop experience, such as whether Dan could manage whose shop and factory effectively. Outcome criteria referred to Dan 's personal quality of the shop supervisor how to supervise whose shop and factory teams effectively. Hence, if I was Dan this electronic company shop supervisor, I shall apply these team concepts to apply to whose shop and factory teams management in this situation.

● Fair compensation solve baseball organization players cooperation challenge

Brooklyn Bluebirds baseball organization was the best professional team for ten years win competition. A new owner, Trudy Mills, who acquired it to rebuild the team by acquiring big name players intention. However, during the first month end, the team was in the first place with a record of 20 wins and 7 losses, but then conflicts problems began. Conflict is a process in which one party perceives that its interests are being opposed or negatively affected by another party. Firstly, Bluebirds organization encountered of conflict between players were reported in the sports columns. Russ Thompson, a five years veteran and starting first baseman team player, publicly stated that who wanted to renegotiate his contract. In fact, the reason to Russ, this baseball team player who caused this conflict, due to he was unhappy that whose baseball team current employer, Trudy had brought many baseball players at much higher salaries than him. Hence, it caused Trudy, baseball team player who felt dissatisfactory to whose current employer, he felt who had fire year baseball competitions experiences and who had fire year baseball competitions experiences and who had helped whose baseball team, such as Brooklyn Bluebirds to win much competitions. Hence, who felt Trudy, current Brooklyn Bluebirds baseball owner could not give him higher salaries than this team's other baseball team players. It was unfair to him. In the result, Russ, baseball team player met with Trudy, Brooklyn Bluebirds baseball team owner and Trudy's lawyer and Bluebird's general baseball team manager to discuss whose salary increasing issue, but the meeting ended in disagreement and both Russ, baseball team player and Trudy, Brooklyn Bluebirds baseball team owner were angry, it was caused by salary could not increased to Russ, baseball team player disagreement to achieve negotiation conflict within Bluebirds organization. It seemed that Russ, baseball team player and Trudy, Bluebirds baseball team employer (owner) whose interpersonal conflict which occurs between their both individuals in this organization. They are personal conflict, it means Trudy, Bluebirds baseball team employer and Russ, baseball team player both conflict that arises out of personal differences between people, such as differing goals, values or personalities, such as the baseball it was possible that Trudy, Bluebirds baseball team owner who would not give high salary to Russ, baseball team player due to who needed to evaluate whose baseball competitions performance with team members to judge whether who ought to increase whose salary, but Russ, baseball team player felt who was unfair to pay him less salary than other baseball players due to who had five years baseball competition experiences.

Thus, their differing values were very
different to cause this personal conflict in this Bluebirds baseball team organization. It also seemed that Trudy, baseball team owner existed substantive conflict that involved work content and goals to Russ, baseball player, such as Trudy needed time to evaluate Russ, baseball competitions performance (work content) whether who could help whose baseball team to win competitors (goals) to decide whether who could increase salary. I felt the main factor to cause their personal conflict was that Russ, baseball player felt Trudy, baseball team owner paid him less salary than other baseball players. Instead of this factor, it had also other factors, such as, baseball team organization needed interdependency co-operation specially. Interdependency means work must be coordinated between groups (such as baseball team) or individuals (baseball players). The more interdependent two
groups on individuals are the more the potential for conflict exists. Interdependency can result from limited resources or from required coordination in the timing and sequencing of activities. Due to Russ, baseball team player needed to co-operate with other baseball team players to attempt to carry on practising to learn how to achieve to win any baseball competitions intention. Hence, it was possible that Russ would listen of conflict between players who were reported in the baseball players in the baseball sports columns about their salary issue, even it was possible that Russ and other baseball players who felt Russ and other baseball players who felt difficult to attempt to co-operate to carry on baseball team training within limited time and sequencing of activities before any baseball competitions.

It would cause this baseball team group conflict occurrence between baseball team individual players because this baseball team individual players and baseball team group had less control over own team cooperation in this situation. Russ, baseball team player felt who individual abilities were exceed to other baseball team players in this baseball team. In fact, Russ's individual abilities did not sum up to influence this baseball team performance. Russ, individual baseball player skill was only moderately good predictor when two or more team players interacted in a precise way. Due to baseball sport team needed more cooperation and interaction to team every players, so it was necessary the importance of individual ability decreases and groups processed increased.

Hence, the more closer the team players were in their abilities, the more likely who would fully put to use their combined abilities . Thus, it was possible that Russ would feel whose baseball skill and ability was exceed to this team other baseball players to cause who felt more difficult interdependent to co-operate with the other team baseball players in this baseball team to cause this team difficult co-operational conflict. Hence, the difficult baseball team cooperation also caused the group conflict due to Russ felt dissatisfactory reward and who felt the other baseball players performance would influence whose performance to be poor to win any further baseball competitions indirectly. Russ, baseball team player was discouraged to leave Trudy, Bluebirds baseball team organization by Marty, baseball team manager indirectly.

Next, Bluebird baseball team organization also encountered conflict between Marty, baseball team manager and Russ and Mickey baseball team players as well as conflict between Marty, baseball team manager and Trudy, baseball team employer (owner) about who planned leaving. Trudy, current baseball employer. This conflict was caused due to Marty, baseball team manager discouraged these two baseball team players both Russ and Mickey continued to serve this employer and encouraged who signed another baseball team employer who could give more salary to them. However, Trudy, this baseball team employer (owner) still felt Russ and Mickey both were the best baseball player and the clients paid to see them player. Hence, Trudy phoned to Marty, baseball team manager to require who to apologize to them and persuaded them did not plan to leave.Then, Marty baseball team manager made conflict with whose employer, Trudy to indicate himself had been a good baseball team manager to manage whose baseball team players effectively and who felt that who did not need to apologize to Russ and Mickey, these two baseball team players because who had not leave Trudy currently and who had already trained them to play further baseball competitions. This conflict was caused because Marty, baseball team manager who encouraged these two team players to leave due to whose salaries were paid less than other baseball team players. Then, Trudy baseball team employer needed Marty to persuade who did not leave his baseball organization, but Marty refused to tell them about whose employer instruction. Thus, it caused group substantive conflict due to Russ and Mickey both baseball team players felt dissatisfaction to work in this baseball team to achieve team cooperation goal with other team players to win any baseball competitions as well as it also caused individual procedural conflict between Trudy and Marty due to that Trudy, baseball team owner gave responsibilities to Marty, such as Marty, baseball team manager needed to apologize to these two team players and persuaded them did not plan to leave, Marty felt it was not whose responsibilities due to who had finished to manage this baseball team effectively and who ought not need to apologize to them due to who was their manager. However, Trudy felt it was also whose responsibilities. Thus, unreasonable responsibility was a factor to cause Marty felt dissatisfactory to Trudy, baseball team employer to require him to do this apologizing issue.

suggestion of solvable method:

● Describe the types of conflict that seem to exist within the Bluebirds organization.

What are the causes?

Is the conflict functional, dysfunctional or both? explain

Dysfunctional conflict is different to functional conflict as below:

Dysfunctional conflict is conflict that interferes with performance to organizational goals and objectives, such as doubting about the organization's future performance in the minds of shareholders; conflict can cause people to exercise their own individual power and engage in political behaviour directed toward achieving their own goals; conflict can have negative effects on interpersonal relationships, so it needs to take time and resources and emotional energy to deal with conflict, both on an interpersonal and an organizational level.

Functional conflict is beneficial to organizational goals and objectives . Any organizations without functional conflict frequency lack the energy and ideas to create effective innovation. Conflict can have a number of functional consequences for organizations, such as facilitation of change, improved problem solving or decision making, enhanced morale within a group, more ability in communication and productivity and creativity and stimulation. I felt this Bluebirds baseball team organization had only dysfunctional conflict, such as Trudy baseball team owner and Marty, baseball team manager who had negative effects on interpersonal relationship. Trudy needed to take time and resources and emotional energy to deal with Marty's individual conflict both on an interpersonal level. For example, in fact, Marty encouraged Russ and Mickey to leave Trudy's baseball team, but Marty refused to follow Trudy's requirement to apologize to them and persuaded them to stay. It would cause this baseball team other players turnover numbers to be increased due to these two the best baseball players leaving influence and Trudy would lose these two the best baseball performance players final.

On conclusion, all of conflicts are caused by unfair compensation to this baseball organizational every players, so this basball organization needs to spend time to decide every player whether whom ought pay the reasonable compensation for his performance. Then, these conflicts will be solved to reduce in possible.

● Fair compensation strategy solves compensation director poor working performance challenge

This is one case applies expectancy theory provides a useful framework for organizing those factors : people will be committed to goals that carrying a reasonable expectation of being attained and are more viewed as desirable to attain. It aims to solve the senior management working performance challenge.

When you are one entrepreneur to manage one compensation director behavior, how you manage him/her successfully. Frances Mead , compensation director for Puma corporation , who paid well to hire Don Coggin to fill position of benefits administrator for her company in corporate personnel department at Puma, headquartered in Salt Lake city, Utah and the job was located in Utah. Hence, Don could always enjoyed the outdoor and he liked to backpack, camp and did some mountain climbing sport entertainment conveniently. Hence, it ensured that this job location could give Dan to enjoy his likely mountain climbing ,camp, backpack sport entertainment conveniently was also an important reason to influence Don to choose this job.In fact, Dan's financial background aided him greatly in his new benefits administrator job, where he was responsible for development and administration of the pension plan, life and health insurance package, employee stock purchase plan and other employee benefit programs within one month. Dan has learned how to do duties. Frances Mead, she was satisfied with her selection for Dan to do this benefits administrator position. Hence, she expected Dan to move up to in the department rank rapidly, but Dan only concern was that who did not seem to have enough time to enjoy his outdoor activities after he had seem promoted to do further duties absolutely. It implied that Dan disliked to promote to spend more time to do more job duties. Even, his salary would not be increased and his rank would be promoted in this moment. After six months, Dan had his job proficiently and who was quite talented and the job did not present a strong challenge to him. During to Frances, compensation director for Puma corporation recognized Dan's talent and wanted him to evaluate Puma corporation's complete benefits package for the purpose of making needed changes without the help of costly outside consultants and Frances believed that Puma's benefits package was outdated and needed to be revised. However, Frances felt Dan disliked to discuss with her to evaluate the total benefits package from her several encouraging because Dan seemed to be constantly thinking of and discussing his outdoor activities and he seemed lack of commitment to do his job. As ERG theory indicated that a person's existence needs don't necessarily have to be satisfied before who can became concerned about whose relationships with others or about using whose personal capabilities, whose desire to meet the existence needs may be stronger than whose desire to meet the two other types of needs, such as relationship with others or about using those personal capabilities, but the other needs may still be important. As this case, Dan , this company 's benefits administrator who chose to serve this company, instead of salary was paid well reason, the other reason was his job was located to let him to enjoy the outdoors sport activities conveniently. Hence, it is Dan's existence needs in this company. Hence, even Frances , this company compensation director accepted to increase Dan's salary to promote him to do higher rank after six months, due to Dan's personal capabilities was very good. Dan whose behaviour performance disliked to discuss with Frances to evaluate and Dan seemed to be constantly thinking of and discussing his outdoor activities and he seemed lack of commitment to his job. As ERG theory indicated Dan could not motivated by Frances because Frances needed him to forgive to enjoy his outdoor sport entertainment when Frances needed him to spend much time to discuss with her to evaluate the total benefits package at this moment. However, Dan felt the reason of his existence was staying in this company was because his new job could located in Utah to always enjoyed the outdoor entertainment. If he could not spend extra time to enjoy this kind of entertainment. It would cause Dan lost commitment to serve this employer.

suggestion of solvable method:

Using ERG theory, explain the reasons for the situation described in the case.

ERG theory suggests people are motivated by three hierarchically ordered types of needs: existence needs (E), relatedness needs (R) and growth needs (G). A person may work at the same time, although satisfying lower order needs often takes place before a person is strongly motivated by higher level needs.Work motivation and job satisfaction means the relationship between the organization and its members is influenced by what motivates them to work and the rewards and fulfilment they derive from it. Motivation is typified as an individual phenomenon. Every person is unique and all the major theories of motivation allow for this uniqueness to be demonstrated in one way or another, it is as intentional to assume to be under the worker's control and behaviours that are influenced by motivation, such as effort expended. Motivation is through an understanding of internal cognitive processes, that is what people feel and how who think. This understanding should help the manager to predict likely behaviour of staff in given situations. The two factors of greatest importance are what gets people activated and the force of an individual to engage in desired behaviour (direction or choice of behaviour). The purpose of motivation theories is predict behaviour. Motivation isn't the behaviour itself and it is not performance. Motivation concerns action and the internal and external forces which influence a person's choice of action.

Maslow's hierarchy of needs theory suggests people are motivated by their desire to satisfy specific needs and that needs are arranged in a hierarchy with physiological needs at the bottom and self actualization needs at the top. People most satisfy needs at lower levels before being motivated by needs at higher levels. However, ERG theory differs from Maslow's theory. Firstly, a person's existence needs don't necessarily have to be satisfied before who can become concerned about whose relationships with others or about using whose personal capabilities, whose desire to meet the existence needs may be stronger than whose desire to meet the two other types of needs, such as relationship with others or about using those personal capabilities, but the other needs may still be important. Otherwise, the need hierarchy theory proposes that the hierarchy is fixed and that physiological needs must be largely satisfied before other needs become important. Hence, using ERG theory to apply to this case, it may explain why Don Coggin did these behaviour. Although, Frances Mead , compensation director for Puma corporation , who paid well to hire Don Coggin to fill position of benefits administrator for her company in corporate personnel department at Puma, headquartered in Salt Lake city, Utah and the job was located in Utah. Hence, Don could always enjoyed the outdoor and he liked to backpack, camp and did some mountain climbing sport entertainment conveniently. Hence, it ensured that this job location could give Dan to enjoy his likely mountain climbing ,camp, backpack sport entertainment conveniently was also an important reason to influence Don to choose this job.In fact, Dan's financial background aided him greatly in his new benefits administrator job, where he was responsible for development and administration of the pension plan, life and health insurance package, employee stock purchase plan and other employee benefit programs within one month. Dan has learned how to do duties. Frances Mead, she was satisfied with her selection for Dan to do this benefits administrator position. Hence, she expected Dan to move up to in the department rank rapidly, but Dan only concern was that who did not seem to have enough time to enjoy his outdoor activities after he had seem promoted to do further duties absolutely. It implied that Dan disliked to promote to spend more time to do more job duties.

Even, his salary would not be increased and his rank would be promoted in this moment. After six months, Dan had his job proficiently and who was quite talented and the job did not present a strong challenge to him. During to Frances, compensation director for Puma corporation recognized Dan's talent and wanted him to evaluate Puma corporation's complete benefits package for the purpose of making needed changes without the help of costly outside consultants and Frances believed that Puma's benefits package was outdated and needed to be revised. However, Frances felt Dan disliked to discuss with her to evaluate the total benefits package from her several encouraging because Dan seemed to be constantly thinking of and discussing his outdoor activities and he seemed lack of commitment to do his job. As ERG theory indicated that a person's existence needs don't necessarily have to be satisfied before who can became concerned about whose relationships with others or about using whose personal capabilities, whose desire to meet the existence needs may be stronger than whose desire to meet the two other types of needs, such as relationship with others or about using those personal capabilities, but the other needs may still be important. As this case, Dan , this company 's benefits administrator who chose to serve this company, instead of salary was paid well reason, the other reason was his job was located to let him to enjoy the outdoors sport activities conveniently. Hence, it is Dan's existence needs in this company. Hence, even Frances , this company compensation director accepted to increase Dan's salary to promote him to do higher rank after six months, due to Dan's personal capabilities was very good. Dan whose behaviour performance disliked to discuss with Frances to evaluate and Dan seemed to be constantly thinking of and discussing his outdoor activities and he seemed lack of commitment to his job. As ERG theory indicated Dan could not motivated by Frances because Frances needed him to forgive to enjoy his outdoor sport entertainment when Frances needed him to spend much time to discuss with her to evaluate the total benefits package at this moment.

However, Dan felt the reason of his existence was staying in this company was because his new job could located in Utah to always enjoyed the outdoor entertainment. If he could not spend extra time to enjoy this kind of entertainment. It would cause Dan lost commitment to serve this employer. Hence, as ERG theory indicated that Dan felt he and Frances relationship would become worse and he would feel this company was not to be valued for whom to grow further and Dan would plan to leave current employer possibly if Frances continue to force Dan to discuss with her to evaluate the total benefits package for her employer. Moreover, ERG theory also indicated that when a need is satisfied, it may remain the dominant motivator if the next need in the hierarchy can't be satisfied. As Dan , benefits administrator who had satisfied whose relatedness needs to Frances, as Frances had believed who was satisfied with her selection to do this benefits administrator position absolutely within this six months. Basically,

Dan felt his existence needs was satisfied with Frances, compensation director relationship. Hence, during Dan was stilling doing this benefits administration position within these six months, it might remain Dan to be this company dominant motivator, even, he could not promote to do higher rank and he could earn higher salary from Frances after these six months. In result, Dan's performance began to be poor after six months, e.g. complaints from employees regard errors and time delays in insurance claims and stock purchases began to increase. Also, Dan was package and thus no progress in the design of new benefit programs and he began to call in sick occasionally. Interestingly, he seemed to be sick on Friday and Monday, allowing for a three day weekend. It was obvious that Dan had the ability to perform the job and even more challenging tasks. In conclusion, Dan changed his behaviour and performance poorly in this company because Dan felt not he had existence needs, as he needed to spend time to discuss with Frances to evaluate the total benefits package employees, she could not let him to have more extra time to enjoy his sport entertainment as well as Dan, benefits administrator and Frances, compensation director both co-operation relationship was broken because the reason of Frances needed Dan to spend much time to discuss with her to evaluate Puma corporation's completion benefits package for the purpose of making needed changes was that she did not without the help of costly outside consultants and Frances was still not ensuring to increase his salary, she was examining Dan's ability in this stage. Hence, Frances's decision would cause Dan lost existence needs and relatedness needs and growth needs in this company. Due to these needs had been found to decrease to Dan as they were not satisfied and the lesser needs were not satisfied and the lesser are desired . Hence, it would cause Dan's behaviour and performance to be poor because Frances could not motivate Dan to get these psychological needs absolutely in this company after six months.

Using expectancy theory, explain the reasons for the situation.

Expectancy theory suggests motivation is a function of an individuals expectancy that a given amount of effort will lead to particular level of performance and judgement that indicates performance will lead to certain outcomes. Expectancy is the subjective probability that a given amount of effort will lead to a particular level of performance. Hence, manager needs to consider the factor of probability that a given amount of effort will lead to a particular level of performance and the second factor individuals consider is the perceived connection between a particular level of performance and important outcomes and the third factor is the importance of each anticipated outcome.Hence, it means individual may have different goals or needs and individual may have different connections between actions and achievement of goals to consider alternatives, weigh cost and benefit and choose action of maximum utility. Different reward can be given to individual as a result of effort or performance. Hence, expectancy theory indicates that people are influences by the expected results of their actions.

Concept of motivation is some driving force within individuals by which they attempt to achieve some goal in order to fulfil some need or expectation. People's behaviours are determined by what motivates them.Their performance is a product of both ability level and motivation. Motivation is a function of the relationship between effort expended and perceived level of performance and the expectation that rewards (desired outcomes) will be related to performance and the expectation that rewards (desired outcomes) are available. Motivation includes extrinsic and intrinsic two kind of motivations. Extrinsic motivation is related to tangible rewards such as salary and benefits, security, promotion, contract of service, the work environment and conditions of work as well as intrinsic motivation is related to psychological rewards, such as the opportunity to use one's ability, a sense of challenge and achievement, receiving appreciation, positive recognition and being treated in a caring and considerate manner.People are capable and willing to perceive fairness in their immediate environment, compare input , ability, skill, age, education, effort and training to outcome like monetary reward, praise, status, improved promotion opportunities to compare reward to others. It implies needs and expectations of staffs at work, it includes economic rewards, social relationships, intrinsic satisfaction. Hence, motivation is as psychological forces that determine the direction of a person's behaviour in an organization and a person's level of effort and a person's level of persistence. It is important that managers attempt to reduce potential frustration, for example, through, effective
recruitment, selection and socialisation, training and development, job design and work organization, equitable human resource management policies, recognition and reward, effective communications,participative styles of management, attempting to understand the individual's perception of the situation. Proper attention to motivation

and to the needs and expectation of people at work will help overcome boredom and frustration induced behaviour.

To apply this expectancy theory to this case study. In fact, Dan who had lack effort and motivation to do this benefits administrator position from Frances after six months, so Dan should choose to perform whose normal job duties poorly. e.g. complaints from employees regarding errors and time delays in insurance claims and stock purchases began to increase. Even, Dan was making no progress in the evaluation of benefit package and thus no progress in the design of new benefit programs and he began to call in sick occasionally. Interestingly, he seemed to be sick on Friday and Monday, allowing for a three day weekend. It was obvious that Dan had the ability to perform the job and even more challenging tasks.The expectancy theory could explain reasons why Dan's behaviour and performance was became poor. Due to expectancy theory suggests motivation is a function of an individual's expectancy that a given amount of effort will lead a particular level of performance and judgement that indicates performance will lead to certain outcomes. Before the six months, Frances could give motivation to Dan, such as she could give good salary and good job location to satisfy Dan's life needs and outdoor sport entertainment needs and Dan and Frances both felt this job's working hours and Dan's ability and performance was very reasonable.

However, after six months, Frances needed Dan to spend much time to discuss with her to evaluate the total benefits package for her employees, but Frances could not tell Dan to ensure to increase Dan's salary and promotion after Dan should finish this extra evaluation job duties with Frances. Even, Dan felt who could not enjoy this outdoor sport entertainment due to he needed to spend much time to discuss with Frances about the total benefits package evaluation to whose employees issue. Hence,Dan would felt that who spent much effort to do this job, but he could not get fair salary and position . It would cause him to decide to change his job performance and personal behaviour to be poor , e.g. complaints from employees regarding, errors and time delays in insurance claims and stock purchases began to increase. Even, Dan was also making no progress in the evaluation of benefit package and this no progress in the design of new benefit programs and he began to call in sick occasionally. Interestingly, he seemed to be sick on Friday and Monday, allowing for a three day weekend. It was obvious that Dan had the ability (effort) to perform to job (benefit administrator position) in this Puma corporation company, but he chose to perform to do this position poorly. The reason was because Dan had judged that his expectancy was not reasonable from Frances demand because Dan needed to spend much time to discuss with Frances and who could not get higher salary and higher rank and who could not have extra time to enjoy his outdoor entertainment. Hence, Dan's decision to make poor performance and bad behaviour, his aim was to make Frances felt who had ability to change another new job possibly. Unless, Frances could change her decision not needed Dan to spend much time to discuss with her to deal this extra job duties. Otherwise, who would find another new job possibly. It implied Dan's job expectancy was not same to Frances's performance need expectancy to Dan to cause Dan's poor performance occurred after six month.

Using the integration framework found in the last major section of the chapter, describe what actions Frances should and should not take.

In fact, Dan Coggin, benefits administrator, whose behaviour performance indicated that who chose to do this job because he felt be well paid and this job was located in Utah to always enjoy the outdoors activities of backpack, camp and do some mountain climbing. Before six months, Dan's job performance was satisfied with Frances, compensation director, so it caused Dan expected Dan to move up in the department ranks rapidly . Due to Frances felt Puma's benefits package was outdated and needed to revised and who proposed to making needed changes, without the help of costly outside consultants. Thus, Frances decided to recognize Dan's talents and wanted him spent extra time to evaluate with her to discuss how Puma corporation's complete benefits package to make changed to satisfy Puma's employees benefits of needs. However, after six months, Dan's performance and behaviour began to be poor, e.g. complaints from employees regarding errors and time delays in insurance claims and stock purchase began to increase. Also, Dan was making no progress in the evaluation of benefit package and thus no progress in the design of new benefit programs and he began to call in sick occasionally. Interestingly, he seemed to be sick on Friday and Monday, allowing for a three day weekend. It was obvious that Dan had the ability to perform the job and even more challenging tasks.

However, why Dan became lazy and who disliked to spend extra time to discuss with Frances to evaluate how to change Puma corporation's complete benefits package to its employees. It was obvious that Frances forced Dan to spend extra time to discuss with her to do evaluation issue that who did not enquire Dan's desire(ideas) whether who liked or disliked to do this issue and Dan would feel who would not have time to enjoy his sport activities in this job Utah location and who also felt it was unfair to him why whose salary was not increased and position was not promoted when Dan needed to spend extra time to do extra job unreasonably.

I shall use integration framework to find whether what Frances Mead, compensation director should take actions and should not take actions. On the one hand, Frances should take these actions as below:

In common, formulating strategies that can deliver competitive advantage is not easy. Senior managers needed to work with other individuals engage in meetings, experiments, discussion and analyses in order to create or modify company strategies. Implementing strategies and engaging in the day-to-day behaviours that help to create competitive advantage also are not easy task. Hence, staffs must be motivated if who are to effectively engage in the behaviours and practices that bring advantage and success to a firm. Hence, Frances mead, compensation director should need to choose to use different strategies to require different types of people (staffs) and behaviours and therefore different approaches to motivation. To fully motivate such Dan, benefits administrator staff, resource for trying new ideas, must be available, including time and opportunities to develop new skills to change old pension plan, life and health insurance package, employee stock purchase plan and other employee benefit programs benefit package. I believe human resources and time was not enough to Frances and Dan two people to evaluate this issue. Frances ought to enquire Dan's idea whether Dan felt what cause whose performance began to be poor, e.g. complaints from employee regarding errors and time delays in insurance claims and stock purchase began to increase. To investigate whether Dan felt the issue of evaluation Puma corporation's complete benefits packageissue with her or other factors that was influenced to his normal job performance to be poor. The benefits were that Frances could let Dan to tell what the reasons were to cause his performance poor honestly and their conservation could let Dan felt France could spend extra time to consider to discuss whether what Dan felt needs and dissatisfaction to cause Dan's performance poorly. Hence, Frances could judge whether Dan's ability could deal to evaluate Puma corporation's complete benefits package and this issues could not influence Dan's daily normal job duties for this benefits administrator position or not. If Frances should prefer to spend extra time to discuss with Dan about what difficulty and needs and dissatisfaction who felt to cause whose job performance began to be poor. Frances should know whether it was job factors or other factors were influenced to Dan to feel dissatisfaction to cause whose performance poorly to let Frances to revise whose strategies. The factors could include such as, unreasonable market salary, poor working environment, increasing job responsibilities and feeling difficulties, lacking opportunity for advancement or promotion, challenging work and potential for personal growth, lacking personal commitment and recognition and achievement needs to this position,lacking work and life balance needs, unreasonable company policies and working conditions and administration procedures, poor interpersonal relationship with peer and poor status security issues.

As goal setting theory suggests challenging and specific goals increase human performance because whose effort and persistence attention can be committed to affect motivation. Due to Frances didn't indicate clear specific goals to let Dan to know whether how and what steps who should use to evaluate Dan's ability to judge whose job performance was achieved to goal to promote higher rank before Dan began to do this job. Hence, Dan should feel doubt why Frances needed him to spend extra time to evaluate with Frances about making changes to Puma corporation's complete benefits package issue after six months. Hence, Frances should need to explain why who needed Dan to spend extra time to evaluate with him and they also needed to discuss further issue for this evaluation report job of about how difficult Dan felt his performance goal should be achieved whether the goal should be easy, moderately difficult or very difficult to achieve to Dan's ability, how the expert outcome should be specific or goals could be more do best what Dan needed to make commitment to achieve this goal; to what extent of feedback needs Dan should be informed of their report in this evaluation progress toward his performance goal. Hence, if Frances could let Dan to know what Dan needed to perform to achieve. Frances goal to evaluate Dan's ability clearly. Then, Dan's could judge whether Frances was a right employer for his continue staying or leaving further decision. An understanding for the factors that motivate workers are critical not only to corporate executive who concentrate on the bottom line, but more importantly to the security of companies as it relates to compete in the global market. However, the internal process view that motivation needs that activate, guide, and motivate behaviour (especially goal directed behaviour) is one of the most important concerns of modern organizational managers , as Frances Mead, compensation director for Puma corporation. The traditional motivator for a worker is his salary, but in many cases that isn't enough. As Puma corporation, Frances Mead, compensation director, it implied to use only material rewards to motivate Dan, benefits administrator staff , it was not enough and it needed to use only motivators to satisfy Dan's needs. Supposing to Dan's tasks such as development and administration of pension plan, life and health insurance and employee stock purchase package etc duties whose solution was obvious extrinsic motivators, e.g. increasing salary reward were working as which should be increase performance, but for task whose solution were more complex, such as revision and evaluation of complete outdated benefits package for the purpose how to make needed changes, extrinsic motivation should have negative effects on performance to Dan. Hence, if the task was complex, the motivation users must be intrinsic e.g. achievement, chance, promotion to give to Dan employee. Due to revision and evaluation of complete outdated benefits package was one complex and if also needed to spend more resources and time discussion tasks for Puma corporation. Hence, Frances should ought to tell Dan who should use job with performance related pay to attract him of higher ability and induced who to provide greater effort. Frances should focuses on Dan's role as an incentive system. Hence, Frances should consider compensation as a return for Dan's services rendered and saw Dan's performance was as a reflection of whose personal worth in terms of skills and abilities as well as whose education and training also had acquired. However, Frances should view compensation from two perspectives: as a major expense and as a possible influence on Dan's attitudes and behaviours through compensation based motivational strategies. This potential to influence Dan's work attitudes and behaviours and subsequently the productivity and effectiveness of Puma corporation.

Attribute theory indicated that when an outcome, such as poor performance is attributed to a stable cause. such as low intelligence, it is logical to expect that the employee's performance isn't going to change in the future. If the same poor performance is attributed to a less stable factor, such as insufficient effort, a employer can expect that the employee could improve whose performance by working harder in the future. Thus, Frances should consider what attributions were to influence Dan's job performance began to be poor, then who should revise whose actions should be changed to solve this issue. The attribution should influence Dan's performance to be poor, internal and stable attribution, such as whether Dan's intelligence could deal his normal job duties and extra job duties of evaluation on Puma's benefits package both at the same time; external and unstable attribution, such as whether Dan had enough effort and time to attempt to discuss with Frances to finish this extra job duties of
evaluation on Puma's benefits package within limited time or external and unstable attribution, such as whether Frances' temporary strategy or decision was without the help of outside consultants to evaluate Puma's benefits package whether which should give pressure or effort to Dan to attempt to help him to finish this evaluation job, it meant that Dan would do this duties, even which should also influence whose normal duties to be poor if Dan felt pressure to attempt to do this extra duties. Frances should need to provide feedback to Dan about whose progress toward performance goals was well established . In fact, feedback on performance was likely to have a positive effect on motivation. Moreover, Dan's feedback was important when benefits package of evaluation of performance goals existed and when Dan was relatively difficult to achieve. Hence, Frances's feedback should encourage Dan to discover (find) errors to know what he should need to improve during evaluation was progressing and Frances should not have due date limitation to let Dan felt pressure to finish this benefit plan evaluation job ,even if influenced to whose normal job duties poorly .

Expectancy theory provides a useful framework for organizing those factors : people will be committed to goals that carrying a reasonable expectation of being attained and are more viewed as desirable to attain. Frances should judge whether human resource inputs were enough to do this benefit package evaluation job with Dan. It was possible that Dan felt human resource inputs were out enough to cause who felt pressure to attempt to dot this extra job duties with Frances and Dan should feel inequity and unfair treatment and unreasonable due to who should need to spend extra time to do this extra evaluation job with Frances. Hence, Frances should need to explain to let Dan to know why who needed Dan to attempt to do this extra evaluation job as well as what benefits were Dan should give reward if Dan's evaluation job performance could satisfy Frances' requirement. Then Dan would be committed to goals that carrying a reasonable expectation of being attained and was more viewed as desirable to attain. On the other hand, Frances should not take these actions as below: Although Dan performance began to become poor after six months due to Dan needed to spend extra time to discuss with Frances to evaluate how to change Puma corporation old benefits package issue. However, Frances should not angry to blame Dan immediately. The reason was that Dan's performance was still good before six months. It meant that who had ability to do this position.Hence, Dan ought have ability to assist Frances to evaluate the changed needs to current benefits package evaluation to Puma corporation's employees with Frances discussion together.

Otherwise, if Frances should blame to Dan. it would cause Dan felt Frances was not a good compensation director to manage and co-operate with him to work together and it was possible that would choose to leave Puma corporation to find any employer immediately. Then, Frances would feel difficult to spend more time to choose applicants to re-employ another new staff to do this benefit administrator position, instead of Dan and Frances should also need to spend more time to train this new staff. Hence, Frances should not blame Dan. Otherwise, Frances should need to enquire why Dan's performance to be poor whether Dan's poor performance behaviour was caused by extra evaluation job duties factor or other personal factors to revise Dan's errors to expect Dan to continue to assist Frances to finish this evaluation job effectively and efficiently.

In conclusion, I did not agree Frances, compensation director should blame Dan immediately because Dan believed himself had owned market competitive ability due to Dan had worked in Puma corporation six months . It should give Dan had confidence to change another new employer if Dan felt Frances' personal attitude was not friendly to arrange any further new jobs to him to do. Hence, Frances should enquire Dan why who performed poorly in order to solve whose personal trouble issues and then Frances should also attempt to find some methods to satisfy Dan's personal needs to motivate and persuade Dan to continue to co-operate with Frances in this company together.

Crisis management and time management strategy solves nuclear factory team cooperation challenge

This case concerns how this nuclear factory repair teams often face difficulties to make any kinds of decisions in suddenly. So, management decision making is one important factor to assist how they can deal any problems in any time when they are working in this nuclear factory. In academic decision theory, one fundamental decision rule is that of maximizing expected utility. This is the idea that when company management needs to make a decision and there are different choices, each choice has a set of possible outcome with different probabilities.

Nuclear factory team making the most right decision challenge:

When you are one nuclear factory entrepreneur, how you manage you nuclear team work efficiently. Dan was the supervisor of technical maintenance in the nuclear power facility factory and who had noticed that several of his people were reluctant to follow maintenance procedures. He had been told that the specifications were too complex to understand, that the procedures were often unnecessary,and that the plant engineers did not really appreciate maintenance problems. On the one hand, Dan realized that most of their complaints were just excuses for doing things their own way. On the other hand, Dan did not really know which procedures were important and which were not. That's why Dan had asked Mary, design engineer to meet with him. Mary, design engineer knew nuclear power plants' procedures are complex and potentially risky and every specification and every procedures had a reason for being there. If Dan, supervisor of technical maintenance ignored one procedure, they might get by with it and nothing happens. But one of them just might do it at the wrong time and it caused serious wrong result in this nuclear power plant. So, Mary needs Dan to explain that they had safety and cost to consider. If they lost expensive equipment how they should lie to pay for it. Dan referred that if they lost a finger or got exposes to much radiation, they would not like that happened either.

However, Mary needed Dan to follow her specification and procedures to do, but Dan told Mary this really wasn't what his maintenance staffs wanted and they hoped for a little flexibility and who felt who would not like it, but they would have to do it. Lately that afternoon, Dan decided to met his unit and relayed the instructions and who reminded them of the rules and disciplinary actions for not following procedures. At the end of the meeting, who couldn't decide whether whose decision had done any better than Mary's decision. Harry, technical maintenance staff noticed that he had been assigned the routinely scheduled maintenance on the three feed water pumps. The pumps were normally used only for start up and shutdown and as emergency backup. When the main feed water system malfunctioned, these pumps would activate to keep the steam generator from drying out. The procedure also specified that the pumps should be serviced and test one at a time and that one pump should be out of service at a time. Harry thought that who needed to take three hours to service the pumps that way, but who could do it in two hours if who shut don together. Finally, who did not follow specification and procedures to do maintenance job from Mary demand and who decided to shorten the normal three time to two hours to finish this pump maintenance service job. This case indicated that the nuclear power plant maintenance job needed Mary, design engineer and Dan, supervisor of technical maintenance to co-operate to give their opinions to make any important decision to follow the specification and procedures to reduce the incident crisis occurrence to cause serious death to workers and damage to nuclear power plants. However, due to Dan who had noticed that several of his people were reluctant to follow maintenance procedures. He had been told that the specifications were too complex to understand, that the procedures were often unnecessary, and that the plant engineers did not really appreciate maintenance problems. In fact, I believe that the bad result would be caused seriously. Hence, Mary needed Dan to discuss this issue urgently. However, Mary needed Dan to follow her specification and procedures to do, but Dan told Mary this really wasn't what his maintenance staffs wanted and they hoped for a little flexibility and who felt who would not like it, but they would have to do it. It implied that Dan still agreed whose technician opinions and refused to accept Mary's opinion to follow specifications and procedure in the maintenance procedure as well as Dan decided to meet whose technicians to notify them the rules and disciplinary actions either who might choose to follow procedures or who might choose not to follow during their maintenance. Hence, it implied Dan gave whose technicians to choose freely and Dan's attitude was not forced to need them to follow easily. I agreed that Dan handled this decision was not the best way.However, it was not right that Dan made decisions to choose of nuclear power plant maintenance job whether technicians ought follow specifications and procedure from Mary or technicians ought not follow specifications and procedure from maintenance units actions in the short time. Because it would increase Dan, supervising maintenance unit technicians death or hurt chance and nuclear power plant damaging change if whose decision was wrong. So, Dan ought need to spend time to discuss and gather information to evaluate whether Mary or technicians' suggestion was more safe and less cost to work in nuclear power plant for long term benefits in their meeting together.

In fact, Dan had not follow the correct steps to make final decision before he accepted whose maintenance units did not need to follow specifications and procedures during who needed to maintain nuclear power plant. The decision making steps include that as defining the maintenance problem, e.g. what maintenance problems were the most important to need technicians followed all specifications and procedures to carry on working; identifying criteria, gathering and evaluating information, e.g. other nuclear power plant maintenance procedure methods; listing and evaluating information; selecting best alternative; implementing and following up and giving feedback to let Mary to know the reason either why who disagreed Mary's suggestion or why who agreed whose maintenance units suggestion or none of final decision was made that Mary and Dan and technicians needed to carry on meeting to discuss clearly. An effective decision was as one that was timely, that was acceptable to those affected by it, and that satisfied the key decision criteria, and it was in the systematic and logical process. Mary and Dan and maintenance units had not ever sat down to discuss this issue in any once meeting together. Dan only met Mary and Dan only met maintenance units individual to discuss this issue separately.He did not give chance to let them to discuss with him in meeting room by face to face contact. Hence, they could not have complete knowledge about all possible alternatives to achieve their potential results effectively because who lacked enough time to make decision making and one good decision making needs a cognitive activity that relies on both perception and judgement. If two people used different approaches to solve problem in the processes of perception and judgement, they were likely to make quite different decision, even if the facts and objectives are identical. As Mary and Dan used different approaches to solve maintenance procedure problem in the process of perception and judgement to decide decision whether the maintenance units needed to follow specifications and procedure or they did not need to follow during technicians did maintenance job in nuclear power plant. Thus, Dan could not ensure technicians' decision whether which was better than Mary's decision because who lacked complete knowledge about all possible alternatives to make final decision before. In conclusion, Dan ought spend time to follow correct decision steps to make decision and who also needed to give them to discuss this issue by face to face contact in meeting and he ought not own objective judgement to agree any one suggestion, who ought give them to make subjective judgement to discuss to accept whose decision freely. Hence, Dan ought to be one participant role and ought not be one controller role in this decision making procedure.

suggestion of solvable method:

Analyze the critical problem in Part A of the case.

Did Dan handle it in the best way?

What decision styles did he use?

Decisions are reflected the person's preference for one of two perceptual styles and one of two judgement styles. Dan seemed to use intuition style decision, who disliked details and time required to sort and interpret them and whose decision made using this style was based on imagination and Dan believed that whose creativity could help Mary and technicians both to choose whose decision was more suitable. For example, Dan did not spend time to follow decision steps to make decision and Dan did not let Mary and maintenance units and him had chance to meet to discuss this issue by face to face contact to decide whether whose decision was less risky and logical to maintenance units work in nuclear power plant easily. Dan was also a feeling style person to make whose judgement. A feeling style meant a decision style focused on subjective evaluation and the emotional reactions of others. Dan preferred to rely on whose emotions and personal subjective judgements to agree maintenance units' decision. At the earlier, Dan had noticed that several of his people were reluctant to follow maintenance procedures. He had been told that the specifications were too complex to understand, that the procedures were often unnecessary, and that the plant engineers did not really appreciate maintenance problems. So, Dan had accepted maintenance units' suggestion to make judge and Dan had not think and analysed their suggestion clearly. So, Dan chose maintenance units decision was based their feeling and emotion reactions. Before,Dan was met to enquire whose suggestion from Mary. Dan would not accept her suggestion easily, even Mary let Dan to know what the serious crisis would have more chance to occur if his maintenance units did not follow specifications and procedure during they were carrying on maintaining job. However, Dan had not change to accept maintenance units' suggestion easily due to they had influenced Dan's feeling and emotion to judge this issue early.

In what important ways is Harry's behaviour different from Marv's?

During the nuclear power facilities occurred problem, Mary and Harry's both behaviour performance could be seemed as these four aspects to evaluate, such as judgement effort and decision making effort and crisis management effort and time management effort aspects.The important ways is Harry's behaviour different from Marv's included as below: Marv Bradbury, technician was working shift time in nuclear power facility plant. In fact, most technicians did not like this shift, but Marv discovered that who enjoyed this job after few months and who also liked sleep in the mornings and many of this co-workers complained his behaviour to influence poor team work. Marv's job in the nuclear power plant was particular important. Marv's primary was to monitor a series of dialsand readouts in the control room. In fact, the system was so automatic, so who did not spend much time to do this duty of control and manage this system. However, if the readings indicated some variance in the system whose responsibilities were great, who would needed to do duty of interpret the readings, diagnose the problem as well as who would needed to do initiate corrective actions if the automatic correcting system failed. For two reasons, Marv never worried about his responsibilities because the system was fault free and self correcting and it was a good system with no weaknesses as well as Marv had confidence to understand about the system and he was trained always knew what he had to do in the event of a problem and was capable of doing it. In fact, the system occurred problem and who attempted to solve, but who felt difficult to deal. Hence, Marv felt the system was in serve trouble and decided to phone to get help. Although, who could not solve this system problem, but who knew the result if the systems dried out, the temperature was really going to go up and that the core was going to be damaged. Hence, the nuclear power facilities would cause to damaged. However, it took minutes to get someone to attempt to solve this system trouble, but it was too late and no one seemed to know what to do.

On judgement effort and decision making effort aspects, Marv's behaviour performance was seemed as team co-operation managed style person. On the one hand, who lacked decision making effort and who could not attempt to solve problem himself and who needed team co-operation to work together to increase confidence to solve problem. On the other hand, who lacked judgement effort to know whether what who ought need to attempt to solve any during crisis occurred. Moreover, Marv also lacked time management and crisis management efforts.

However, Marv needed to wait eight minutes to get someone to attempt to solve this system trouble, but it was late and no one seemed to know what to do. If the technicians took longer time to arrive, even Marv could not phone to contact them successfully. The result would be more poor seriously. It seemed that Marv could not have confidence to continue to maintain this system. Otherwise, if Marv could attempt to maintain, it was possible that the system could be maintained successfully.

Because Marv felt to make decision making have some degree of risk at this immediate accident occurrence, it would seem that risk taken by a group should be the same as the average risk that would have been taken by the individual group members acting alone (himself). Hence, who decided not to do action to attempt to solve this trouble, who decided to phone other technician team members to wait their arrival after eight minutes to attempt to solve this trouble, but it was too late and no one seemed to know what to do. However, if who could attempt to solve this trouble within eight minutes, it is possible that this trouble would solve from himself alone.

Harry, technical maintenance staff noticed that he had been assigned the routinely scheduled maintenance on the three feed water pumps. The pumps were normally used only for start up and shutdown and as emergency backup. When the main feed water system malfunctioned, these pumps would activate to keep the steam generator from drying out. The procedure also specified that the pumps should be serviced and test one at a time and that one pump should be out of service at a time.

Harry thought that who needed to take three hours to service the pumps that way, but who could do it in two hours if who shut don together. Finally, who did not follow specification and procedures to do maintenance job from Mary demand and who decided to shorten the normal three time to two hours to finish this pump maintenance service job. Two hours later he was done and he packed up his tools and hurried to get home.

On crisis management and time management effort aspects, Harry's behaviour performance was seemed as self managed style. He could attempt to accept risk to decide how to solve problem from himself effort and who had effort to judge how to deal in any crisis occurrence and time management. Hence, it could prove who could deal any crisis occurrence alone and who did not spend time to wait any team members (technician group) assistance, although who could not ensure whose decision whether it was right or wrong. Hence, it implied who was one confident person.Harry, technical maintenance staff noticed that he had been assigned the routinely scheduled maintenance on the three feed water pumps. The pumps were normally used only for start up and shutdown and as emergency backup. When the main feed water system malfunctioned, these pumps would activate to keep the steam generator from drying out. The procedure also specified that the pumps should be serviced and test one at a time and that one pump should be out of service at a time. Harry thought that who needed to take three hours to service the pumps that way, but who could do it in two hours if who shut don together. Finally, who did not follow specification and procedures to do maintenance job from Mary demand and who decided to shorten the normal three time to two hours to finish this pump maintenance service job. Two hours later he was done and he packed up his tools and hurried to get home. On judgement and decision making effort aspects, Harry's behaviour performed who can attempt to judge what action was possible more right to solve this trouble, although who could not ensure whose action is right or wrong, who could make decision to attempt to finish whose job and who felt who would not need to spend time to wait other team members (technicians) to make any decision to work together. Hence, who performed that who was one confident person. In conclusion, risk exist when the outcome of a chosen course of action is not certain. Most decisions in business carry some degree of risk. In choosing between less and more risky options, an individual's risk taking propensity, or willingness to take chances, often plays a role. Two persons with different propensities to take risks may make different decisions when confronted with identical decision situations and information. One who is willing to face the possibility if loss, for example, may select a riskier alternative, whereas another person will choose for taking risks. As Harry and Marv who were working in this same nuclear power facility plant, when the crisis occurred, whose performance would have different to decide to cause different result. Due to Harry performed behaviour was more confident and more judgement effort and self managed person who could accept risk to attempt to make decision alone and disregarded whether the result was right or wrong . Otherwise, Marv performed behaviour was lacked confidence and less judgement effort and team managed person who could not accept risk to attempt to make decision alone and regarded whether the result was right absolutely. Hence, their performance caused the result was also different, as Harry decided to spend two hours to solve the system trouble alone. Although Marv was not sure that Harry's action whether was correct or incorrect and it needed time to wait whether the system would occur trouble again or not. However, Harry had attempted to finish whose duties. Otherwise, Marv decided to phone to ask technicians to assist whom and they arrived after eight minutes and who attempted to co-operate to work together. But it was too late and no anyone seemed to know what to do and the system trouble would not still be solve. Hence, it was ensure that the system must be existed trouble and Marv decided not to continue to solve this problem individually and it seemed that Marv could not finish whose duties definitely. Otherwise, Harry could attempt to solve this system trouble alone although it needed time to wait. It seemed that Harry, technician had more strategic decision ability and performed better to compare Marv to deal any crisis occurrence in the nuclear power plant and it seemed that who could assist Dan, supervisor technical maintenance in whose team effectively, although the system needed time to wait to confirm whether it was needed to maintain or needed not maintain again after Macv spent two hours to attempt to maintain. However, it seemed that Harry had more judgement and decision making and crisis management and time management efforts to compare Marv to do this technician position in this nuclear power plant.

How might group decision making be applied at the end of Part B?

The group decision making might be applied to Marv, technician shift team as below:

In general ,in high involvement organizations, associates participate in many decisions with lower level and middle level managers and where low level and middle level managers participate in decisions with senior level managers as well as teams of associates can also make some decisions without managerial input. In this way, human capital throughout the organization is utilized effectively. However, group decision making is similar in some ways to individual decision making because the purpose of group decision makes to arrive a preferred solution to a problem, the group must use the same

basic decision making steps: such as defining problem, identifying criteria, gathering and evaluating information, listing and evaluating alternative, choosing the best alternatives and implementing it finally. Groups are made up of multiple individual, however, resulting in dynamic and interpersonal processes that make group decision making different from decision making by individual. For instance, some members of the decision group will arrive with their own expectation, problem definition and predetermined solutions. These characteristics are likely to cause some interpersonal problems among group members. Also some members will have given more thought to the decision situation than other members' expectation about what is to be accomplished may differ. Thus, a group leader may be more concerned with a collection of individuals into a collaborative decision making team than with the development of individual decision making skills.

In fact, group processes that occur during decision making often prevent full decision of facts and alternatives. Group norms, member roles, dysfunctional communication pattern, and too much cohesiveness may deter the group to produce ineffective decisions. Marv Bradbury, technician was working shift time in nuclear power facility plant. In fact, most technicians did not like this shift, but Marv discovered that who enjoyed this job after few months and who also liked sleep in the mornings and many of this co-workers complained his behaviour to influence poor team work. Marv's job in the nuclear power plant was particular important. His primary was to monitor a series of dials and readouts in the control room. In fact, the system was so automatic, so who did not spend much time to do this duty of control and manage this system. However, if the readings indicated some variance in the system whose responsibilities were great, who would needed to do duty of interpret the readings, diagnose the problem as well as who would need to do initiate corrective actions if the automatic correcting system failed. For two reasons, Marv never worried about his responsibilities because the system was fault free and self correcting and it was s good system with no weaknesses as well as Marv had confidence to understand about the system and he was trained always knew what he had to do in the event of a problem and was capable of doing it. One day, the system occurred problem and who attempted to solve, but who felt difficult to deal. Hence, Marv felt the system was in serve trouble and decided to phone to get help. Although, who could not solve this system problem, but who knew the result if the systems dried out, the temperature was really going to go up and that the core was going to be damaged. Hence, the nuclear power facilities would cause to damaged. However, I felt that it was wrong decision that Marv decided to phone to technicians to wait eight minutes to attempt to find them to solve this system trouble, but it was too late and no one seemed to know what to do. In the beginning, Marv could attempt to solve this system trouble by individual decision, but then who decided to phone to technician team members to assist who because who wanted to reduce whose action risk alone. After eight minutes, these technician team members arrived the nuclear power plant. Marv did not anticipate any actions finally and Marv did not tell technicians how to attempt to act, so who did not anticipate any group decision among their actions finally. In the result, these technicians group decided to auxiliary pump room and discovered that the three valves were still closed and they decided to open the valves, but it was too late and no one seemed to know what to do. During these technicians group decided to do any actions immediately, their group leader would think to build a positive image (believing this system trouble could solve immediately) under threat (nuclear power facilities would occur damage possibly). Hence, this technician group leader had already failed possibly and who would decide to attempt to maintain this system together and who decided not to enquire Dan, supervisor of technician to assist them immediately. It was possible that who felt time was not enough to wait supervisor assistance or who could attempt to solve by themselves. Because Marv believed that group think decision making was more successful than individual decision making.

Although, group think did not guarantee a better decision but simply increased that likelihood of such a result. When good judgement and discussion were suppressed, the group decision could be more effective to compare to individual decision, Hence, it was possible that , the group decision making could give some benefits to Marv's individual decision making, which included that group decision making could reduce more errors to than Marv's individual decision alone; group decision making could reduce pressure when technicians gave their opinions to solve this system trouble at the same time; members who could been quiet were assumed to be in complete this job together; they could build complex rationales that effectively discount warnings or information that conflict with their thinking; they could reduce chance to cause them to ignore any dangers when they worked at the time and they could discussed any facts, criticisms or evaluations to solve this trouble together at the short time possibly. Hence, it implied that group making decision still had these benefits to compare to Marv's individual making decision.

What alternatives do you use for reducing the possibility of a similar problem in the future?

In academic decision theory, one fundamental decision rule is that of maximizing expected utility. This is the idea that when company management needs to make a decision and there are different choices, each choice has a set of possible outcome with different probabilities. The problem with this procedures

is that in real life the probabilities and utilities are often different to determine. Of course, if the outcomes are more or less certain. There might be more than one item you like and you might have a hard time to choose just one, but choose any one of choice will be a rational choice. More generally, what we should be when we make decisions is to list the pros and cons of each option available to use (the reasons supporting the option and the reasons against it). Management then choose the option that on balance has the most reasons in its favour. A good decision process requires all time parts being implemented correctly. For example, Is it clear what we have to decide? What is the most important or urgent decision? Are all the options realistic? Are there other options we should consider? Are we

overlooked any good or bad consequences of an option? Is there any special criteria for the decision, we should be aware of?
Have the criteria been applied wrongly?

Main reasons why people are failure in their creative idea because failure due to lack of part knowledge and relevant skills and failure of concept and wrong with the initial idea or theory and failure of judgement due to management can have the right idea, but make the wrong decision in executing and developing it and due to failure of attitude and forging a new path where others have not gone before requires courage and the right balance of attitude and due to fear to failure to cause management to abandon an idea before it comes to success.

I recommend that Harry, engineer and Dan, supervisor and Dan's group of normal shift and part time technicians who needed have group discussion to decide what were the serious or common problems as well as whether these system problems which needed to follow specification and procedures
or which needed not to follow specification and procedures during who needed to carry on working daily in this nuclear power plant. Because who should not have enough time to predict or evaluate to judge whether which system troubles issues were serious and which system troubles issues were common to decide whether which needed to follow specification and procedures to carry on maintaining job.

Thus, this decision ought be more fair between Harry and technicians to reduce their conflicts. However, in this situation, group decision making (Harry, engineer and Dan, supervisor of maintenance groups and technicians discussion together) must be better than individual decision making (Harry, engineer and
Dan, supervisor of maintenance group discussion together).
The group decision making advantage is better quality, or least a significant chance of better quality, particularly when complex decisions are being made. The advantage is based on the fact that groups bring more knowledge and facts to make decision and engage in a richer assessment of alternatives. Other advantages include making better of decisions and greater satisfaction in the organization and personal growth for group members. However, time is one several disadvantages associated with using a group to make a decision. Thus, if they had already discussed this issue to make group decision making before any system troubles existed trouble . Then, these technicians would know whether which system troubles were more serious and which system troubles were common to judge whether either which system troubles needed to follow specification and procedures or which system troubles did not need to follow specification. For example, as the shift time technician, Marv and another full time technician who could not judge whether system troubles were serious or not, so who should felt doubt and difficult whether who ought follow all instruction to finish system maintained work or who ought not follow al instruction to finish system maintained work. Even, Marv decided to phone to technicians to ask their help. Marv would cause these technicians felt difficult to make group think to make decision in the short time. Group think is a more extreme problem where the pressure to conform hinders critical analysis and creativity, resulting in poor decision making, it might include outsiders who disagree and morality superior. These members are likely to feel more comfortable with each other, but who might also mistakenly perceive themselves as creative. In conclusion, group decision making ought be needed between Harry, engineer and Dan, supervisor of maintenance and technicians before other new system troubles occurred. Hence, if this nuclear factory management can have crisis management and time management strategy to know how to assist these different repair teams to work together, then their cooperation challenge must be solved more easily.

- Time management hotel staff workplace stress emotion challenge

When you are one hotel entrepreneur, how you manage chef have high moral performance. Walt and Tony were working in the Frontier hotel, Walt was head waiter and Tony was head chef. Then, Tony encouraged Walt to start a restaurant and who promoted himself to be Walt's restaurant's head chef. Finally, after several meetings and a lot of planning, Walt and Bill decided to open a Italian restaurant and employ Tony to be head chef. After then, Walt and Bill both partners tried to encourage Tony to join them in partnership, but Tony had refused and his personal reason was to lose his freedom. However, Walt dissatisfied Tony's performance because Tony had begun waking up late for work and who had missed several shifts altogether and who also often liked to drink alcohol. Hence, Tony performed bad behaviour to cause this conflict with Walt. Although their age were late thirties years old and before they were head positions in the Frontier hotel, but Tony had personal problem, such as marriage was broken and who liked to spend much time to meet girlfriend and who often drank alcohol in his private life. Tony's private life was seemed to influence whose head chef cooking job in Walt's Italian restaurant. Although, the Italian restaurant could expand to a large location. Walt and Bill two partners could earn profit and Tony head chef could earn Frontier hotel and Italian restaurant both employers' salaries in the same time within one year. However, Tony's performance was became poor, e.g. who didn't come to work and who had called in sick to Walt. In fact, who told lie to Walt, Tony spent sick time to meet whose girlfriend. Sometime, Tony arrived Walt's restaurant to work , but sometimes who was absent. Tony had also often drunk alcohol for two years during who had worked in Frontier hotel and Italian restaurant in the period.

suggestion of solvable method:

Could Tony's problem with alcohol be stress related?

Explain why or why not?

Walt and Tony were working in the Frontier hotel, Walt was head waiter and Tony was head chef. Then, Tony encouraged Walt to start a restaurant and who promoted himself to be Walt's restaurant's head chef. Finally, after several meetings and a lot of planning, Walt and Bill decided to open a Italian restaurant and employ Tony to be head chef. After then, Walt and Bill both partners tried to encourage Tony to join them in partnership, but Tony had refused and his personal reason was to lose his freedom. However, Walt dissatisfied Tony's performance because Tony had begun waking up late for work and who had missed several shifts altogether and who also often liked to drink alcohol. Hence, Tony performed bad behaviour to cause this conflict with Walt. Although their age were late thirties years old and before they were head positions in the Frontier hotel, but Tony had personal problem, such as marriage was broken and who liked to spend much time to meet girlfriend and who often drank alcohol in his private life. Tony's private life was seemed to influence whose head chef cooking job in Walt's Italian restaurant. Although, the Italian restaurant could expand to a large location. Walt and Bill two partners could earn profit and Tony head chef could earn Frontier hotel and Italian restaurant both employers' salaries in the same time within one year. However, Tony's performance was became poor, e.g. who didn't come to work and who had called in sick to Walt. In fact, who told lie to Walt, Tony spent sick time to meet whose girlfriend. Sometime, Tony arrived Walt's restaurant to work , but sometimes who was absent. Tony had also often drunk alcohol for two years during who had worked in Frontier hotel and Italian restaurant in the period.

I believe Tony's problem could be with alcohol stress related. I shall give these reasons as below:

Stress means a feeling of tension that occurs when a person perceives that a situation is about to exceed whose ability to cope whose ability to cope and consequently can endanger whose well being and who feels whose capabilities or resources or needs don't match the demands or requirements of the job. In fact, it was possible that Tony would feel stress because Tony was working two head chef positions in Frontier hotel and Italian restaurant at the same time. He should feel very busy to work and who could not use enough time to meet his girlfriend. Although Tony could earn double salaries from these two employers, but he felt stress after one year. Hence, after one year, Tony did poor performance (behaviour) to let Walt to know, e.g. Tony had begun waking up late for work, who had missed several shifts although. Thus, Tony's stress had poor consequences to Walt's Italian restaurant and to Tony's himself. These poor consequences followed from the effects on Tony's individual's performance that include lower motivation, dissatisfaction, low job performance, increased absenteeism and lower quality of relationships at work, increased safety risks in kitchen and increased health care and increased costs to Tony's alcohol drinking problem. Thus, stress would cause Tony's bad behavioural consequences, e.g. abusing alcohol, late work, absenteeism and Tony's individual's frequently missed work due to stress related illness personal problems. In fact, Tony needed to do two head chef cooking jobs for two employers at the same time. It would cause psychological stress to Tony, e.g. anxiety, depression, low self esteem, sleeplessness, frustration or family problems(marriage was broken). Tony's drinking alcohol problem would increase stress to influence whose job performance to be poor. It caused Tony could not wake up early to work lately, Tony would absent to work to follow shift time often and Tony could not cooperate with kitchen cookers team and waiter team easier and became increasing isolated with them. Thus, Tony's problem with alcohol influenced whose work and private times could not adopt to cause a serious source of stress related. Due to Walt's restaurant work demands had increased to Tony to need spend longer working hours, fast and short time cooking speed needs to satisfy client increasing numbers needs. The most important, Tony needed to work for head chef two jobs for Frontier hotel and Italian restaurant both employers at the sane time. Hence, Tony's work overload could be quantitative increasing too much cooking work. In conclusion, Tony's bad behavioural habit, such as abusing alcohol drinking problem could be caused to stress related due to influence his sickness, woke up late for work and lacked enough nervous and energy to do cooking job and felt not enough sleeping time. Thus abusing alcohol drinking problem was cause nervous stress to Tony's cooking job performance absolutely.

What should Walt do in this circumstance to help Tony cope?

In fact, it implied Tony would feel stress to perform those behaviours, such as who had begun waking up late for work, who had missed several shifts altogether to work to Walt and Bill two partners' Italian restaurant. Due to Tony was working Frontier hotel and Italian restaurant as two head chef positions as the same time. It was possible that Tony felt who needed to spend too much nervous and energy to do cooking job in these two employers and who needed to do shifts job duties for Walt's Italian restaurant and Frontier hotel both as well as Tony had also bad drinking alcohol habit two years, it would influence who could not have nervous to concentrate on cooking job in Walt's Italian restaurant's Kitchen. Because cooking head chef job was needed to spend too much energy (effort) and nervous and time if Tony hoped to cook good tactic foods to Walt's Italian restaurant's clients to eat and who hoped to lead his cooking team work efficiently with waiters team to provide good service to Walt restaurant clients. However, Tony had missed several shifts, it was possible that Tony preferred to spend his private time to meet whose girlfriend, who felt who spend shift time to work in Walt's Italian restaurant which would reduce he could enjoy his private life time with her as well as Tony had begun waking up late for work, it was possible that Tony had alcohol drinking abused problem long time , it would caused Tony has serious psychological stress responses, e.g. depression, low self esteem, sleeplessness, frustration or family problems(marriage broken). The most important, although Tony could earn double salaries due to who had been working Frontier hotel and Italian restaurant both employers at the same time, but Tony would enough lack nervous and energy and who would feel difficult to adopt to arrange time to do cooking jobs with whose team efficiently. So, Tony would feel very hard to earn double salaries after Tony had begun to choose to do Walt's Italian restaurant and Frontier hotel cooking jobs at the same time after one year. However, I shall recommend that Walt should attempt to use these methods to help Tony cope in this circumstance.

Workplace stress can occur when individual (Tony) perceive the demands of the workplace to outweigh whose resources for coping with those demands as well as workplace demands are aspects of the work environment that job holder (Tony head chef) must handle. Hence, Tony was current stressor but who had little control over this situation from Walt's fear authority to him. The most important, Walt should not let Tony to feel who gave more stress to Tony's cooking duties because Tony should choose to leave Walt's cooking job to serve only Frontier hotel employer or who should perform to lead whose cooking team to influence waiter team co-operation poorly and who could not cook better taste to foods to satisfy clients needs if Walt's behaviour should let Tony to feel more stress and unhappy to work. Hence, Walt needed to use organizational stress management method to help Tony to reduce stress or helped Tony to deal more efficiently with Tony's stress. Walt could attempt to let Tony to increase his individual's autonomy and control to his working time, e.g. Tony could choose to arrange what shift working times were the most suitable to him to work every day in order to make Tony could arrange what shift times to work in Frontier hotel or Italian restaurant every day.Walt should ensure that Tony was compensated properly and maintained job demands / requirements at healthy levels to ensure that Tony had enough nervous and energy and time to prepare to cook and lead whose cooking team to co-operate with waiter team efficiently. Demand control model that suggests experienced stress is a function when demands are high , but individuals have little control over situation. The two factors can create situations of job strain and the experience of stress include the workplace demands faced by employer and the control that an individual has in meeting those demands. In fact, Tony felt pressure due to who needed to do both shift time jobs at the same time. If Walt could employ more cookers to assist Tony to do cooking job and Walt could change Tony to do part time shift job. It would reduced Tony nervous workload to do both cooking jobs and it could let Tony had more relax time to sleep. Effort reward imbalance model that suggests experienced stress is a function of both required effort and rewards obtained. Stress is highest when required effort is high but rewards are low. It focused two factors include the effort required by employer and the rewards an individual receives as a result of the effort. Hence, it was possible that Tony felt who required effort and nervous and time were high but rewards were low to work in Walt's Italian restaurant to compare to Frontier hotel employer. It implied that Walt needed to increase Tony's salary if who hoped Tony could serve whose Italian restaurant long time. Otherwise, Tony would choose to leave Walt's cooking job.

Is Tony saveable?

Do the benefits outweigh the costs of trying to save him?

Tony can be attempt to saveable to work in Walt's Italian restaurant in the one to three months probationary period to evaluate whether the benefits outweigh the cost of trying to save Tony or not save.

Effort required relates to performance demands and obligations of the jobs. It is more narrowly focused on the job itself rather than on broader aspects of the overall work environment. It indicates a combination of strong required efforts and low rewards to any employees in organization to cause whose have strong negative emotions and harmful changes. Although a individual facing such a situation could simply exist, many stay because of limited opportunities in the labour market, hope for changes in the situation and excessive work related over commitment. (it is driven by achievement , motivation and approval motivation). In fact, Tony had enough effort and cooking skill and experience to choose which hotel or restaurant employer who liked to work in this labour market. Hence, Tony felt no worry his poor behaviour to cause Walt should dismiss him. Moreover, Tony was also working head chef shift job in another hotel at the same time. So, it was possible that Tony performed absent and woke up late to work and told lie to sickness and drunk alcohol of bad behaviour that who wanted Walt knew that they ought to discuss salary rising issue. Otherwise Tony should leave Walt's employment.The reason was because Tony felt spend much effort and time and nervous to do head chef job in Walt's Italian restaurant, but Walt could not give reasonable rewards to Tony to compare Frontier hotel employer at the same time. Hence, Tony begun waking up late for work and who begun to miss several shifts after he worked one year in Walt's Italian restaurant. Hence, Tony did action to complaint Walt to imply whose dissatisfaction to Walt's employment. However, Walt could attempt to increase Tony's salary and let Tony to choose to change to do part time shift.

Even who could let Tony to choose what shift time who preferred to work and who could suggested Tony who would not spend much time to meet girlfriend and drunk alcohol , who would spend time to sleep to prepare to do cooking job every day. Walt could enquire Tony whether who needed extra cookers and assistant head chefs staffs to assist him when the restaurant was busy time. If Tony felt who lack enough cookers and assistant head chef to assist him to do cooking job in kitchen when the restaurant was busy time. Walt ought need to spend extra salaries to employ extra staffs to assist Tony. Hence, Walt needed to discuss with Tony about how to change his shift job time and whether Tony accepted full time or accepted part time shift job and whether how many extra cookers and assistance head chefs who needed . After they had negotiated successfully, Walt could begin to give one to three months probationary period to evaluate whether Tony was suitable to do whose staff or not.

In conclusion, Walt could give one to three months probationary period to evaluate(measure) whether Tony could have enough effort and nervous to continue to do this cooking job. However, if Walt felt Tony's performance was still dissatisfactory. Walt needed give final chance to Tony to chose either who didn't work full time shift head chef job in Frontier hotel or leave Walt's job immediately.

Marketing mix strategy solves supermarket store organizational cooperation challenge

- This case concerns chain involved in the supply of fresh
fruit and vegetables to Tesco stores cooperation challenge

The place(P) of the traditional marketing mix decides about channel intermediaries or middlemen to use an outdated, yet user friendly, term and the management of physical distribution. Placing products involves managing the process supporting the flow of goods or services from producers to consumers.

The process has sometimes been described as developing the best routes to market for a firm's products. Products must be made available in the right quantity, in the right location, and at the times when customers wish to purchase them. Marketing channels can perform an important role in the later stages of a value chain, in particular outbound logistic (e.g. order processing, storage and transportation); marketing and sales (e.g. market research, personal

selling, sales promotion) and after sales service. However, it depends on which kinds of business to need outbound logistic, such as Tesco supermarket only needs ordering fresh fruit and vegetables from local farmers, then these foods need to be stored in refrigerate in warehouse and transport these foods to different supermarkets by vans. So, Tesco value chain only needs outbound logistic activity, but it does not need marketing and sales and after sale service to sell its fresh fruit and vegetables to its clients from its supermarkets (stores). In fact, Tesco stores is such UK farmer's intermediaries which can add value by breaking bulk. This might involve purchasing in large quantities of fruits and vegetables from UK local farmers and then selling smaller, more manageable, to keep volumes of fresh food stock in warehouses, then its vans will deliver these fresh fruits and vegetables to different stores daily. Discrepancies of fruit foods quantity are reduced by Tesco (intermediary) who provides every store clients with individual preferable fresh foods items that suit their needs daily. Tesco stores can offer superior knowledge of a target market compared with farmers, for example by ensuring which kinds of vegetables or fruits foods numbers are stocked in every store to match the economic and lifestyle needs of Tesco store shoppers who live in the area. Probably the most important gaps between Tesco store shoppers and UK local farmers in channel management are indicated at those of location and time. A location gap occurs owing to the geographic separation of farmers and the store shoppers of their fresh fruit and vegetables foods. UK farmers generally want to grow their fruits and vegetable food in one central location (farming), but farmers' food buyers typically want to buy their growing foods locally. A time gap arises when the UK local farmers' fresh foods buyers want to buy whose fresh growing foods at a time when a UK local farmer may considerate it inconvenient to make the available. UK local farmers may like to grow fresh fruits and vegetable foods at night from 8:00 PM to 12:00PM, then who will collect these fresh foods
from 5:00 AM to 7:00 in the morning, but their buyers may want to buy in the evenings or at weekends afternoon. Tesco stores (intermediary) need to facilitate vans to transport these fresh fruits and vegetables foods from farmers' farming to its one central warehouse to deliver to different stores to sell the budget numbers of different kinds of foods to every local store consumers more exactly (Adrian, P. 2012).

Tesco stores is one of the world's largest retailers, it has social responsibility to protect fresh fruit and vegetable to sell to clients. It had attempted to predict customer behavior about hope much fresh fruit and vegetable and what kinds of fresh fruit and vegetable whose consumers will buy from data statistic in warehouse. It aims to reduce excess fruit and vegetable stocks in warehouse to cause perishable. In the winter might have seen choice reduced to basic items such as potatoes, cabbage, apples, supplemented by canned fruit and vegetables. Look in a Tesco supermarket today, and clients may find difficult to tell the season of the year or the distance from the countryside, simple based on the fruit and vegetables with are on display. In UK supermarket sector is intensely competitive, and has seen continuous innovation in the way it seeks to satisfy customers' needs. As consumers have become wealthier, the supermarkets realized that buyers would no longer be content with the staple foods such as cabbage and potatoes in the depths of winter-significant numbers of them now wanted excitement on a plate, and all year round. Furthermore, if they were planning a menu, they wanted to be sure that when they went to their local supermarket.

By and large, supermarkets have been key drivers of the value for the groceries that they sell. They have been close to their customers and identified their changing needs. They have built confidence with their customers, who can trust freshness and provenance of food they sell and the reliability of supply. It is therefore the supermarkets who have gone seeking sources of supply, rather than growers aggressively seeking to sell the produce that they have available. Before, the development of very large supermarket chains, retailers were more
fragmented. They did not have the power or resources to innovate with new product lines which they could then commission a grower to produce. Today, supermarket such as Tesco invest heavily in their food technology laboratories, and can then go to suppliers and place large orders with exacting standards with regard to price, quality, and delivery. Above all else, supermarkets have put themselves at the center of a slick distribution system which connects an international networks of growers through transport networks of trucks, ships and planes to put fresh produce in their network of stores, every day, all year around. The efficiency of the logistics, and the bargaining power of the supermarkets has often led to the price being charged at a British supermarket being lower than the price changed in supermarkets thousands of miles away where fruit and vegetables were grown. Tomatoes grown in

Bulgaria and sold in Britain can be cheaper in Britain in local Bulgarian shops. The bizarre situation has occurred where the supermarkets import apples from France to be sold in Kent, the traditional home of British apple growing, plums from Poland to be sold in the grown product in Lincolnshire. Supermarkets argue that sourcing from overseas is not just an issue of cost saving more importantly, the supermarkets seek a continuity of supplies from large growers who can guarantee to deliver a specified quantity at a specified quantity at a specified time and place. The supermarkets capable of achieving this. British supermarkets are among the most efficient in the world, and their desire to ensure that customers can always get what they want may explain the mass transport of food. Local farmers' market may could environmentally friendly, but they rarely guarantee a continuity of supplies. As part of their drive for efficiency, supermarkets have a tendency to move food , such potatoes could being transported several hundred miles between distribution centers before they end up on a supermarket shelf just a few miles from where potatoes were grown. The environmental campaigning group Sustain has estimated that the average children travels 2,000 between the farm where it was grown and the supermarket shelf and furthermore the distance products travel from farm to end customer increased by an estimated 25 per cent between 1980 year and 2007 year (Priesnitz 2007).

Global warming had become an important issue with many clients and there was growing concern that supermarkets' practice of transporting fresh produce long distances around the world was irresponsibly adding to greenhouse gas emissions. Hence, distance travelled was one of value chain factor Terso supermarket needs to consider their fruit and vegetables food to keep fresh in refrigerate to transport to retailers to sell in UK. The most contentious food miles are clocked up by fresh fruit and vegetables flow in by plane from overseas. Although, air freighted produce accounted for less than 1 per cent of total UK food miles, it was the fastest growing way of moving foods around. One response By Tesco was to introduce a greatest proportion of local produce. To achieve this, it placed buyers and marketing teams in the regions in order to get a clear picture of local markets and to develop relationships with suppliers. By 2007 year, Tesco claimed to have 7,000 regional lines from throughout the UK, which were promoted as local produce, supporting local growers and reducing greenhouse gas emissions. Throughout its history, Tesco has demonstrated its ability to listen to what customers want, and this has been true in respect of its distribution system. The weaknesses of commodity systems are particularly for major customers, such as Mc Donalds, commodity systems do not lead to reliability in supply, quality, quantity or price nor high rates of innovation on which they can differentiate their offer from their competitors. The opportunity and challenge of fresh food product differentiation, so Tesco stores need to innovation to give rise to a number of strategic options to keep vegetables and fruits to be fresh in the short time to sell full numbers. If a firm, such as Tesco is the lowest cost producer than commodity market strategy can be an attractive strategic option. As Tesco stores fresh food sale that it's larger competitors shall find difficult to copy. Otherwise, Smaller size stores can sometimes be a competitive advantage.

Tesco stores (fresh food retailer) need to co-operate with suppliers and fresh food growers to align the whole chain to the changing needs of consumers. The food chain strategy aims to deliver superior value to specific groups of customers.

Tesco stores work closely with its fresh food suppliers to develop specific products for each range. Both the supplier and growers understand the Tesco marketing strategy and their role in the innovation process. Tesco is actively seeking new

chain ideas and is prepared to pay for such efforts. From a primary producer and supplier perspective the range of brands enables Tesco to work with suppliers to market the total crop .

2. Critically discuss the factors influencing Tesco's sourcing of fresh fruit and vegetables.

At a time when the media enjoyed the big supermarkets, such as Tesco, being seen to source fresh fruit and vegetables food locally and being good to the environment helped to restore. One observe from Friends of the Earth noted the local produce sold at a branch of Tesco in Excess had in fact travelled served hundred miles as it was moved from the grower to a regional processing center, then to a regional distribution center, and finally back to the supermarket where it was sold. There has also been debate about where sourcing fruit and vegetables locally actually reduces greenhouse gas emissions. There is an argument that Tesco supermarket would be better for environment to grow them in countries where fresh fruit and vegetables need less heating and fertilizers than if they were grown in

British. The greenhouse gas emissions resulting from growing them locally in Britain may be more than the emissions associated with transporting them from warmer countries.

The first factor influences Tesco's sourcing of fresh fruit and vegetables is the main stages of horticultural value chain are as follows: The first stage is inputs elements needed for production, such as seed, fertilizers, agrochemicals fungicides and pesticides, farm equipment and irrigation equipment, production for export includes the production of fruit and vegetables and all processes related to the growth and harvesting of the produce, such as planting, weeding, spraying and picking, packaging and cold storage means grading, washing, trimming, chopping, mixing, packing and label are all processes that may occur in this packing stage of the value chain . Once the produce is ready for transport, it is chilled produce is ready for transport, it is chilled and placed in cold storage units ready for export, processes fruit and vegetables include dried, frozen, preserved, juices and pulps. May of these processed add value to the new foods by increasing the shelf life of the fruit and vegetables and the final stage is distribution and marketing means the produce is distributed to different channels, including supermarkets and small scale retailers and wholesalers and food services.

The second factor indicates several basic conditions must be for a country to enter the fresh fruit and vegetables value chain. These include climate allowing for year found supply, adequate road and transport infrastructure, such as ports and airports, essential for moving fragile foods to market efficiently, establishment of sanitary and to prevent disease spreading. The value chain needs to upgrading into the packing segment and processing segment. Upgrading into parking is dependent on understanding the market needs investment in capital goods and availability of supporting activities within the country, such as United Kingdom. Maintaining open lines of communication regarding demand preferences in fresh foods, quality, packing and fostering buyer involvement is critical in all stages of the value chain. For example, organize trips to key markets and they observe interactions at the point of fresh food purchase, a wide variety of equipment to attain very high standards of hygiene within the pack house operations as well as on site laboratories for fresh fruit and vegetables research and staff health tests, horticultural sector has been greatly inhibited in its upgrading along the value chain by the lack of fresh food quality packing materials. Much of produce destined for the Europe is shipped to neigh countries where it is repackaged, resulting in a significant of value. However, upgrading into the processing segment of the value chain has been difficult to achieve for low income developing countries since the processing of fruit and vegetables is cost prohibitive at low levels of crop production. Therefore, countries must gain a level of expertise during the production stage to increase output to a level that will enable the country to upgrade to the fruit and vegetable processing stage. For example, given the importance of ability to read pesticide labels and understand barcodes amongst others, standards have led to additional training initiatives to improve adult literacy. Skills training must be carried our in all job categories of value chain to maximize growth and upgrading opportunities. Investments in training are required for all job categories, from farm workers to managers, such as farming activities and the workforce within the agriculture sector, packing and storage positions and the processing stage in which workers are classified under the industrial workforce. Hence, fresh fruit and vegetables packing and processing services, such as washing, chopping, mixing as well as bagging, branding and applying bar codes are often carried out at the fresh foods source rather than at the end market destination. These processes which were previously based in the developed country, such as UK have created considerable new employment opportunities in developing countries.

The third factor influences Tesco's sourcing of fresh fruit and vegetables, which indicates today, the fruit and vegetables sector operators as a buyer driven value chain and large supermarket chains are the leading actors both in key export markets with controlling market and shares across the Europe and United States as well as increasing in emerging markets. These buyers including Sainsbry's Marks and Spencer and Walmart seek enhanced cost competitiveness, consistency and product differentiation, such as convenient, ready to eat fresh foods from their global supply chains. It causes considerable value chain method how fruit and vegetables are produced, harvested, transported, processed and stored to achieve how fresh fruit and vegetables characteristics of quality, size, pesticide use and the social and environment conditions of cultivation and post-harvest handling will influence buyer behavior decision. This ensures that the perishable food reaches its destination in good condition cold storage units are used throughout the chain to keep the produce fresh and both air and sea freighting supported by the cold chain are key elements to ensure timely delivery. Export is divided between production for fresh and vegetables and fruit consumption and production for processed fruit and vegetables that are not accepted for sale as fresh produce are as well as inputs for the processing stage, but in order cases, such as orange juice or preserved peaches a specific variety and grade quality is required and production occurs separately. The next segment is packaging and cold storage unacceptable low grade produce will be redirected to processing plants or the domestic market. Washing, trimming, chopping, mixing, packaging and labelling are other processes that may occur in this stage of the value chain. Once the produce is ready for transport it is chilled and placed in cold storage units ready for export. Packaging usually requires economies of scale due to the high costs of cold storage and other capital investment necessary at this stage .Processed fruit and vegetables include dried, frozen and preserved produce as well as juices. Processing plants purchase fruit and vegetables inputs from the producers. These firms may export their products under their own brands as well as under the buyer's brand. The last stage of the value chain before consumption is distribution and marketing. In this final stage, the produce is distributed to different channels including supermarkets, small scale retailers, wholesales and food services. Air freighting for horticultural foods and more cold storage segment of value chain in order to increase their access to key markets and avoid competition form new countries entering cold storage technologies allow suppliers to adapt to geographic constraints, such as size and distance to market.

3. Assess the level of power that Tesco exercises in the supply chain for fruit and vegetables.

The themes identified were the perceptions of freshness, having good relationships with growers and suppliers , good quality of fresh fruits and vegetables, competitive and pleasant environment for shoppers. Globalization of the fresh fruits and vegetables, retailer system has impacted on the distribution and marketing of fresh modern supply chain outlets now dominate the fresh food retail market. The increasing population and rising personal income is resulting in significant shifts in fresh food demand. Supermarkets are perceived to be the place where more wealthy consumers choose to shop. Consumers purchase almost everything there including fresh fruit and vegetable, meat, children and fish and other household supplier like dry food, bread, detergents, stationary and toys in supermarkets, such as Tesco stores, not choose to buy from fruit and vegetable markets or food retailers. The traditional markets and grocery stores comprise wet markets, fresh markets, farmer's markets are popular among consumers when purchasing fresh food are the oldest food distribution channel.

The traditional market has been defined as a market with little central control or organization that lacks refrigeration and doesn't process fresh foods into brands foods for sale where each vendor specialized in one fresh food line (meat, fish, fruit or vegetable) or in a sub line (fruit and vegetable). A fresh market and/or wet market generally occupies one or two floors of a building that is located adjacent to a housing area where there is a high population density and high traffic flow. The ground floor is normally rented to retailers who sell fresh food or ready to eat items.

The upper live level is occupied by retailers who sell ready to items or non food products/ These stores are family owned retailers that sell a limited variety of foods ,such as fish, fruit and vegetable, bread and milk, stationary , toys and household supplies. However, consumers may limit their purchase from these stores due to the high prices and limited product lines. Another distribution power level to Tesco supply its fruits and vegetable to deliver to its clients in the short time. Tesco faces its customers occurred with respect to its home delivery service. With the launch of its Tesco online service, it effectively extended the supply chain right through to customers' own homes, adding value to its product offer by avoiding the need for customers to even visit a supermarket. Was it good for the environment to have fleets of delivery vans around town and countryside? Simple evaluations were difficult to make supermarket buyers again, Tesco was keen to be seen as a good citizen in this final leg of its chain, for example by launching electric delivery vehicles which Tesco decided to reduce global warmth when its vans do not need to deliver fresh foods and vegetables to different supermarkets from its warehouse in the long distance. Tesco stores is a retailer to UK local farmers that buys their fresh fruits and vegetable for the purpose of reselling them to end consumers in its different local stores daily. The Tesco stores are large, self service stores carrying a very wide range of different kinds fresh fruits and vegetable foods to sell in its different local value chains from UK local farmers supply daily. For example, Tesco stores are often the first with new store shoppers initiatives such as loyalty cards and low fresh food prices are based on large scale efficiency to sell in Tesco smaller independent stores to match. Hence, the factors can influence Tesco stores channel selection power include that the expectations of store shoppers who expect to buy local stores or who prepared to travel to a retailer that the farmers' fresh fruit and vegetables keep to save more than one day or more days to buy. This might mean taking into consideration factors such as a geographical preference to buy locally, or a tendency to feel more comfortable visiting a particular type of store; Tesco fresh foods attributes can be important, fresh produce that is highly perishable requires fairly short channels. Bypassing channels, a UK local farmer may seek to cut out intermediaries , such as Tesco stores by dealing directly with the public and Tesco may feel difficult to open up any new local stores for the farmers. Over saturation, a farmer may be accused of using too many fresh fruits and vegetable food distributors within a given geographical area, making it difficult for any individual distributor to achieve a satisfactory level of fresh foods sale , such as Terco stores. Too many links, in the supply fresh foods chain, Tesco stores may be required to buy excessive fresh fruits and vegetable foods from any farmers daily, who may be perceived as a fresh food farming competitor, rather than a cooperative channel member. New channels, these can have a similar effect to bypassing an intermediary, for example, many UK local farmers have opened up internet sales channels, thereby taking fresh food sales away from established intermediaries, such as Terso stores. Cost cutting, in order to increase volume fresh fruit and vegetables food sales, a UK local farmer may seek to distribute through higher volume, low cost intermediaries, which may make it more difficult for a smaller, full service intermediary , such as Terso stores sell the farmers' any fresh foods and UK local farmers can give incentives and rewards to other intermediaries to help them to sell in UK any stores to raise Terso's competition in UK foods supply market.

A national chain of restaurant mobile advertising promotion strategy

1. Critically assess the likely opportunities and problems
of mobile advertising for a national chain of restaurants.

A global crisis in the advertising industry largely linked to the impact of the internet is transforming the business models of media industries, the content they create and distribute, and the audiences who consume that contents. Such as consumers can use whose mobiles to find where the chain of restaurants are located and meal and drink prices and meal and drink types and
restaurant opening and closing time etc. information for the national chain of restaurants from internet advertising when who leave at home conveniently. The opportunity to mobile advertising for a national chain of restaurants, it can expand its national chain of restaurants brand to different countries visitors and instead of its self country visitors to let them to know whether where its chain of restaurants can provide what kinds of food or drink to serve to them to eat before they prepare to go to any one of the national chain of restaurants immediately. Hence, when visitors travel to its country, it will be more easy to let them to remember where any one of the national chain restaurants are located in the nation when who enter the national chain restaurants website or enter yahoo website to type" national chain restaurants" word, then who can seek any one of the national chain restaurants from whose mobiles easily.

In fact, if a national chain of restaurants chose to use television advertising, due to the national chain of restaurants which locate at itself country locally. It is only concentrate on promoting it's country's domestic eating consumers target to know it's existence when its country's domestic eating consumers are watching television at homes. Usually, working people need to work and students need to go to school to study from morning 9:00AM to 6:00 PM at night. Hence, the national chain of restaurants can only advertise at night time. Furthermore, the overseas travelers watch the nation's television when who are staying in the nation's hotels at night time. Hence, the national chain of restaurants can only use television to advertise to attract the largest numbers of local and foreign visitors to watch its advertisement at night time possibly.

Due to mobile advertising exists, television advertising is more difficult to attract the durability of audience segmentation models to build upon demographic and it also lacks new opportunities to implement psychographic and behavioral models for understanding audiences. Such as, many young people who accept to use mobile to communicate, so it implies every family usually has a mobile to use and mobile advertising also have much opportunity to help any businesses to promote whose services or products to let many families to know whose advertising. In fact, mobile users can use mobile to watch movies or news, so who ought to link internet to watch during who are sitting on any transportations or walking, so when the nation's people who feel hungry, who can use their mobiles to link to internet to seek any restaurants to decide which restaurants are the most close to their locations to choose. As a national chain of restaurants, it is more effective to advertise it's different chain of restaurants' locations to let any it's different locations of national mobile users to seek its any one of chain restaurant conveniently when who are walking on the street if who feel hungry who can turn on mobile to find map to seek the national chain of restaurants immediately. In fact, the global households who the average viewing audience composition, the number of global households using the television set and the various times it is in use, the average audience (home viewing during an average minute of a program) and the total audiences (homes viewing the program in excess of minutes) which are decreasing. Otherwise, the mobile phone users view mobile advertising numbers are increasing. Broadcast channels as well as whatever is available on their various devices, including computer, mobile devices, gaming devices, time-shifting devices or internet enables devices. As such, it is providing more and more difficult to track the audience and known who they are and the best way to target them. Additionally, the rise of social media adds another dimension to audience research. Social media provides new ways of segmenting audiences that currently can not be done on television. Hence, a national chain of restaurants can get better ways of segmenting its viewers from mobile advertising over a variety of platforms.

So mobile networks can be better package to the nation chain of restaurants advertising programming and the national chain of restaurants advertiser can make a more effective to attract foreign visitors or domestic visitors to make them to enter its website to view its advertising from their mobiles. For example, car owners, such as those who own a BMW or Audi famous brands cars, which have very homogeneous demographic characteristics, but each car brand has a specific type of owner with a unique personality. A similar look as television audiences could allow advertising of those car brands (who attend the upfront presentations every year) to match their car buyers to specific television shows. Demographics have not caught up with these changes and presume that viewers are still watching in only the conventional way. For instance, there is not yet a way for the networks to get credit for online viewers and it is as more viewers more to online platforms, like a network in landing site.

Instead, a psychographic profile of the audience, one based on psychological segmentations , such as behaviors, attitudes, interests, values, opinions feelings which is a valid and valuable way of narrowing down the audience into segments for an advertiser. So, psychographic data can measure, such as peoples' activities how who spend whose time, their interests what they place importance on in their immediate surroundings, their opinions how their view of themselves and the world around them and some basic characteristics, such as their stage life cycle and income and education and residence location. The result of the research then provides a detailed profile that allows the marketer to be better visualize the target audience.

Psychographics start with people and reveal how the people feel client specific subjects, which can lead to be more effective marketing. When psychographic segmentations are used, the consumers are divided into group based on lifestyle and personality, often with all of this in mind, the research questions proposed here as follows: What psychographic measurements are being used right now to determine the television audience or mobile advertising ?

How are the various branches of the industry , such as restaurant industry adaptive to the new television landscape ,such as mobile advertising and what actions are they taking?

What are some challenges and resistances to psychographic measures between television advertising and mobile advertising?

What incentives or lack are there to change between television and mobile advertising?

What would be helpful for advertisers , such as a national chain of restaurants or networks , such as internet advertising to know or do in order to more towards wider use of psychographics?

A reason behind dividing audiences based on engagement can be illustrated with the Pod mobile phone, such as the national chain of restaurants organization has shown that audiences' attachment to specific the restaurants' brand corresponds directly to how much the audience will pay attention to the national restaurant brand's advertisements from mobile and how likely who are the actually to choose to go to the national chain of restaurants to eat lunch or dinner or breakfast more than its other restaurants.The problem is how the national chain of restaurants to advertise it's foods taste, price and service and locations uniquely to win its other restaurant competitors from mobile specific program, providing the network to be best convenient that it's restaurant brand to advertise on that specific program. Another key problem is trend segments viewers based on domestic and foreign consumers' behavior are more specifically their viewing behavior mixed with their restaurants choosing eating behavior in whose countries, watching the national chain of restaurants television advertising from whose mobile , what who are watching to know its existence and on how to let them to know what their actual eating taste to the national chain of restaurants can provide. Hence, I suggest the national chain of restaurants can attempt to use surveys to carry on researching the different countries foreign visitors and domestic visitors whether what whose tastes are preferable to choose what kinds of foods and drinks who hope to eat in this national chain of restaurants from mobile advertising website. The problem is who may choose not to fill its surveys from its mobile website advertising. If they use computer to fill its surveys at home, it will have more opportunities to gather data from survey due to who can sit down to fill surveys in quiet environment. Hence, I suggest it ought use computer internet to do market research about what whose tastes are preferable to eat in its restaurants. When it estimates whether the foreign visitors and domestic visitors numbers, how many people choose to eat different kinds of foods and drinks to its identifications. After it can achieve mobile advertising to promote its restaurant brand more confidently in this mobile marketing advertising strategy.

2. Discuss methods that could be used to assess the effectiveness of mobile advertising.

Measuring social media marketing , such as mobile advertisement, effectiveness and identifying the target market. The use of social media sites as part of company's marketing strategy has increased significantly. Regardless its popularity, there is still very limited information to answer some of the key issues concerning the effectiveness of social media marketing , ways to measure its return on investment and its target market. The social media was started around ten years ago. It began with linked in, which was launched in 2003 year, followed by both My space and face book in 2004 year. You tube in 2005 year and Twitter in 2006 in year. The popularity of social media sites has also spread to companies as part of their strategies. Executives are concerned with their budget justification for a social media plan in computer or media online advertising, when there is lack of supporting materials to confirm the effectiveness of the social media platform , i.e. conversion rate, the relation between buyer-seller relationship and increase in sales and the rate of return investment that they can earn from this plan. Others also believe that their companies' performance are not affected by their lack of involvement in the social media sites.

Clearly, the fact that social media marketing is still relatively new among business practitioners has raised some major concerns , such as its effectiveness, the main purpose of including social media mobile advertising in a company's media platforms, it's relation to the existing platforms and the target audience of this strategy. The methods to assess effectiveness of mobile advertisement include that marketing research method is about target client segment of respondents' social media activities and buying decisions relationship survey. Survey questions can include whether how long time and how often who turn on mobile phone to use internet, such as a week is less than 20 hours average or a week is between 20 hours and 30 hours average or a week is between 30 hours and 50 hours or a week is more than 50 hours, why who like to use mobile to use internet and not use home computer to use internet, e.g. reducing to use home electricity, interesting, convenience, no computer at home, what who will seek to see from mobile advertisement, e.g. advertisement , news ,email , message, movie, whether who decide to buy products or consume services choice is from which kinds of channel advertisement influence mostly, such as television, radios, newspapers, magazines, computer internet, mobile internet. It aims to gather target client segment of respondents' social media activities and buying decision relationship to estimate whether there are how many numbers of target client will decide to buy the company's product or use it's service from mobile advertisement channel.

Hence, the survey result can indicate these five respondent groups, such as highly affected, somewhat affected, neutral somewhat not affected and not affected at all groups. Mobile phone advertisement is needed to any organizations to use internet to operate. Hence, to access the effectiveness of mobile advertising which may begin by using measures that were very easy to capture and understand, such as the number of website hits or percentage of users who clicked on an advertisement. These measures were very useful fro examining trends in traffic patterns, but the impact of this traffic on sale and other marketing objective was sales and other marketing objectives were little understand. Standardized approaches for capturing and summarizing websites behavior were eventually developed to help make sense of web traffic and patterns. Metrics, such as number of unique visitors and the amount of time who spent viewing web pages provided marketers with new insights into who was assessing the site and how who were using it. But even with a high level of detail about how customers were interacting with the company via the web, marketing manager often lacked the information how user behavior data translates into increased profits and business value. For example, organizations using websites primarily for after sales support have used exactly the same kinds of metrics as these selling directly from the site. This is not due to a lack of available data. Many organizations using web analytics gather and store vast amounts of information and develop large, complex databases to house it. But much of that information is never used. Because organizations who first began to market over the internet often lacked a clearly formulated strategy. In addition, the rapidly changing internet environment made it difficult for marketers to formulate clear expectation about the impact of activities. Both the amount of returns and amount of investments are difficult to measure. I suggest organizations may estimate the value of a visit to a particular web page by estimating the number of visitors who will become customers and then multiplying that number by the average value of all clients to estimate returns. What the 'clicks and hits' and 'measurement driven' approached have in common organization's strategic objectives and provide quantified models that plan and track internet marketing investments from intermediate outcomes to financial results. Hence, it can indicate how marketing expenditures in mobile internet advertising method to lead to increase shareholder value aim. I think investment in internet marketing , organizations will need follow these stages. In the beginning is inputs stage:

Organization and business unit strategy includes structures, systems, resources as well as marketing strategy includes structures, systems as well as information strategy includes structures, systems and market strategy transfers to websites, search marketing , advertisement and public relations, mobile marketing and marketing research. Next, it is outputs stage: It includes intermediate outputs, such as awareness and perceptions, attitudes and intentions, value provisions, channel optimization and market information as well as it includes final outputs, such as marketing assets: customer value, brand equity, knowledge as well as financial flows: increased revenue, cash flows, reduced revenue, lower cost, lower working capital, lower fixed capital and reduced risk. Finally, it is outcomes stage includes shareholder value, return on investment and corporate profitability. For example, Donald restaurant uses its website to promote lower calorie food and fruit options as well as its global campaign tied to the Olympics, nutrition (Business week 8-7-06). Each organization should carefully identify the outputs it seeks to achieve. How can process produce these outputs? Organization can attempt to enhance of website functional or initiation of an email campaign. The final question to organizations which will ask : How outputs contribute to the long term financial performance of the organization from mobile advertising ? Is critical for organizations seeking to enhance return on investment from mobile advertising? In addition, whether mobile advertising can give these benefits to any companies, such as market capitalization and shareholder value can be enhanced by increases in marketing assets (customer value, brand equity and knowledge base) that produce future corporate financial flows from mobile internet advertising method. Hence, marketing assets include customer value, such as using dynamic pricing to manage demand, supporting sales through online information sites, shipping directly to reduce need for inventory possession, shifting in store sales to online sales, eliminating clients with prior post sales problems from promotion lists; brand equity, such as additional revenue through brand premiums, using customer relationship to speed adoption of next generation products target marketing to loyal clients during predicted slow periods, reducing customer turnover and support costs, shifting responsibility and risk for inventory management to major suppliers, pool inventories with suppliers and clients to reduce warehouse space across the supply chain, using trust in brand to reduce unwarranted lawsuits, knowledge base, such as developing mass customization capability, reducing time to market through online concept trials, time promotions to smooth demand, eliminating product features that are not valuable to clients. Watching production timing to demand, direct in store sales to products that generate high contribution margin per square foot of fixed space and anticipating and respond to stakeholder concerns. Finally, customer value and brand equity and knowledge base shall transfer to financial flows aim, such as increased revenue, accelerated cash flow, reduced revenue volatility, lower cost, lower working capital requirement, lower fixed capital requirement and reduced risk.

However, Metrics can be used to access effectiveness of mobile advertising, both financial and non financial metrics are needed to effectively measure performance. Some non financial items , such as market research activities are difficult to measure and companies often avoid measuring those items. However, if the item plays a critical role in delivering organizational value. Measuring it, preferably in quantifiable terms, such as monetary changes or percentages. Even when such measures are difficult to obtain or depend a rough estimates, they provide a basis for examining trends over time and can provide useful information to managers. For example, two metrics for the output awareness are: The number of emails opened recipients and the number of clients that clicked on a promotional mobile advertising. Those two metrics can provide different perspectives on the meaning of awareness, thus the choice of metrics helps clarify the objectives, just as clear objectives can help in identifying specific and to be relevant must be specific and to be relevant they must be customized to meet the unique dynamics of the organization . It aims to achieve the best to capture and reflect the organization's unique sets of activities and results some may be relevant to all organizations and many can be readily adopted to be useful for decision making.

3. Discuss the relationship between mobile advertising and other elements of the promotion in campaign planning.

Mobile advertisement defines as the use of the mobile medium, it is as a communications and entertainment channel between a brand and an end user. In basic terms, it is the process of planning and execution conception, pricing, promotion and distribution of products and services through the mobile channel. Advertising is a form of communication intended to convince an audience (viewers, readers or listeners) to purchase or take some action upon products, information or services etc. The relationship between independent variables elements and mobile advertising which are environmental response and emotional response with behavioral aspect of consumer buying behavior with mobile advertising. It is time that people purchase those brands with which who are emotionally attached elements. Almost every one grows up in the world which is flooded with the mass media, e.g. television, films, videos, magazines, movies advertising and internet channel is either mobile advertising or computer advertising. Advertising is a subset of promotion mix which is one of the 4'p in the marketing mix, i.e. product, price, place and promotion. As a promotional strategy, advertising serve as a major tool in creating product awareness in the mind of a potential consumer to take eventual purchase decision. Advertising, sales promotion and public relations are mass communication tools available to marketers.

Telecommunication technology, such as mobile advertising enables business and industry to grow at a faster pace when contributing to the economic development and at the same time telecommunication infrastructure can be reliable. Cellular phone industry has been one of the profitable businesses in Asian. The country's growing population and huge demand potential have always been an attraction for many high-technological multinational companies. Societies used symbols and pictorial signs to attract their produce users. There elements were used for promotion of products. A company can't make dream to be a well known brand until which invests in their promotional activities for which consumer market have been dominating through advertisements. As the primary mission of advertiser is to reach prospective customers and influence their awareness, attitudes and buying behavior.

The major aim of advertising is to impact on buying behavior, however this impact about brand is changes or strengthened frequently in peoples' memories. Memories about the brand consist of their associations that are related to brand name in consumer mind. These brand cognition influence consideration, evaluation and finally purchases. The promotion in campaign planning to mobile advertising focuses on young people because who choose advertising information and characters as whose role models, who may not only identify with them but also intend to copy them in terms of how who dress and what who are going to buy. As the market is surplus with several products or services, so many companies make similar functional claim, so it has became extremely difficult for companies to differentiate their products or services based on functional attributes alone. Differentiations based on functional attributed, which are shown in advertisement, are never long lasting as the competitors could copy the same. Mobile advertising may differentiate companies' products or services promotion channel to attract client's attention, e.g. the company can use movable product images on internet video to show on mobile. However, mobile advertising time ought depend on the business nature, e.g. facial health products target segment is female, so it's mobile advertising time ought choose form 9:00 AM to 6:00 PM working time between Monday to Sunday, due to housewives or working women shall go back home to cook, who shall not turn on mobile phones at home. Hence, if the company had differentiated which brand and it had chose what time is the more popular to accept to let mobile users to turn on their mobile from mobile advertising. The company mobile advertising will have more promotion effort. For example, if the company sold toys, it's target segment would be 3 ages to 10 ages old. It's mobile advertising ought let every family to find its company website easily. If the family didn't know it's brand, but is was difficult to let the family to find what its toys sale from whose mobile phone because there are many toy companies were using internet advertising to promote which toys. So, it might let every family types " toy" word on yahoo, Google websites, then this toy company name would appear on their websites, the family only clicked its name on their mobile phone, it could show it' toys images, prices, which country manufacturing and which year manufacturing different kind of toys, sale payment and delivery method, e.g. visa card payment, air or land or shipping transportation flight delivery, toys manufacturing ingredients indication from website advertising and it's toys advertising time ought to choose family working time, such as between 9:00 and 6:00 PM , due to who shall bring their mobile to work usually. Hence, the toy company needs to consider family will choose what time to use mobile phone. It ought not choose night time to advertise its toy products from mobile due to family would not turn on whose mobile at home at night time usually. Economic theory has sought to establish relationships between selling prices, sales achieved and consumer's income, similarly before the company chooses to spend mobile advertising expenditure, it ought frequently compared it with sales actual income each month.

Social media marketing, such as mobile advertising effectiveness is highly influenced by three aspects: content quality, involvement and integration with the other media platforms methods to assess whether effectiveness of mobile advertising.

On the first aspect, content quality isn't quantity. It shows that managers should not totally reply on the monitoring software to measure and analyze their social media campaign. For example, the twitter website analysis show that some brands/companies, e.g. Microsoft used their Twitter account to connect and to

communicate with customers . Their Tweets were about communicating and connecting with their follows, through some personal conversations in subjects. That were relevant to their customers . As a results, Microsoft clients were able to

beat their main competitors in financial performances and Twitter activities. So, Microsoft can use twitter website to assess whether how many numbers of people use internet service to enter phone, then who decide to buy its software products . If Microsoft found the result of the number of buyers who decide to buy its software from mobile phone Twitter website advertisement channel which is more than mobile phone Yahoo or Google websites advertisement channel after who turn on mobile to see advertising. On the another aspect, building trust and long term relationship to mobile advertising to indicate to how to persuade to increase many shippers to decide to buy any products or seek service, e.g. travel tickets booking service after who use mobile to seek advertising habitually. Today, media marketing is about building relationship and trust through effective two way communications , e.g. talk about something that customers are interested in and creating products or service that will help to solve customers' problems from mobile advertising. Some of today's social media marketing campaigns are still driven by the old fashioned marketing and focus on short-term effect sales, which is also known as incentive induced behavior. To assess trust and genuine buyer/seller relationships achieved through consistent and engaging conversation will increase the messages (SMM) level of influence. Trust is the key factor to get the followers to actually to something , i.e. change in buying decisions influence their peers and turn it into revenue for the companies. It is crucial to build a strong relationship with customers and enhance brand loyalty. Hence, it implies mobile phone companies need to build trust relationship to let them to pay extract internet charges to aim to read email, news, watch movie habitually. Then, it will increase chance to let potential buyers to prefer to seek advertisement to choose to buy and products or consume service from mobile websites habitually. Hence, assessment of mobile internet habitual users who use mobile internet time per week from survey is one effective method. Also, firms should start their involvement by inviting their customers or prospects to join their social media community. For example, firms can post the icons of the social media main websites or giving some special deals to customers who become their fans or followers . In the online community, firms should start writing more effective posts. An effective post should reflect honesty and conciseness, it is as key elements of an effective post. It should also be informative to satisfy clients‘ need for information and experts; opinions. Effective contents should be able to actions from the audience (conversion) so that by the end of this process. Followers will place on order, subscribe newsletter or participate on online surveys. In the offline community, managers should share expertise with their speaker in the local community, which will help to attract more followers or fans and to strength connection with the community. A debate has been going on whether or not consumers are willing to receive mobile advertising. America consumers seem to willing to accept mobile advertising to subsidize the cost of other mobile services , such as email and news services.

A study conducted by HRI Research on behalf of Nokia brand found that the core mobile phone subscriber market (16 to 45 year old) is not only receptive to experiencing mobile advertising, but also actively welcoming mobile advertising in the form of electronic coupons promotion. The relationship between mobile advertising and the four key elements contributing to mobile advertising's acceptance of the promotion in campaign planning. There were mobile advertising should allow users to decide whether or not to receive messages, users could bypass sales messages easily, users should be filter the message received and users want to get mutual benefits of something back. The SMA advertising campaigns of mobile advertising industry plays and consumers have been made afraid of the spam phenomenon deriving from negative email spamming experiences. The personal nature of the website phone markets spamming especially invasive compared to spam received via other channels and devices. Mobile advertising has the potential to be one of the most powerful one to one digital advertising mediums of utilized in the right manner. SMS trials across the would have show the power of mobile advertising in building direct one to one relationship. The online companies like AT&T, AOC wireless, Microsoft and Nokia to mention few companies that are focused on the potential of mobile marketing via mobile handsets. Factors contributing to the success of mobile advertising include that ability, setting up research. measurement, tracking systems, availability of specialist expertise in agency, service provide and establishing consistent rate mobile cards. Other factors impact of drivers on the development of mobile advertising include that personalized medium, users able to opt in , call to action , i.e. immediate response possible , location specific, interactive profiling, appeals to younger customers , one to many communication.

In conclusion, the relatively between mobile advertising and other elements of the promotion in campaign planning include as below: The first element is by utilizing mobile advertising, companies can run marketing campaigns targeted to tens of thousands of people with a fragment of the costs compared to other direct marketing mediums, such as direct mail or telephone and this in just few seconds of line. The advertising industry uses two types of cost calculation cost per thousand impressions (CPM) and cost per rating point (CPP). CPM is used for both print and electronic media when CPP is more popular for electronic media. For instance, if an advertising campaign costs US$5,000 and has an audience of 300,000 consumers, the CPM will be approximately to the initial CPM measure in media selection , such as quality of the audience, audience attention probability and believability of media selection when the CPM for direct mail is between UA$500 to US$700. For email the CPM ranges from US$5 to US$7. However when email marketing is losing its efficiency, mobile advertising offers new ways to promote products and services. A significant factor contributing to consumers' willingness to accept mobile advertisement is the capability of mobile handsets to service certain type of messages , such as multimedia messages. Evidently, most consumers in the future will carry on smart phone with them. The smart phones allow advertisers to reach consumers in different locations with personalize messages at a given time. Another element is the industry of SG or 4G network service is faster connection speed is a obvious enables users to receive digital photographs, moving wide images, high quality sound for their mobile handsets. From advertisers; perspective this opens various opportunities to plan and implement more advance m-advertising campaigns and integrate those with existing marketing channels. However, to develop and provide applications, for example, interfaces to the carrier's wireless network need to be provided in multiple areas: location, presence, billing, personalization, provisioning, packet network, transport and messaging systems. Next element is location awareness cab be seen as the driving force of many wireless applications and suits also well types of mobile advertising. When mobile phones are almost always carried with and intelligent location awareness technical solution are available. The final element is personalization means building customer loyalty by building a meaningful one to one relatively by understanding the needs to each individual and helping to satisfy a goal that efficiently and knowledgeably addresses each.

Personalization is about mapping and satisfying of client's goal in specific contest with a business's goal in its respective context. Personalization means understanding different kinds of individual preferences , needs, mindsets and lifestyles and cultural as well as geographical differences. Mobile are already equipment with a profiting options, e.g. silent, meeting, outdoors. For example, the utilization of time and location awareness as personalization variables has the benefit that mobile advertising is a marketing medium has features that other marketing channels lack. Hence, email advertising needs to keep every mobile users' personal information to be confidential, solicited message, relevance to users need and the right frequency.

A global crisis in the advertising industry largely linked to the impact of the internet is transforming the business models of media industries, the content they create and distribute, and the audiences who consume that contents. Such as consumers can use whose mobiles to find where the chain of restaurants are located and meal and drink prices and meal and drink types and

restaurant opening and closing time etc. information for the national chain of restaurants from internet advertising when who leave at home conveniently. The opportunity to mobile advertising for a national chain of restaurants, it can expand its national chain of restaurants brand to different countries visitors and instead of its self country visitors to let them to know whether where its chain of restaurants can provide what kinds of food or drink to serve to them to eat before they prepare to go to any one of the national chain of restaurants immediately. Hence, when visitors travel to its country, it will be more easy to let them to remember where any one of the national chain restaurants are located in the nation when who enter the national chain restaurants website or enter yahoo website to type" national chain restaurants" word, then who can seek any one of the national chain restaurants from whose mobiles easily.

In fact, if a national chain of restaurants chose to use television advertising, due to the national chain of restaurants which locate at itself country locally. It is only concentrate on promoting it's country's domestic eating consumers target to know it's existence when its country's domestic eating consumers are watching television at homes. Usually, working people need to work and students need to go to school to study from morning 9:00AM to 6:00 PM at night. Hence, the national chain of restaurants can only advertise at night time. Furthermore, the overseas travelers watch the nation's television when who are staying in the nation's hotels at night time. Hence, the national chain of restaurants can only use television to advertise to attract the largest numbers of local and foreign visitors to watch its advertisement at night time possibly.

Due to mobile advertising exists, television advertising is more difficult to attract the durability of audience segmentation models to build upon demographic and it also lacks new opportunities to implement psychographic and behavioral models for understanding audiences. Such as, many young people who accept to use mobile to communicate, so it implies every family usually has a mobile to use and mobile advertising also have much opportunity to help any businesses to promote whose services or products to let many families to know whose advertising. In fact, mobile users can use mobile to watch movies or news, so who ought to link internet to watch during who are sitting on any transportations or walking, so when the nation's people who feel hungry, who can use their mobiles to link to internet to seek any restaurants to decide which restaurants are the most close to their locations to choose. As a national chain of restaurants, it is more effective to advertise it's different chain of restaurants' locations to let any it's different locations of national mobile users to seek its any one of chain restaurant conveniently when who are walking on the street if who feel hungry who can turn on mobile to find map to seek the national chain of restaurants immediately. In fact, the global households who the average viewing audience composition, the number of global households using the television set and the various times it is in use, the average audience (home viewing during an average minute of a program) and the total audiences (homes viewing the program in excess of minutes) which are decreasing. Otherwise, the mobile phone users view mobile advertising numbers are increasing. Broadcast channels as well as whatever is available on their various devices, including computer, mobile devices, gaming devices, time-shifting devices or internet enables devices. As such, it is providing more and more difficult to track the audience and known who they are and the best way to target them. Additionally, the rise of social media adds another dimension to audience research. Social media provides new ways of segmenting audiences that currently can not be done on television. Hence, a national chain of restaurants can get better ways of segmenting its viewers from mobile advertising over a variety of platforms.

So mobile networks can be better package to the nation chain of restaurants advertising programming and the national chain of restaurants advertiser can make a more effective to attract foreign visitors or domestic visitors to make them to enter its website to view its advertising from their mobiles. For example, car owners, such as those who own a BMW or Audi famous brands cars, which have very homogeneous demographic characteristics, but each car brand has a specific type of owner with a unique personality. A similar look as television audiences could allow advertising of those car brands (who attend the upfront presentations every year) to match their car buyers to specific television shows. Demographics have not caught up with these changes and presume that viewers are still watching in only the conventional way. For instance, there is not yet a way for the networks to get credit for online viewers and it is as more viewers more to online platforms, like a network in landing site.

Instead, a psychographic profile of the audience, one based on psychological segmentations , such as behaviors, attitudes, interests, values, opinions feelings which is a valid and valuable way of narrowing down the audience into segments for an advertiser. So, psychographic data can measure, such as peoples‘ activities how who spend whose time, their interests what they place importance on in their immediate surroundings, their opinions how their view of themselves and the world around them and some basic characteristics, such as their stage life cycle and income and education and residence location. The result of the research then provides a detailed profile that allows the marketer to be better visualize the target audience.

Psychographics start with people and reveal how the people feel client specific subjects, which can lead to be more effective marketing. When psychographic segmentations are used, the consumers are divided into group based on lifestyle and personality, often with all of this in mind, the research questions proposed here as follows: What psychographic measurements are being used right now to determine the television audience or mobile advertising ?

How are the various branches of the industry , such as restaurant industry adaptive to the new television landscape ,such as mobile advertising and what actions are they taking?

What are some challenges and resistances to psychographic measures between television advertising and mobile advertising?

What incentives or lack are there to change between television and mobile advertising?

What would be helpful for advertisers , such as a national chain of restaurants or networks , such as internet advertising to know or do in order to more towards wider use of psychographics?

A reason behind dividing audiences based on engagement can be illustrated with the Pod mobile phone, such as the national chain of restaurants organization has shown that audiences' attachment to specific the restaurants‘ brand corresponds directly to how much the audience will pay attention to the national restaurant brand's advertisements from mobile and how likely who are the actually to choose to go to the national chain of restaurants to eat lunch or dinner or breakfast more than its other restaurants.

The problem is how the national chain of restaurants to advertise it's foods taste, price and service and locations uniquely to win its other restaurant competitors from mobile specific program, providing the network to be best convenient that it's restaurant brand to advertise on that specific program. Another key problem is trend segments viewers based on domestic and foreign consumers' behavior are more specifically their viewing behavior mixed with their restaurants choosing eating behavior in whose countries, watching the national chain of restaurants television advertising from whose mobile , what who are watching to know its existence and on how to let them to know what their actual eating taste to the national chain of restaurants can provide. Hence, I suggest the national chain of restaurants can attempt to use surveys to carry on researching the different countries foreign visitors and domestic visitors whether what whose tastes are preferable to choose what kinds of foods and drinks who hope to eat in this national chain of restaurants from mobile advertising website. The problem is who may choose not to fill its surveys from its mobile website advertising. If they use computer to fill its surveys at home, it will have more opportunities to gather data from survey due to who can sit down to fill surveys in quiet environment. Hence, I suggest it ought use computer internet to do market research about what whose tastes are preferable to eat in its restaurants. When it estimates whether the foreign visitors and domestic visitors numbers, how many people choose to eat different kinds of foods and drinks to its identifications. After it can achieve mobile advertising to promote its restaurant brand more confidently in this mobile marketing advertising strategy.

2. Discuss methods that could be used to assess the effectiveness of mobile advertising.

Measuring social media marketing , such as mobile advertisement, effectiveness and identifying the target market. The use of social media sites as part of company's marketing strategy has increased significantly. Regardless its popularity, there is still very limited information to answer some of the key issues concerning the effectiveness of social media marketing , ways to measure its return on investment and its target market. The social media was started around ten years ago. It began with linked in, which was launched in 2003 year, followed by both My space and face book in 2004 year. You tube in 2005 year and Twitter in 2006 in year. The popularity of social media sites has also spread to companies as part of their strategies. Executives are concerned with their budget justification for a social media plan in computer or media online advertising, when there is lack of supporting materials to confirm the effectiveness of the social media platform , i.e. conversion rate, the relation between buyer-seller relationship and increase in sales and the rate of return investment that they can earn from this plan. Others also believe that their companies‘ performance are not affected by their lack of involvement in the social media sites.

Clearly, the fact that social media marketing is still relatively new among business practitioners has raised some major concerns , such as its effectiveness, the main purpose of including social media mobile advertising in a company's media platforms, it's relation to the existing platforms and the target audience of this strategy. The methods to assess effectiveness of mobile advertisement include that marketing research method is about target client segment of respondents' social media activities and buying decisions relationship survey. Survey questions can include whether how long time and how often who turn on mobile phone to use internet, such as a week is less than 20 hours average or a week is between 20 hours and 30 hours average or a week is between 30 hours and 50 hours or a week is more than 50 hours, why who like to use mobile to use internet and not use home computer to use internet, e.g. reducing to use home electricity, interesting, convenience, no computer at home, what who will seek to see from mobile advertisement, e.g. advertisement , news ,email , message, movie, whether who decide to buy products or consume services choice is from which kinds of channel advertisement influence mostly, such as television, radios, newspapers, magazines, computer internet, mobile internet. It aims to gather target client segment of respondents‘ social media activities and buying decision relationship to estimate whether there are how many numbers of target client will decide to buy the company's product or use it's service from mobile advertisement channel.

Hence, the survey result can indicate these five respondent groups, such as highly affected, somewhat affected, neutral somewhat not affected and not affected at all groups. Mobile phone advertisement is needed to any organizations to use internet to operate. Hence, to access the effectiveness of mobile advertising which may begin by using measures that were very easy to capture and understand, such as the number of website hits or percentage of users who clicked on an advertisement. These measures were very useful fro examining trends in traffic patterns, but the impact of this traffic on sale and other marketing objective was sales and other marketing objectives were little understand. Standardized approaches for capturing and summarizing websites behavior were eventually developed to help make sense of web traffic and patterns. Metrics, such as number of unique visitors and the amount of time who spent viewing web pages provided marketers with new insights into who was assessing the site and how who were using it. But even with a high level of detail about how customers were interacting with the company via the web, marketing manager often lacked the information how user behavior data translates into increased profits and business value. For example, organizations using websites primarily for after sales support have used exactly the same kinds of metrics as these selling directly from the site. This is not due to a lack of available data. Many organizations using web analytics gather and store vast amounts of information and develop large, complex databases to house it. But much of that information is never used. Because organizations who first began to market over the internet often lacked a clearly formulated strategy. In addition, the rapidly changing internet environment made it difficult for marketers to formulate clear expectation about the impact of activities. Both the amount of returns and amount of investments are difficult to measure. I suggest organizations may estimate the value of a visit to a particular web page by estimating the number of visitors who will become customers and then multiplying that number by the average value of all clients to estimate returns. What the 'clicks and hits' and 'measurement driven' approached have in common organization's strategic objectives and provide quantified models that plan and track internet marketing investments from intermediate outcomes to financial results. Hence, it can indicate how marketing expenditures in mobile internet advertising method to lead to increase shareholder value aim. I think investment in internet marketing , organizations will need follow these stages. In the beginning is inputs stage:

Organization and business unit strategy includes structures, systems, resources as well as marketing strategy includes structures, systems as well as information strategy includes structures, systems and market strategy transfers to websites, search marketing , advertisement and public relations, mobile marketing and marketing research. Next, it is outputs stage: It includes intermediate outputs, such as awareness and perceptions, attitudes and intentions, value provisions, channel optimization and market information as well as it includes final outputs, such as marketing assets: customer value, brand equity, knowledge as well as financial flows: increased revenue, cash flows, reduced revenue, lower cost, lower working capital, lower fixed capital and reduced risk. Finally, it is outcomes stage includes shareholder value, return on investment and corporate profitability. For example, Donald restaurant uses its website to promote lower calorie food and fruit options as well as its global campaign tied to the Olympics, nutrition (Business week 8-7-06). Each organization should carefully identify the outputs it seeks to achieve. How can process produce these outputs? Organization can attempt to enhance of website functional or initiation of an email campaign. The final question to organizations which will ask : How outputs contribute to the long term financial performance of the organization from mobile advertising ? Is critical for organizations seeking to enhance return on investment from mobile advertising? In addition, whether mobile advertising can give these benefits to any companies, such as market capitalization and shareholder value can be enhanced by increases in marketing assets (customer value, brand equity and knowledge base) that produce future corporate financial flows from mobile internet advertising method. Hence, marketing assets include customer value, such as using dynamic pricing to manage demand, supporting sales through online information sites, shipping directly to reduce need for inventory possession, shifting in store sales to online sales, eliminating clients with prior post sales problems from promotion lists; brand equity, such as additional revenue through brand premiums, using customer relationship to speed adoption of next generation products target marketing to loyal clients during predicted slow periods, reducing customer turnover and support costs, shifting responsibility and risk for inventory management to major suppliers, pool inventories with suppliers and clients to reduce warehouse space across the supply chain, using trust in brand to reduce unwarranted lawsuits, knowledge base, such as developing mass customization capability, reducing time to market through online concept trials, time promotions to smooth demand, eliminating product features that are not valuable to clients. Watching production timing to demand, direct in store sales to products that generate high contribution margin per square foot of fixed space and anticipating and respond to stakeholder concerns. Finally, customer value and brand equity and knowledge base shall transfer to financial flows aim, such as increased revenue, accelerated cash flow, reduced revenue volatility, lower cost, lower working capital requirement, lower fixed capital requirement and reduced risk.

However, Metrics can be used to access effectiveness of mobile advertising, both financial and non financial metrics are needed to effectively measure performance. Some non financial items , such as market research activities are difficult to measure and companies often avoid measuring those items. However, if the item plays a critical role in delivering organizational value. Measuring it, preferably in quantifiable terms, such as monetary changes or percentages. Even when such measures are difficult to obtain or depend a rough estimates, they provide a basis for examining trends over time and can provide useful information to managers. For example, two metrics for the output awareness are: The number of emails opened recipients and the number of clients that clicked on a promotional mobile advertising. Those two metrics can provide different perspectives on the meaning of awareness, thus the choice of metrics helps clarify the objectives, just as clear objectives can help in identifying specific and to be relevant must be specific and to be relevant they must be customized to meet the unique dynamics of the organization . It aims to achieve the best to capture and reflect the organization's unique sets of activities and results some may be relevant to all organizations and many can be readily adopted to be useful for decision making.

3. Discuss the relationship between mobile advertising and other elements of the promotion in campaign planning.

Mobile advertisement defines as the use of the mobile medium, it is as a communications and entertainment channel between a brand and an end user. In basic terms, it is the process of planning and execution conception, pricing, promotion and distribution of products and services through the mobile channel. Advertising is a form of communication intended to convince an audience (viewers, readers or listeners) to purchase or take some action upon products, information or services etc. The relationship between independent variables elements and mobile advertising which are environmental response and emotional response with behavioral aspect of consumer buying behavior with mobile advertising. It is time that people purchase those brands with which who are emotionally attached elements. Almost every one grows up in the world which is flooded with the mass media, e.g. television, films, videos, magazines, movies advertising and internet channel is either mobile advertising or computer advertising. Advertising is a subset of promotion mix which is one of the 4'p in the marketing mix, i.e. product, price, place and promotion. As a promotional strategy, advertising serve as a major tool in creating product awareness in the mind of a potential consumer to take eventual purchase decision. Advertising, sales promotion and public relations are mass communication tools available to marketers.

Telecommunication technology, such as mobile advertising enables business and industry to grow at a faster pace when contributing to the economic development and at the same time telecommunication infrastructure can be reliable. Cellular phone industry has been one of the profitable businesses in Asian. The country's growing population and huge demand potential have always been an attraction for many high-technological multinational companies. Societies used symbols and pictorial signs to attract their produce users. There elements were used for promotion of products. A company can't make dream to be a well known brand until which invests in their promotional activities for which consumer market have been dominating through advertisements. As the primary mission of advertiser is to reach prospective customers and influence their awareness, attitudes and buying behavior.

The major aim of advertising is to impact on buying behavior, however this impact about brand is changes or strengthened frequently in peoples' memories. Memories about the brand consist of their associations that are related to brand name in consumer mind. These brand cognition influence consideration, evaluation and finally purchases. The promotion in campaign planning to mobile advertising focuses on young people because who choose advertising information and characters as whose role models, who may not only identify with them but also intend to copy them in terms of how who dress and what who are going to buy. As the market is surplus with several products or services, so many companies make similar functional claim, so it has became extremely difficult for companies to differentiate their products or services based on functional attributes alone. Differentiations based on functional attributed, which are shown in advertisement, are never long lasting as the competitors could copy the same. Mobile advertising may differentiate companies' products or services promotion channel to attract client's attention, e.g. the company can use movable product images on internet video to show on mobile. However, mobile advertising time ought depend on the business nature, e.g. facial health products target segment is female, so it's mobile advertising time ought choose form 9:00 AM to 6:00 PM working time between Monday to Sunday, due to housewives or working women shall go back home to cook, who shall not turn on mobile phones at home. Hence, if the company had differentiated which brand and it had chose what time is the more popular to accept to let mobile users to turn on their mobile from mobile advertising. The company mobile advertising will have more promotion effort. For example, if the company sold toys, it's target segment would be 3 ages to 10 ages old. It's mobile advertising ought let every family to find its company website easily. If the family didn't know it's brand, but is was difficult to let the family to find what its toys sale from whose mobile phone because there are many toy companies were using internet advertising to promote which toys. So, it might let every family types " toy" word on yahoo, Google websites, then this toy company name would appear on their websites, the family only clicked its name on their mobile phone, it could show it' toys images, prices, which country manufacturing and which year manufacturing different kind of toys, sale payment and delivery method, e.g. visa card payment, air or land or shipping transportation flight delivery, toys manufacturing ingredients indication from website advertising and it's toys advertising time ought to choose family working time, such as between 9:00 and 6:00 PM , due to who shall bring their mobile to work usually. Hence, the toy company needs to consider family will choose what time to use mobile phone. It ought not choose night time to advertise its toy products from mobile due to family would not turn on whose mobile at home at night time usually. Economic theory has sought to establish relationships between selling prices, sales achieved and consumer's income, similarly before the company chooses to spend mobile advertising expenditure, it ought frequently compared it with sales actual income each month.

Social media marketing, such as mobile advertising effectiveness is highly influenced by three aspects: content quality, involvement and integration with the other media platforms methods to assess whether effectiveness of mobile advertising.

On the first aspect, content quality isn't quantity. It shows that managers should not totally reply on the monitoring software to measure and analyze their social media campaign. For example, the twitter website analysis show that some brands/companies, e.g. Microsoft used their Twitter account to connect and to communicate with customers . Their Tweets were about communicating and connecting with their follows, through some personal conversations in subjects. That were relevant to their customers . As a results, Microsoft clients were able to beat their main competitors in financial performances and Twitter activities. So, Microsoft can use twitter website to assess whether how many numbers of people use internet service to enter phone, then who decide to buy its software products . If Microsoft found the result of the number of buyers who decide to buy its software from mobile phone Twitter website advertisement channel which is more than mobile phone Yahoo or Google websites advertisement channel after who turn on mobile to see advertising. On the another aspect, building trust and long term relationship to mobile advertising to indicate to how to persuade to increase many shippers to decide to buy any products or seek service, e.g. travel tickets booking service after who use mobile to seek advertising habitually. Today, media marketing is about building relationship and trust through effective two way communications , e.g. talk about something that customers are interested in and creating products or service that will help to solve customers' problems from mobile advertising. Some of today's social media marketing campaigns are still driven by the old fashioned marketing and focus on short-term effect sales, which is also known as incentive induced behavior. To assess trust and genuine buyer/seller relationships achieved through consistent and engaging conversation will increase the messages (SMM) level of influence. Trust is the key factor to get the followers to actually to something , i.e. change in buying decisions influence their peers and turn it into revenue for the companies. It is crucial to build a strong relationship with customers and enhance brand loyalty. Hence, it implies mobile phone companies need to build trust relationship to let them to pay extract internet charges to aim to read email, news, watch movie habitually. Then, it will increase chance to let potential buyers to prefer to seek advertisement to choose to buy and products or consume service from mobile websites habitually. Hence, assessment of mobile internet habitual users who use mobile internet time per week from survey is one effective method. Also, firms should start their involvement by inviting their customers or prospects to join their social media community. For example, firms can post the icons of the social media main websites or giving some special deals to customers who become their fans or followers . In the online community, firms should start writing more effective posts. An effective post should reflect honesty and conciseness, it is as key elements of an effective post. It should also be informative to satisfy clients' need for information and experts; opinions. Effective contents should be able to actions from the audience (conversion) so that by the end of this process. Followers will place on order, subscribe newsletter or participate on online surveys. In the offline community, managers should share expertise with their speaker in the local community, which will help to attract more followers or fans and to strength connection with the community. A debate has been going on whether or not consumers are willing to receive mobile advertising. America consumers seem to willing to accept mobile advertising to subsidize the cost of other mobile services , such as email and news services.

A study conducted by HRI Research on behalf of Nokia brand found that the core mobile phone subscriber market (16 to 45 year old) is not only receptive to experiencing mobile advertising, but also actively welcoming mobile advertising in the form of electronic coupons promotion. The relationship between mobile advertising and the four key elements contributing to mobile advertising's acceptance of the promotion in campaign planning. There were mobile advertising should allow users to decide whether or not to receive messages, users could bypass sales messages easily, users should be filter the message received and users want to get mutual benefits of something back. The SMA advertising campaigns of mobile advertising industry plays and consumers have been made afraid of the spam phenomenon deriving from negative email spamming experiences. The personal nature of the website phone markets spamming especially invasive compared to spam received via other channels and devices. Mobile advertising has the potential to be one of the most powerful one to one digital advertising mediums of utilized in the right manner. SMS trials across the would have show the power of mobile advertising in building direct one to one relationship. The online companies like AT&T, AOC wireless, Microsoft and Nokia to mention few companies that are focused on the potential of mobile marketing via mobile handsets. Factors contributing to the success of mobile advertising include that ability, setting up research. measurement, tracking systems, availability of specialist expertise in agency, service provide and establishing consistent rate mobile cards. Other factors impact of drivers on the development of mobile advertising include that personalized medium, users able to opt in , call to action , i.e. immediate response possible , location specific, interactive profiling, appeals to younger customers , one to many communication.

On conclusion, the relatively between mobile advertising and other elements of the promotion in campaign planning include as below: The first element is by utilizing mobile advertising, companies can run marketing campaigns targeted to tens of thousands of people with a fragment of the costs compared to other direct marketing mediums, such as direct mail or telephone and this in just few seconds of line. The advertising industry uses two types of cost calculation cost per thousand impressions (CPM) and cost per rating point (CPP). CPM is used for both print and electronic media when CPP is more popular for electronic media. For instance, if an advertising campaign costs US$5,000 and has an audience of 300,000 consumers, the CPM will be approximately to the initial CPM measure in media selection , such as quality of the audience, audience attention probability and believability of media selection when the CPM for direct mail is between UA$500 to US$700. For email the CPM ranges from US$5 to US$7. However when email marketing is losing its efficiency, mobile advertising offers new ways to promote products and services. A significant factor contributing to consumers' willingness to accept mobile advertisement is the capability of mobile handsets to service certain type of messages , such as multimedia messages. Evidently, most consumers in the future will carry on smart phone with them. The smart phones allow advertisers to reach consumers in different locations with personalize messages at a given time. Another element is the industry of SG or 4G network service is faster connection speed is a obvious enables users to receive digital photographs, moving wide images, high quality sound for their mobile handsets. From advertisers; perspective this opens various opportunities to plan and implement more advance m-advertising campaigns and integrate those with existing marketing channels. However, to develop and provide applications, for example, interfaces to the carrier's wireless network need to be provided in multiple areas: location, presence, billing, personalization, provisioning, packet network, transport and messaging systems. Next element is location awareness cab be seen as the driving force of many wireless applications and suits also well types of mobile advertising. When mobile phones are almost always carried with and intelligent location awareness technical solution are available. The final element is personalization means building customer loyalty by building a meaningful one to one relatively by understanding the needs to each individual and helping to satisfy a goal that efficiently and knowledgeably addresses each.

Personalization is about mapping and satisfying of client's goal in specific contest with a business's goal in its respective context. Personalization means understanding different kinds of individual preferences , needs, mindsets and lifestyles and cultural as well as geographical differences. Mobile are already equipment with a profiting options, e.g. silent, meeting, outdoors. For example, the utilization of time and location awareness as personalization variables has the benefit that mobile advertising is a marketing medium has features that other marketing channels lack. Hence, email advertising needs to keep every mobile users' personal information to be confidential, solicited message, relevance to users need and the right frequency.

Reference

Stredwick. J, (2005). An Introduction to human resource management. Elsevier Ltd, UK.

CHAPTER FOUR

LEARNING AI ASSISTS ORGANIZATIONAL DEVELOPMENT

AI Management accounting organizational behavior how applies to Amazon ecommerce organization
Management accounting concept can help organizations to do management budget strategies, e.g. margin analysis, capital budget, inventory valuation and product cost budget, trend analysis and forecast . Management accounting also called managerial accounting or cost accounting, is the process of analysis business costs and operations to prepare internal financial report, records and managers decision making process in achieving business goals.
However, management accountants depend on standard financial statements containing the earning statement, cash flow statement and balance sheet. In addition , it also makes use of additional finds reports in analysizing the information of the organization including budget performance and cost reports. I shall attempt to explain how management account science can help organizations to analyze cost , why and how changes in order to avoid expense increases or excess cost cases or loss increases.
For Amazon e-commerce publish organization example, Amazon publish is a famous publish organization. It applies internet (online) channel to help authors to sell electronic books and paper books to different countries readers. It also cooperate to other publishers to deliver any its anthors books to their webstores, so when one reader chooses its publish partner webstores to buy Amazon any author books, then Amazon publish will share royalty income between them. Hence, Amazon publish may be book distribution partner to its other e-publish partners.

- How management accounting cocept can help Amazon publish to manage its cost effectively in order to increase its profit or e-books or paper books sale ability.

Amazon publish is a e-comerce organization. It depends high internet speed to help global authors to register Amazon publish's individual author account , then any global authors may download their book files to produce any ebooks and papers to sell from Amazon publisher webstores as wellas global any readers can apply Amazon publish webstores to buy any author individual paper or ebooks from its web-publish stores rapidly. So, Amazon publish must need have fast speed internet technology to support its books sale ability,
It brings this question: How much does Amazon publish internet expenditure need? Does it need to pay shops rent per month? Because Amazon publish has none any actual book shops to locate in any countries. So, Amazon publish must not pay rent to any countries for its shops. Although Amazon publish does not need to pay rent for any book shops, but Amazon publish needs to pay extra internet expenditure to US internet service provider to support its electronic webstores daily electronic books and paper books every purchase transaction, any countries author individual book electronic files download per day 24 hours . So, Amazon publish must need to pay more expenditure for internet service to support its authors and readers their electronic books and paper books purchase and sale transaction per day 24 hours.
As Amazon publish case, in its financial report indicates , it does not pay any book stores rent expenditure or book stores (shops) building building expediture on its profit and loss account, but Amazon publish must need to pay internet service expenditure to US internet service provider. Moreover, this internet service expenditure must be more amount, due to it needs to provide its webstores online book (electronic books and paper books) to sell and

electronic library e-book lending service to global readers, 24 hours. Thus, internet service expenditure must be Amazon publish long-term influential transaction expenditure because, any electronic books and paper books, even e-library books borrow service and readers must need to pay visa card for borrowing book month service fee and purchase books from amazon publish e-publish webstores in any time every day.

Hence, Amazon publish must need have good management account strategy in order to predict whether different countries will have how many readers click to its different countries e-publish webstores to spend time to choose different authors books to buy or borrow to read from intenet channel. So, any countries readers budgeting number, readers reading habit behavior, e.g. US has about one million online readers click Amazon e-publish webstores , but it has only three thousands readers pay visa card to buy its ebooks and paper books from its Amazon electronic publish webstores, in this week , but next week, US has about seven thousands online readers click Amazon e-publish webstores, but it has three thousands readers pay visa card to buy its ebooks and paper books. Hence, it seems tha although this week has one million online readers click to Amazon publish electonic webstores to seek any books, but the book buyer number has only three thousands. Otherwise, although next week, it reduces three thousands e-readers click to visit Amazon e-publish webstores e-readers number , but it still keep same three thousand e-readers to choose to buy Amazon publish's books to read.

I assume that Amazon publish needs to pay a fixed internet service expenditure, e.g. US $500,000, but it design this e-publish webstores can help it to do its different countries e-publish webstores, their daily e-readers visiting number, daily electronic book and paper book sale number and daily e-readers visiting time statistics. It's electronic publish webstores can help it to record any countries' reading habits and reading taste , e.g. how many fiction , story books have sold in the week, how many non fiction books have sold in the week , e.g. business topic books have sold next week.

So, Amazon publish can use its e-publish webstores to gather above data in order to make author book topic sale choice, e.g. whether this week, US market ought sell how many consumer psychological topic book, US market ought sell how many management topic book next week. If this week US market can only sell one thousand consumer psychological topic book to compare its budget is less than one thousand consumer psychological topic books budget sale number reduces, e.g. in the week, there are two thousands readers choose to buy consumer psychological topic books from European market in this week. It implies that there are many European readers who like to read consumer behavior books recently. Hence, Amazon can attempt to concentrate on encouraging authors to write more consumer psychological books to let European readers to read within next several months.

Basic on above effects, Amazon needs to provide rapid internet service to European libraries, schools ,e-book partners to help them to promote Amazon consumer psychology topic books in order to let the European consumer psychological students, consumer psychology lecturers, consumer psychologists to know Amazon publish can provide more different topics concern consumer psychology research in order to increase Amazon 's consumer psychology book European market book buyers bumber.

As above case, I assume Amazon publish needs to pay a fixed internet service expenditure , e.g. US$500,000 per month. Amazon needs webstores to evaluate whether it is value, if it helps European schools, libraries organizations to pay internet fee, in order to let they can let many consumer psychology students and teachers and consumer psychologists to know that Amazon publish may have enough different consumer psychology books to be provided to European publish libraries, schools readers to read. For example, I assume next several month, Amazon publish needs to pay US two million internet service expenditure to global different European countries to help Amazon publish itself to promote its al different authors' consumer psychology topic books as well as it evaluates that it will sell different European countries; students , teachers and consumer psychologists readers, they have about three million readers at least choose to buy its one million consumer psychology topic authors; paper books and electronic books next several months as well as it also needs to evaluate whether it can earn more than US ten million at least royalty income after reducing author royalty from all European countries book markets.

Thus, if Amazon publish makes decision to help European countries schools, public libraries to pay internet expenditure to help it to advertise its one million consumer psychology topic authors electronic and paper books to sell. It must needs to pay fixed US$500,000 internet expenditure for Amazon publish its all e-bpublish webstores and it also needs to pay extra two million internet service expenditure for global all European countries libraries and schools per month. If next month, Amazon publish can earn more than US tem million at least royalty income after reducing author royalty from all European countries book market. Then, Amaozn publish ought attempt to make this internet service expenditure for all European schools, libraries organizations, if it had confidence to earn this royalty amount from European consumer psychology book readers, such as this Amazon publish.

On conclusion, , this Amazon publish organization case, it may attempt to apply management accounting science method to make book sale number budget, royalty income budget, even analysis to reader individual reading habit, book topic choices, book sale price evaluation in order to judge whether the kind or topic book ought concentrates on selling to which countries marekts, such as Amazin publish case, it also may choose different consumer psychology topic books to concentrate on selling to different European countries in next several months, if it can earn all European royalty income more than its internet service expenditure to European schools, libraries, then Amazon may attempt to make this decision. Otherwise, it won't be good decision.

Hence, it implies that management accounting is one kind of business management science, it can apply number to help any organizations to do right or reasonable reason more accurate as well as it is different to traditional financial acounting, it only helps organizations to record and income and expenditure, earn or loss record function. Hence, management accounting may help any organizations to attempt implement useful or effective strategies in order to improve themselves performance.

How management accounting concept applies to investment

Can we apply management accounting concept to investment decision aspect? An organization's investment decision may make risk, so they need risk evaluation to decide whether the project can bring ehat benefit before they want any decisions. Risk management is the process of assessing, managing and mitigating losses . This applies to both business and investing risk management exists in many forms throughout the financial world, such as one individual investor decides to buy low risk government securities, instead of high yield corporate bonds in an example of risk managment companies and investors frequently use financial managment method like options, and future and strategies, like portfolio and investment diversification, in order to effectively manage risk.

For investment management strategy example, it is professional asset management of various securities, including shareholdings, bonds and other assets, such as real estate, in order to meet specified investment goals for the benefits of investors. Investors may be insurance companies, pension funds, corporations, charities, educational organizations or private invetors.

The term asset management is often used to refer to the management of investment funds. So managerial accounting is the process of identifications, measurement , analysis and interpretation of accounting information that helps business leaders make financial decisions and efficiently manage their day operation . The main objective of managerial accounting is to maximize profit and minimize losses . It is concerned with the presentation of data to predict inconsistencies in finances that help managers make important decisions, such as investment decision for Amazon publish book sale country market choice for which topic of books which are the most popular, in order to concentrate on selling the topic of books to the country market. So, Amazon publish needs to gather past different kinds for any one country, number data may include each author ebook and paper books sale prices, each author different book topic books sale number , in order t make which topic of book sale to which countries investment decision aims to increase readers number t o the country book sale market. So, Amazon publish may be apply these tools of management accounting to gather datas to concern book sale record. They may include: Financial accounting, financial statement analysis, book cost accounting, fund flow analysis , cash flow analysis, standard costing, marginal cost, budgetary control , management accounting tools.

- How to apply mental accouting method to predict investor behavior?

The main aim of management accounting to investment includes planning, controlling and evaluating. Thus, the advatanges to investment may include; better decision making, increase business efficiency, simplify financial statement, raises profitability, motivates employees, cost control, reliability. Hence, management accounting means " mental accouting", it is a concept in the field of behavioral economies. Mental accouting refers to the different values of person places on the same amount of money, based on subjective criteria, often with detrimental results.

Mental accouting is a concept in the field of behavioral economies. Developed by economist Richard H, it contends that individuals classify funds differently and therefore are prone to irrational decision making in their spending and investment behavior. It refers to the different values people value on money, based on subjective criteria, that often has detrimental results, mental (managerial)accounting decisions and behave in financially counterproductive or detrimental ways, such as funding a low interest savings account when carrying learge credit card balances, to avoid the mental (managerial) accounting bias, individuals should treat money as perfectly used tools when they allocate among different accounts, be it a budget account (everyday living expenses), a spending account or a wealth account (saving and investment). Also abother author indicates that managerial accounting means mental accounting, which appeared in the Journal of behavioral decision making, the begins with this definition, " mental accounting" is the set of lognitive operations used key individuals and households to organize, evaluate , and keep tracks of financial activities. He considers of how mental accounting leads to irrational spending and investment behavior.

- How mental (managerial) accounting concept helps Amazon publish to make investment decision?

I believe that Amazon publish may apply mental accounting concept to help it to predict whether which topic of books will be the most popular to sell to the country market more accurately. The reason concerns that it can apply all data gathering to analyze whether past has how many readers paid visa to buy the topic of electronic or paper books to prepare to the country , e.g. in this year, Jan. it had 40,000 readers buy fiction electronic books and paper books from Amazon publish US market website to read , it had 100,000 readers buy fiction electronic and paper books to read in European market website and the year Feb. It had 70,000 readers paper books from Amazon publish US market website, it had 200,000 and paper books from Amazon publish European market website. Now, it is Mar. So, Amazon publish may make assumption that fiction (story) topic book is accepted to read by American and European readers, due to US fiction readers had increased 30,000 number in past one month and European fiction readers had increased 100,000 number in past one month.

However, US and European readers number data is not enough to evaluate whether US and European fiction readers number may still keep to increase. It depends on other factors, e.g. fiction e-book and fiction paper book sale price, if one author's ficton's ebooks and paper books rising prices whether it will influence US and European fiction book buyers make book purchas decision to the author's any fictions. So, Amazon publish need s to make the author's past different kinds of fiction books sale prices record in order to judge whether his fiction book's variable price (changing price) will bring negative or positive impact to his readers' fiction book purchase decision. For exmaple, if the author (A)'s one fiction price increased 10% to ebook and paper book sale price between Jan and Feb. His fiction readers number won't be influenced to reduce, even his fiction readers number can still increase 10%. So, it implies that this author's fiction is attract or popular to US and Eurpopean fiction reader market. Amazon publish ought concentrate on helping this author (A) to advertise his fiction to let many US and European readers to know.Hence, it explains that Amazon publish may attempt to gather past every author individual writing book topic book sale proce whether it is increased or decreased how much %, book sale number in order to make book sale investment decision to concentrate on helping whom to advertise to sell to which book sale country market.

So, it seems that mental accounting concept can be applied to Amazon publish to help it to do any author individual book sale country market advertisement investment decision. For example, if Amazon publish can only spend US$10,000 advertieing expenditure to help author (A) to sell fictions to US and European both markets in Mar. , then it can help author (A) to increase 20% more fiction sale number to US and European both markets. This advertisement expenditure is worth to spend for this author (A) in fiction market.

Hence, it implies that mental accounting concept can be applied to publish investment market, such as choosing which country to sell which topic of books, e.g. US sells more which fiction or European sells more fiction or Japan sells more management business topic books or UK sells more consumer psychology business topic books. All of these issues will be any publisher's important book sale market decision . It may influence their royalty income because if the publisher makes wrong decision to sell not popular topic books to the country market, e.g. in the month, US ought have many business topic readers to choose any business topic books to buy from any publishers, if the publisher makes wrong decision to find many fiction authors to help it to increase fiction stock to prepare to sell to US book market. Then, excess fiction stock may cause low fiction price (fiction book supply or publisher's

fiction stock number) is more than fiction book demand (readers). Otherwise, it can not increase business topic books royalty inocme to US book market, because it has not enough different topic, such as management, consumer psychology , accounting, economy , marketing topic business books stock to be putted on book shelves to let US readers to choose when they visit US any book shops in the month.
On conclusion, it explains why mental (managerial) accounting has close relationship to influence customer behavior in behavioral economy view. Mental accounting is a management science or behavioral science tool to help any businessmen to make the most effective or the most reasonable busines decision in nowadays society.

Management science accounting concept how predicts market changing
Accounting aims to help any organizations to record whether the year has what kinds of expenditures, how much of every kind of expenditure finds what factors to cause the kind of expenditure needs to be spent too much in order to avoid excess spending, measurement profict or loss level why what factors cause the year had loss or profit growth in order to achieve long term performance improvement or avoiding loss. Hence, accounting system is not only for bookkeeping record financial performance aim. Accoungint may be one kind management science concept to be applied to explain why and how market changes in order to predict whether the company ought implement which strategies to grow up its business groth or increase clients number.
The question concerns why the organization can apply accounting concpet to predict how the market will change in order to avoid profit falls down or loss causes. I shall attempt to explain as below:
For a watch product sale organization example, this watch sale compay own 100 expensive price watch brand products stock to prepare to sell, their sale prices are between US$3,000 to US$5,000 , so the watch brand prices are below than US$3000, they belong to low prices. It has 100 low price watch brand products stock to prepare to sell. Hence, every month, it keeps exact 100 high price of brand watch products stock and exact 100 low price of brand watch products stoc to prepare to sell. I assume this watch company can sell 100 low price watches and 100 high price watches in this month, but next month, it can sell 50 low price watches and 0 high price watches. Hence, it means that next watch , low prices watches sale number falls 50 number and high price watches sale numbe falls 100 number. It ensures that this company's profit may be influenced to fall by the high and low watch price client reducing number factor. However, this company still lacks data to know whether its competitors ; watch price is the main factor to influence its watch buyers number reduces or whether other factors influence its watch buyers number reduces, e.g. whether its high and low watchs are attractive or not attractive to high its watch design buyers number reduces or whether smart phone product invention influences watch users begin feel watchs have not be importnt to help them, because smart phones have time record function, they can replace traditional watch products or this month has higher unemployment rate, so it causes people do not like spend easily , in special, watch is not one kind essential product. Hence, it seems that this watch company can investigate its every month whether its low and high price watch stock sale record in order to attempt tp find whether what are the main factor to cause its watch sale number increases or decreases? I shall follow above every possible points to be investigated by accounting concept in order to explain why its watch low and high price customer number sudden reduces.
I assume that this watch company's last month and this month every high and low price watch brand's sale prices are stable. So, it seems that the influential factor won't be its " increasing sale price" to cause its high and low watch price customers number sudden reduces. If it gathered data concerns its watch competitots similar famous watch brands of general price range. It discovered their general sale prices do not have much difference between itself and their famous brnad of watchs. Also, it discovered that their these famous brand high and low price watch sale number is more than its sale number, e.g. the another similar famous watch brand company can sell 200 high price watchs and 200 low price watchs last month and 400 high price watchs and 400 low prcice watch this month. So, it seems that its high and low price of watch is not main factor to influence its watch sale number, because its high and low price watch's their price level had not changeed within these two months . Moreove, its watchs manufacture material costs had not increased within these two months. So, it ensures that its profit falls must not be influenced by watch manufacture cost increasing factor. Hence, it may depends on its accounting record to conclude the main factors influence its high and low price watch sale number reduces, they may include; poor watch design feeling to watch buyers factor, smart phones increasing need factor, unemploymenr rate rising factor.

The next step concerns how this watch company can apply accounting concept to find whether the main factor is poor watch design feeling factor, or smart phones are popular accepted to replace watch product feeling factor, or rising unemployment rate factor which one influences it s high and low price range watch sale number decreases can apply accounting cencept to investigate which is the main factor to influences its watch sale number decreased in this two months? I shall attempt to confirm this possibility as below:

Firstly, I assume this watch company's accounting record has marketing promotion expenditure, its expenditure includes advertisement fee, exhibition expense only, however, in its expenditure group accounting record, it has none design expenditure with these two months. Hence, it seems that its high and low price range fanous brands watches had not been improved by its improvement design skill method in order to improve their watch style, picture, shape, colour, function , design to satisfy watch buyers'changing watch fashion need in this competitive market. Hence, it seems that poor watch design feeling factor may be one main factor to influence its watch sale number decreases. It implies that accounting record may help it to find lacking new fashion watch design factor may be one main influential factor to cause watch buyers choose to buy other similar famous brands' watch products.

Next, whether accounting concept can help this firm to judge whether smart phones influences its watch sale number? I assume that smart phone products had been selling more than 10 years in this country in this case indicates US country. So, smart phones mus be its long time similar time seeing function competitors in US. I assume that its past 10 years high and low price range famous brand watches sale number must be more than these two months as well as it had not increases high and low price range of watches prices within this 10 years. Hence, it can depend on its past 10 years accounting record to judge whether smart phones product invention may influence watch buyers number decreases within these two months. basic on its past 10 years , accouniting record indicated that its high and lw price range watch sale number had been increasing, and it s watch price had not beedn increased and its markting advertisement promotion expense had been reducing much within 10 years. Thus, its past watching expense and watch price sale amount and profit accounting record may help it to conclude that smart phone product sale to US market is not the main factor to influence its recent high and low price range watchs sale number falls.

Finally, I shall explain whether this watch company may apply accounting concept to explain whether this month's high unmployment rate factor can influence geeral watch buyers' consumption desire as below:

I assume that this watch company employed 20 watch salespeople and their salaries range are between US$2,000 to US $4,000 per month in the first years . It operated till to this month total 20 years . However, its accounting record indicated that its watch salespeople number had been increasing from 20 to 50 number recently and their salaries range had been increading between US$3,000 to US$6,000 permonth. Hence, within these 10 years , this watch company employees number and their salaries range had been continue increasing. . It may depend on its past 10 years accounting record for salespeople salaries and employee number to reflect whether higher unemployment rate is the main factor to influence its watch sale number reduces.

I assume that within these 10 years, its unemployment rare was between 1% to 10%, in US society , although it may had 1% to 10% young people unemployed within 10 years. But, this watch company, I could also increased salespeople employees number and their salaries could also increase more significantly, even their salaries had not decreased in these 10 years. Hence, its accounting record of salsepeople salaries increasing trend , it may reflect this US watch market's local and overseas watch buyer individual buying watch desires ought not be influenced by slight rising unemployment rate factor, it is based on that this watch company will like to increase salespeople employee number, when it discovered there were many potential watch buyers visited its any watch shops every day within past 10 years. Hence, it implies higher unemployment rare won't influence watch potential buyer individual visiting to any one watch shops in US within these 10 years. So, this watch company's past salespeople salaries, employees number, and their salaries rising range record can reflect whether US higher unemployment ratio level can influence its recent high and low price range of watchs sale number decreases in US local watch sale market.

On conclusion, we can depend this watch company past 10 years accounting record to judge whether which one may be the most main fluential factor to influence its recent watch sale number reduces. I make the final conclusion that its poor watch design feeling factor ought be its main factor to influence its recent watch sale number reduces, due to it had not spend any design expenditure to improve its watch style in order to attract many watch buyers' choices within these 10 years. So, I believe that accounting concept can help any companies to revise whether what factos influence their businessess to be better or worse, instead of general booking record function.

Accounting trademark loyalty theory

In accounting theory view, any organizational goodwill or trademark, they are intangible asset because they can not touch, they are the company name. However, when the organization grows up a long time, ususally more than 10 years, if they are famous when consumers choose to buy the kind of product, they will must remember, then the organization's trademark or goodwill, company names will become the company's intangible asset in their balance sheet , financial report, e.g. Cock Coke soft drink, " Coca Coke" may be this soft drink company's trademaek , intangible asset to this soft drink company. Because any country's soft drinkers, they must remember Coca Coke brand soft drink before they make any brands of soft drink purchase choice. The reason may be Coca Coke soft drink . Its brand had been popular to be accept to be the first soft drink choice to any countries people. Hence, Coca Coke soft drink compnay must put is brand name to be intanginle asset in balance sheet, (B/S),

Why does Coca Coke's brand name (intangible asset) value may increase or decrease in B/S. The reason is simple, when general consumers feel Coca Coka drink has better taste to compare other brands soft drinks. Then, they wil choose other brand soft driks to replace Coca Coke soft drink. So, if the year, Coca Coke's any taste of soft drinks sale number decreases, then it will feel its intangible asset of trademark value is devaluation, but if its soft drink sale number increases in this year. Its intangible asset of trademark value will increase in its B/S.

Hence, it explains why Coca Coke 's trade mark value can reflect its soft drink sale number whether it increases or decreases in the year. Thus, any firms mist hope their trademark , goodwill valuation can often increase every year. The question concerns how they can often keep their trademark valuation to increase? Can the firm increase sale number , it can represent that it has long term goodwill valuation increases? Can other factors influence or impact the firm's goodwill valuation changes? I shall attempt to give examples to explain these questions as below:

In fact, goodwill or trademark represents the company's famility whether how many consumers can remember its brand name , when they choose to buy the kind of product . So, if the firm's products are famous in market, Its products must have many consumers can remember it before they choose to buy the kind of product. So, product's familiar to publish,which ill be one measurement tool to judge whether what may be its goodwill valuation. If there are many consumers remember its brand before they want to buy the kind of products, the firm ought raise its goodwill valuation. It may make market research to enquire whether consumer will choose to buy which brand of product among several similar brands of product. It many people choose to prefer to buy its brand. Then, its brand familiar level to publis will be high grade. It may raise to goodwill valuation inB/S.

So, I think that goodwill fact valuation can not be measured by sale number or sale price or profit or loss amount. It ought be measured by market familiar level. If the product can have many people know its brand exitence in market. Then, its goodwill , intangible asset valuation ought be increased. Otherwise, if there are not may people know or they are familiar its brand existence in market. Then, its probable valuation ought need to decrease . Hence, any firms' goodwill valuation ought reflect their market familiar level for standard.

Do you feel firm goodwill valuation can represent its market value or product sale effort? In accounting principle, goodwill valuation must be measured by money. For example, Coca Coke brand goodwill valuation, in fact, Coca Coke had not pay another in B/S. Its goodwill valuation increases, it is not due to it pays its firm pays cash to buy goodwill. It is due to its capital increase. But, in fact, it does not need to increase cash to capital balance amount in B/S. Because coca Coke has not increase its cash amount, due to goodwill valuation increases. Its goodwill valuation increases, it supposes that is capital amount also be influenced to increase. So, Coca Coke 's goodwill valuation can not represent it has profit growth. Goodwill valuation only represents it has profit growth. Goodwill valuation only represents Coca Coke's present market valuw whether it increases or decreases in soft drink market. It is not actual cash available value. So, why firms need have goodwill valuation. The reason is simple. If one day, the firm hopes to sell its busines to another. When the another potential business buyer feels this firm's goodwill valuation is high. It may persuade b make business purchase decision more easily. because he believes that there are many people are famkliar this product brnad , then they will choose to buy theis product in preference . So, good goodwill valuation can build good business sale image to help the firm can raise business sale price to anyone . Such as Coca Coke soft drink goodwill case, if it can keep high goodwill valuation, then it can persuade any businesses buyers accept to pay high business purchase price. so, B/S goodwill valuation may help any famous business to sell to anyone in the high business sale price more easily.

Can goodwill valuation help the firm to predict market environment changes? For Coca Coke soft drink case example, I assume that it estimated its goodwill valuation is US 3 million , but this year, it estimates its goodwill valuation falls down to US one million. What factors influence Coca Coke feels its goodwill valuation reduces US two million in this year? I believe that is current year goodwill valuatin falls, it has relationship to whole global soft drink taste changes to global soft drinkers. The factors influence global drink makes taste changes , they may include: global soft drinkers begin to dislike to choose to drink any brands of soft drink in preference, if they feel soft drink is one kind of bad health drink. They may choose to buy freash fruits to eat to replace any soft drink. I assume that the other soft drink brand companies' goodwill valuations are decrased. It means that if other soft drink brands' goodwill valuation can increase. Then, Coca Coke may believe that there are many soft drinkers prefer to choose other soft drink brands' soft drinks to drink. So, global soft drink markets still have competitive effort. Coco Coke nees to learn how to change its taste and let soft drinkers believe its soft drink can bring health to them to compare other soft drink brands. So, it seems that goodwill valuation also helps any organizations to eveluate how market changes to influence itself product sale effort. It explains why goodwill valuation is one kind of good market changing predictable tool t any businesses in accpunting concept, instead of sale business valuation measurement tool.

On conclusion, accounting principle or accounintg concept is not only be applied to bookkeeping financial record aspect. If the organization hopes to find what factors to influence its customer number or they hope to predict whether market will ought how to change to be netter or worse. It may attempt to investigate its past every year some kinds of expenditure amount record in order to find how any why the firm itself needed to pay more or less to the kind of expenditure. It aims to research what factors may influence its past and present expenditur changes in order to find whether what the most influential factors are influenced itself buyers number increases or decreases . Hence, accounting is one kind of makret research scientific method to any organizations.

Accounting science how predicts e-commerce consumer behavior

Cash e-commerce organizations apply accounting record to predict consumer behaviors? If it is true, how e-commerce organizations can use past accounting record to predict consumer behaviors? In general, e-commerce sale transactions must need any individual e-buyers to register higher address to their e-store in order to deliver products to any one-buyer homes. For Amazon e-commerce organization, when one China client buys a furniture from US Amazon e-commerce organization, when one China client buys a furniture from US Amazon e-store. The furniture is putted to Amazon US itself warehouse. So, when the China e-buyer pays visa to buy the furniture . He needs to register his address to amazon e-store. When amazon confirms that it can receive cash from the China e-buyer visa card, then amazon will deliver the furniture from US amazon warehouse to the China e-buyer home by plane.

So, amazon must have any e-buyer address record and the product sale price record for any one country e-buyer after it comfirms that the e-buye visa card has enough money to buy the product. Thus, amazon can apply past every online transaction to follow these data to do market research, they may include: which country person buys the product, what the product is, how much to the product price, how many of different product number e-buyer purchase within the year. So, amazon can collect all above data to analyze any one country has the highest e-buyer number,e.g. in the year, there ar one million US e-buyers number, there are two million China e-buyer number,which kind of products are the most popular, e.g. soap , computer, furniture, cloth, shoe, shirt, towel, electronic products etc. what the age range is, e.g. young , old, students , workpeople, they choose to buy the kind of product, how many number , the family buys the kind of product to the e-transaction, how many goods return number to the year total e-transaction, how many goods return number to the year total e-transactions.

Hence, amazon can gather all past every e-transaction data to prepare how to predict whether how every country e-transaction will consumer behavior to predict whether how every country e-transaction will influence consumer behavior will change next year in order to let it to prepare how to implement new market strategy,e.g. how to advertise its product, which countries need to spend more advertise to promote its products, evaluate whether amazon needs to spend how much advertisement expenditure to earn more e-sale transactions number to the targe sale country.

Why does amazon's any one e-transaction's accounting record assists it to predict consumer behavior? For china target e-buyers market example, when one Shanghai city e-buyer pays visa to buy one computer from amazon e-store, if the e-transaction can be accepted . Amazon can gather the e-buyer is living in China Shanghai city, which brand of computer , he chooses to buy, how much sale price to the computer, how many of computers number , he buys, how many e-transaction times to the China, Shanghai city buyer within the year. Hence, when amazon needs know where China target market has how many e-buyers number to every city, how many e-transaction return goods and refind number, which kinds of product are the popular to China e-buyers' purchase needs, which is the highest price and the lowest price sale level to China, Shanghai city target e-commerce market every e-transaction . Thus, when amazon collestc all above China, Shanghai past one year any individual e-transaction data, it can compare whether how its China, Shanghai city.

Nest year, e-buyers behavior change in order to analyze whether which kinds of product price ought need to reduce in order to attract many China e-buyers to click amazn webstores to pay visa to buy its products or which kinds of product price may increase, when the kind of product is popular to sell to China target market, or make out of e-stock shelf decision to the kind of product when Amazon discovers the kind of product is not accepted to buy in popular from its e-store. Thus, it seems that Amazon's past any one e-transaction accountning record can help it to analyze whether how every target market its e-buyer behavior is changing in order to change next year sale changing strategy is more reasonable . Hence, it explains why e-commerce organization's accounting record may help it to analyze how future market changes as well as record how every old e-buyer customer whether he/she will choose to buy the kind of old product again or buy new product, even not buy anything from Amazon e-stores this year.

Hence, any e-commerce organization's e-stores can apply online technology skil and accounting concept to help it to learn how to analyze every year post efficient countries‘ cities different e-buyer individual product behavioral choice in order to judge/revise whether it ought need to change to buy its products from its e-stores conveniently. So, any e-commerce organization explains why it can attempr to apply its post every accounting e-buyer sale transaction record to make every country consumer behavior marketing analysis to compare transaction visiting shop business model more easily, because visiting shop sale model can let the seller to sell its products in its shop, when it locates in the country. But e-commerce sale model can let the product can be sold to different countries more easily.

So, it seems that if the e-commerce organization can have good accounting record system to keep its past all e-transactions record can gather all data concerns any countries e-buyer individual address , how much sale price for the product, how many sold, and refund to the country e-buyers and the e-buyer age is young or old , male or female e-buyer purchase habit.

Can the e-commerce organizatin predict consumer behavior if it implemented inefficiency accounting record system? Firstly, we need to know good or right accounting record system can help the organization to track or find past any transactions more easily. So, if the organization has none good accounting record system , its accounting record system can not be improved efficiently. Then, its accounting record may bring wrong sale price record, wrong profit (over -profit) or less profit or wrong loss (over loss) number record. Then, this wrong sale transaction record may mislead financial performance to publis to know, e.g. current year, its sale performance is improved, but in fact, its current year sale number is less than last year sale number. Consequently, this organization can not predict its consumer behavior. Whether know to change exactly, due to it often has wrong sale number record, e.g. higher or lesser sale price record, and more or less sale number may influence its gross profit earns high amount, even if its any kinds of expense record is more orless, it will influence its net profit is more or less or less is more or less, for example, if the organization earns US one million dollar prodict this year, but due to it smore sale number transaction to cause over profit. So, its financial performance report indicated its earned US two million dollar. So, it believes its buyers number can increase, if its sale prices do not change. This wrong financial performance report many mislead it has good consumer behavior in this year. Then, it will continue implement its old marketing strategy. Consequently, its next year financial performance may be caused worse to compare present. So, it implies that wrong financial record may cause wrong consumer behavior judgement.

Can robots perform management accounting analysis
tasks

Our future will experience artificial intelligent development stage. Nowadays, we had had some tasks which can be done by robots, e.g. warehouse delivery, restaurnt kitechen dish cleaning tasks, transport tasks, even non drive manual auto driving tasks, shopping center service etc. cleaning or customer service simple jobs duties. If one day, robots cab be applied to do office tasks, e.g. accounting record tasks, they may replace account clersk, even accountants to deal simple accounting record tasks, even complicate management account analysis tasks in office working environment. If future robots can be developed to help accounts clerks as well as accountants to do simple bookkeeping debit and credit every income ot expense transaction record in order to analyze marketing research tasks, then it brings this question: Can future robots replace accounts clerks and accountants to do their accounting tasks in any organizations. I shall attempt to research the relationship between robots and accounting tasks questions as well as whether robots will bring what social influence if robots can replace future human to do any simple and complex accounting tasks for any organizations.

What is need for development of artificial intelligence to accounting tasks aspect? The first computer language used to create artificial intelligence is USP. This language is quite flexible and extensive . Features such rapid prototyping and macro are very useful in creating AI. LISP is a language that makes complex tasks simple. So it seems that it is possible tobots can learn human to do any kinds of accounting tasks, e.g. financial account record, audit check, management account analysis etc. different kinds of acounting tasks for financial , management account, audit check functions in any organizations.

However, scientists believe that artificial intelligence can help accountants be more productive and efficient. Robotic process automation RPA) allows machines or AI workers to complete repetitive, time-consuming tasks in business processed, such as document analysis, handling that are plentiful in accounting . AI can also significantly reduce financial fraud and maintenance accounting errors. Hence, the stages of AI development to accoutning industry, they may include: internet AI, business AI, perception AI, and autonomous AI ., Internet AI is thr simplest stage of AI, business AI has a limted memory, perception AI. This is the first stage in the future of AI. A key feature of this perceptive form of AI is the ability to compile and draw from past experiences, much like human to accounting tasks. The design phase is essentially in literative process comprising all the steps releveant to building the AI or machine learning model, data acquisition, exploration, management and analsis tasks. So, it seems that future robots may be developed to help human to do simple and complex accounting tasks. Combining AI with other technologies, such as robotic, process automation can follow accountants to redirect the time that they used to spend on multiple tasks, toward performing high-value, high -impact taaks. Adding AI to accounting operation can also increase output quality by miniizing human errors. So, AI and automation won't be replacing finance and accounting professionals in the foreseeable futue.

On the contrary, as AI automates many aspects of business, there is a bug opportunity for accounting and finance professsionals to upskill themselves to meet the requirements of the 21 centurey. For AI audit task aspect, AI enables the analysis of a full populatin of data and can identify outliers or expectations. By making it possible for auditors to work better and smarter. AI will help them to optimize their time, enabling them to use their human judgement to analyze a boarder and deeper set of data and documents.

Can AI be used in auditing and accounting ? In the assurance practice, AI is being used to perform auditing and accounting prcedures, such as review of general ledgers, tax compiance, preparing workpapers, data analytic, expense compliance, fraud accounting skills. So, it seems that future AI can replace market research analysists, compensation and benefits managers , instead of financial accountants, management accountants an auditors in any organizations.For bookkeeping clerks position example, these simple account jobs are expected to decrease, by 8% 2024, and it's non surprise because most bookkeeping is getting automated if it has not been as of now, Quickbook, Peachtrss etc. accounting software that does not need any more, because robots do not need any kinds of accounting software to help them to do any simple or complex accounting tasks.

How has teachnology changed the accounting industry? Computers and accounting softeare has changed the industry complexity, with but when robots develop, it will change global accountancy professional more complex. Can robots replace accountants? Automation had brought significant changes the accounting profession over the last decaed. When some tools have made accountants lives easier. However, since robots invention, it developed these tools have also created a false debate about whether automation will overtake the global accounting industry compexity and make accountants irrelvant . The question should not be whether automation will take over accounting, but where its rreal value lives.

In fact, I believe that no any software can match the critical thinkning and trusted counsel that a human advisor offes, as valued accountants, have become business partners, where software is limited to evaluating concrete inputs, accountants can understand clients business goals and observations voice to make decisions. This allows them to serve as advisors to their clients, whether by adjusting business models in real time, or managing emplyer wellbeing . Sok, future AI development ought not replace human accountant's this kind of skill more easily.

- How robotic process automation impact on accouting industry changes?

Searching for methods to efficiently perform accounting tasks can be dated book to the 1950 s, when process mechanisation involved the use of punched cards to store and retrieve transaction data (Keenoy, 1958). Since then IT ad automation have transtormed the way accountants collect, store, process and share data through a variety of tools (Ellis, 1986); Kaye, Nicholson, 1992; Rom, Rohde, 2007). However, robotis process automation is a technology solution that allows end-users to comfigure a software robot to use existing applications to perform accounting transactions manipulate data and communcation with other systems (introduction to robotis, 2015).

Software robots can be easily programmed or trained to perform repetitive, rules-based , high volume operations by replicating human actions when accessing multiple systems, applications, and documents (Embracing robotic automation 2018). Hence, robotic accounting software can bring cost reduction to counting and finance tasks, e.g. one robotic accounting software can replace two to five full time accounting clerks, increased process speed, software robots perform routime tasks faster than employees would manage mamually (Cacity, Willcocks, 2016) . They do not get distracted or tried and thus avoid delays, cycle times decreases significantly improved process control and performance visibility, e.g the collected analytical information is much more detailed and can be used for audit and compliance checks, higher quality data (accuracy, consistency, compliance), e.g. robots can validate the data before reporting or using them future. Assuming that the appropriate rules have been thoroughly tested beforehand, data inaccuracy and quality risk decrease fill tracking and logging robots' action make internal and external audits easier and reduce compliance risks, continuous operation 24 hours a day, or none working day limits. So, robots are applied on accounting task aspect, it can bring positive impact on employees, repetive tasks taken over by robots release employees' times. They can shift their focus on higher value added tasks, solve employee morale proble,. Any accounting department staffs may feel tired when they need over time works, often but robotic accounting staff won't have tired or bored feeling.

However, robotic process, automatin may be applied on these accounting tasks aspect, they may include: internal control period end clising, general ledger, subledgers, closing , validatin of journal entries, low-risk accounts, reconsiliation, consolidation, reporting-monthly , quarterly close, internal performance and management reportng aggregating and analysing financial and operational data, external statutary report, accounts receivable and payable record-maintaining updating customer/supplier data, creating processing, posting payment, collections, billing, matching invoices, aganist sales and purchase orders, cash management, general accoutning, inter-company transactions, inventory accountancye, travel and expenses reimbursement request, audit and document expense report, payroll, stock keeping, fixed asset accouting record, tax accounting. So, the general simple accounting tasks robots will have effort to finish.

- Can robots perform the same management accounting analytical decision making skills to human management accountants tasks?

Although, robots can perform simple bookkeeping audit accounting tasks, but whether complex management accounting analytical and decision making tasks, robots can do the same level of management accounting analytical, decision making tasks to human management accountants?

I shall attempt to answer this question. How robots impact of mental accounting in valuation? No retailers show this price without considering the " 99" in end. This indicates to our mind that the price is cheaper. Its popularity can be verified gas stations all around the world. The difference between robots mental accounting issue and management accountants.

The Anchoring theory was used to verify its possible impacts on capital venture tech finds decisions, during equity trading for an initial investment starting. Management accountants ususally arrange 68% of the finds use-valuation as a basic, when 21% proposed other methods . But still use valuation and only 11% of the investors said they did not consider valuation at allo. the context considered that the human management accountant will consider that the investment would be made in a startup in early stages. That is with little or any real accounting information can image the amount of uncertainty that exists in the type of analysis?

Moreover, why do even experienced fund managers invest based on an impossible calculation> In simplity, it explains that human management accountant in order to do any investment decision. Although robotis will use alaytic mind more than calculating to estimate any investment risk in order to make investment decsion for any organizations. AI's analytic skill and human management accountant calculation risk skill be their difference on how dealing management accounting investment risk issue aspect. Even, the difference between human management accountant and robotic management accounting automation is their robotic management automation can apply mental accounting theory to judge consumer behavioral choice.

It is a new model of consumer behavior is developed using a hyrod of psychology and microeconomics. The deveopment of the model starts with the mental coding of combinations of risks and losses using the prospect theory value finction. Then, robotic management accounting automatin can attempt to evaluate of consumer purchase for the product is modeled using the new concept of " transaction utility", e.g. one family electronic firm, it is seeling rice cooker, television radio, household electronic products, it can learn how to mental accounting method to help this houseold electronic product firm to predict how any why its different kinds of household electronic products choice may change to its consumer behavior next week, e.g. robots can gather wlectronic product competitors prices data to compare itself company's same kinds of electronic product data e.g. rice cooker prices and its competitors' rice cookers prices, whether its high price , rice cookers price factor or other factors influence its rice cookers sale number decreases in this week. Consequently robotic management accounting software may help this household elecronic product company to analyze whether what are the actual factors to influence its rice cookers prces reduce in this week. It is human management accountants feel difficult to collect past price data in order to make accurate consumer behavior changes, prediction or find whther are the main factors to influence product sale number increases or decreases.

Hence, future robotic management accounting automation can learn the valuation of purchase modeled using the new concept of transactin utulitym such as this houseold electronic product case, robotic management accounting automation many learn the household budget process ,the characterization of mental accounting, in order to find whether household purchase behavior to the company's products whether what the main factors may influence its household producys sale number increases or decreased.

On conclusion, future robots can do simple bookkeeping, audit check , general daily accounting tasks, even robots can also do complex management accounting tasks, they can learn how to apply mental accounting knowledge to gather the company's past all every month different price variable data, sale number, in order to conclude whether what are the main factors to influence the kind of product sale number increases or decreased more accurately to compare human management accountants in any organizations.

Applying HR management accounting learns consumer behavior

Managerial accounting purposes to be used by management in "making by business decision: It includes product caost, budget , forecast and various financial analysis consumer behavior is the series of behaving of patterns that consumers follow before making a purchase through consumer behavior, you can also earn how customers interact with and the year products. So, any organizations may attempt to find any management account past year past per month transaction records to bring consumer behavioral change predictiver knowledge, it can help future decisions about product creation more easily.

Hence , the management accoutning knowledge focuses the process of creating organization goals by identifying, measuring, analyzing, interpreting and communicating informations to managers is call management or manerical accounting. Management accounting focuses on all accounting aimed at informing management about operational business metics. Also, any managers may attempt to gather past product number presentation date to find whether what the main factors can influence consumer buying behavioral change in its any kinds of products, the level of motivation also affects the buying behavior of customers, e.g. whether the products‘ sale prices sight rise, to influence customer number reduces, or whether the product's traditional old design is not more attractive or popular to accept to compare other linds of competitors' similar product design, or whether the kind of product is not popular to be accpeted to use, the another how invention of similar product ot the market is recession , it need to change another new sale market, if replaces its existence etc. different factors.

Hence, management accounting can help managers to attempt to gather past the product's sale and production past data to carry on analyzing whether what the main factor to influence its customer number reduces or increases in other to improve its sale strategy.

- Computer sale applies management accounting to predict consumer behavior

For computer sale product example, the computer saller may attempt to apply management accounting to analyze why computer buyer behavioral changes, e.g. a study of consumer behavior will reveal what kind of consumers buy computers, could they buy for home and personal use or for office, what features , they look for, what benefit o they seek including post purchase service, huw much they are willing to pay how many they are likely to buy . All of these computer buyer individual purchase behavioral analysis, the computer seller can follow its different models of laptops, desttops, prices, sale number, house or office ise design kind etc. data to research and analyze and predict hether future computer buyer individual need will how changes, in order to prepare and learn how to design new kinds of desktops and laptops to raise competitve effort.

In fact, in computer industry, the factors may influence computer buyer behavioral change, they may include core technical features, past purchase services, price and payment, conditions, physical appearanre, value added features and connectivity and ability are the main seven factors that are influencing consumers‘ laptop purchases choices.

- How can the laptop computer seller applies management accounting data to analyze whether which is the main factor to influence laptop buyer behavior changes?

for last month, I assume that laptop model (A) laptop computer sale price si per US$1000 and it can sold 1000 number and laptop model (B) laptop computer sale price is per US$1,500 and it can sold 2000 number.SO, it implies that although laptop model (B) computer sale price is more than US$500 to compare laptop model (A) computer, but the model (B) laptop computer can still sell more than 1000 number fo compare model (A) laptop computer last moth. It seems that model (B) laptop's attractive dsign, more fuction, rapid connectivity and mobility and attrative physical appearance main factors may influence laptop (B) model computer products sale number is more than laptop (A) model computer products last month. But, in this month, it has significant change between laptop model (A) and laptop (B). In this month, laptop modle (A) and laptop model (B) prices are not changes, but laptop model (A) can sell 3,000 number and laptop model (B) can sell only 500 number. Consequently, their sale numbers have significantly changes, laptop (A) can increase more 2,000 sale number, but laptop model (B) can decrease 1,500 sale number between these two months. It explains that although it seems that laptop (B) model has possible own attractive physical appearance, and rapid connectivity and mobility, more function to cause it can sell more than laptop (A) model computer produc. But, it ensures that all of anh one these possible factors can not help it to raise sale number in long time. It means that laptop model (B) may have other factors to influence itss sale number, e.g. other brand of laptop computers' physical appearance, more function, connectivity and mobility , features , even they can provide better value added sale service, repair service, product delivery service, feature to compare this brand of laptop seller, or its laptop model (B) buyers had lost confidence to use its laptop model () computer products, because they often need to repair and pay extra repair service fee frequently, e.g. one year has one time to two times at least per year. SO, their past poor frequent repair experience influences they choose to buy other brand of laptops. Otherwise, why laptop model (A) computer products number can sell more 2,000 number , the factor may include non rising price, none frequent past repair experiences to any one model (A) laptop buyer , their individual psychological positive feeling factor . So, it seems that gather these two laptop model (A) and model (B) past sale number, sale price data to conclude whther what main factors may influence its model (A) and model (B) laptop sale number to increase or decrease in long term.

However, this laptop computer seller can not only depend on the gathering these two months short time sale numbers ans sale prices data to model (A) and (B) laptops, in order to make the final conclusion concerns whether what the main factor can influence model (A) and model (B) laptop product sale number changes absolutely. It must need to continue to keep the long time management sale umber and sale prie data record for laptop (A) and (B) in order to conclude whether what the most accurate influential factor is that it can influence laptop model (A) and B() sale number both change in order to implement the improvement strategy for them both.

- Management accounting data can also help this laptop seller to predict future market development or whether which market will have high sale effort, e.g. Japan laptop sale market may have the highest market share ratio, among different Asia countries, or Germany laptop sale market may have highest market share ratio among different European countries next year. For example, in the last year, this laptop computer seller had sold 50,000 laptops to Japan computer market, it has sold 500,000 laptops to China computer market, it has sold 100,000 laptops to US computer market and 50,000 laptops to Germany computer market, in this year. its these laptop markets sale prices are not changed, it has sold 200,000 laptops to japan computer market, it has sold 400,000 laptops to China computer market, it had sold 200,000 laptops to US computer market and 200,000 laptops to Germany computer market . Hence, it ensures that Germany laptop market has increased 4 times sale number from last year and Japan has increased 4 times sale number from last year. Otherwisem China laptop sale number has decreased 100,000 laptops from last year and US laptop sale number has increased 1 time from last year. So, it can imply that Germany and Japan future laptop sale number may grown rapidly to compare US and CHina laptop sale markets. It also indicates this sale trend also may help this laptop computer to attempt to find whether what factors may influence its US and China laptop sale number fells down,e.g. whether this local laptop choices increasing factor, it laptop physical appearance is not more attraction, or slow connectivity and mobility speed ,even their model (A) and () laptop prices are higher to compare US and China local other similar brands of laptops prices.

In summary, I believe that management accounting technique can be attempted to apply to help any kinds of products to find whether what main factor(S) to influence their product sale number changes, it is one kind of good data gathering and analytical tool to help any businesses to attempt to predict consumer behavioral changes.

Organization management accounting strategy

What is organization management accounting strategy? As its most basic an organization management accounting strategy is a plan that specifies how your business will allocate resources, e.g. money, labour, and inventory to suppoty production, marketing, inventory and other business activities. IN general, the foure organizational straategy and the culture of the organization categorized into four types: Adhocracy, market and hierarchy.

The purpose of an organization management accounting strategy can be defined as the direction an organization takes with the aim of achieving future business success. Strategy sets out how an organization intends to employ its resources, including the skills and knowledge of its people as well as financial and material assets, in order to achieve its mission or overall targets. So, the key element of an organizational strategy may include: define vision, create mission, set objectives, develop strategy, outline approach, get down to tactics. However, an organizatinal strategy plan is an organizational management activity that is used to set priorities, focus energy and resources, strengthen operations, ensure that employees and other stakeholders are working toward common goals established agreement crowd intended outcomes/ results, and access organizational missions.

Adhocracy strategy is a form of business management accounting that emphasizes individual initiative and self organization in order to accomplish tasks. This is in contrast to bureaucracy which relies on a set of defined rules and set hierarchy in accomplishing organizational goals. The term was popularized by Alvin Toffler in the 1970s. Examples of adhocracy include most project or marix organizations. Among private-sector organizations, high technology firms, particularly young firms facing fierce competition are sometimes organized as adhocracies.

However, important examples of adhocracy do exist in government. Hence, adhocracy is a flexible, adoptable and informal form of organization that is defined by a lack of formal structure that employs specialized multidisciplinary trams grouped by functions. Adhocracy is characterized by an adoptive , creative and flexible behavior based on non-performance. Adhocray culture in a business context, is a corpoate culture based on the ability to adapt quickly to changing conditions. Adhocracies ar characterized by flexibility, employee empowerment and an emphasis on individual initiative.

The five basic marketing strategies may include: product, price and promotion and people in management accounting strategy aspect. They are key marketing elements used to position a business strategically. A market strategy refers to a business's overall game plan for reaching prospective consumers and turning them into customers of their products and services. For example, the BSC business 2 customed marketing strategies may include : social networks and viral marekting, paid media advertising, internet marketing, email marketing, direct selling, point-of-purchase marketing, co-branding, cause marketing, conversational marketing. Hence, marketing strategy or management accounting strategy is a long term toeard looing approach and an overall game plan of any organization or any business with the foundemental goal of achieving a competitive advantage by understanding the needs and wants of customers.

Hierarchy strategy describes a relations of corporate strategy and sub-strategies hierarchically and logically consistent at the level of vision, mission, goals, and metrics , e.g. HR strategy (human resource strategy), to general, the three levels of strategy are: corporate level strategy, this level answers the foundamental question of what you want to achieve, business unit level strategy focuses on how you've going to grow.

The management accounting strategy planning hierarchy is the organization's mission and vision both of ,which should be long-lasting and motivating. At the base of the hierarchy are the shorter term strategies and tactics that unit members will use to achieve the vision. So, the basic levels of management accounting strategy are: corporate, business, functional and operational level strategy. The strategic hierarchy aims to be concept used to understand the different types of strategy decision made in a organization, e.g. michael porter , three generic strategies (cost leadership, differentation, and focus) that can be implemnted at any organizations. So, hierarchical levels of strategy managment accounting may be concerned with selection of which is the right generic strategy to implement, sale method, such as low product sale price, lot differentiation of product choice, and focus an main product feature market sale methods etc.

● The relationship between organizational management accounting strategy and avoiding resource waste

If an organization can implement good managment accounting strategy whether it can assist it to reduce any organizational internal resource waste, e.g. exceed human resource employment cost, facility used cost, using cost, efficient administration or management cost etc. essential organizational cost. Because any organizations must need to use resources in order to achieve efficient providivities, service activities, if the organization can implement effective strategy in order to measure its performance, whether strategy can assist it to judge how to avoid not essential resources spending. Can efficient strategy help organizations to avoid to waste resources? I shall attempt to explain as below:

Whether formal strategy implement can avoid formal technical measurement of scale and concentrates on the loca resource mobilization using aspect os small, medium and large organization? What does resource mobilization strategy mean? Resource mobilization refers to all activities involved in sesuring new and additional resources for your organization. It also involves making better use of and maximizing , existing resources.What are the stepd in resource mobilization?

Firstly, any organizations need to plan od designing a resource moilization strategy and action plan, secondary , finding key elements of a resource mobilization strategy, thirdly,act of practical step to implementatin, fourth identify, fifth step, engagement, sixth step, negotiate, eventh step, manage and report, final step, communicating results.

What are the source of resource mobilization to any organizations? For example includes spreading flyers, holding community meetings, and recruiting volunteers. Material may include financial and physical capital, like office space, money, equipment, and supplies . Human resources, such as labour experience, skills and expertise in a certain field. How does an entrepreneur mobilize resources? To exploit opportunities, entrepreneurs monilize and recombine a variety of resources, such as financial capital (e.g. cash, ot loan from a bank , human capital e.g. skills from a employees, and social capital e.g. information obtained from social contracts. Hence, the overall objectives of the resource mobilization strategy is to securce the necessary funds to deliver on the source mobilization strategic outcomes. To achieve this accurate resource used number and expenditure budget and emergency appeals will need sufficient preditable and contrributions. So, the aim of resource mobilization strategy outlines how secretariat will organize the process of prioritising, plannin, selecting projects, monitoring: broadening the resource channels, as well as coordinating with staffs for mobilising and effectively utilizing resources.

So, the genesis of resource mobilization strategy is a good, solid strategic plan, it should articulate activities that are more routine in nature and can be finded through the organizational internal efficient resource mobilization. Resource mobilization refers to all activities involves in securing . These new directions or new business opportunities are pursued using a distinct resource mobilization strategy .

On conclusion , an efficient resource mobilization plan is a term resource mobilization, it refers to all activities undertaken by an organizations to secure new and additional financial, human and material resources to advance its mission. Inherent in efforts to mobilize resources is the drive for organizational sustainability . So, resource mobilization is about an organization getting the resources that are needed to be able to do the work it has planned. Resource mobilization is more that just fundraising, it is about getting a range or resources from a wide range of resource providers for donors, through a number of different mechanisms. How does an entrepreneur mobile resources? To exploit opportunities, entreprensurs mobilize and combine a variety of resources, such as financial captial , e.g. cash or loans from a bank, human capital e.g. skill from an employee and social capital e.g. information obtained from social contract.

Why do organizations need resource mobilization strategy? The reasons may include: The principles of resource mobilization wih examples, it focuses on forging partnerships built on trust and mutual accountability . So, as to attract adequate and more predictable contributions, with the future goal of sustainability, it refers to all undertaken by an organizatin to secure new and additional financial , human and material resource to advance its mission, in efforts to mobilize resources is the drive for organizational sustainability, community mobilization is the process of bring together as many stakeholders as possible to raise people's awareness of and demand for a particular programme to assist in the delivery of resources and services, and to strengthen community participation for sustainability an dself -reliance, resource mobilization is often referrred t as " new business creaating chance" , the organization has a strong, yet flexible structure , such as writing proposal how to spend the least respurce expenditure in order to achieve the most satisfactory effective result to the organization.

Hence, developing a resource mobilization strategy plan , as the source of new business opportunities to the social and behavioral change considerations must be needed the organization as well as resource mobilization target at a minimum level should be needed to raise at transformational change happen on the ground and advocate for the products and may have to develop new business proposal.

- Can resource mobilization change improve organizational performance?

I believe that resource mobilization can help any organizations to change or improve performance to the better, even the best. I shall explain as below:

What are the sources of organizational change? Change originates in either the external or internal environments of the organization. External sources include political, social, technological or economic environment, externally motivated change may involve government action, technology development, competition , social values and economic variables.

How do organizational resources affect change? Results indicate that organizations possessing greater stocks of historically valuable resources were much less likely to engage in adaptive strategic change, but also that this resoure-driven towards change tended to have a even beneficial effect on performance . Wonder of organizational change management is easier spoken about than achieved by resource mobilization strategic in possible? Can create enterprise level value by effective process for resource allocation?

The key to success involves managing organizational change , so it leads to real and lasting improvements, tailoring to resource allocation how mobilization strategy. So, nowadays, organizational capacty for change: Increasing change capacity and avoiding change overload, organization, today risk is overcommitting resources, resulting in an overload condition wih which it how allocates its resources to tbe used efficiently or inefficiently. For example, on new government regulations, ne products development or growth aspect, organizational change efforts often run into some form of human resistance. First, management staffed its human resource departments with spend most of that time in efficiency. So, whether how organizational change is better, it depends on how it changes its old resources, e.g. human resource, facility, equipment resources, even management time resources to change new improvement resources change to be better . It means providing the resources, budget, authority, credibility and commitment for the effort to truly organizational change on improvement.

● Why does organizational resource budget need?

For example, managing a human resource department involves budget planning and execution . The human resources budger refers to the finds that how HR allocates to all HR processes. Unit should include in an HR budget. It may include: number of employees, projected for next year, benefits cost increases or decreases, salary cost increases or decreases, projected turnover rate, calculation, actual cost incured in the current year, new employee welfare benefits. programs planned, other changes in policy, business strategy , it may impact costs on HR cost aspect. So, an organization needs to budget whether it will have how much on what kinds of resources spending aspect, including human resources, facility, equipment and water , electricity etc. natural resource , it budget is a tool used for planning and controlling financial resources. It is a guideline for future plan of action, espressed in financial terms within a set of period time, knowing organization's priorities, objectives and goals helps it prepare organization resource budget. Effectively leveraging people and budget, resource management is critical for organizations to ensure . They are optimizing and allocating resources to the right initiations, e.g. from a human resource perspective, the data needed to create a new budget include the following number of employees, working arrangement tasks time, management time, employee salary cost, due to costs that only impact the human resource department and impacts the entire organization both aspects. So, efficient HR cost budget can help refine goals that reflect realistic resources and how memebers of the organization to use fund because employee retirement can be expensive and it can b increased or decreased expense in any time, when the month needs increase or decrease employees number to any departments. It depends on whether tasks rate is needed to increase or decrease. So, an organization's HR cost budget can help how it makes the most accurate HR resource expenditure.

Organizational facility, equipment, shop, office, warehouse space resource budget why is important. Office space is as an enabling resource, equipment and furniture to enhance the organization's ability to achieve efficient operations and activities of the best organizational performance. In view of this analysis, facility planning personal would be one important factor to influence whether the organizatin can spend the least expenditure to use its resource. During business growth, any facility equipment, office , shop, warehouse space must increase , moreover staff puts increasing number on existing resources, so be sure to budget in order to make another option is to least equipment instead of buying it, whether you need moving insurance for important equipment and machinery, set budget to help prevent overspending.

All of the tasks that are include in maintaining a facility, such as equipment maintenance and building facilities whether are needed to improve, facility oversight, warehouse and special equipment whether is qpproriate space for customer service and uses resource dynamic of an organization's work patterns with work. It depends partly on the resources an organization is willing to invest or not, when it feels this facility resources are very important to influence its performance.

● What does organization office , shop , warehouse space resource management strategy?

Organization and using space must be land resource, if the organization can manage how to use its space in efficiency, then it can improve service performance or productive efficiency. Space management can be defined as a practice where an organization manages its physical space invnetory which includes tracking , control, supervision and utilization, planning of the space available. So, space management is the mangement of an organization's physical space inventory. Ths involves the tracking of how much space an organization has managing occupancy information and creating spatial plans. So, one efficient space resource using organization, it needs to undertake annual property assessment reviews, leverage individual projects to drive portfolio evoluation applya planning methodology on all project rises, utilize planning to define direction and scope focus on mathematics before graphics, define and collect only the required data on warehouse, shops, office, buildind space using aspect. For example, a space management ffice can give the organizatin an accurate picture of how many employees , it needs to have space for an average day, and show it the trends of demand for this space across weeks and months. This can help the organization to determine how many permanent desks could be converted to hot desks in office, warehouse or shop , saving space. For example, space managementin retail aspect, it is the process of managing the floor space adequately to facilitate the customers and to increase the sale.

Shop space management is very crucial in retail as the sales volume and gross profitability depends on the amount of space used to generate those sales. Space management is a multi-step process that requires data gathering, analysis , forecast and strategizing. In prective, it involes creating a space management system that occupants throughout your organization, so whether the organization realizes it or not, every organization needs to know how to manage its space one way or another , if it hopes to improve its service or productive performance. Make use of these strategic space management and planning techniques, efficient and an unplanned, unmanaged office is not likely to magically transofrm into a well organized of productivity. So, space management is the management of an organization's physical space inventoty , employee working environment, shop product putting sheleves locatin, equipment, desk putting location. All of this tangible space physical factor may influence overall organizational service and/or productive performance and /or sale performance. So, space may be an organization's land usng resource because any organization's land using space must be limited size, they must have land space using shortage challenge if their products stock number increases, but warehouse space can not increase or shop products shelves number can not increase, but product sale number increases.

- The relationship netween organization behavior and resource using management accounting

Has organizational behavior and resource spending, they have close cause and effect direct relationship ? When one organization can perform better, whether it represents that it must spend much resource to use or when it perform poor, it represents that it must not spend much resource to use. Organizational behavior is a field of study that investigates the impact that organizational psychology and human resource management, the cause and effect relationship.

How organizational behavior effects an oganization? Organizational behaviors propose that inventives are motivational factors that are crucial for employees to perform well. It changes the way people make decisions, e.g. decision to increase or decrease resources to use, when the organization feels that it has resource shortage or excess. However, businesse that are able to encourage risks in decision making within the company culture can enhance innovation and creativity.

In fact, organizational behavior has four main elements, people, structure, technology and external environment. So , tangible and intangable resources may influence organization behavior when it is needed to change by management, e.g. human behavior in a work environmen and determines its impacts on job structure, performance, communication, motivation, leadership etc. for example, when the manager has less time to prepare how to organize this meeting process to his client. His short managing meeting plan time , intangible time resource, it can influence his business proposal to be either accepted or rejected to this client. So , time resource whether it is enough or not. It can influence this manager's client proposal meeting whether it is accepted or rejected in possible.

Every employee behavior can determine the importance of group departments in business productivity. So, it seems that resources whether they are enough , they can impact on employee's performance. As a result, managers are able to maintain better relation with their employees by effective utilization of human resource. So, cause and effect relationship plays an important rolw in how an individual is likely to behave in a enough tangible and intangible resource provided or not enough organization.

Modern organizational behavior is characterised by the acceptance of a human resource model, e.g. whether the plant can provide enough productive equipment facility and space shelf for product putting location in order to raise or improve logistic transport efficiency in warehouse. So, plant warehouse space management and shelf putting location productive equipment facility these tangible resource factors may influence warehouse productive performance. It seems that tangible resource provision amount and space management or intangible resource time management resource, they have close relationship to influence organizational behavior. Consequently, it can achieve the result either performance improvement or worse performance. So, resource and performance organizations , they ought have cause and effect relationship in resource management mobilization strategy view.

- How applying artificial intelligent management accounting solution accounting challenges

One of the biggest challenges for management accountants nowadays is the preparation to face globalization in local and global market. Globalization competition is changing government regulation and innovation in technology had to change in the market environment which have greater impact to an organization. The role of managemet accounting to AI, it may help managers to make any management strategy decision, e.g. evaluate sale price is the most reasonable, sale market choice, customer age target evaluation etc. within any organizations. Also known of cost accunting, management account of the process of identifying, analyzing and communicating information to managers to help to achieve business goals. However, the most important job of management accountant is t condoct a relevant cost analysis to determine the existing expenses and give suggestion for the future activities and make better management accounting, when management accountants need to learn how to apply these management accounting data: financial planning, financial statement analysis, cost accounting, find flow and cash flow analysis, standard , marginal cost and budgetary control, they can be made by AI.

In general, the job dutures of management accountant may include: generate sale among client accounts, operates as the point of contact for assigned customers, develops and maintains long term relationships with accounts, makes sure clients receives requested produsts ans services in a timely fashion . So, they need to learn these different management accounting technique: margin analys, capital budget, inventory valuation and product cost, tend analysis and forecasting. Future AI may be taught to learn all of these any one management accounting technique to assist organizations to make more reasonable management account strategy implementation.

The basic principles of management accounting include communication presents insight which is crucial , irrelevance information is valuable, the influence one value is estimated, credibility,recognizing the requirement, good accounting manager, they need to learn how conflict, be open to new ideas: In management accounting tehnology apply, there are three elements of management control system to develop to future Artificial intelligent management accounting technology delegated decison authority , performance evaluation and measurement systems and compensation, reward system.

Hence, accounting technology in AI development has always played a past in making the accountant's job just a played a part in making the accountant's job just a easier. Its own knowledge of technology increased to have the accountant's ability to analyze statistical values. Technology advancements have enhanced the accountant's ability to interpret data efficiently and effectively.

- Future AI management accountant may help human to the honest accounting record

However, any one managment accountant needs have good professional personal quality, honestly and integrity play vital roles in accounting because they allow investors to trust the information they receive about companies in which they invest. Honesty in accounting is the primary characteristics of the profession that allows financial decision-makers to make appropriate judgement . So, the main focus of management accounting is to assist the management of a company in efficiency performing its function-planning, organizaing, divesting and controlling . Management accounting helps with these functions in the following ways: provides data, it serves to a vital source of data for planning, for product costing method example, it is used to cost methods available are process costing, job and different production and decision making. for 3 types of controls may include: internal controls are typically procedures or technical safe guards that are implemented to prevent problems and protect organizations' assets. Future AI technology may help an organizations to do above all management accounting decision jobs ,even replace human in offices to avoid losses. The traditional management accounting technique includes" the use of performance measures, three ROI , budget systems for planning and control, divisional profit reports and cost-profit volume relationship, and breakeven analysis for decisions. The management accounting reports may include order information report, project report, competitor analysis. They are either internally aor outsourced. All of these management accounting methods, future AI can replace human accountants to do .

- Can AI be applied to help organizations to implement management account strategies ?

The two widely used types of accounting are: Financial and management accoutning, for the strategic cost management techniques example, it is the cost management techniques that aims at reducing cost , when strengthening the position of the business. It is a process of combining the decision making structure with the cost information in order to do the strategy as a whole . Hence the role of management account in the organization is to support competitive decision making by collecting, processing and communicating information that helps management plan, control and evaluating business processes and company strategy . So, the strategy management accounting can be defined as the process of identifying, collecting , selecting and analyzing accounting data . So, future AI can be applied to assist accounting teams in strategic decision making and organization effectiveness assessment must be defined.

Future AI can be applied to these management accounting aspect: For methods and techniques of costing management , it may include: Job costing, advestment, salepeople,bonus, contract cost, long periods of time job, batch cost, process cost, one operation (unit or output) , cost service or operating costing, farm cost, multiple cooperation unit. The tools of cost analysis, breakeven analysis, budget cost control marginal cost analysis, cost control , minimum price analysis, standard cost development , target cost. All of these management strategies, AI can do .

The various tools and technique of marginal costing may include: contribution, profit volume ratio, contribution : sale value , p/v ratio, features of profit volume , break even point . Hence, the AI tools can control cost monitoring in execution. For that AI can help organizations to make cost control budget, it is defined as a AI tool that is used by the management of an organization in regulating and controlling of a manufacturing organization. AI can also perform cost budget for material to any manufacturing organizations to help them to reduce the manufacturing cost , e.g. making material choice for the cheapest price.

AI can gather the product material price, e.g. standard cost and normal cost. Then , AI can help the manufacturing organization to choose the best quality of the cheapest material in order to compare whether which kinds of material to produce the kind of product can bring the high economic benefit to let consumers get more satisfactory feeling. Thus, it is future management accounting development direction for AI.

CHAPTER FIVE

ORGANIZATIONAL BEHAVIOR HOW INFLUENCE ECONOMIC GROWTH

Human Behavioral network job brings social economic benefits

What does human network job mean ? Why may human network job be popular? Why human network job behavior may influence economy ?

Nowadays internet is popular to use. We can apply internet to find data , search any new things, even earn money. Why does internet
may become huma network job source. For example, e-publish may be one kind of new human network job. Any authors may apply internet
channel to help them to sell electronic or paper books from e-publisher web store. They may apply facebook, you tub etc. any online
channel to promote themselves new books to let new readers to know whether when they may buy themselves favourable new topic books to read
from electronic publisher web store.

Thus, future electronic publisher industry may help any authors to build internet network platform to help them to sell and promote
ot advertise their any one new electronic or paper book topic to let global any one reader to choose to buy their any new topic books from electronic publisher web store easily and conveniently. However, it implies that electronic network platform author may be one kind of future new human network job in our societies.

How electronic network platform author job may bring economy benefit in macro economy view? A person can have few friends, contacts and still be very influential if these few
friends and contacts are themselves highly influential, e.g. one author must not need to know any one reader in global society. When they like to choose any electronic books from electronic internet network platform. They may become the author's any one topic book buyer, when they feel the author's any one topic book is fun and attract they make decision to buth the strange author whose the topic book from electronic book publisher's platform web store conventiently in short time. Although, they are strangers, they do not know themselves , but the reader can understand what it way that made Google from writing platofrm to create new creative mind and typing network job method to replace traditional hand writing book method for global authors. It will be one kind of new human network writing job.

Hence, global any one reader can apply an innovative search engine , such as google.com to find whether whom author personal new topic books are value to read from internet.

Then, the electroniuc publisher's web store may be new book store platform sale network to help the author to sell many electronic or paper books from electronic network platform

in short time. So, internet may be future new network plaform to help global any one author to create network writing job absolutely. Furthermore, internet may be popular social media
to help any one author to build goold relationship between his/her readers. It is one kind of new network, human network job. New authors do not need to buy many paper books to prepare to put in any one book shop warehouse. Their every book can print on demand to reduce out of book stock in any one book shop. They may choose to sell either electronic books or paper books both from any one book publisher web store. So, electronic network platform may be one kind of good writing channel to help human authors to create income and it can also help authors to bring new creative mind and new topic fun content books to let readers to know and buy to read from electronic publisher network platform.

Why does human behavior may be one kind of new human network job to bring global economic advantages. ALthough, it may be free income or without inocme, but the person does the network behavior, his/her behavior may be bring advantages to influence many other people's health. For this case, when a worker in a coffee shop in an airport gets a vaccination aganinst the flu, it does not only helps him or her stay healthy, but also helps the many travellers who might otherwise have been inflected if that workers caught the flu. So, the externality , the result implies the vaccination of even a part of a community conveys benefits to the whole community. For example, governments pay special attention to the vaccinations of school children, teachers, health mothers, and the elderly, categories of people particularly susceptible not only to catching, but also to transmitting a disease.

It is not accidential that governments are heavily involved with vaccination . When there are externalities, free market, fail to persuade individual incentives with society's
their the worker's decision of whether to get a vaccine ends up attracting whether other people get sick. The workers might not fully take all these other people's potential suffering into account when making her or his vaccination decision.

As Stanford University does many suggestions, understand this and tries to help them make the right decisions and so providers free flu vaccines for its staff and students.
Small pockets of unvaccinated individuals can allow a disease to gain a spread more widely well-being. For example, parent weighing the costs and benefits of a vaccine for their child is not always thinking of the consequences of that vaccination to other people. THese are markets in which subsidizing or regulating behavior can make everyone better off. Because the reason for requiring that a child be vaccinated before enrolling in school is not just to protect that child, because each child's vaccination affects others via potential contagions.

Robots take our jobs behavioral and economy influences

Robot job behavior brings economy influences

If one day robots can replace human to do simple, even complex jobs. They will bring what influences to our global societial economy.The popular economic refrain declares that the
global middle class is dying and robots will soon take our jobs, e.g. shopping center customer service jobs, library service jobs, cinema ticket sale jobs, restaurant kitchen cooker jobs,
even, bus drivers, taxi drivers etc. public transport driving jobs, accountant, doctors etc. professional jobs. Whether it is beautiful or petty matter if our future societies have many human jobs can be replaced to do from robots. Businessman must may reduce to employ employees and reduce to pay salary or wage, when robots can be replaced to do their employees tasks. But, societies must bring unemployement rate rises , due to societies will have many people loss jobs when their employers choose to buy robots to serve their clients or do any office tasks or customer service or cleaning etc. tasks.

In micro economy view, employers may save money in long term, but in macro economy view, it will cause unemployment ratio rises , even crime rate rises when there are many people lose
jobs in societies. These models of doom, though, fail to account for the hundreds of businesses riding the waves of change in their industries when robots may be invented to replace human to do many simple , even complex tasks in our future societies.

WE may image that one small factory needs to manufacture fishes canes to sell to supermarket, the small , cheaper stuff and higher margin parts of the fishes manufacture industry. Before, this factory needs to employe many human factory workers need to help every fresh customer makeing the perfect fishing gear, designed for performance, durability, and cost in order to achieve to manufacture every fish cane in whole fished processing manufacturing stages. Every worker needs to spend about 15 to twenty minutes to finish every fish cane , till to delivery to any supermarket to sell. If this fish canes manufacturing factory can apply manufacturing robots to help them to finish any one working tasks , every robot can only spend five minutes to finish whole fresh fish cane manufacturing process. Thus, every robot can

help this factory save 10 to 15 minutes time to finsh every fish cane manufacturing process. IN fact, time is money, because when every robot can help this factory to reduce 10 to 15 minutes time to compare human worker. Then, this factory can finish about 20 fish canes in one hour if it can use robot to help it to manufacture fish canes. Otherwise, if this factory still use human workers to help it to manufacture fish canes, then it can finsh about 3 to 4 fish canes in one hour. SO, the manufacturing efficiency ensures that robots must help this fish manufacturing factory to raise fish canes number more than human workers. So, in robotic behavioral economy view, manufacturing robots must help this fish canes manufacturing factory to raise fish canes manufacturing number and deliver increasing number to supermarkets to prepare to sell every day. Robots can help this fish canes manufacturing factory bring manufacturing time saving, rising manufacturing efficiency, improving performance and reducing wages expenditure long time advantages in micro economy view. However, manufacturing robots can also bring disadvanages to society, e.g. increasing unemployment ratio, increasing crime rate,

this factory workers will lose jobs and income, they need earn social welfare from government and increasing government finance pressure in short time, even long time in macro economic view.

Stanford University graduate program in economics, Scott lecturer explained that "in demand and supply economic theory for robots supply and demand case, robots supply number increasing may influence human workers demand number decrease. It sometimes calls " the efficient frontier".

No specific human beings were mentioned in any of economics classes. As robots supply and demand in market case, They (robots) may be purely theoretical " agents" who reached to the most reasonable sale prices in order to persuade any one businessman buyer to make manufacturing robot buying decision whether robots can help him / her to bring how much saving time , saving money, saving cost, improving performance, efficiency economic benefit before he/she plans to reduce workers number when he/she decides to apply robots to replace human workers in his/her factory or office or any service department, e.g. cinema ticket sale service, shopping center customer service, shopping center cleaning , supermarket customer service etc. service or sale tasks. When robots can replace human to do any one of these tasks in any organizations. So, robots may be human worker agents who reached to prices the way robots would react to a software

command. There was nothing that explained why some people thrived and others did n't or why truly brilliant, hardworking people could fail when much lazier folks succeeded." Having been admitted to the Stanford University graduate program in economics, Scott lecturer hoped to get his answers there.

How robots influence our future social changing? Using the right technology can be a boon to your business in this economy. For internet example, it is easier than ever to find well-matched customers all around the world, to stay in contact with them, and to more quickly design the products they want. If you focus solely on being cutting -edge, though you risk letting the technology

take over what should be very robust relationships with your customers , employees, and colleagues. IN nowaddays society, technoligical advances and cutomation, personal

relationships in business are more crucial than ever. I mean that robots can not replace human to serve clients to let them to feel more comfortable and passion more easily. For shoe shop case example, if the shoe shop apply one robot to serve its clients to replace human shoe salesperson to serve its shoe customers. Robots ensure that they can not persuade every shoe potential buyer to make shoe buying decision more easily when robots need to contact every shoe potential buyer. The reason is simple, because robots can not touch any one shoe buyer individual emotion very easier.

If the shoe buyer needs the robots to help him/her to choose any right shoe styles when he/she can not feel himself / herself can make the most right shoe style choice decision. The robots can not replace human shoe salesperson to make shoe style choice judgement more easily. They must need longer time to analyze whether which shoe style may be the most suitable to the shoe buyer. Otherwise, human shoe salesperson may attempt to make the most right shoe style choice decision to help any one shoe buyer to chooce the most right style shoe because he/she owns shoe style sale experience, shoe style knowledge, the most important reason is that they can feel every shoe customer individual emotion to touch whether he/she will feel comfortable or happy when they attempt to help every shoe customer to seek the most right shoe style in every shoe customer whole shoe searching processing. Othwerwise, serving robots are only one machine, they can not touch or feel every shoe customer individual emotion whether he/she feel comfortable or unhappy or happy when they need to contact them in whole shoe searching processing. Hence, I believe that some tasks robots can
not repalce human staff to do very easily. Otherwise, robots may bring disadvanatges to let any one businessman to loss his/her customers, due to robots can not touch every customer
emotion to compare human staff in service tasks more easily. Robots serving customer behaviors may cause money lose and customers number lose to the shop in micro economic view.

Intellectual human economic behaviors

What does intellectual human economic behaviors mean ? I believe that when we choose or decide to do intellectual behaviors, then our societies will be influenced to bring economic growth in consequence.I shall attempt to indicate pollution case to explain how and why eithet our intellectual or foolish behaviors may bring economic growth or recession in consequence as below:

On one hand, for air pollution social case aspect example, if we only consider to buy cars to drive for working aimr or holiday leisure aim. Then, our societies air will be polluted. Our health will be influenced to bad. Our car driving behaviors may cause global environment air pollution serously. In long tiem, global air pollution will bring our bodies health to be bad. Although, ourselves car driving behaviors may bring our driving travelling leisure enjoyment and comfortable feeling in short time, also we so not need to pay public transport fare often, but we need to compensate ourselves health economic intangible loss due to air pollution , when cars number increases, dirty air will cause ouselves health to become bad.

In the result, we will need to pay more medical expenditure when we are old age, due to ourselves bodies will become bad, due to we breathe global dirty air every day, due to ourselves cars pollute air in long time, e.g. 10 to 20 years, even 30 more without limited air pollution environment. So, driving cars behavior may be one kind of human foolish behavior and our foolish behavior may bring ourselves future long time medical expenditure absolutely.

One the other hand, water pollution social aspect, if we often keep much rubblish to pollute sea, oil exploration porcessing pollute ocean , ships gas pollute ocaen, then fishes will eat polluted food and drive dirty water, due to global ocean is polluted.

In fact, because human only to conside how to buy boats to carry on leisure enjoyment activities, or catch cruises to travel on the sea. Also, oil manufacturers only consider researching anywhere to find new oil exploration places to manufacture oil product, when their oil exploration processes pollute ocarn . Consequently, global fishes drink polluted warer or eat polluted food. They will have poison. SO, human will have high chance to eat poison polluted fishes, due to fishes are poison or are polluted.

So, human is doing foolish activities, we only hope to find oil exploration places to pollute ocean or we only spend money to buy ticket to catch ships to travel anywhere in global ocean. All of these human foolish behaviors will bring pollution to global ocean. On consequently, we will need to compensate to eat polluted or dirty or poision fishes, ourselves bodies health will be bad. In long time, we need have high chance to pay medical expenditure when we are old. So, pollution case may be one good example to explain how and why human foolish behavior may influence ourselves future need to compensate serious medical loss.

All of these human foolish behavior will bring pollution to global ocean. On consequently, we will need to compensate to eat polluted or dirty or poison fished , ourselves bodies health will be bad. In long time, we will have high chance to pay medical expenditure, when we are old. So, pollution case may be one good example to explain how and why human ourselves intellectual or foolish behaviors may influence future long time economic loss or economic growth or recession in micro and micro economic view.

On another water pollution aspect hand, if we often keep rubbish to sea, oil exploration processing pollutes ocean and ships' gas pollute ocean, then fishes will eat polluted food and drink dirty water, due to fishes will eat polluted food and drink dirty sea water because the global ocean is polluted seriously.

In fact, because human only consider how to buy boats to carry on any leisure water activities, or catches cruises to travel on the sea. Also, oil manufacturers only consider any where to find oil exploratin places to manufacture oil products from ocean, when their pol exploration processes can plooute ocean. Consequently, global fishes drink polluted water or eat direty food. They will have poison. So, human will have high chance to eat poison fishes.

Otherwise, such as pollutin case, it can infuence inflation or deflation. Consequently, the reason indicates supply and demand theory. If air pollution is serious, then we will consider health issue, global cars demand number may be influenced to reduce, when global cars number demand will reduce, global car prices and supply number will need to change to fall down in order to attract or persuade global car consumers choose to make car purchase decision.

Hence, global car manufacture number and car price will be influenced to reduce, due to global air pollution issue. Consequently, deflation will occur because when the country citizen usually does not spend much extra saving money to buy car expensive goods. Money value will be low. Otherwise, if global cair pollution is not serious, human considers to buy cars to enjoy driving leisure lives. So, global car demand is influenced to increase , also global car price will also influenced to increase.

Consequently, gobal human will choose to buy cars to drive. Due to we accept to spend extra saving to buy expensive car goods. Car sale price and supply may be influenced to rise up. Money value is influenced to reduce. Inflation may be influenced, due to global car consumers number increases, we would not have extra money to spend easily. Car expensive goods expenditure influences our spending habit to avoid to make car purchase decision more easily. So, human intellectual or foolish activities may bring inflation or deflation consequency in possible indirectly in macro economic view.

On conclusion, above pollution case explain that how and why human intellectual or foolish economic behaviors may bring inflation or deflation consequency as wll as economic growth or recession consequency as well as any goods demand and supply increasing or decreasing consequency. It implies that human behavior may have indirect relationship to influence any goods demand and supply number to either increase or decrease result as well as any goods price will be influenced to increase or decrease in micro and macro economic view.

The relationship between social change and human behavior

Why does economic changes may influence human individual behavioral change? I shall attempt to indicate shopping behavior and staying at home behavior to explain their case and effect relationsip as below:

Human behavior can be influenced by economic change or economic change can be influenced by human behavior? Why does recession may influence consumers reduce shopping desire? In social recession suitation, it is possible that many people lose jobs suddenly, due to businessmen lose many customers. They need to make decision to reduce employees number in order to continue to keep businesses. Consequently, many firms (organizations) their employees may lose jobs. When they have much time, due to lose jobs, they will feel to avoid to spend too much time and money to go to shopping often. Many losing jobs people, they will often stay at homes.

So, they will reduce time to go to shopping, then non essential products won't their preferable choice purchase products. Hence, recession will change many losing jobs people their shopping or consumption desires to avoid to buy non essential products often . Usually when economic boom, many people have jobs to do because consumers number must increase when many people have jobs to do. Then, many people can accept to spend money to buy non essential products often. Many people feel spend time to go to shopping can satisfy their purchase of any kinds of new products useful psychology or desire. So, recession is one good example to explain it can influence many people do not like often to leave homes to go to shopping easily. Many people like to stay at homes, becaue they feel worry about spending too much shopping time when they leave homes. Their staying home time is one good negative shopping behavior example. So, economic change may influence human individual behavior changes , they have direct cause and efect relationship in behavioral economic view.

May human behavior influence economic change? Is it possible that human behavior may bring the country social economic change in macro economic or micro behavioral economic view ? I shall indicate publishing industry example. Do you feel that if there are many students feel learning is very important when they read many books or many of students feel interesting to read or they have reading new books in habit, then it is possible that the country will have many students like to spend time to go to any book shops to choose the books, they feel that they can help they learn new knowledge. Then the country will increase students number, they often spend time to visit any one book shop every week. Their visiting book shops behavior which may become their habits. So, the country will increase students number, they often spend time to visit book shops. Also, it implies that visiting book shops behaviors may be their behavioral habits.

So, when the country has many students often spend time to visit book shops , their visiting book shops behaviors may help any one book shop to raise books sale chance. So, the country's student individual often visiting book shop behaviors, their habitual visiting book shops behaviors must may assist help any one book shop to increase books sale number absolutely.

Consequently, any one book shop , its books sale bumber must be influenced to increase to increase because the country will have many students like or feel need visit book shops habit in order to choose any suitable books to buy to read at home in order to raise themselves learning effort. When the country has many bok shops often have many students visit their book shops, then their books sale number may be influenced to increase. It explain why student individual visiting book shop behavior may help any one book shop sale number increases also.

How human productive behavior may influence economic development

May any country which citizen behavior assist themselves country development? It is one cause and effect economic question. I mean that if the country itself citicen can not concentrate mind or energy to choose to do one kind of industry in order to let themselves country can bring the most benefit, then whether the counry itself economy can bring the most serious economic benefit. I shall attempt to indicate these countries themselves indistry choice to explain whether these countries themselves citizen productive behavior may help themselves countries to achieve the largest economic benefits. I shall indicate as below:

New Zealand farmer individual wine productive behavior

For New Zealand country example, this country concerns itself effort is foucs on farming agricultural aspect. So, this country has many farmers concentrate on farming agricultural aspect. May New Zealanders choose to spend time to produce different kinds of wines, e.g. wine or red grape wine is for the people are eating meat, or they are eating dinner.

When these New Zealanders their behaviors choose to do farming or agriculture to grow and produce different kinds of taste of white or red grape wine drinking products job. Themselves grape agriculture behavior will influence these New Zealanders themselves, they can learn how to improve different kinds of grape wine drinking products in order to achieve every kinds of white or read grape wines taste improving aim during their white or red grape producing process.

Why can New Zealander every individual white or read grape wine producers improve their white or read grape wine taste more easily? In behavioral economic view, it can explain that why any one New Zealander white or read grape wine producer can be encouraged or excited or persuaded to concentrate nervous and energy and effort to learn how to improve their white or red grape wine products easily.

In fact, New Zealand is one agricultural food export country. It has good natural environment resource , e.g. land, seed to provide any one farmer to produce themselves any kinds of agricultrual food products, e.g. fruit, or wine food products. Because New Zealanders know themselves country has enough natural resource . So, in common, many New Zealanders choose to attempt to do farming agricultural jobs in order to export themselves any kinds of fruit or meat or wine products to overseas or sell to domestic in order to earn profit.

So, when these New Zealand farmers number has been increasing every year. This country farmers will feel themsleves competition between this New Zealand farmers themselves are serious due to they may feel New Zealanders choose to do agriculture businesses in order to export themselves different kinds of farming food to overseas or sell to local to earn profit.

Hence, when many New Zealand farmers feel that farmers number has been increasing every year. They will feel themselves competition is serious. They must need to spend much time and nervous and effort to research what method is the best how to produce the best taste of white or red grape wine products in order to let local or overseas wine buyers to choose to buy his/her producing white or read grpae products to drink.

Hence, in competition psychological view, may influence many New Zealand white or reaad wine producers had been beginning to change their learning behavior on researching what method is the best in order to produce the best quality of taste red or white wine products to sell in order to attract overseas or local white or read grape wine drinkers to choose to buy his/her wine products. Their behavior will focus on learning how to raising or improving white or read grape wine taste method more than only focus on producing a large number white or red grape wine products. They believe wine quality is more important to compare wine producing number. So, New Zealand wine producers themselves wine producers behaviors have been changing on concentrating on researching wine quality method aspect more then wine producing number aspect in behavioral economic view.

America high technological productive behavior

For America example, US is one high technological country, it owns many high technological knowledge talent inventors, e.g. computer science inventors. Hence, US must attract many diferent countries owning high technological computer inventors choose to go to US to develop their computer science profession career. Also, it seems that when many computer science inventors or professions choose to go to US to develop themselves computer science new career. In behavioral economic view, due to their leaving themselves countries choice, which may bring influence themselve country job behaviors need to be changed. They must need to adapt US new live. Because they will forgive their past computer science job. These computer science professionals need to spend time to adapt US new lives. They " past computer science job behaviors" will need to be changed to their new US any computer employer's new computer science job model.

Because their traditional computer science jobs needed to be forgot in their themselves countries. They will feel their old computer science job knowledge and behavior needed to change in order to let their US any one new of computer company employer feels satisfactory to accept their new working behavior in any one US computer organization.

So, on the other hand, many US computer company employer will feel that they must need time to accept any one new overseas computer science professions their working behaviors, their working attitude daily, because these foreign comouter science professional, their past computer working behaviors and working attitude must be different to US domestic computer science professions.

In behavioral economic view, these overseas computer science professions, their working behaviors and attitude must be needed to change in order to adapt any one US new computer company itself domestic or local computer science professional stafs themselves daily working behaviors and attitude because these overseas and local computer science professionals must need to team work together.

In behavioral economic view, it is only one way that foreign computer science professionals must need to change themselves past country traditiona daily working behaviors and attitude in order to cooperate with these US local computer science professionals in teams more easily.

Consequently, if these foreign compute science professionals can change their past working behaviors and attitude to let any one US local computer science professional feels to cooperate with them easily in short time. Then, the US computer company itself whole computer professional teams themselves efficiencies will be influenced to raised or improved by the changing past working attitude and working behaviors of these foreign computer science professionals. So, in behavioral economic view, only if US any one computer company hopes itself computer teams themselves efficiency can be raised or improved when it decides to employ foreign computer science professionals and US domestic computer science professionals. They need to work in teams together. They must need to let these foreign computer science professionals to know how to change their working behaviors and attitude to let their domestic computer science professionals feel easy to work together. Then, the US computer company itself whole team efficiency must be rasied or improved easily in short time.

- China share market investing behavior

For China share market example, economic development depends on financial market. Because if many Chinese have

interest to invest to carry on shares buying and selling activities in orde to learn how to earn shares interest and share profit when the China shareholder can make decision to sell himself/herself shares in the the high price, then he/she can earn money when he/she can sell the China company's shares in the high sale share price position.
If China has many Chinese like to spend time to carry on investing shares activities. Themselves shares buying and selling behaviors will influence China has many companies can increase fund from many Chinese shareholders in order to have enough money to expand or develop themselves businesses in China in long term.
Consequently, when China can have many Chinese like to attempt to carry on buying and selling shares investing behaviors in China share market. Themselves buying and selling shares behaviors can help many Chinese companies have effort to increase enough money or capital in order to continue to do their businesses in long term absolutely. So, it explains why when many Chinese become shareholders , they can assist China will have many companies continue to develop their businesses if many Chinese like to carry on shares buying and selling investing behaviors in long time in China financial investment market nowadays in behavioral economic view.

Why has any individual country have many people invest share behavior which can influence the country's macro consumption desire?
I shall apply shares market buying and selling investment behavior to explaiin why shares investment behavior which may impact the country's overal consumption desire as below:
In behavioral economic view, I assume that when the coutry has many people have interest to attempt to carry on shares buying and selling investment behavior, then their frequent shares buying and selling behaviors which may bring negactive consumption desire or shopping desire of these shares investors their consumer behavior.
The reason is simple, when the country has many share buyers number suddenly been increasing rapidly. Consequently, these large group share investors must need to spend much time to research any kinds of company shares variations, whether when their share prices will rise up of fall down in order to achieve buying the company's shares in the lowest price and selling the company's shares in the highest price level in order to earn profit.
Basic on this reason, they must need to spend much extra time to research share prices changing behavior every day, e.g. one working person will wait to leave his/her job, after he/she can spend time to gather data to research the day's share price changing behavior after dinner. So, the working person's right time may be his/her share price market research behavior. Before he/she may spend his/her night time to go to shopping after dinner, but nowadays, he/she will fogive to do his/her shopping behavior before dinner or after dinner at hight sometime. He/she will make decision to spend much night time to turn on computer to click on share market website to research his/her share purchase choice to investigate whether his/her share price whether it rises up or falls down at the moment in order to make his/her share buying or selling decision at ever night time.
I mean the when the country has many people are share investors, their shares investment behavioral spenging time which will influence many shops lose customers at might often because the country will have many people feel need to spend night time to turn on computer or watch television to investigate share price variation. So, the country will have many people / share investors choose to stay at home in order to carry on share price variation investigation behavior, they need to listen share market update news from radios or watch the share market update news from computer or TV at home every night. Consequenly, they must reduce times to leave themselves homes at night. So, their shopping behavior also will be reduced. Because these share investors feel need to spend time to investigate share price variation news at homes which can bring economic benefits (high opportunity benefits) when they choose to forgive to leave homes to go to shopping times (opportunity cost) every night.
On conclusion, it seems that when the country has many people are share investors, then their share price investigating behavior may bring negative shopping emotion at night. Consequently, the country's any one shop may lose many customers from this share investor consumer group in behavioral economic view. Hence, when the country's share investors number had been increasing rapidly, it will influence any shops lose many customers from this share investing customer group at night frequenly in short time, even long time in behavioral economic view, because their shopping desires or shopping emotion will be brought negative feeling when they make decisions to spend much time to listen radios or watch TV or computers share price update nes at night. Hence, share market will bring negative impact to influence consumer shopping desire or negative shopping emotion in behavioral economic

view.

Can technology influence human shopping behavioral change?
Nowadays, technological development has reached mature stage, whether technological mature stage may bring positive or negative shopping emotion influence to global consumers. I shall aplly internet inventin or ecommerce shopping channel tool to explain whether internet technology can bring postive or negative influence to global consumer behavior in behavioral economic view.

Internet is a good technological tool, it brings e-commerce business chance. In fact, commonly, global has have many businessmen choose to use internet channel to carry on their products transactions between global online-buyers and their electronic websites. So, global many shoppers had begun to feel online shopping is more convenient to compare visiting shops shopping. Their shopping behaviors have been changed from internet technological tool. Global has many shoppers choose to buy any products from any overseas or local businessmen their web stores. They only need to spend time to find any businessmen their webstores to choose the most suitable products to pay visa to buy from their webstores. at homes. So, in general, global had have may shoppers had changed their shopping behaviors from visiting shops to visiting webstores at homes often.

So, it seems that internet technological tool had influenced global many shops disappear, but internet webstores will be replaced their actual shops on streets. Some of businessmen either they choose webstores to replace shops or choose websotes and shops both or still keep shops only. Hence, internet tool influences global businessmen have three kinds of products sale channels to let globa local and overseas consumers to choose how to buy their products. However, in fact, many of global shoppers, youngers and olders had begun to accept to buy any products from webstores. They feel to spend time to leave homes to visit shops , their shopping behaviors will be wasted time to not essential part to their daily lives. Hence, since internet technological invention, it had changed many consumers their traditional visiting shops shopping habit to change to buying products from webstores channel.

However, on the one hand, internet creates webstores ecommerce shopping channel to let global many consumers do not need to leave homes to go to shopping. It brings negative visiting shops shopping emotion to global general consumers nowadays. But on the other hand, it also brings positive visiting internet webstores shopping emotion to global general consumer nowadays. So, it seems that global many consumers feel that they often do not need to spend much time to go out shopping. Many global consumers feel convenient and enjoy to choose any products to buy from different internet webstores, when the online buyer chooses the most suitable product, he she only needs to pay visa card to buy the product from the online seller's webstore conveniently at home.

Hence, online shopping can bring economic benefit to online buyers, e.g. avoiding walking time or spending transport fare to visit the shop to go to shopping, shortening or reducing shopping time to do another important matter.

On conclusion, global many consumers began feel online shopping can bring more economic benefits on shortening shopping time, avoiding transport fare spending aspect. So, online shopping will be popular shopping behavior for future long time. It may encourage global many shoppers can make rapid shopping decision in short time in order to carry on any products buying transaction to global any one online shopper in short time easily in behavioral economic view. So, global many businessmen had begun to build themselves one attraction webstore in order to persuade different countries consumers to choose to click themselves webstores from internet channel to buy any kinds of products in short time easily.

So, internet technology had changed consumers traditional shopping behaviors to build positive online shopping emotion as well as raise online sellers' any products sale chance easily in behavioral economic view.

Why and how human behavior may influence the country's economic growth or recession?
When one country has many people choose to do the same matter for one period, whether their behavior may influence the country's pvera; economic growth or recession . I shall attempt to indicate cases toexplain their relationship as below:

For flowing rubblish behavioral case example, do you feel that when the country has many people often flow rubblish on the streets, instead of their flowing rubblish behavior may bring streets dirty? But, their flowing rubblish behavior may explain that this country has people may have enough money to buy food to ear, or enough cloths to wear, enough bottles of water to drink, even they may have enough money to buy new television, radio, refrigeraters , washing machines, desktops or laptops electronic home products from old to new to use in order to satisfy their living needs. So, when they flow old electronic home products, their flowing old home electronic products behaviors may seem that they have enough money to buy other new home electronic products to replace old home electronic products to use at homes.

However, it seems thaat this country ought have many people have jobs to do. So, many of them, they can easy to make purchase decison to flow any old home electronic products and buy any new home electronic products to use . Because this country has many people have jobs to do. So, they can often not use old home electonic products to become rubblishs to flow on streets after they had bought any kinds of new home electronic homes.

In fact, it also implies that this country's economy grows rapidly. So, many businesses can glow up rapdly. When they expanded their businesses, they must need to increase employees number in order to let they help themselves to raise productivity or serve their clients absolutely. So, when the country has many businesses can grow up, it seems that its economy must be better or it is improved to compare past. Due to many different kinds of home electronic products had been often bought to use by this country people in this period. So, this country's any streets can be observed that expensive electronic home products were flowed on streets anywhere. then, this country will have many electronic home products sellers can sell their home electronic products very easily. When this country has many people can find any kinds of jobs to do easily. So, due to unemploymen rate had been decreasing.

In behavioral economic view, as this many electronic home products rubblish country case, we can observe this country may have many people have jobs to do. So, consumption number has been increased long time. So, cheap food, or expensive home electronic products may be rubblish on any streets. This country's people , their flowing rubblish behaviors may be explained that many of people have enough jobs to do, so they have ability to buy any good taste food to eat or buy any kinds of expensive electronic home products to use. So, this country's economy may be improved for this long period. So, in behavioral economic view, when this country can have many electronic home products rubblishs are flowed on anywherer in streets frequently. It seems that this country will have many people have jobs to do, so it causes they often change old home electronic products or replaced them easily, when they have enough income to spend to buy any kinds of new home electronic products to use at homes easily. Moreover, their flowing old electronic home products behaviors also indicate that this country has many people their salaries may be increased in possible from their emplyers. When this country can have many different kinds of home electornic products are sold. It means that this country's electronic home products needs or demand had been increasing, due to many people have jobs to do and income increases to excite their living of needs also improve. Consequently, this country may seem have better economic improvement. We can observe from this country's electronic home products rubblish increasing income in theis period.

On conclusion, this country ought experience economic growth at this period. So, " flowing expensive electronic home rubblish increasing number " may seem that this country's economic growth is rapidly in this period, due to many people have jobs to do as well as salaries increase in this period.

Technology how impacts human behavior changing?

Technology how influences human behavior to bring changing? For example, online share purchase and sale transaction from smart phone brings share investor can do share buying or selling transation in any where and any time conveniently, non manual driving auto vehicle, bring car owner feels comfortable and spends free time to do other matter, e.g. reading, listening mucis in himself or herself car freely. electrical energy vehicle can help car owner to reduce air polluton and it can brings the drivers do not feel drive long time in any journeys in order to avoid air pollution for environmental protection responsible car drivers in our societies. Thus, they will drive long time in any journeys when they can drive electronic energy cars to replace oil energy cars.

However, online technology can also bring consumers can choose to stay at homes to buy any things from seller individual online webstore conveniently. Such as online technology can bring shoppers do not need to spend much time to visit shops to buy any things. They can choose any kinds of products from any online sellers individual online webstores conveniently at homes. Online technology excite busy consumers can make purchase decision easily as well as it can help online sellers sell any kinds of products from internet easily.

In behavioral economic view, technology can change human behavior to be improved, it can let human feels comfortable, more free time ro use, rapid making any decisions, such as apply smart phones to make share purchase or sale transaction decision, online shopping decision, even travelling any where decision in short time, when the traveller finds the most cheap hotel accommodation room price and air ticket price frm any travel agent online tourism webstore, then the potential travel customer can follow the online hotel accommodation price and air ticket price data to make decision when to buy the air ticket from the airline travel agent or make decision when to prebook which hotel accommodation room to go to the country to travel from online travel agent tourism webstores. So, technology can encourage global any country travelers to make anywhere to trvel rapidly. If the traveler can find the country's general hotel rooms and airline tickets prices had been decreasing more sightly. The traveler may make travel decision to choose the country to travel in short time, then he/she can prebook the country;s any hotel room and airline ticket to pay by visa fraom the country's any hotel and airline travel agent webstores., before one week, even one month or more easily. Hence, online technology can also encourage traveler individual frequent travel times to be increased, due to global travelers can find any hotel rooms and airline tickets prices from internet conveniently at homes. They do not need to spend time to visit any airline travel agent to enquire travel choice country's hotel rooms prices and airline ticket prices. They can compare global travel of countries choices ' all hotels rooms and airline agents air tickets prices to make prebook airline seat and hotel room decision before one week, one month even six months early.

On conclusion, online technology can encourage global travelers can make travelling any where and when traveling time desicions easily. It can excite tourism industry develops in long time. Also, such as electricity cars invention can encourage environment protection car owners do car purchase decision easily, because they can choose to drive electronic energy cars to replace oil energy cars in order to avoid air pollution occurs easily. So, electronic cars can increase electronic car purchasrs number, due to many of environmental protection attitude of car owners can choose to drive electricity cars to bring air cleans, even non -manual driving cars can encourage lazy driving and free time driving car owners to choose to buy non-manual (artificial intelligent) cars to drive , because they can spend much free time to read, listen music or do any matters in themselves cars, they do not need to drive cars, robotic (AI) auto driving machine is such one non-manual driver to help them to drive themselves cars confidently. So, non-manual driving cars can attract lazy and enjoying free time driving car owners to choose to buy to replace traditional manual cars to drive easily. Moreover, online share transaction can help any share investors to make share buying and selling decision in short time easily. When they can apply smart phones technological tool to carry on share buying and selling activities easily. They can observe any share rising or falling price suitation from smart phones in any where any any time easily. So, smart phone technology can help global any shareholders to make share purchase and sale transaction easily. So, technology can encourage human makes decision in short time rapidly.

How and why employees behaviors may influence economy development?

In behavioral economy view,I believe the country's any organizational employees behavior may bring indirect relationship to influence the country's long term economic development. I shall indicate past manufacture industry social development period to explain their relationship. For many countries' past business activities had belonged to manufacturing industry, such as US, UK past before 1980 year, it focused on steel manufacturing and steel manufacturing related machine products. So, US, Uk developed countries manufacturing industries may be past main country's economic income sources. I assume US , UK past had one million number different kinds of industries. They ought had about seven houndred thousand number organizational businesses were belonged to manufactured industry. They may include:

Steel manufacturing and steel related machine manufacturing, e.g. vehicle manufacturing, home appliances, e.g. washing machine, television, radio, refrigerate cooler, heater, air condition etc. different kinds of different kinds of steel -related manufacturing machine, they were manufactured from US, UK steel machine manufacturers. So, US, Uk the other three hundred thousand number industry may be general service industry, e.g. hotel service, restaurent, cinema, public transport service, tourism lesiure , wine bar, supermarket etc. different kinds of non-manufacturing industries business organizations were operated in UK, US past before 1980 year.

So, in UK, US developed countries industry development history, they ought have high percentage of businesses belonged to steel related manufacturing machine and steel products. Also, in the past before 1980 year, US, Uk business employers , they employed many workers are manufacturing workers. They needed to spend long time to work in factories. They were skillful workers, and they are trained to manufacturing cars, washing machine, television, heater, etc. even steel itself different kinds of steel related products to prepare to deliver to their shops to sell to US, Uk local or overseas clients.

So, I believe that past UK, US ought employ many employees, they belonged to skillful manufacturing workers, manufacture increasing steel machine or steel related machine number of products rapidly daily. So, if UK, US had had many of these manufacturing factories owned high skillful workers, then their manufacturing steel-related machine or steel both kinds of products number must be influenced to raise rapidly. Consequently, their steel machine manufacturing products would been exported to overseas or would been sold to local both markets , they may be influenced to raise sale number. They (these manufacturing workers) needed to be trained to know how to manufactur these different kinds of machine products in the efficient teams and they ought to be trained to raise their efficiencies in order to shorten time to manufacturing many kinds of steel related manufacturing machine or steel itself products rapidly. So , if their efficiencies and manufacturing performance was improved, these US, UK any one manufacturing worker and their teams ought achieve raising productivities significantly.

Hence, when past UK, US manufacturing industry development period, if these two countries‘ any manufacturing factories could have many manufacturing workers could be trained to be skillful and proficient manufacturing workers. Then, in past every day to these factories workers, they ought help their steel or steel related manufacturing employers to raise any kinds of machine or steel products number in every team. So, when past in the manufacturing industry development, US, UK could have many factories' manufacturing workers themselves steel or steel related machine products manufacturing skill could be trained to to improve to any kinds of these machine or steel manufacuring products quality as well as their products number could be influenced to raise by themselves skillful improvement significantly every day.

Then, what would be influenced to occur to past UK, US manufacturing industry period? In behavioral economic view, when these two manufacturing industry developed countries, such as UK, US , if they had many factories workers can be trained to improve their skill in order to achieve any kinds of steel or steel-related machine products quality could be improved as well as products manufacturing number could be also increased absolutely.

In consequence, past UK and US both countries ought increase themselves any kinds of steel and steel related machine products number to be supplied to themselves local shops to let local clients to choose any one kind of machine manufacturing products to buy easily as well as they could also export to supply overseas any countries to buy their different kinds of steel or steel related machine products to let overseas steel or steel related manufacturing machine product buyers, they can have many of these different kinds of these steel or steel-related different kinds of manufacturing machine from UK and UK these both countries easily to compare other countries.

On conclusion, I believe that past US, and UK macro manufacturing industry income GDP would increase significantly. So, they would have good economic growth performance because when many of these manufacturing workers themselves manufacturing effort could be improved. So, it explained when employees manufacturing abilities can influence economic growth indirectly.

www.ingramcontent.com/pod-product-compliance
Ingram Content Group UK Ltd.
Pitfield, Milton Keynes, MK11 3LW, UK
UKHW061830190726
13853UKWH00009B/2533